Mathematics for Primary Teachers

Edited by
Valsa Koshy, Paul Ernest and Ron Casey

London and New York

First published 2000
by Routledge
11 New Fetter Lane, London EC4P 4EE

Simultaneously published in the USA and Canada
by Routledge
29 West 35th Street, New York, NY 10001

Routledge is an imprint of the Taylor & Francis Group

© 2000 Valsa Koshy, Paul Ernest and Ron Casey selection and editorial
matter; © 2000 individual chapters their contributors

Typeset in Times
by HWA Text and Data Management, Tunbridge Wells
Printed and bound in Great Britain
by TJ International Ltd, Padstow, Cornwall

British Library Cataloguing in Publication Data
A catalogue record for this book is available from the British Library

Library of Congress Cataloging in Publication Data
Koshy, Valsa, 1945–
     Mathematics for primary teachers / Valsa Koshy, Paul Ernest, and
  Ron Casey.
        p.   cm.
     Includes bibliographical references and index.
     1. Mathematics–Study and teaching (Primary)   I. Ernest, Paul.
     II. Casey, Ron.   III. Title
     QA135.5.K67   2000   99-33554
     372.7'044–dc21   CIP

ISBN 0-415-20090-3

Mathematics for Primary Teachers

In England, and internationally, numeracy standards in primary schools are the cause of as much concern as literacy standards. Often the greatest problem with maths at primary level is the teacher's own understanding of the subject. *Mathematics for Primary Teachers* aims to combine accessible explanations of mathematical concepts with practical advice on effective ways of teaching the subject. It is divided into three main sections:

* Section A provides a framework of good practice
* Section B aims to support and enhance teachers' subject knowledge in mathematical topics beyond what is taught to primary children. Each chapter also highlights teaching issues and gives examples of tasks relevant to the classroom
* Section C is a collection of papers from tutors from 4 universities covering issues such as the teaching of mental mathematics, children's mathematical misconceptions and how to manage differentiation. They are centred around the theme of effective teaching and quality of learning during this crucial time for mathematics education.

Valsa Koshy is Senior Lecturer in Education at Brunel University with responsibility for mathematics in-service courses. **Paul Ernest** is Professor in Mathematics Education at Exeter University. **Ron Casey** is Senior Research Fellow at Brunel University.

Contents

SECTION C

Contributors

Margaret Brown is Professor of Mathematics Education at King's College London and a member of the National Numeracy Task Force. She was in the working party who wrote the mathematics National Curriculum and has been involved in many of the major initiatives in this country in Mathematics Education. She has directed a number of research projects in numeracy in the last few years which have guided shaping national policy.

Jean Murray is Director of Primary Education at Brunel University. She is also responsible for the development of the mathematics components of the PGCE and BA courses and teaches on the mathematics education in-service programme of the University. Prior to entering Higher Education she taught in primary schools in Inner London.

Valsa Koshy is Senior Lecturer in Education at Brunel University. Prior to joining the University she was a member of the ILEA mathematics advisory team for a number of years. She co-ordinates the mathematics in-service programmes at the University and teaches Initial Training students. She has published many practical books for teachers: the most recent ones are on the teaching of 'mental maths' and 'effective teaching of Numeracy' in the primary school.

Christine Mitchell lectures in primary mathematics at the School of Education, University of Exeter. She has taught in primary schools in the UK and has provided consultancy and in-service support in assessment and management. She researches the development of mathematical reasoning in young children.

William Rawson lectures in primary mathematics at the School of Education, University of Exeter. As well as having taught in primary and secondary schools in the UK, he has a wide experience of teaching in South America, Africa and Asia

Lesley Jones is Head of Primary Initial Teacher Education at Goldsmith's College, University of London. She joined Goldsmith's College after being a teacher for a number of years and is currently involved in teaching mathematics education to Initial trainees and practising teachers. She edits *Mathematics in School*, the professional journal of the Mathematical Association, and has written many books on practical applications for teachers.

Barbara Allebone is Lecturer in Education at Goldsmith's College, University of London where she teaches mathematics education to both Initial Training students and teachers. She has taught in primary schools for a number of years and has led in-service training of teachers in LEAs prior to joining Goldsmith's College. One of her major research interests is the education of Able Children and the role of questioning in extending children's thinking.

Acknowledgements

This book attempts to bring together the two strands which we believe contribute to the quality of teaching and learning of mathematics and raise pupils' achievement in one book – the development of teachers' Subject Knowledge and Pedagogical Skills. The authors wish to acknowledge and thank various people who helped to make this book a reality.

First, we thank the large numbers of practising teachers and Initial Training students whom we have taught for many years, and who provided us with valuable insights into aspects of mathematics education. These insights helped us to select the aspects of mathematics education included in the book. We are particularly grateful to those who looked at the drafts and provided critical commentary at various stages of writing the book.

Thanks to Barbara Allebone, Margaret Brown, Lesley Jones, Christine Mitchell, Jean Murray and William Rawson who wrote papers on topics of current significant interest for Section C of this book. These people, from four universities, are active at both national and institutional level in policy-making and research relating to mathematics education. We acknowledge their willingness to find time, within their busy schedules, to contribute to the book.

Thank you also to Professor Martin Hughes and Professor Tony Crocker for acting as referees to the papers in Section C.

The amount of support and incisive and constructive comments provided by Helen Fairlie, former Senior Editor at Routledge, has been invaluable. We thank her for that.

Valsa Koshy, Paul Ernest and Ron Casey

Introduction

As we approach the millennium, primary mathematics teaching is at a crossroads. The primary teacher cannot afford to take the wrong path. This book, we hope, will both assist in selecting the right path as well as illuminate the journey along it.

Evidence from Ofsted inspections and findings from international comparisons have caused concern about children's mathematical performances. As a result, raising the level of achievement in mathematics is now strongly on the national agenda. One of the recommendations of the Numeracy Task Force for improving standards and expectations is the need for primary teachers to be supported in order to 'cover mathematics subject knowledge relevant to the primary curriculum and pupils' later development, and effective teaching methods' (DfEE, 1998). The Teacher Training Agency (1998) introduced a National Curriculum for Mathematics for Initial Teacher Training students which requires them to demonstrate knowledge and understanding of mathematics as well as the pedagogical skills required to secure pupils' progress in mathematics. From September 1999, primary school teachers are expected to introduce a structured 'daily mathematics lesson' – often referred to as the 'numeracy hour'– as part of the National Numeracy Strategy. Much emphasis is placed on 'focus', 'pace', 'balance of knowledge and skills' and 'development of processes'. The message is clear. **Teachers need to develop their subject knowledge and have clear ideas about how to teach mathematical ideas**.

We believe that opportunities for developing greater understanding of mathematical topics and considering the most effective teaching skills will greatly enhance the quality of mathematics teaching in our schools. This belief has prompted us to write this book. In selecting the content and style of this book, the authors have drawn on their considerable experience of being involved in both in-service and initial training of teachers. Both these groups have been consulted at different stages during the writing of this book.

What contributes to the effective teaching of mathematics? Askew *et al.* (1997) identified a group of 'effective' teachers who they described as 'connectionists'. Askew summarises (Askew, 1998) that these teachers emphasised the connections by:

- valuing children's methods and explanations;
- sharing their own strategies for doing mathematics;
- establishing connections within the mathematics curriculum, for example fractions and decimals.

The research team at King's College, London, found that the children in these teachers' classes achieved higher average gains in tests in numeracy in comparison with other groups. (You can read about this research in Margaret Brown's paper in Section C of this book.)

In listing aspects of good practice in teaching and learning mathematics the HMI (1989) attaches much importance to pupils' motivation:

> Distinctive, good work in mathematics was generally accompanied by a high level of motivation and engagement in the task: the pupils showed interest, commitment and persistence (p. 26).

How can teachers support their children to be motivated, to show interest and commitment? A teacher's own enthusiasm is an important factor. They play a crucial role in developing the right attitude in the children. We have all heard people attributing their success or failure in learning mathematics to a particular teacher or a group of teachers in a particular school. The problem, however, is that many adults experience anxiety and fear when they talk about their own learning of the subject. Discussions with teachers and students have often highlighted these anxieties and their lack of confidence about teaching the subject. Their concerns usually have origins from their school days. The reasons for their insecurities have seldom been lack of willingness or ability to learn. What we have listed below are some of the articulated reasons for their dislike of the subject. A close look at these reasons will be a good 'first step' when considering how to develop and enhance one's own mathematics teaching. The following are among the most often mentioned comments:

- I never understood much of the mathematics at school, so I don't have enough confidence to teach it to children.
- Could not follow teachers' explanations.
- It was all too fast for me, I couldn't keep up.
- I just learnt the rules in order to pass the examination.
- By the time I got to the final years of my schooling, the gaps in my knowledge base were so wide that I gave up.
- Maths lessons were so boring and irrelevant.
- I was afraid of failure, especially of being shown up to be useless.
- I don't have the basic mathematics knowledge to risk giving my children very challenging work.
- The word 'maths' makes me have a panic attack.

A consideration of the above list in itself should greatly assist you in your personal journey towards improving your mathematics teaching. Besides offering what we hope will be therapeutic reading , these comments will raise the most important question – how can I, as a teacher, ensure that my pupils will not develop any of the anxieties in the above list?

The three sections of this book are designed to support you in your efforts to develop your practice. In Chapter 1, Paul Ernest provides a framework for reflecting on many issues which should support your understanding about mathematics teaching and learning. He focuses on the aims of mathematics teaching, the nature of mathematics teaching, teaching styles and the requirements of the National Curriculum and Statutory Assessment. Other aspects of learning mathematics - special needs, equal opportunities and cultural issues – are also considered.

Chapters 2 to 8, in Section B, deal with mathematical topics which cover the requirements of the National Curriculum beyond Key Stage 2, the National Curriculum for teacher trainees (TTA, 1998) and the *Framework for Teaching Mathematics* for the National Numeracy Strategy. In each of these chapters we consider specific areas of mathematics. Each chapter deals with mathematics subject knowledge at your own level providing explanations with examples as well as interconnections between topics. Key issues in the teaching of these topics to children are also very briefly dealt with. Our belief is that as you read this section, many mathematical ideas which were 'not understood' before or 'forgotten' will begin to make sense. At the end of section B, you are provided with some self-assessment questions and a grid for auditing your achievement and planning personal learning. After undertaking the assessment you may need to re-visit parts of that chapter or discuss the ideas with others – tutors and friends.

Section C contains five chapters dealing with topics which we consider to be topical and important in the context of our pursuit of excellence in mathematics teaching and learning. In these chapters mathematics educators from four institutions share their expertise and research findings with the reader in order to facilitate reflection and informed choices. We recommend that you make notes on the key ideas in each chapter and share your thoughts with your colleagues.

References

Askew, M. (1998) *Primary Mathematics. A guide for newly qualified and student teachers,* London: Hodder and Stoughton.

Askew, M., Brown, M., Rhodes, V., William, D. and Johnson, D. (1997) *Effective Teachers of Numeracy: A report of a study carried out for the Teacher Training Agency*, London: King's College, University of London.

DfEE (1998) *Numeracy Matters. The preliminary Report of the Numeracy Task Force*, Department for Education and Employment.

HMI (1989) *The Teaching and Learning of Mathematics*, Department for Education and Science. London: HMSO.

Teacher Training Agency (1998) *Initial Teacher Training National Curriculum for Primary Mathematics*, (DfEE Circular 4/98).

Section A

Chapter 1

Teaching and learning mathematics

Paul Ernest

Why teach mathematics?

Every teacher of mathematics should ask themselves the following basic questions. What is mathematics? Why teach mathematics? The immediate reason why we teach mathematics is that we have to, and our children must learn it, because it is in the National Curriculum. But why is it there? There must be a reason why it is thought to be so important. Answering this question explains why everyone thinks mathematics is so important, and what we should emphasise to our children. Also, having a clear idea why we teach mathematics can serve as a source of inspiration, a vision of what our children can gain from learning the subject.

The first and most obvious aim is for children to gain knowledge that is useful. But there are uses of mathematics at several levels. To get the fullest benefit children should be:

- learning basic mathematics skills and numeracy and the ability to apply them in everyday situations such as shopping and the world of work;
- learning to solve a wide range of problems, including practical problems;
- understanding mathematical concepts as a basis for further study in mathematics and other subjects, including information technology;
- learning to use mathematics as part of citizenship, as part of a critical understanding of society and the issues of social justice, the environment, etc. This involves being able to look critically at statistical claims and graphs in advertising, political claims, etc.
- learning to successfully use their mathematical knowledge and skills in tests and examinations, to give them the qualifications they need for employment and further study and training.

These are already ambitious aims which go beyond the basic uses that many have in mind for mathematics. But these skills are needed to prepare children for the advanced post-industrial world of the twenty-first century and the social and environmental problems it will bring.

Second, we must aim for children to gain and grow personally as individuals from the study of mathematics. Children should be:

- gaining confidence in their own mathematical skills and capabilities;
- learning to be creative and express themselves through mathematics, including exploring and applying mathematics in their own hobbies, interests and projects.

Mathematics should be contributing in this way to the education of fully rounded individuals who are confident and able to use what they have learned, sometimes in original and creative ways.

Third, we should aim for children to gain some appreciation of mathematics, by understanding some of its big ideas and appreciating their importance in history, society and the cultures of the world. We live in an information society, and children should appreciate that mathematics is the language of information and computers. We are all part of the family of humankind, and mathematics is one of the most important central threads that runs through our history and our present life.

These are some of the most important aims for the teaching and learning of mathematics. Children should gain useful knowledge and skills, they should grow and be enhanced as developing persons by it, and they should gain a broader appreciation of the subject. Together, they provide a good if not complete answer to the question, why teach and learn mathematics?

What is mathematics?

Too few teachers in the past have asked themselves the question, what is mathematics? Our view of the nature of mathematics affects the way we learn mathematics, the way we teach it, and will affect the way the children we teach view mathematics. In teaching and in learning mathematics, too often we move on from one topic to the next, from one skill to the next. It is all too rarely that we stand back and take a broader view of mathematics, let alone share this view with the children we teach. So this is a very important question, one that is essential to consider, especially at the beginning of a book like this.

There are different answers to the question according to whether we ask mathematicians, philosophers, psychologists or educational researchers. Perhaps the most useful answer for teachers comes from the review of research on the teaching and learning of mathematics carried out by Alan Bell and colleagues (1983). This influenced both the Cockcroft Report (1982) on the teaching of mathematics and the Ofsted analysis of the aims and objectives of teaching mathematics (HMI, 1985).

Bell *et al.* distinguished the different things that can be learned from school mathematics. These include the learning of facts, skills and concepts; the building up of concepts and conceptual structures; the learning of general mathematical strategies; and the development of attitudes to, and an appreciation of, mathematics. These different learning components of mathematics are explored in more detail below.

Facts

These are items of information that just have to be learned to be known, such as Notation (e.g. the decimal 'point' in place value notation; '%'); Abbreviations (e.g. cm stands for centimetre); Conventions (e.g. $5x$ means 5 times x; knowing the order of operations in brackets); Conversion factors (e.g. 1 km = 5/8 mile); Names of concepts (e.g. odd numbers; a triangle with three equal sides is called equilateral); and Factual results (e.g. multiplication table facts, Pythagoras' rule).

Facts are the basic 'atoms' of mathematical knowledge. Each is a small and elementary piece of knowledge. Facts must be learned as individual pieces of information, although they may fit into a larger more meaningful system of facts. When they fit in this way they are much easier and better remembered, but then they become part of a conceptual structure. For example $9 \times 6 = 54$ is a fact. But when a child also knows that $9 \times 6 = 6 \times 9$, and that 9×7 has one more ten and one less unit, and 9×5 has one less ten and one more unit, and $9 \times 6 = (10 - 1) \times 6$, and so on, this fact is part of that child's conceptual structure.

Skills

Skills are well-defined multi-step procedures. They include familiar and often practised skills such as basic number operations. They can involve doing things to numbers (e.g. column addition), or to algebraic symbols (e.g. solving linear equations), or to geometrical figures (e.g. drawing a circle of given radius with compasses), etc.

Skills are most often learned by examples: first seeing worked examples, and then 'doing' some. That is, repeated practice of the skill, usually on examples of graduated difficulty.

Seeing how learners actually perform skills is a valuable lesson. For as well as learning skills, children make errors, often on the way to learning the skills. Many of these errors are part of a repeated pattern. They often seem to come from children learning some of the parts of the skill but missing out a part, or putting them together incorrectly. Other errors come from misapplying a rule. For example, in adding fractions, many children simply add the top numbers together, and the bottom numbers. Researchers found that about 20% of secondary school children made the following mistake: $1/3 + 1/4 = 2/7$ (see Hart, 1981). Why should they do this? It seems likely that they are misapplying the easier multiplication rule for fractions, but adding instead of multiplying.

Error patterns in skills suggest that children absorb some of the different components they have been taught, and put them together in their minds in their own individual ways. This leads to the important conclusion that children themselves construct their skills and knowledge, based on their teaching and learning experiences, and is called the constructivist theory of learning. This also explains how some children invent their own correct but unusual skills.

Concepts and conceptual structures

A concept, strictly speaking, is a simple set or property. This is a means of choosing among a larger class of objects those which fit under the concepts. For example, the concept red picks out those objects that we see which are red in colour. The concept of negative number picks out those numbers less than zero. The concept square picks out just those plane shapes which have four straight equal side sides and four equal (right) angles. A concept is the idea behind a name. To learn the name is just to learn a fact, but to learn what it means, and how it is defined, is to learn the concept.

A conceptual structure is set of concepts and linking relationships between them. It is complex and continues to grow as the child adds more concepts and links through learning. For example, 'place value' and 'quadrilateral' are conceptual structures. Place value is the system of numeration we use which sets the value of a digit, e.g. 9, according to its position or placing. So 9 in the units, tens, hundreds and tenths place has the value 9, 90, 900, 0.9, respectively, with zeros and the decimal point showing its position. Understanding place value means knowing this, and that each column is worth ten times more than its right-hand neighbour, and a tenth as much as its left-hand neighbour. So multiplication by 10, 100, 1000 means moving the whole number train (all the digits in a number) one, two or three places, respectively, to the left. It also means knowing that there is no end to the supply of places to the left and right, and that that numbers of any size can be expressed with ten digits and a dot.

'Quadrilateral' makes up a simpler conceptual structure. But it includes knowing the relationships between polygons, quadrilaterals, trapeziums, rhombuses, parallelograms, rectangles, squares and kites.

The conclusion that children construct their own knowledge applies even more to conceptual structures. Our memory of all that happens to us, both in and out of school, is put together in a unique way in our mind. I have certain pictures I associate with the numbers 1 to 100, but other people will have different pictures, or other feelings or associations. In other words, our conceptual structures for whole number are different. Of course they should share some features, such as the fact that 11 comes before 12.

Some researchers drew a very thorough map of the basic knowledge and skills making up two-digit subtraction, with about 50 components, not counting individual number facts such as $5 - 3 = 2$ (see Denvir and Brown, 1986). They tested quite a few primary school children and found that although the map was a useful tool in describing personal knowledge patterns, it didn't help predict what the children would learn next, even given teaching targeted very carefully at specific skills. Many children did not learn what they were taught, but more surprisingly learned what they were not taught! This fits with the constructivist theory that children follow their own unique learning path and construct their own personal conceptual structures.

Most of the mathematical knowledge that children learn in school is organised into conceptual structures, and the facts and skills they learn can also be fitted in or linked with them. The more connections children make between their facts, skills and concepts the easier it is for them to recall the knowledge and to use and apply it.

General strategies

Solving problems is one of the most important activities in mathematics. General strategies are methods or procedures that guide the choice of which skills or knowledge to use at each stage in problem solving.

Problems in school mathematics can be familiar or unfamiliar to a learner. When a problem is familiar the learner has done some like it before and should be able to remember how to go about solving it. When a problem has a new twist to it, the learner cannot recall how to go about it. This is when general strategies are useful, for they suggest possible approaches that may (or may not) lead to a solution. Open-ended problems or investigations may require the learner to be creative in exploring a new mathematical situation and to look for patterns.

The first area in which most children learn general strategies is in solving number problems. If asked to add 15 and 47 mentally, children learn to look for ways to simplify the problem. Thus they will often try to make ten with part of the units. They might take 3 from the 5 to add to the 7 to make 10 ($15 + 47 = 12 + 50 = 62$) or they might take 5 from the 7 to add to the 5 to make 10 ($15 + 47 = 20 + 42 = 62$). Some will simply add the tens and units separately ($15 + 47 = 50 + 12 = 62$). The general strategy is that of simplifying the problem through decomposing and recombining numbers.

The following are some typical general strategies that learners have been seen to use on a variety of more complex problems and investigations:

- representing the problem by drawing a diagram;
- trying to solve a simpler problem, in the hope that it will suggest a method;
- generating examples;
- making a table of results;
- putting the results in table in a helpful (suggestive) order;
- searching for a pattern among the data;
- thinking up a different approach and trying it out;
- checking or testing results.

General strategies are usually learned by example, or are invented or extended by the learner. They are recognised as important in the National Curriculum for children of all ages, and the first attainment target Using and Applying Mathematics is mainly concerned with developing and using general strategies. Three types of general strategy are included in National Curriculum mathematics. The first is 'making and monitoring decisions to solve problems' concerning the choice of materials, procedures and approaches in problem solving. The second is 'developing mathematical language and communication' which concerns the oral communication and written recording and presentation of problem solving and its results. The third is 'developing skills of mathematical reasoning' concerning mathematical thinking, and the use of reasoning to arrive at, check and justify mathematical results.

Attitudes

Attitudes to mathematics are the learner's feelings and responses to it, including like or dislike, enjoyment or lack of it, confidence in doing mathematics, and so on. The importance of attitudes to mathematics is widely accepted, and one of the common aims of teaching mathematics is that after study, all learners should like mathematics and enjoy using it, and should have confidence in their own mathematical abilities. As well as being a good thing in itself, a positive attitude often leads to greater efforts and better attainment in mathematics. However, too many youngsters and adults sadly say that they dislike mathematics and lack confidence in their abilities. Some even feel anxious whenever it comes up.

Attitudes to mathematics cannot be directly taught. They are the indirect outcome of a student's experience of learning mathematics over a number of years. However, sometimes a particular incident can change a student's attitude, such as teacher encouragement and interest in the learner's work (positive effect), or public criticism and humiliation of the learner in mathematics (negative effect). However, these effects are unpredictable and they depend on the learner's own response to the situation.

Appreciation

The appreciation of mathematics concerns understanding the big picture. It involves some awareness of what mathematics is as a whole (the inner aspect), as well as some understanding of the value and role of mathematics in society (the outer aspect). This outer appreciation involves some awareness of the following:

1 mathematics in everyday life;
2 the social uses of mathematics for communication and persuasion, from advertisements to government statistics;

3   the history of mathematics and how mathematical symbols, concepts and problems developed;
4   mathematics across all cultures, in art, and in all school subjects.

School mathematics too often treats only the first of these, with a little of the second. Often the outcome is that mathematics is seen only as a bag of tools, a set of basic skills, mostly in arithmetic, to be used when needed. But mathematics is much more than this. It is a central element in human history, society and culture. Mathematical symmetry has been a central element in religion and art since long before recorded history began. The development of mathematical perspective heralded a breakthrough in Renaissance painting. Every culture around the world uses mathematical patterns and designs in their art, crafts and rituals. Science, information technology, and all the subjects of the school curriculum draw upon aspects of mathematics. So to neglect the outer appreciation of mathematics is to offer the student an impoverished learning experience. This neglect may be for the best of reasons, to cover the necessary knowledge and skills of school mathematics. But when an outer appreciation is neglected, not only does school mathematics becomes less interesting and the learner culturally impoverished, it also means that mathematics becomes less useful, as learners fail to see the full range of its connections with daily and working life, and cannot make the unexpected links that imaginative problem solving requires. An outer appreciation of mathematics is not a luxury or an optional extra. It should be a part of every learner's educational entitlement.

An inner appreciation of mathematics involves some awareness of such things as the following:

1   big ideas in mathematics such as symmetry, randomness, paradox, proof and infinity;
2   the different branches of mathematics and their connections;
3   different philosophical views about the nature of mathematics.

Too often the teaching and learning of mathematics involves little more than the practice and mastery of a series of facts, skills and concepts through examples and problems. This fits with the well-known view that 'mathematics is not a spectator sport', i.e. that it is about solving problems, performing algorithms and procedures, computing solutions, and so on. Such activities are of course at the heart of mathematics. But if they become the whole of school mathematics, students may not see the big ideas behind what they are doing, let alone meet and wonder at the big ideas which are not in the National Curriculum, such as paradox, infinity, or chaos. Yet ideas like this are what fires the imagination of many young people, as well as the growing readership of popular mathematics books. Similarly, getting an appreciation of the different branches of mathematics and their links, e.g. that of algebra and geometry through Cartesian graphs, or becoming aware of controversies in accounts of the nature of mathematics, is not on the agenda of school mathematics. But any understanding of mathematics without some elements of this inner appreciation of mathematics is superficial, mechanical and utilitarian. I am not proposing something that is unrealistic or excessively idealistic, for in my view this is within the grasp of virtually all learners of mathematics. For example, many primary school children are fascinated by the idea of infinity, and have a sense of the 'neverendingness' of counting. Why should we not try to draw and build upon this interest, and their wonder and awe, in the teaching of mathematics?

Views concerning the nature of mathematics as a whole form the basis of what is called the philosophy of mathematics. There are many different views about mathematics, but most fall into one of three groups.

First, there is the dualist view that mathematics is a fixed collection of facts and rules. According to this view, mathematics is exact and certain, cut and dried, and there is always a rule to follow in solving problems. This view emphasises knowing the right facts and skills. The back-to-basics movement which emphasises basic numeracy as knowledge of facts, rules and skills, with little regard for understanding, meaning or problem solving, can be regarded as promoting a dualist view of mathematics.

Second, there is the absolutist view that mathematics is a well-organised body of objective knowledge, but that any claims in mathematics must be rationally justified by proofs. The traditional mathematics of GCE 'O' levels and 'A' levels where the emphasis is on understanding and applying the knowledge, and writing proofs, fits with the absolutist view.

Third, there is the relativist view of mathematics as a dynamic, problem-driven and continually expanding field of human creation and invention, in which patterns are generated and then distilled into knowledge. This view places most emphasis on mathematical activity, the doing of mathematics, and it accepts that there are many ways of solving any problem in mathematics.

Although the first (dualist) view is primitive and not philosophically defensible, both the second and third views correspond to legitimate philosophies of mathematics (see Ernest, 1991). However, it is important to distinguish between students' views of school mathematics, teachers' views of school mathematics, and teachers' views of mathematics as a discipline in its own right, for these may be very different. In addition, teachers' and learners' views of the nature of mathematics are not necessarily conscious. They may be implicit views which teachers or students have not stopped to consider consciously.

The Assessment of Performance Unit (1985) conducted extensive investigations into perceptions of mathematics, as well as towards attitudes to it. They found that students distinguished mathematical topics as hard–easy and as useful–not useful, and that these categories played a significant part in their overall view of mathematics. They also found that students tended uniformly to regard mathematics as a whole as both useful and important, reflecting a realistic perception of the weight that is attached to the subject in the modern world.

Mathematics in the National Curriculum

What mathematics is, is one thing, but what children have to learn is another. However, most of the elements discussed above are included in mathematics in the National Curriculum. This is the published curriculum that all children 5–16 years of age in normal state schools have to follow. Furthermore, although private schools are not bound by law to follow it, virtually all of them do, because they are aiming at the same tests and examinations for their children.

The structure of the National Curriculum

Overall the National Curriculum is organised in four key stages (see Table 1.1).

Primary schooling covers Key Stages 1 and 2. It includes the following National Curriculum subjects: English, mathematics, science, technology (design and technology, and information technology), history, geography, art, music, and physical education. The only

Table 1.1 National Curriculum key stages

Key stage	Pupil's ages	Year groups
Key stage 1	5–7	Years 1–2
Key stage 2	7–11	Years 3–6
Key stage 3	11–14	Years 7–9
Key stage 4	14–16	Years 10–11

exception is in Wales, which also includes Welsh (and English is omitted in Welsh-speaking classes for Key Stage 1).

For each subject and for each key stage, there are programmes of study which set out what pupils should be taught. There are also 'attainment targets' which set out the standards that pupils are expected to reach in particular topics. For example, in mathematics the four attainment targets are: Using and Applying Mathematics; Number (including Algebra, for older children); Shape, Space and Measures; and Handling Data. In mathematics, as in most subjects, each attainment target is divided into eight levels of increasing difficulty, plus an additional higher level for exceptional performance (beyond GCSE), for gifted students.

Mathematics in the National Curriculum

At Key stage 1, for pupils aged 5 to 7 years, the programme of study in mathematics has 3 elements, which can be summarised as follows:

1　**Using and Applying Mathematics.** Pupils should learn to use and apply mathematics in practical tasks, in real-life problems and in mathematics itself. They should be taught to make decisions to solve simple problems, to begin to check their work, and to use mathematical language and to explain their thinking.
2　**Number.** Pupils should develop flexible methods of working with number, orally and mentally; using varied numbers and ways of recording, with practical resources, calculators and computers. They should begin to understand place value, develop methods of calculation and solving number problems. They should also collect, record and interpret data (later this becomes part of Handling Data).
3　**Shape, Space and Measures.** Pupils should have practical experiences using various materials, electronic devices, and practical contexts for measuring. They should begin to understand and use patterns and properties of shape, position and movement, and of measures.

The programme of study in mathematics at Key Stage 2 for pupils aged 7 to 11 years has 4 elements.

1　**Using and Applying Mathematics.** Pupils should learn to use and apply mathematics in practical tasks, in real-life problems and in mathematics itself. They should begin to organise and extend tasks themselves, devise their own ways of recording, ask questions and follow alternative suggestions to support the development of their reasoning skills.

There should be further development of their ability to make and check decisions to solve problems, to use mathematical language to explain their thinking, and to reason logically.

2   **Number.** Pupils should develop flexible methods of working with number, in writing, orally and mentally, using varied resources, and ways of recording, and calculators and computers. They should develop an understanding of place value and the number system, the relationships between numbers and methods of calculation, and of solving number problems. They should begin to understand the patterns and ideas which lead to the basic concepts of algebra.

3   **Shape, Space and Measures.** Pupils should use geometrical ideas to solve problems, have practical experiences using various materials, electronic devices, and practical contexts for measuring. They should begin to understand and use patterns including some drawn from different cultural traditions and extend their understanding of the properties of shape, position and movement, and of measures.

4   **Handling Data.** Pupils should learn to ask basic statistical questions. They should collect, represent and interpret data using tables, graphs, diagrams and computers. They should begin to understand and use probability.

This summary of the National Curriculum contains many of the different elements of school mathematics discussed above. First of all, it specifies in detail the facts, skills and conceptual knowledge that children need to learn in the areas of number, geometry and measurement (Shape, Space and Measures), and probability, statistics and computer mathematics (Handling Data). Secondly, the general strategies of problem solving are given an important place, both in the special attainment target Using and Applying Mathematics, but also in the others too. Three main types of strategy are included in the first attainment target. First, there are strategies for *using mathematics*, so that it becomes a powerful tool for children to apply in solving problems across a range of contexts. Second, there are strategies for *communicating in mathematics* so that children can talk, listen, read and write mathematics with understanding. Third, there are strategies for *developing ideas of argument and proof*, so that children can make and test predictions, and can reason, generalise, test and justify mathematical ideas and arguments.

Attitudes to and appreciation of mathematics are the elements discussed above which are missing from the National Curriculum. But these are things that cannot easily be taught or tested, perhaps not at all. In the early development of the National Curriculum, the first report of the Mathematics Working Group (Department of Education and Science, 1987) included large sections on attitudes and appreciation. But in the end it was decided that because it was not possible to spell out exactly how they should be taught and tested, they should permeate the whole curriculum. A supplement to the National Curriculum was published, called the *Non-Statutory Guidance for Mathematics* (National Curriculum Council, 1989a). This emphasises teaching mathematics so that learners develop positive attitudes to and an appreciation of mathematics. For example it states the following:

Mathematics provides a way of viewing and making sense of the world. It is used to analyse and communicate information and ideas and to tackle a range of practical tasks and real life problems.

Mathematics also provides the material and means for creating new imaginative worlds to explore. Through exploration within mathematics itself, new mathematics is created and current ideas are modified and extended (p. A2).

After describing the usefulness of mathematics in everyday life, work, and other school subjects, the document continues as follows:

> As a complement to work which focuses on the practical value of mathematics as a tool for everyday life, pupils should also have opportunities to explore and appreciate the structure of mathematics itself. Mathematics is not only taught because it is useful. It should also be a source of delight and wonder, offering pupils intellectual excitement and an appreciation of its essential creativity (p. A3).

There are also other sections which stress the importance of developing mathematical appreciation, such as section F on the importance of cross curricular work for mathematics. The document also includes recommendations for good mathematics teaching, including the following.

Activities should enable pupils to develop a positive attitude to mathematics.
Attitudes to foster and encourage include:
* fascination with the subject;
* interest and motivation;
* pleasure and enjoyment from mathematical activities;
* appreciation of the power, purpose and relevance of mathematics;
* satisfaction derived from a sense of achievement;
* confidence in an ability to do mathematics at an appropriate level (p. B11).

So this document pays particular attention to the development of positive attitudes and appreciation in mathematics, and the importance of these elements for the National Curriculum. Overall, it is clear that the National Curriculum in mathematics emphasises all of the elements of school mathematics listed above, including facts, skills, concepts, general strategies, attitudes and appreciation, some directly and some indirectly.

Teaching and learning mathematics

The previous sections discuss different elements of school mathematics. Each of them plays an essential part in all mathematical work and thinking including using and applying mathematics. Facts, skills and conceptual structures make up the necessary basic knowledge for applying mathematics and solving problems. General strategies are concerned with the tactics of applications: what to do and how to use this knowledge to solve problems. Appreciation and attitudes also contribute to using and applying mathematics by providing interest and confidence and through fostering persistence, imaginative links, and creative thinking.

The distinction between these different elements of school mathematics and their importance was part of the message of the landmark Cockcroft Report, which influenced the development of the National Curriculum. This report argued that each of these elements requires separate attention and different teaching approaches. On purely scientific grounds, the report concluded, it is not sufficient to concentrate on children learning facts and skills, if numeracy, understanding, and problem solving ability are what are wanted. So the more extreme claims of the back-to-basics movement in education were rejected: basic skills alone are not enough. And this argument still remains valid.

On the basis of its review of psychological research the Cockcroft Report made its most famous recommendation.

Mathematics teaching at all levels should include opportunities for
* exposition by the teacher;
* discussion between teacher and pupils and between pupils themselves;
* appropriate practical work;
* consolidation and practice of fundamental skills and routines;
* problem solving, including the application of mathematics to everyday situations;
* investigational work (Cockcroft, 1982, paragraph 243).

So the teaching approaches needed to develop the different elements of mathematics at any level of schooling include investigational work, problem solving, discussion, practical work, exposition (direct instruction) by the teacher, as well as the consolida- tion and practice of skills and routines. Figure 1.1 shows how these teaching approaches can help to develop children's appreciation of mathematics, strategies for tackling new problems, conceptual structures in mathematics, as well as their knowledge of mathe- matical facts and skills.

The connecting lines in Figure 1.1 show some of the more important influences of different teaching and learning styles on the learned elements of school mathematics, but further lines could be added. The most important point made by the Cockcroft Report is that if we want all of the outcomes listed on the right-hand side to be developed, then we need to use the mix of approaches listed on the left-hand side of the figure.

The Cockcroft model of teaching strategies is a balanced one, because it says that no one method should dominate, and the method we choose should depend on what we want the children to learn, and what is suitable for the resources available and for the children and

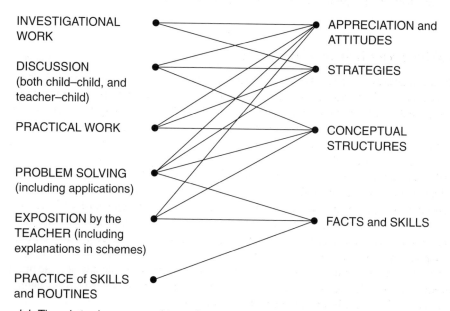

Figure 1.1 The relation between teaching styles and learning outcomes

school. Nevertheless, teaching approaches can be controversial according to whether traditional or progressive approaches are in fashion.

A quick look at the history of primary mathematics confirms this. In the 1950s children mainly worked on arithmetic and measures in the form of old-fashioned sums, not all that different from Victorian arithmetic. In the 1960s primary school children not only began to study 'modern mathematics', instead of just arithmetic, but there was also a new emphasis on practical work, problem solving and 'discovery learning' in mathematics. This was due to the influence of a new way of thinking expressed in the Nuffield primary mathematics project and Her Majesty's Inspector Edith Biggs' widely read report on primary mathematics. In the 1970s there was a reaction, the back-to-basics movement, but the most significant development was the widespread adoption of individualised primary mathematics schemes in school, which children worked from at their own pace. Although these persisted in the 1980s, this decade also saw the endorsement of problem solving and investigational work in mathematics by the Cockcroft Report and HMI, and later the National Curriculum through the attainment target Using and Applying Mathematics. So primary school teachers worked hard to include this in the mathematics curriculum too, although many were worried and did not feel they fully understood what was involved. In the mid-1990s there has been an official turn against 'progressive teaching approaches' and whole-class interactive teaching has been endorsed by OFSTED and the government Department for Education and Employment. Thus the new 'numeracy hour' requires (or rather strongly recommends) that skills practice and whole-class teaching should be used daily in primary mathematics.

The Cockcroft model of teaching should satisfy all of these changes in fashion, because it argues that children need to experience all approaches in a balanced way, not just learner-centred approaches (problem solving, investigational and practical work, pupil-to-pupil discussion) or teacher-centred ones (teacher exposition, consolidation and practice of basic skills, teacher-led discussion). Furthermore, the so-called 'child-centred' approaches are necessary if children are to be able to make practical use of the mathematics they learn, as teaching Using and Applying Mathematics makes very clear.

The different purposes of four main different teaching approaches are as follows. First of all, in *direct instruction*, the teacher states and shows the class the rules, skills or concepts to be learned, and provides the class with exercises to apply this new knowledge, often showing worked examples. The students listen and watch, and then apply the new knowledge to the exercises set. In so doing they are learning and applying or practising and reinforcing facts, skills and concepts.

In *guided instruction* the teacher arranges practical tasks or a sequence of examples which have a pattern or indirectly embody a concept or rule. What the learner has to do is to work through the tasks and spot the rule or learn the concept or skill implicit in the given examples. The learner has to work to gain the new knowledge, and as well as developing understanding learns to spot patterns and to generalise.

In *problem solving*, the teacher's role is to present problems, but leave the solution methods open to the students. Learners have to attempt to solve the problems using their own methods, and learn to become independent problem solvers, as well as developing their general strategies.

In *investigatory mathematics*, the teacher presents an initial mathematical topic or area of investigation, or may approve a student's own project. The learner's role is to ask themselves relevant questions to investigate in the project area and to explore the topic freely, hoping to develop some interesting mathematical ideas. So this approach encourages creative thinking as well as the use of problem-solving strategies.

Table 1.2 summarises what is involved in these four teaching approaches. For each approach it shows what the teacher does, what the learner does, and the processes involved.

Needless to say, this is a very simplified picture of what goes on in the different teaching approaches. For example, in investigatory mathematics the teacher does much more than just presenting an initial area of investigation or approving a student's choice; such as maintaining an orderly classroom, circulating among the children asking questions to get them thinking in new ways, or getting them to check their work; controlling the use of time and equipment, and so on. To be worthwhile such activities must take place within an overall curriculum plan for teaching the National Curriculum.

Two things should be stressed about this range of teaching approaches. First of all, in each case the learners are involved, taking an active part in their own learning. This is essential for successful learning, and is discussed more in the next section. Second, although sometimes child-centred teaching approaches are regarded as inefficient and wasteful of time, they provide something that teacher-centred approaches cannot. This is practice in creative uses and applications of mathematics. Recently there have been a number of international comparisons of achievement in mathematics. British children at ages 9 and 13 have come out below average on number skills. This is something that needs to be improved upon, and has been much criticised in the press. In contrast children in Japan, Singapore and other Pacific Rim countries have come out top in this area. Experts have been sent out to the Far East to find out what their secret is. However, in problem solving and the practical applications of mathematics, British children came out very nearly top. This is something we should be proud of, but little has been written about it in the papers. Interestingly, the Japanese experts are saying that their own students are not creative enough in their thinking, and future economic success will depend upon developing this. So they are sending experts to Britain and the West to find out how we teach creative problem solving so well. So we should try to keep up the tradition of using a variety of teaching approaches because this is what is helping to develop

Table 1.2 The role of teacher and student in different teaching approaches

Teaching approach	Role of the teacher	Role of the learner	Process involved
Direct instruction	To explicitly teach rules, skills or concepts, and provide exercises for application	To apply the given knowledge to exercises	The direct applications of facts, skills and concepts
Guided instruction	To give practical tasks or a sequence of examples representing a concept or rule implicitly	To identify the rule or concept implicit in the given examples	Generalisation, rule spotting, concept formation
Problem solving	To present a problem, leaving solution methods open	To attempt to solve the problem using own methods	Problem-solving strategies
Investigatory mathematics	To present an initial area of investigation, or approve a student's project	To choose questions to investigate in project area and to explore the topic freely	Creative thinking and problem-solving strategies

all the skills and capabilities our children will need for the world of the twenty-first century, including creative problem-solving skills.

Learning mathematics

In the past few decades we have come to know much about how children learn mathematics. The Swiss psychologist Jean Piaget made extensive studies of children learning, paying special attention to mathematics. He had the great insight, based on his observations, that children interpret their situations and school tasks through schemas that they have built up, which are the conceptual structures discussed earlier. These structures guide what children understand, what they expect, and how they act or respond. His theory places great emphasis on operations, whether physical, imagined or mathematical, and such features as whether they can be undone, once done, and what stays the same during operations. These ideas have direct applications to mathematical operations where, for example, the operation of addition can be undone (subtraction), and changing to equivalent fractions leaves the value unchanged.

Piaget also had a theory that children's development goes through fixed stages, with different kinds of thinking at each stage. While there is some truth in this on the large scale, for example children usually have to master the more basic ideas of number before they move on to the more abstract ideas of algebra, it has been shown that language and the social context have more influence on the child's development than Piaget thought.

One of the important theories based on Piaget's work is called constructivism, which was mentioned above in discussing conceptual structures. This is the theory that first of all, all learners (indeed all persons) make sense of their situations and any tasks in terms of their existing knowledge and schemas (conceptual structures). So existing schemas act like a pair of tinted spectacles, everything seen is seen through them and coloured by them. Secondly, all new knowledge is built up from existing ideas and knowledge extended or put together in a new way. This means that we only understand new things in terms of what we already know. Thirdly, all learning is active, although this activity is primarily mental, so being told or shown things may suggest new ways for the learner to interpret or connect her existing knowledge, but cannot directly 'give' the knowledge to the learner. Children do not just 'receive' knowledge, they have to reconstruct it. In other words, for proper learning we need to fully understand new ideas before we can make them our own. Fourth, because of the active nature of all learning, mistakes are a natural part of the same creative process that results in standard (correct) knowledge and skills. Learners need to be guided to test and to adjust their understandings towards the standard knowledge. So mistakes are a necessary and good thing, as steps on the way to proper understanding. Children need to feel free to try things out and make mistakes without any shame, fear or feeling the need to hide them, so that they can correct them and continue to learn without the interference of any bad feelings.

These are important ideas, with obvious applications in the teaching and learning of mathematics. However Piaget's is not the only the theory of learning and many people also look to the theories of the great Russian psychologist Lev Vygotsky (1978). His idea is that language and social experience play a dominant role in learning. He argues that most new knowledge is learned through language and other symbolic forms including pictures, diagrams and mathematical symbols, and we first meet these when they are presented to us by other persons. So we learn language by hearing it used, by imitating, through being guided and corrected, and from this we attain basic mastery which we expand through use and practice. Vygotsky describes what a learner can do as in terms of zones. The first zone consists of what the student can do unaided, so it is made up of the abilities developed so far. The second zone consists of what student can do with help from someone else, their teacher, peers or parents. These make up the tasks and abilities within reach, but not yet attained. This zone is called the Zone of Proximal Development. Vygotsky's theory is that teaching should be directed at this zone, because it extends what the leaner can do unaided. So the student can be shown simple worked examples to imitate, and after this experience will gradually master the skills or types of tasks. Indeed, understanding may not come until later, after the skill has become routine.

Cross-curricular dimensions

This book is about the teaching and learning of mathematics in the primary school. However, what you actually teach is children, and they do not necessarily do all their learning in separate 'subject boxes'. Mathematics is just one of these 'boxes', and in teaching it we always need to be aware of how it links with other subjects, and with children's own experiences and their lives. One important innovation in the National Curriculum is to pay special attention to these links, in the form of cross-curricular dimensions, themes and skills (National Curriculum Council, 1990). These are cross-curricular links and ideas which are common to all of the subjects of the school curriculum, and which are supposed to weave them all together into a unified whole. The cross-curricular skills are numeracy, literacy, oracy, information techno-logy skills, and personal and social skills. Clearly children must learn number and the use of calculators and computers in mathematics. But they also must learn to read and write, listen and speak in their mathematics lessons. Personal and social skills come up everywhere, in learning to work together, in learning to listen, respect and value each other's ideas and contributions, and so on. So these skills are not difficult to see and include in mathematics teaching.

The cross-curricular themes include economic and industrial understanding, careers, health, citizenship, and the environment. Even in the primary school, children need to be developing an understanding of the economic basis of society and an awareness of the world of work, and the central role of mathematics in these areas. They must also begin to understand their roles as future citizens and how their choices affect their health and the environment. So much of the information about health and the environment, whether local, national or global is best displayed mathematically, using numbers and graphs. Even from a very young age children care about what is happening to the environment and teachers can build on this both to teach them mathematics and to help them grow into caring and responsible citizens.

The cross-curricular dimensions identified by the National Curriculum Council are equal opportunities, multicultural, and special educational needs. Equal opportunities are about the different opportunities given to boys and girls, and the importance of fairness in their treatment. In the past, mathematics was thought of as a boy's subject, and often boys were encouraged and girls discouraged in mathematics. Mostly this was done in unintended ways, like teachers asking boys more challenging questions, and maths schemes showing fewer pictures of girls and women, and then mostly in passive or traditional roles. Since the 1980s this has changed, and now girls do as well in mathematics as boys throughout all of primary and secondary schooling, and most teachers expect as much from girls as boys. However there is still a residual belief in society that mathematics is a male subject, and research shows that girls are still, on average, less confident about their mathematical ability than boys

(Walkerdine, 1998). So it is just as important today that teachers should provide equal opportunities in their classrooms, and try to develop confidence in all of their children.

The multicultural dimension is the second in the set of links identified by the National Curriculum Council. There is a mistaken view that multicultural mathematics is about accommodating the needs of ethnic minority students in the classroom. Actually, multicultural mathematics is about the appreciation of mathematics discussed at the beginning of this chapter. It includes appreciating the historical and cultural roots and uses of the subject. Through learning about the Middle Eastern (Mesopotamia) and African (Egypt) origins of mathematics children develop an understanding of the global interdependence of all humankind. They need to be aware of the Hindu and Mayan origins of zero, without which we couldn't calculate effectively or have computers, and the role of the Greek and Arabic civilisations in the invention of geometry and algebra. Children can learn about symmetry by making Hindu Rangoli patterns, Islamic tessellations and African sand drawings, so developing their mathematical understanding through enjoyable creative work. Modern Britain is a multicultural society, it is part of a united Europe and part of a global village. A multicultural approach not only enriches the teaching and learning of mathematics and the experiences of children. It also prepares them to be citizens of a multicultural society, and of the world!

The last cross-curricular dimension in this set is that of special educational needs. At any one time, one in five schoolchildren may experience a 'special educational need' (Warnock, 1978). This may be even more common in mathematics because of the wide spread of achievement levels. There are many possible special needs in mathematics. Children may be low achievers in school mathematics, and may need extra work to help them understand and master concepts and skills. Children may display exceptional ability in part or all of mathematics ('mathematical giftedness'), and need additional enrichment work to keep them challenged and interested. Children may have specific learning difficulties in some area of mathematics, such as fractions, and may need extra attention and work to help them get over this stumbling block. Sometimes poor reading skills and language difficulties, including dyslexia, make learning mathematics difficult, and these need special attention. There are yet other types of special needs that can surface in mathematics, such as difficulties due to physical impairments (e.g. children who are hard of hearing), and children who have emotional or behavioural difficulties which interfere with their mathematical learning and performance. In each case, the teacher must find an individual solution that suits the needs of the particular child, calling on the help of others if necessary. Whatever their special needs, all children are entitled to a broad and balanced curriculum and learning experience in mathematics (National Curriculum Council, 1989b). Teachers must be especially careful not to prejudge what a child can do, and to put a ceiling on it. It is the teacher's responsibility to bring children on as far they can go, in their mathematics learning. We never know how far forward that is until we see what they have achieved!

This chapter summarises some of the more important ideas about the teaching and learning of mathematics in the primary school. Many of them are difficult ideas, but they will come to mean more as you continue to use them in teaching mathematics and in watching and helping children to learn. Being a teacher means undertaking a lengthy and exciting journey of lifelong learning. We wish you luck as you continue on this career, and we hope to help you to further develop the most important things to take with you: an informed eye and the desire to keep on learning and inquiring.

References

Assessment of Performance Unit (1985) *A Review of Monitoring in Mathematics 1978 to 1982*, London: Department of Education and Science.

Bell, A. W., Küchemann, D. and Costello, J. (1983) *A Review of Research in Mathematical Education: Part A, Teaching and Learning*, NFER-Nelson: Windsor.

Cockcroft, W. (Chair) (1982) *Mathematics Counts, Report of the Committee of Inquiry into the Teaching of Mathematics*, London: HMSO.

Denvir, B. and Brown, M. (1986) Understanding of Number Concepts in Low Attaining 7–9 Year Olds: Parts I and II, *Educational Studies in Mathematics*, Volume 17, pp. 15–36 and 143–164.

Department of Education and Science (1987) *The Interim Report of the Mathematics Working Group*, London: DES.

Ernest, P. (1991) *The Philosophy of Mathematics Education*, London: Falmer Press.

Hart, K. (ed.) (1981) *Children's Understanding of Mathematics: 11–16*, London: John Murray.

HMI (1985) *Mathematics from 5 to 16*, London: HMSO.

National Curriculum Council (1989a) *Non-Statutory Guidance for Mathematics*, York: National Curriculum Council.

National Curriculum Council (1989b) *A Curriculum For All (Curriculum Guidance 2: Special Educational Needs in the National Curriculum)*, York: National Curriculum Council.

National Curriculum Council (1990) *The Whole Curriculum*, York: National Curriculum Council.

Vygotsky, L. S. (1978) *Mind in Society. The development of the higher psychological processes.* Cambridge, MA: Harvard University Press.

Walkerdine, V. (1998) *Counting Girls Out* (2nd edn), London: Falmer Press.

Warnock, M. (Chair) (1978) *Report of the Committee of Enquiry into the Education of Handicapped Children and Young People*, London: HMSO.

Section B

The aim of this section is to support you to enhance your subject knowledge in mathematical topics. The topics included in this section are selected on the basis of what is considered to be necessary for a sound understanding of the contents of the National Curriculum at Key Stages 1, 2 and 3, the requirements of the Initial Training National Curriculum in mathematics set by the Teacher Training Agency and the *Framework for teaching mathematics* to implement the National Numeracy Strategy.

The following objectives guided the style and content of the chapters in this section. They are designed to:

* encourage you to think about the mathematics you already know;
* identify gaps in your knowledge and understanding of mathematical topics;
* consider mathematical topics at your own level through relevant contexts;
* make connections with various strands of mathematical topics;
* acquire or revise the correct terminology and language of mathematics;
* consider some key issues in the teaching of the topics to children.

Each chapter in this section begins with a list of the mathematics topics covered; sub-headings are used to guide the reader through the various topics included in the chapter. Mathematics is developed through examples. Emphasis is placed on addressing the underlying principles of a topic with the aim of facilitating greater understanding of the topic. Many of the principles are explained in order to facilitate thinking, in depth, about why many 'procedures' and 'rules' actually work. It is hoped that you will read the chapters in this section slowly and systematically; as the intention is to provide explanations of complex ideas rather than offer superficial discussions about mathematical topics. Within the text, key ideas about teaching the topics are briefly referred to , where appropriate, but it is assumed that you will refer to textbook schemes and sources for other practical ideas.

We recommend that you take time to read each section of the chapters. You may read a section about a topic that you are teaching to your class, or about a topic that is being covered on your course. Before reading a section it is a good idea to think about or write down the ideas you already know about the topic, also aspects of the topic you may feel anxious about or have difficulties with. While you read the section make notes about new ideas and vocabulary you come across. As you read through the text, it is also a good idea to give yourself some questions to tackle before you try the exercises at the end of the chapter. Teachers who trialled these sections found it useful to look at sections of children's textbooks and teachers' handbooks and relate the ideas to what is taught to children.

The chapters dealing with 'number' are longer than the rest. This is because the 'number' sections in both the National Curriculum and the TTA National Curriculum are substantially longer than the rest of the other sections. Also, in view of the emphasis placed by the National Numeracy Strategy on developing numerical skills and understanding, it was felt that you would appreciate opportunities to reflect on aspects of 'number' in greater detail than you have done in the past.

Finally, remember that learning and understanding mathematics takes time. As you read the chapters in this section, you should gain more insight into what each mathematics topic is about and develop your expertise and confidence to teach it. This, in turn, should enable you to teach it in such a way that the children you teach will both enjoy learning mathematics and understand what they are learning.

Auditing your subject knowledge

At the end of the Chapters 2 to 7 two types of tasks are provided. The first is a collection of tasks which enable you to think about the implications for teaching particular topics to children and the other is a set of tasks for you to try. Two sets of tests are included at the end of Chapter 8, which you may use for auditing your knowledge. The Record of Achievement and the audit grid in the appendices may also be of help.

Chapter 2

Whole numbers

This chapter focuses on:

2.1 Development of number concepts in the early years
2.2 The role of algorithms
2.3 Place value representation of numbers
2.4 Number operations
2.5 Factors and prime numbers
2.6 Negative numbers

Something to think about:

We have ten toes on our feet and ten fingers on our hands. It is natural for us to use a counting system based on ten. The sounds and sights we interpret to get information about our surroundings are received by two ears and two eyes. Is it therefore natural for us to use an information technology based on two?

2.1 Development of number concepts in the early years

Cardinal and ordinal numbers

Early experiences with counting make children deal with two aspects of number: the *ordinality* and the *cardinality* of number. Counting 'one, two, three, four' goldfish in a bowl or counting 'one, two, three, four' paws on a cat involves using 1, 2, 3 and 4 as ordinal numbers. Recognising that the goldfish and the paws of the cat have something in common – that they both consist of four things – involves insight into their common cardinality; the cardinal number 4 is used to describe the *fourness* of the goldfish and the paws. The same number symbol is used for both aspects – the ordinal and cardinal. The two aspects allow each number to have two roles. When 4 is being used in counting up to 4, it is playing its ordinal role, but when 4 is being used to indicate the size of a group of 4, it is playing its cardinal role.

Which aspect of number is involved when you see that a person or team is ranked fourth?

Somehow, you need to count towards the person or team to see that the position is fourth; here, the *ordinal* aspect of the number four is involved.

Immediately spotting the cardinality of a group of things is possible, for most people, perhaps for small numbers.

The cardinality of a group of things is the number of things which are in the group.

Here is an activity for you to try.

Counting strategies
This activity is designed to help you to gain insight into the ability of adults and children to spot the cardinality of a small group of objects. Show a few adults and children a small collection of things, say 5, 6, 7 or 8. Find out how they determine the number in that set of things.
Do they count 1,2,3 and so on?
Do they use their fingers to count?
Do they count in their heads?
Do they 'just know' immediately by observing?
How large a group of objects can they spot immediately, without consciously doing anything?

Young children need to be provided with experiences to learn about the three aspects of number. Two have already been dealt with – the cardinal and the ordinal numbers. The third is the use of number symbols.

The cardinal aspect of a number is used to describe the number in a set: 10 beads in the set.

The ordinal aspect of a number refers to a number in relation to its position in the set: colour the fifth bead red.

A number symbol, say 9, is used both to express the cardinality of the number 'nine' and to show something in the 9th place. It is also sometimes used as a label: A9 or B9 (as a road).

Counting in groups

When you are counting the number of objects in a set, does it make a difference if the things are arranged in some smaller groups of two or three or four? Does this allow the cardinality to be arrived at by spotting multiples of two, three or four?

Show some children the following picture and ask: how many leaves are there? Then ask how they worked it out.

You may find that one of the following strategies were used.

- Recognise that the leaves are arranged in threes and add 3 repeatedly to get the total.
- Use the knowledge of the 3 times table and work out 6 lots of 3 to be 18.
- Count in ones from 1 to 18.

Here is another activity for you to try with a few children.

Give a child a large bag of beans – about 50 or so.

Ask that child to find out how many beans there are.

As well as observing the child, conduct an interview to carefully determine the strategy used by the child.

In what way is the child's strategy different to yours?

Repeat the experiment using 2p coins instead of beans.

In what ways have your findings changed?

Try this with more children.

The results of this experiment should illustrate an important and very useful principle in learning mathematics.

The best way of doing something depends on the context and on the individual, but children need to be shown and taught a range of strategies for doing mathematics so that they can choose the most efficient strategy.

For example, a child who decides to count 50 objects in 'ones' can be shown that counting in groups is a more effective way of counting.

2.2 The role of algorithms

The idea of an algorithm will be developed throughout the text. So the following statements are worth reflecting on:

1   An algorithm is a procedure for doing something. You can perform a calculation using different algorithms. For example, to add 35 + 36, you may use 'double 35 + 1 = 71' or you may choose a 'standard' algorithm, for example one you have learnt at school – writing the two numbers vertically as a sum to add them.

2   An efficient algorithm is one which does the job better than other algorithms.

3   Although learners of mathematics should be taught algorithms for calculations, these can be mental and written; there are times when the learner can judge the context of the procedure and find a more efficient algorithm for dealing with the calculation. When asked to subtract 398 from 500 on a worksheet, a child may decide to use a mental strategy which is based on a number line: from 398 to 400 is 2, 400 to 500 is 100 making the answer 102.

Discipline is required for item 2 above, but item 3 requires a degree of freedom for the learner so that teachers may adopt a different role of facilitator of a creative and flexible attitude in the learner.

2.3 Place value representation of numbers

Efficient ways of handling numbers depend very much on how the numbers are represented. Understanding algorithms and finding more efficient algorithms, in turn, depends on how well a learner appreciates our present number system. This appreciation may be enhanced by considering some aspects of the Roman number system – no longer used for computation, but still appearing on some documents.

Recall that the following symbols are used in the Roman system:

- I for one
- V for five
- X for ten
- L for fifty
- C for one hundred
- M for one thousand.

Are there any advantages in this system?

In order to write a number – up to 999 in our present system – a Roman needed to know only five symbols rather than ten.

The Roman symbols make various simplifications possible:

- instead of IIIII they could write V
- instead of VV they could write X
- instead of XXXXX they could write L
- instead of LL they could write C.

In some ways there are 'place value' conventions in the Roman system. Consider the difference between IX, representing nine, and XI, representing eleven. The meaning of the 'I' depends on its position relative to the 'X'; to the left of X the I means 'one less than' whereas to the right of X the I means 'one more than'. Does this convention always hold? For 32 the Romans wrote XXXII. The II indicates 'two more than', but the 30 is represented by XXX. Here the convention breaks down. The XXX means 'ten and ten and ten'. Spending a little time considering the good as well as the not-so-good features of the Roman system will be useful preparation for making a balanced appraisal of our present system which uses the ten symbols 0, 1, 2, 3, 4, 5, 6, 7, 8 and 9. When you next observe young children counting with their fingers you may be reminded of the Roman system. Can you link it with the human hand? Does 'I' look like a finger? When 'V' was used for five instead of 'IIIII', was one open palm being symbolised rather than five fingers?

If the Roman system can be imagined as linked with one hand, then our present system can be linked with two hands. Yet are there some similarities between the two systems? What about 555? The first 5 means five hundred, the next 5 means fifty and the rightmost 5 simply means five units. Is there some similarity between 555 and XXX? Think about it! In the hundreds, tens and units system the meaning of a 5 depends on its position in the number. In contrast, the meaning of each X in the Roman number is the same regardless of its position in the number. However, the 555 makes use of a compacting technique just like that used in XXX. It is a compact way of writing 500 + 50 + 5, as 30 is thought of in the Roman system as X and X and X. Learning how numbers can be split into the sum of parts is a very useful skill which can enhance your understanding of numerical algorithms and will be considered in the next section.

The base ten representation of numbers

The place value numeration system is based on two fundamental principles:

- the grouping aspect – grouping in tens. The system is referred to as the 'base ten' system;
- Using ten digits: 0, 1, 2, 3, 4, 5, 6, 7, 8, 9, 10 in different positions you can write any number. The position of digits from left to right determines the value of the number. For example: 546 means 6 singles, 4 tens and 5 hundreds
  304 means 4 singles, 0 tens and 3 hundreds.

Key issues in teaching place value to children

As a starting point, it is useful to remind ourselves that a good understanding of place value of whole numbers and its extension to decimal numbers is vital because it is the basis of both our mental and written calculations. There is evidence (Brown, 1981; Koshy, 1988; SCAA, 1997) to show that children at all key stages have difficulties in understanding many aspects of place value. Some of the areas which cause concern include difficulties with zero as a place holder, reading and writing large numbers, problems remembering rules of algorithms for adding and subtracting numbers which involve carrying or exchanging.

One possible reason suggested by SCAA (1997) for young children's difficulty in internalising the principle of place value is the nature of the names of numbers between 10 and 59. The reason for Japanese students acquiring a greater understanding of the place value concept is explained in terms of the Japanese number system having number names, up to hundreds, 'consistent with the numbers they represent', e.g. the Japanese for twenty-two shows there are two tens. It is suggested that in the 'English system, the naming of numbers in relation to their place value does not begin to appear until numbers containing hundreds, e.g. three hundred and twenty-nine'. Restricting young pupils to numbers up to 20 may be doing them a disservice because it is not until one gets to the 'sixties' that the place value and number names come together: six-ty, seven-ty, eight(t)y and ninety. 'Twenty and thirty instead of two-ty and three-ty do not make the structure explicit' (SCAA, 1977, p. 7–8).

When working with numbers, it is useful to bear in mind the *two* aspects of number:

- the 'number-line aspect' which deals with the order in which numbers appear on a numberline, and
- the grouping concept which focuses on considering numbers in groups of hundreds, tens and units and so on.

The *Framework for teaching mathematics* (DfEE, 1999) to support the implementation of the National Numeracy Strategy places much emphasis on teaching place value.

Teaching place value

In the following section, some specific teaching resources for teaching place value are dealt with:

- place value arrow cards
- base ten materials
- sets of 0–9 digit cards for discussing place value.

The arrow cards, as shown below, have been found particularly useful by teachers to support children's understanding of place value. To make a set of arrow cards, you need nine cards printed with 100 to 900, nine cards printed with 10 to 90 and nine cards printed with 1 to 9.

By overlaying three cards from the different sets you can make any 3-digit number, e.g. 687:

By targeting questions such as: *make a number with 3 hundreds in it, can you make a number between 350 and 450, make the number 235, you have 467 – how many more is needed to make 500?* and so on, you are focusing on the important principle that the value of a digit depends on its position in a number. For a class activity you will need several sets of arrow cards. During an introduction of a lesson, you could ask a group of children to choose three cards – one from the hundreds, one from the tens and one from the units – and make a 3-digit number. Ask the group of children to stand in 'order' based on their numbers, for example, smallest first. Ask the children whose number is the nearest to 400.

Here is an activity which demonstrates the grouping and regrouping principles of place value.

Ask the children to make a 3-digit number using the arrow cards: say 356 was made by one child. Ask the child what number needs to be subtracted (taken away) in order to show a zero in the tens column. Quite often, children will say 'subtract five' and are surprised that you are in fact taking away 50!

Place value blocks, below, usually referred to as base 10 material, are commonly used to show the relative sizes of singles (units), tens, hundreds and so on. Base 10 blocks can be used for making a model of 389 as: 3 hundreds, 8 tens and 9 singles. These were designed by Z.P. Dienes specifically to model the place value system of number. Most schools have these materials; their effective use will depend on the way children are encouraged to study how their structure relates to the way numbers are constructed.

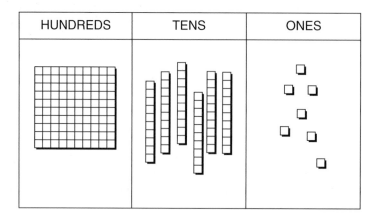

Base 10 materials can also be used to demonstrate number operations which are dealt with later.

Activities which use digit cards 0 to 9 and place value boards also provide opportunities for enhancing children's understanding of the principle that the value of a digit is determined by the position it occupies. An example is given below.

Try playing this game with up to 4 players.

You need a few sets of shuffled 0–9 cards, placed face down and a place value board for each player.

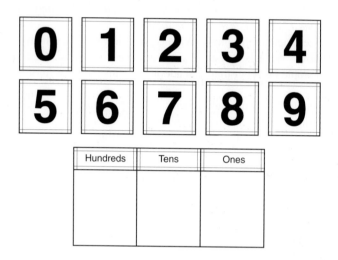

Before the game starts decide whether the lowest or the highest number wins. Take it in turns to place a card on the board in any position, bearing in mind the criteria – lowest or highest – selected for winning. Once a card is placed, it cannot be moved. Change the criteria as often as you wish and include a new criterion 'nearest' to a number, say 450.

All the three teaching aids described above are useful for modelling the principles of place value. However, it must be stressed that simply using materials does not guarantee children's acquisition of concepts; appropriate questioning, discussing and explaining ideas are also very important.

2.4 Number operations

Some useful principles

As an introduction it is useful to consider the four basic operations as linked in pairs.

Multiplication can be thought of as *repeated addition*, whilst *division* can be thought of as *repeated subtraction*. Let us spend a little time trying to understand what is involved in the links between the pairs of operations.

During a public examination a pupil needed to find the result of multiplying, without a calculator, the numbers 17 and 35. He wrote down the number 17 thirty-five times and then proceeded to add the 17s together to find the total.

What is your assessment of this pupil? What is your view of what is being attempted? What does the pupil know? What is it that he does not seem to know? Can you think of two procedures which would be better than that adopted by this pupil for finding what 17 × 35 is equal to?

This pupil certainly has some deficiencies in carrying out numerical work efficiently. What is being attempted is the addition of thirty-five 17s, on paper, by lining up the 7s in a column of units and the 1s in a column of tens and proceeding to use an algorithm for addition. He seems to appreciate that the required thirty-five 17s can be found by the process of repeated addition. Unfortunately, he does not seem to know an algorithm – a step-by-step procedure – for performing the operation of multiplication on whole numbers.

The first thing this pupil could have chosen to do, instead of writing down 17 thirty-five times, was to write down 35 seventeen times; this would have still involved doing multiplication by repeated addition, but with the amount of writing required cut by almost half.

Of course, the second thing which could have been done was to opt for a multiplication algorithm – a mental method or a written one. This would have been far more efficient in the sense that it would have been quicker so that more time could have been given to other parts of the mathematics examination.

From the above discussion we can derive another useful piece of information. The fact that 35 × 17 and 17 × 35 are both equal to 585 indicates that multiplication is *commutative*. It should also be pointed out that 35 + 17 and 17 + 35 both equal 52, showing addition also being commutative. This is a very useful and important teaching point.

The operation '+' performed on integers (whole numbers) is commutative means that addition can be performed in any order, whether it is carried out horizontally or vertically. In using vertical addition, whether somebody writes the 17 above the 35 or the 35 above the 17 does not matter!

Additive identity

You may not have heard of it before, but it is worth spending a little time on this section because it contains an important principle which helps understanding some complex mathematical ideas.

Think of a number. What number can you add to it so that the result is the same number you originally thought of? Regardless of the number you thought of the same number does the trick. That number, of course, is the number 0 (zero).

Add 0 to any number and the result is the same number.

0 is called the additive identity or the identity for addition.

Asking children to add 0 is useful, in fact its role as an additive identity turns out to be very useful when trying to understand, for example, operations with negative numbers.

Multiplicative identity

Again, think of a number. What number can you multiply it by so that the result is the same number you originally thought of? Regardless of the number you thought of the same number does the trick. That number, of course, is the number 1 (one).

Multiply any number by 1 and the result is the same number.

1 is called the multiplicative identity or the identity for multiplication.

Again, asking children to multiply a number by 1 too is useful, as the notion of a multiplicative identity turns out to be very useful in understanding, for example, some operations on fractions.

Let us now take a look at the connection between subtraction and division, restricting the examples considered for the time being to those involving the subtraction of positive integers from positive integers greater than them.

Consider the case of subtracting 3 from 18. The result is 15. Take 3 away again, but this time from the 15 and the result is 12. Repeat the process to get, in succession, 9, then 6, then 3, then 0. What has happened? Starting with the 18, the number 3 has been subtracted six times until 0 remains.

What is 18 divided by 3? It is 6.

So division can be thought of as repeated subtraction. Just how useful is this link? Can someone who does not know an algorithm for division, nevertheless do division by changing it into a repeated subtraction even though the 'division' will take longer to do that way?

In what cases will there be a snag?

A simple example of such a case would be $23 \div 4$. The result of 5 leaves a remainder of 3. It may be of interest to check what children understand about this remainder concept when they have mastered a division algorithm.

So $\div$ is the odd one out. Whereas the other three operations on whole numbers – addition, subtraction and multiplication – always yield an exact integer result, the operation of division can sometimes produce a result which is not exactly an integer because of the remainder.

Have you noticed that all the examples considered so far have involved two numbers being operated on by one of the four operations: $+$, $-$, $\times$ and $\div$. Is it possible to perform one of these operations on three positive integers? This brings us to another link between $+$ and $\times$.

Adding $8 + 6 + 29$ is possible and can be done in two ways. The result of $8 + 6$ could be obtained first and then the result of 14 added to the 29 to produce the final result of 43. Alternatively, the 6 and 29 could first be added to get 35 which can then be added to the 8 to again produce the result, 43, of adding the three numbers 8, 6 and 29. The mathematical language for describing this feature of addition is given by the following:

- *+ is a binary operation*
- *+ is associative.*

A binary operation is an operation which is performed on two things at a time. Check that $\times$ is also a binary operation.

Saying that $+$ is associative simply means that if more than two numbers have to be added, then any two may be added (associated) together first before the next number is added to the total. The procedure can be clarified with the aid of brackets as follows:

$$8 + 6 + 29 \qquad = (8 + 6) + 29$$
$$= 14 \quad + 29$$
$$= 43$$

or

$$8 + 6 + 29 \qquad = 8 \quad + (6 + 29)$$
$$= 8 \quad + 35$$
$$= 43$$

You should now be able to check that $\times$ is also an associative, binary operation.

The other two operations of subtraction and division are , of course, binary operations but they are not associative as is easily illustrated.

Consider the example of $26 - 17 - 5$.

Since subtraction is a binary operation two numbers have to be chosen for the first subtraction. The selection does affect the result as the following demonstrates.

$$26 - 17 - 5 \qquad = (26 - 17) - 5$$
$$= 9 - 5$$
$$= 4$$

whereas

$$26 - 17 - 5 \qquad = 26 - (17 - 5)$$
$$= 26 - 12$$
$$= 14$$

Select one simple example to convince yourself that the operation, division, is also not associative.

The fact that division can produce a remainder leads quite naturally to the consideration of fractions, since a fraction can be thought of in terms of division.

Flexible calculations

When asked to add $563 + 99$ mentally, children and adults are likely to use strategies which are not the same as they would use in written algorithms.

To carry out the above calculation mentally, for example, one may use: $563 + 100 - 1$ as a possible strategy. It is quite common to see children conditioned in such a way that if asked to do the above calculation, they would use a written algorithm as a vertical addition sum. This, of course, involves a more complex methodology for the job in hand.

The same applies to other operations. Sometimes you may find children writing out a vertical sum for carrying out the subtraction: $5000 - 1 =$ and spend a lot of time working it out, even when they are perfectly capable of carrying out the operation in their head within seconds. It makes sense to highlight to a child who is spending considerable time working out 25×20 as a long multiplication or $2000 \div 25$ as a long division sum that they may be able to do these operations much faster and with accuracy if they used facts they already know such as '25 times 2 is 50' or that 'four 25s make one hundred'. The Mathematics *Framework* provided for the National Numeracy Strategy provides a great deal of support to teachers in developing flexible and efficient methods of calculations. Focusing on the use of the most efficient method for the job in hand should discourage children from selecting a 'taught' method automatically when there are more effective alternatives. The chapter on mental mathematics in Section C of this book provides a very detailed exposition of the issues relating to teaching 'calculations' to children.

Although we recommend the use of mental calculations and the need for children to be flexible when engaged in calculations, we believe that children should also be familiar with written algorithms. When calculating larger numbers – both whole numbers and decimals – written algorithms provide children with another option, which always works.

Standard written algorithms

Addition

The standard written algorithm taught in schools is based on the 'grouping' principle of place value. In the written algorithm, addition is conventionally carried out from right to left. The idea that ten 'singles' or 'units' can be 'exchanged' for one 'ten' and 'ten tens' can be 'exchanged' for a hundred and so on is the basis for the 'carrying' aspect of addition.

When adding

$$
\begin{array}{r}
2\;\;5\;\;1 \\
+\;\;5\;\;4\;\;7 \\
\hline
7\;\;9\;\;8 \\
\end{array}
$$

you add the two sets of units, tens and hundreds – there is no 'carrying' because none of the columns produces an answer of over 9, which necessitates 'carrying'. But in the example

$$
\begin{array}{r}
3\;\;6\;\;7 \\
+\;\;5\;\;5\;\;8 \\
\hline
9\;\;2\;\;5 \\
\scriptstyle 1\;\;1\;\;\;\;
\end{array}
$$

however, you add 7 and 8 to get 15, which is one ten and 5 units. The ten is 'carried' to the tens column. Adding 6 tens and 5 tens gives you 11 tens, then of course you need to add the 'carried' one which gives you 12 tens. Ten tens makes one hundred so one hundred is 'carried' to the hundreds place and added to the total of 3 hundreds and 5 hundreds. This principle can be used for adding any place values with increasing number of digits or for any number of rows of numbers.

When teaching children how to add vertically, it is useful to *stress* and reinforce the principles of place value used in the operation, so that children relate the word 'carrying' to what is actually happening rather than learn it as a rule that helps to produce correct answers. Periodically, when engaged in a written sum, it is a good idea to ask children to write next to it (in a circle) what the estimated answer would be. This process of checking for 'reasonableness' can be used for all operations and has many benefits. First, it reminds children what the operation is all about so that they do not adopt a mechanical mode and perform a skill without thinking about what is actually happening. Secondly, it provides a checking mechanism for children which reduces the number of mistakes. Many mistakes are made because of forgotten or partly remembered rules. Children's mistakes are discussed in detail in Section C of this book.

Subtraction

The written method commonly used in schools for subtraction is based on 'decomposition'. Textbooks too use this method. This method, as in the case of 'carrying', is based on the *'grouping'* and *'exchange'* concepts of our place value system. This algorithm can also be explained using base 10 material.

$$
\begin{array}{r}
5\ 8 \\
-\ 4\ 6 \\
\hline
1\ 2 \\
\hline
\end{array}
$$

In this example of vertical subtraction you can take 6 units from 8 units and 4 tens from 5 tens without any rearrangement or exchange. But, when you have to carry out the subtraction:

$$
\begin{array}{r}
{}^{5}\!\!\not{6}\ {}^{1}6 \\
-\ 4\ 8 \\
\hline
1\ 8 \\
\hline
\end{array}
$$

the 'decomposition' procedure is used: take eight units from 6, you cannot do this without some rearrangement, so you 'break' one of the tens taken from the 6 tens into ten units and show the rearrangement. 8 from 16 units is 8, 4 tens from 5 tens is 1 ten.

When carrying out a vertical sum with hundreds

$$
\begin{array}{r}
6\ 4\ 5 \\
-\ 2\ 3\ 4 \\
\hline
4\ 1\ 1 \\
\hline
\end{array}
$$

no exchange is necessary, but to perform the written vertical algorithm

$$
\begin{array}{r}
{}^{7}\!\!\not{8}\ {}^{1}{}^{6}\!\!\not{8}\ {}^{1}2 \\
-\ 2\ 7\ 9 \\
\hline
5\ 9\ 3 \\
\hline
\end{array}
$$

you have to decompose the hundreds and tens, (or 'break it down into …') and rearrange the number to enable you to carry out the calculation.

The 'equal addition' method which was used commonly in the past (some teachers still use this method for their own calculations) is not based on the exchange principle, but on remembering a rule.

For example in the following example

$$
\begin{array}{r}
\not{6}\,{}^{1}6 \\
-\,{}^{6}\not{5}\;8 \\
\hline
8
\end{array}
$$

take 8 from 6; can't do it, so you borrow 'one' from the next column which makes the 6 into 16. 16 take away 8 gives you 8. As you have 'borrowed' a one you pay back a one which is added to 5 which is 6, 6 take away 6 is 0. This is a paper exercise which was popular in the olden days, but is losing its popularity because it is difficult to explain to children why it works in terms of the place value system. Nevertheless, it is useful for a teacher to be familiar with this for communicating with parents and for history's sake! Beware of the word 'borrow' when you use the decomposition method because there is no borrowing, only exchanging and some rearrangement.

Multiplication

When teaching children to carry out multiplication using a vertical method, it is useful to remind them that this algorithm uses the 'carrying' aspect already dealt with in addition.

$$
\begin{array}{r}
4\;6 \\
\times\quad 8 \\
\hline
3\;6\;8
\end{array}
$$

Here you multiply 6 units by 8 = 48, carry the 4 tens and place the 8 in the unit column. Then multiply the 4 tens by 8 which is 32, add the carried 4 tens to 36, giving the answer 368.

Some teachers teach children the 'tens first' method which is then used as a basis for carrying out long multiplication. Here

$$
\begin{array}{r}
4\;6 \\
\times\quad 8 \\
\hline
3\;2\;0 \\
4\;8 \\
\hline
3\;6\;8
\end{array}
$$

Multiply 4 tens by 8 = 320; then multiply the units 6 × 8 = 48. Add 320 + 48 = 368.

The traditional way of multiplying by 2-digit numbers can be based on this:

$$
\begin{array}{r}
4\ 6 \\
\times\ 2\ 8 \\
\hline
9\ 2\ 0 \\
3\ 6\ 8 \\
\hline
1\ 2\ 8\ 8 \\
\hline
\end{array}
$$

Some teachers teach this procedure starting with units and 'adding a zero' when you start multiplying with the tens:

$$
\begin{array}{r}
4\ 6 \\
\times\ 2\ 8 \\
\hline
3\ 6\ 8 \\
9\ 2\ 0 \\
\hline
1\ 2\ 8\ 8 \\
\hline
\end{array}
$$

If you are using this method, it is important to make children think about why the zero is added. It is also good practice to ask them make a 'reasonable' estimate of what the answer will be like because many mistakes are made as a result of forgetting the rule of adding a zero.

Division

You have already been introduced to the idea of division being 'repeated subtraction' earlier in this chapter. Written procedures for division are usually termed 'short' or 'long' division. Traditionally, 'short' division is used for dividing by a 1-digit number. When carrying out division, the decomposition aspect of subtraction is also in use; this can be pointed out to children.

Divide 455 by 8 by the short method:

$$
\begin{array}{r}
5\ 6 \quad r = 7 \\
8\,\overline{)\ 4\ 5\ ^5 5}
\end{array}
$$

It can also be carried out by the long method which shows division as repeated subtraction.

$$
\begin{array}{r}
5\ 6 \quad r = 7 \\
8\ \overline{)\ 4\ 5\ 5} \\
-\ 4\ 0\ \downarrow \\
\hline
5\ 5 \\
-\ 4\ 8 \\
\hline
7
\end{array}
$$

To divide 2457 by 56 using long division; we will need to rely on children learning a method – assisted by the principles of place value and the understanding that the division operation is based on 'repeated subtraction'.

$$
\begin{array}{r}
4\ 3 \quad r = 49 \\
56\ \overline{)\ 2\ 4\ 5\ 7} \\
-\ 2\ 2\ 4\ \downarrow \\
\hline
2\ 1\ 7 \\
-\ 1\ 6\ 8 \\
\hline
4\ 9
\end{array}
$$

2.5 Factors and prime numbers

Number 12 can be written as the product of :

3 and 4 or 6 and 2 or 12 and 1.

In this case 1, 2, 3, 4, 6 and 12 are factors of 12.

Number 21 has four factors: 1, 3, 7, and 21.

All natural numbers can be written as products of their factors.

When you *factorise* a number you are writing that number as a *product* of its factors.

A *prime number* has only two factors; 1 and itself, which means it can only be divided by 1 and itself without a remainder.

2, 3, 5, 7, 11, 13, 17, 19 are prime numbers.

When you factorise 24 you get the following factors:

1, 2, 3, 4, 6, 8,12 and 24.

When a number is written as a product of prime numbers, we can refer to the factors as its *prime factors*.

For example, consider number 12 again:

Start with the factor 2

$12 = 2 \times 6$

Now factorise 6

$6 = 2 \times 3$

2 is a factor again.
So $12 = 2 \times 2 \times 3$: all the factors of 12 are prime.
We have, therefore, *prime factorised* 12.

2.6 Negative numbers

Any number can be represented on a number line. In the number line given below, positive numbers are shown on the right of the line and negative numbers on the left.

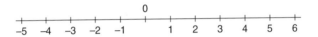

If you want to add a positive number to any number on the line, you move to the right: to add 6 to 3, you start at 3 and move to the right; $3 + 6 = 9$ giving a result of 9.

If you want to subtract a positive number, you move to the left. To carry out the subtraction $6 - 4 = 2$, you have to move two places to the left from, 6. What if you subtract 7 from 4? You will move to the left, but this time you will arrive at –3.

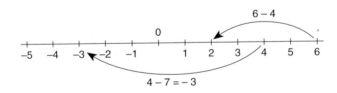

Say you want to add or subtract a negative number. To add a negative number, you move to the left and to subtract a negative number you move to the right. If you add $3 + (-4)$ the result is –1.

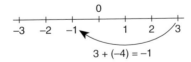

See what happens when you carry out the subtraction 3 – (–2). You move two places to the right and your answer is 5.

$$3 - (-2) = 5$$

Some key issues in teaching negative numbers

Children are often fascinated when they are introduced to negative numbers, but this abstract concept needs much discussion using contexts such as measuring temperature or in diving. Children may come across negative numbers while using a calculator and this may be an opportunity for introducing negative numbers. Calculators provide a very useful resource for exploring number patterns and sequences, positive and negative.

Tasks relating to the classroom

1 Suppose you asked a child, say in Year 1, to count out 5 objects from a tray full of objects and make a set; then show in some way to someone else that there are 5 objects in that set. Make a list of what a child needs to know to be able to carry this out.

2 Study the following statement: a child who can count up to 30 correctly should surely be able to recognise the cardinality of a set of objects. Comment.

3 The following are mistakes and misconceptions collected from children's work. For each one write down the possible reasons for making the mistakes and what the implications are for teaching.
(a) Add 1 to 3499: Alison wrote 4000.
(b) Write five hundred and three in figures: Daniel wrote 5003.
(c) How many bags of 10 sweets can I make from 1500 sweets? Jason did a sum:

$$\begin{array}{r} 1\ 5 \quad r = 0 \\ 10\ \overline{\smash{)}1\ 5\ 0\ 0} \end{array}$$

(d) What is the change in price of a car when a salesman changes the price from £2540 to £2340? Natalie answered £2.

Tasks for self-study

1 Ask 6 people to do 243 – 87 in their heads and tell you how they did it. Analyse the strategies used.
2 Estimate the answers before working them out, using any method
(a) 1237 + 637
(b) 350 + 351
(c) 432 – 179
(d) 23 × 9

    (e) 76 × 34

    (f) 416 ÷ 6

    (g) 376 ÷ 22

3   Explain to someone, using base 10 material, how to do addition and subtraction.

4   Which of the four operations – addition, subtraction, multiplication and division – are commutative? Show an example to prove your point.

5   Using the digits 1, 2, 3, 4, 5, and 6 make up sums following the instructions. Use the digits only once each time. The first one has been done for you:

    (a) The answer is 390

        2   3   4   +   1   5   6   =   390

    (b) the largest answer possible

        ☐ ☐ ☐ + ☐ ☐ ☐ =

    (c) the smallest answer possible

        ☐ ☐ ☐ – ☐ ☐ ☐ =

    (d) the largest answer possible

        ☐ ☐ ☐ × ☐ ☐ ☐ =

    (e) a division sum with an even 2-digit answer

        ☐ ☐ ☐ ÷ ☐ ☐ ☐ =

6   Picture a number line in your mind and carry out the following calculations:

    (a) What integers (whole numbers) lie between –6 and 4?

    (b) The temperature on a thermometer shows –5. When the temperature has gone up by 4 degrees what reading does it show? After another rise of 3 degrees, what is the new reading?

    (c) Order the following numbers : –3, 6, 0, and –8 from the largest to the smallest.

7   Write down all the multiples of 7 between 50 and 100

8   Which of the statements are true?

    (a) All prime numbers are odd numbers.

    (b) There are 12 prime numbers between 10 and 80.

    (c) There are 2 prime numbers in this set.: 23, 59, 49, 91, 121.

Chapter 3

Fractions, decimals and percentages

This chapter focuses on:
3.1 Fractions
3.2 Decimals
3.3 Indices
3.4 Standard index form
3.5 Percentages

3.1 Fractions

In the progression of mathematics topics presented to children, the study of fractions can be the first departure from the restriction to the positive integers, which are usually referred to as whole numbers. A fraction is usually introduced as a concept enabling reference to be made to 'a part of a whole'.

For example, 3/8 can be thought of as three parts of a whole one which has been split into eight equal parts. A diagram can be used to illustrate this particular fraction.

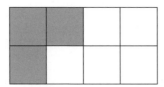

What if the top number of the fraction is an integer (whole number) greater than the bottom number of the fraction? Does this undermine the notion of a fraction being 'a part of a whole'? Two examples will illustrate an appropriate answer to this question.

Consider first the fraction 18/3. Its top number is greater than its bottom number. A diagram could be used to give an interpretation of this fraction.

Each unit (whole) is split into three equal parts. One of those parts, in the left-most unit, is shaded. That shaded part represents 1/3. In the entire diagram there are 18 such thirds. Those 18 thirds, therefore, represent 6 units. So 18/3 = 6.

What about 18 divided by 3? That is also equal to 6.

So the fraction 18/3 may be interpreted in two ways:

- it may be thought of as eighteen thirds or
- it may be thought of as 18 ÷ 3.

Both interpretations are equally correct. The appropriate way in which to consider 18/3 depends on your purpose or the context.

For example, if you have eighteen sweets to share between three children then your situation requires you to think of 18/3 as 18 ÷ 3. As division is repeated subtraction, you are in principle taking away three from eighteen six times, so each child gets six sweets. This illustration gives some justification for sometimes calling division by another term 'sharing' as well as sometimes calling subtraction by its alternative 'taking away'.

What if the top number (called the numerator) is smaller than the bottom number (called the denominator) of the fraction? Does this affect the possible interpretations of the fraction?

Consider the fraction 2/3 for the purpose of illustration.

This can also be represented by a diagram.

The outer rectangle, as previously, represents 1 or unity. It is split into three equal parts and two of those parts are shaded to represent 2/3. What about the other interpretation, according to which 2/3 may be thought of as 2 ÷ 3?

If this is considered in terms of a diagram, then the numerator may be represented by two rectangles which have to be split into three equal parts. This can be achieved by splitting each rectangle into three, as in previous diagrams.

Of the six smaller rectangles one third need to be shaded. This can be done in two ways – either as it is done in the diagram or by shading two of the smaller rectangles within one only of the rectangles representing 1. What has been achieved by this twofold approach? Just that 2/3 of 1 is the same as 1/3 of 1 plus 1/3 of 1. More simply there has been a diagrammatic 'proof' of the statement that:

$$2/3 = 1/3 + 1/3.$$

When the fraction 18/3 was selected above, there was a special feature which limited the usefulness of the chosen fraction; the numerator is an exact multiple of the denominator. 18 is six times 3. What if the numerator is not an exact multiple of the denominator, but still larger than it?

Let's consider, for example, the fraction 11/3. Showing this on a diagram is awkward because eleven units (rectangles) does not easily split into three equal parts. Why is this? $3 \times 3 = 9$ and $4 \times 3 = 12$; 11 is not an exact multiple 3 or, expressed another way, 3 is not a factor of 11. In this case, the alternative way of viewing a fraction can be helpful in promoting an understanding of what is signified by the fraction.

Here the fraction 11/3 can be considered as 11 divided by 3, which in turn can be thought of as taking 3 from 11 as many times as possible. The snag, of course, is that there is a remainder of 2. Look at the diagram below.

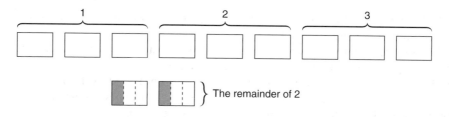

} The remainder of 2

If 11/3 is 11 divided by 3 which comes to 3, leaving a remainder of 2, what sense can be made of the remainder? Again, look at the same diagram. The remaining 2 can be split into three as was done to illustrate 2/3. The outcome of the diagrammatic representation of 11/3 is, therefore, to show that it equals three and two thirds.

More concisely, this may be written as:

$$11 / 3 = 3\tfrac{2}{3}$$

Note the contraction on the right-hand side of 3 + 2/3. $3\tfrac{2}{3}$ can be thought of as a compact way of writing 3 + 2/3.

Top-heavy fractions and mixed numbers

A *top-heavy fraction*, usually referred to as an '*improper fraction*' such as 11/3, can immediately be seen to be greater than 1. The denominator, 3, indicates the 'segments' forming 1. The numerator, 11, indicates the batches of three segments available – three batches with two segments left over. So, given eleven thirds as a top-heavy fraction it can be changed into what is called a 'mixed number', consisting of an integer part and a fraction part less than 1, by thinking:

3 into 11 goes 3 times. 3 times 3 is 9. There are two left over which are two thirds. So eleven over three is three and two thirds.

What of the reverse process? Suppose you have a *mixed number* and want to change it into a *top-heavy (improper) fraction*. Reasons for needing to do so will be considered when operations on fractions are illustrated.

Consider the mixed number $4\tfrac{3}{5}$

The 5 is an indication of fifths. There are five fifths in 1. So altogether there are $4 \times 5 = 20$ fifths, plus three fifths, giving 23 fifths in total. More compactly,

$$4\tfrac{3}{5} = 20/5 + 3/5$$

$$= 23/5$$

Since any integer can be expressed as a fraction, integers can be thought of as special fractions.

An integer is a fraction in which the numerator is a multiple of the denominator.

One implication of this is that fractions can be operated on by the same four binary operations as were considered in relation to integers.

Will the algorithms for performing those operations be very different to those used with integers? It turns out that the algorithms are substantially different and will need to be considered differently. The multiplication of fractions cannot be usefully thought of as repeated addition and the division of fractions cannot be usefully thought of as repeated subtraction Many people find operations on fractions difficult to follow. So, read the next section *slowly*. It may also help you to make notes while you read it.

Operations on fractions

Addition of fractions

To make an algorithm for the addition of fractions comprehensible a simple example, illustrated with a diagram, will be helpful.

Consider an imaginary situation in which a man leaves his fortune to his wife, his only child and a registered charity according to the following instruction.

7/12 of my fortune is bequeathed to my wife. 3/8 is bequeathed to my daughter and the remainder is bequeathed to charity.

What fraction of the man's fortune was left to charity?

What is needed here is an algorithm for finding the sum of 7/12 and 3/8.

To invent a diagram on which the addition can be displayed, the focus must first be on the two denominators; here twelfths and eighths are involved. If a rectangle is used to represent 1 (the whole fortune), then the rectangle must easily split into 12 as well as 8 equal parts.

What is the smallest number of subdivisions of the rectangle required?

24 are required. How can you arrive at that number? Start with the largest of the numbers 12 and 8. 12 is not a multiple of 8 so you double it to get 24; 8 is a factor of 24. So you start with a rectangle split up into 24 squares.

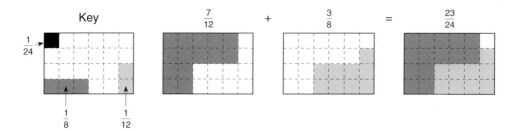

The diagram on the left, providing the key, enables you to spot two *equivalent fractions*. Comparison of the rectangles for 1/12 and 1/8 with the square representing 1/24 shows that 1/12 = 2/24 and 1/8 = 3/24.

Study the diagrams for a while. They illustrate the conclusion that 1/24 of the man's fortune is left to charity.

The diagrams are meant to serve two purposes:

• to justify a procedure for adding two particular fractions; and
• to suggest a general procedure – that is, an algorithm – which can be followed to add any two fractions without a diagram.

At this stage, recollect what you know about adding fractions; you may remember some rules but may not have thought about why the rules actually work!

With the above four diagrams in mind, let us see if the steps of an algorithm can be formulated. It turns out that only three steps are required.

1   *Find a common denominator for the fractions to be added.*
     This can be done by taking successive multiples of the largest of the denominators until the other denominators divide into the current multiple being tried.
2   *Express each of the fractions to be added as its equivalent fraction with the common denominator found in step 1.*
3   *Add the new numerators to find the numerator of the sum of the fractions.*
     Place that numerator over the common denominator.
     The fraction obtained by the three-stage algorithm is the sum of the original fractions.

Step 2 may require further explanation. Suppose you want to add the fractions 1/3, 5/12 and 7/20. Taking multiples of 20 in turn you find that 60 is the required common denominator. How do you find the corresponding numerators for each of the fractions?

Consider 1/3. Remember, from Chapter 2, that 1 is the multiplicative identity. Multiplying 1/3 by 1 does not change its size. You need 1 expressed in appropriate form. What is that? You need to replace the question mark in 1/3 = ?/60. So the appropriate form of 1 is 20/20. (3 goes into 60 twenty times.)

You then proceed with: $1/3 \times 20/20 = 20/60$
followed by: $5/12 \times 5/5 = 25/60$ (since 12 goes into 60 five times)
and finally: $7/20 \times 3/3 = 21/60$
Now you are in a position to simply add the new numerators.

$$1/3 + 5/12 + 7/20 = 20/60 + 25/60 + 21/60$$
$$= 66/60$$

What do you find curious about this result?

It has two curious features: its numerator and denominator have common factors; it is also greater than 1.

The highest common factor of 66 and 60 is 6. A procedure called *cancelling* can be followed so that 6 can be cancelled into 66 to give 11 and 6 can be cancelled into 60 to give 10. This leads to the equality:

$$66/60 = 11/10$$

Subtraction of fractions

The algorithm for subtracting fractions can be obtained from that for the addition of fractions simply by changing *step 3* to:

Subtract the numerators to obtain the numerator of the difference of the two fractions.

Look back to the diagrams illustrating the addition of fractions and check that you can see that

$$\frac{17}{24} - \frac{3}{8} = \frac{8}{24} \ or \ \frac{4}{12} \ or \ \frac{1}{3}$$

Check that the three alternatives are equal. Of course, 1/3 is the simplest form of the result.

The algorithms for the other two operations on fractions have special features. Many of you may have felt in your school days that the algorithm for division of fractions was the most difficult to understand.

Multiplication of fractions

Let us try to make some sense of something like 2/3 × 3/4.

Can this be illustrated by a diagram, so it has a kind of physical meaning? See the diagram below.

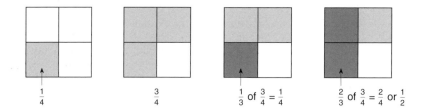

When doing multiplication with integers, such as 5 times 4, how can it be thought of? As 5 lots of 4. As 4 repeated 5 times. If you start with 3/4 rather than 4, it makes no sense to talk of 2/3 lots of 3/4 or of 3/4 repeated 2/3 times. To try to get a form of language which helps to make 2/3 × 3/4 a bit more meaningful, perhaps the following may help:

Think of 5 × 4 as 'start with 4 and then take 5 of it'. This could then lead to thinking of 2/3 × 3/4 as 'start with 3/4 and then take 2/3 of it'.

Now let us see how diagrams can be used to calculate the result.

A square can be used to represent 1; it is shown split into quarters. The sequence of diagrams illustrates how the product of 2/3 and 3/4 may be obtained.

It is likely that the difficulty children will have with the multiplication of fractions will focus on the third diagram. If they have been introduced to the concept of a fraction by a verbal definition along the lines of 'a fraction is a part of a whole' then that definition can be an obstacle to appreciating that you can have a fraction of less than a whole. Look at the third diagram and try to think only of the geometry of it; cast out thoughts of the fractions involved. Focus on the three shaded squares. One third of three squares is one square. That square represents a quarter. So a third of three quarters is one quarter. How could this have been done without the diagram?

$$1/3 \ of \ 3/4 = 1/3 \times 3/4 = 1/4.$$

You could have multiplied the numerators to get 3 and the denominators to get 12, producing 3/12. Cancelling 3 finally gives the result of 1/4.

A more efficient procedure, however, would have involved cancelling the 3 in the denominator of 1/3 and in the numerator of 3/4 to give:

$$1/3 + 3/4 = 1/1 \times 1/4$$
$$= (1 \times 1) / (1 \times 4)$$
$$= 1/4$$

Think how an algorithm for multiplying fractions be extracted from this illustration, so that future multiplications can be done without a diagram.

Again a three-step algorithm has emerged:

1   *Look for factors common to any numerator and a denominator; cancel each of the common factors you have found into a numerator and a denominator.*
2   *Multiply the remaining numerators to get the numerator of the result; multiply the remaining denominators to get the denominator of the result.*
3   *Check the fraction you have obtained for the product. If you can find no further factors to cancel then your result of the product of the fractions is expressed in its simplest form.*

The fraction obtained by applying this three-step algorithm to the given fractions is the product of the given fractions.

When multiplication of integers was considered it was suggested that it could be thought of as repeated addition. What about mutiplication of fractions? Can that be thought of as repeated addition of fractions? No, except when the multiplier is greater than 1. Such would be the case with, for example, $4\frac{1}{5} \times 2/3$. The product can be thought of as

$$2/3 + 2/3 + 2/3 + 2/3 + (1/5 \text{ of } 2/3),$$

involving the notion of repeated addition, but for the purpose of finding the product it is much simpler to apply the three-step algorithm as follows:

$$4\frac{1}{5} \times 2/3 = 21/5 \times 2/3$$

changing the mixed number into a top-heavy equivalent 21/5
Cancelling 3 into 3 and 21 gives

$$7/5 \times 2/1 = 14/15.$$

Division of fractions

We will proceed as before with a particular example illustrated with diagrams.

Consider the case of 7/8 ÷ 2/5. What would be an appropriate diagram for this?

Key

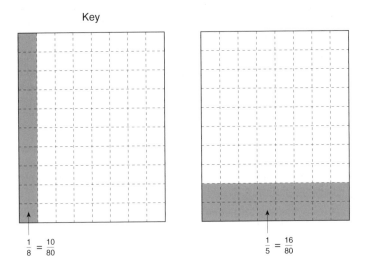

$$\frac{1}{8} = \frac{10}{80} \qquad\qquad \frac{1}{5} = \frac{16}{80}$$

One whole in this illustration is represented by a rectangle enclosing 80 squares as shown in the key. Notice that the diagram representing 7/8 encloses 70 squares and the diagram for 2/5 encloses 32 squares.

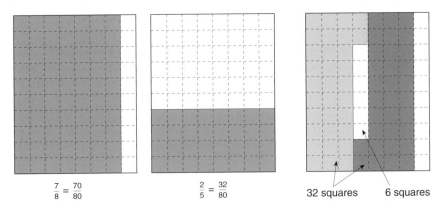

$$\frac{7}{8} = \frac{70}{80} \qquad\qquad \frac{2}{5} = \frac{32}{80} \qquad\qquad \text{32 squares} \qquad \text{6 squares}$$

Remember that the division of integers could be thought of as repeated subtraction. Can this view be adopted to help towards an understanding of the division of fractions? To pursue this question, focus on the representations of 7/8 and 2/5 in terms of squares.

Then the appropriate question becomes:

How many lots of 32 squares can you get from 70 squares? So the question 'what is 7/8 divided by 2/5?' has become translated into 'what is 70 divided by 32?' The result is 2 with a remainder of 6. What should you do with the 6? Put it over the 32 to get the fraction 6/32 which, in simplest form, is 3/16.

So the final result, illustrated in the last diagram is $2\frac{3}{16}$.

Thinking of the division of fractions in terms of repeated subtraction, as the above illustration amply demonstrates, is very cumbersome. Let us then explore the extraction of an algorithm from the diagrammatic illustration of the particular case of 7/8 ÷ 2/5. The mixed number $2\frac{3}{16}$ obtained as the result is equal to 35/16. Notice that 35 equals 7 times 5 and 16 equals 8 times 2. This is very curious, because if the 2/5 is inverted to become 5/2 and the operation of division is changed into multiplication a correct result is obtained for that multiplication:

$$7/8 \div 2/5 = 7/8 \times 5/2$$
$$= 35/16$$
$$= 2\frac{3}{16}$$

The algorithm for the division of fractions is yet again a three-step procedure with the third step requiring a transformation of the division into multiplication.

1   *Change the division sign into multiplication.*
2   *Invert the fraction which was on the right of the division sign.*
3   *Use the multiplication algorithm for the product of fractions obtained from carrying out steps 1 and 2.*

This concludes the presentation of the algorithms for the four binary operations on fractions. They have been shown to include the integers as special cases. Their denominators may be any of the infinite collection of integers and are liable to be changed for the convenience of whoever is operating on them. In spite of the multitude of useful applications of fractions in financial and scientific work, it is those fractions with denominators which are multiples of ten which have acquired great popularity. We may have ten fingers and toes, but try not to regard fractions with denominators which are not multiples of ten as somehow less worthy of attention. The following lines may help to sustain suitable empathy with the whole collection of fractions regardless of their particular denominators.

A fraction's life is full of strife
A little line cuts it in two.
Its top and bottom get cancelled down
By lots of pupils told what to do.
Yet without more factors it can survive
In simplest form and stay alive
Until decimals and powers of ten
Begin the attack all over again.

Something to think about

Before leaving this section, here is something to reflect on. You often hear people debating whether we ought to teach fractions at all. We believe it is useful for many reasons and here are few of them:

- In real-life contexts we use the words and symbols for 'half, 'quarter' and so on. Supermarkets and department stores use these all the time. Children need to be familiar with these ideas.
- When we measure using arbitrary units, for example when moving furniture at home, for sewing or for cooking, we often use the concept of fractions.
- Decimal numbers, which are an extension of the place value system, are based on the idea of fractions. Percentages and ratio are also concepts related to fractions.
- Learning how to operate on fractions is necessary for tackling algebraic work and for undertaking calculations in probability.

3.2 Decimals

Decimal numbers can be thought of as combined integers (whole numbers) and fractions restricted to those with denominators which are multiples of ten.

The decimal numbers form what is called the *denary* system, based on ten, just as binary numbers form what is called the *binary* system, based on two.

The decimal numbers incorporate the notion of place value, but extend it beyond the integers to its fractional parts. The separation of its integer and fractional parts is accomplished by a simple and ingenious device, the decimal point. This is one example of a section of mathematics in which the choice of sign creates the possibility of enormous thinking development.

One question of interest, which will to be dealt with later, is the mathematical connection between decimal numbers and the integers and fractions. For the moment let us be concerned with the practical importance of decimal numbers in decimal currency systems.

Pounds sterling is a decimal currency. One pound is equivalent to one hundred pence. In more mathematical notation this is written as:

$$£1 = 100p.$$

This enables prices to be written in decimal form, such as £4.37.

The number read as 'four point three seven', however, is written as $4 \cdot 37$. The difference between the two is just the position of the point. This is more a matter of convenience; a full-stop on the word processor keyboard was used for the first whereas the decimal point was imported from a collection of symbols available in the word processing package. The United Kingdom currency is a decimal money system; the dot separating the pounds from the pence is essentially a decimal point in its function.

The important aspect of the price £4.37 is that it can be thought of as a decimal number given to two decimal places. The value of each digit in the number depends on its place. The 7 indicates seven pence or 7 hundredths of a pound. The 3 indicates thirty pence or three tenths of a pound. The 4 to the left of the decimal point indicates 4 units or 4 pounds. All this, of course, is quite familiar to you. The purpose in mentioning it is to recall the basic features of decimal numbers as a positional representation system in which the value or meaning of each digit depends on its position in the number.

To the left of the point the digits refer to, from right to left, units then tens then hundreds then thousands and so on; the values are multiplied by ten each time the place shifts one place further to the left as shown in the diagram.

Thousands	Hundreds	Tens	Units		Tenths	Hundredths	Thousandths
1000	100	10	1	•	0·1	0·01	0·001

To the right of the point the digits refer to, from left to right, tenths then hundredths then thousandths then ten thousandths and so on; the values are multiplied by one tenth each time the place shifts one place further to the right.

Now to move away from what is familiar to what may be less familiar, but useful in understanding the usefulness of using decimal numbers.

Consider the following exchange rate between pounds sterling and USA dollars which appeared on the 31 December 1998.

$$£/\$ \ 1.6743$$

This indicates that one pound is worth 1.6743 dollars. Why should the American equivalent be given to four decimal places? The American system is also a decimal system with one hundred cents to the dollar. What do the digits indicate in the exchange rate?

The 6 indicates 6/10 of one dollar which is sixty cents. The 7 indicates 7/100 of one dollar which is seven cents. So far this indicates that one UK pound can be exchanged for one dollar and sixty-seven cents. What about the other digits? The 4 indicates 4/1000 of one dollar and the 3 indicates 3/10000 of a dollar. There are no coins worth 1/1000 of a dollar or 1/10000 of a dollar, so what purpose is served by the inclusion of the 4 and the 3 in the exchange rate? Basically, they will affect very large transactions. Ten thousand UK pounds, for example, would exchange for sixteen thousand, seven hundred and forty-three dollars rather than just sixteen thousand, seven hundred dollars if the 4 and the 3 were not included in the exchange rate.

What this illustrates is that the accuracy of a decimal number, in a practical application, does not become absurd just because no tangible things correspond to the degree of accuracy.

Staying within the currency application of decimals, consider the launch of the euro on the 1st January, 1999. The euro zone created in the eleven European countries involved became controlled by the following list of irrevocable conversion rates, so that from now on one euro equals:

13.7603 Austrian schillings
40.3399 Belgian francs
1.95583 German marks
5.94573 Finnish marks
6.55957 French francs
0.787564 Irish pounds
1936.27 Italian lire
40.3399 Luxembourg francs
2.20371 Netherlands guilders
200.482 Portuguese escudos
166.386 Spanish pesetas

(Sterling, not within the euro zone at the time of the launch was given a value of 70 pence to one euro. That conversion rate will fluctuate and be expressed to four decimal places.)

Take a good look at the eleven rates. What do you notice about the numbers? Do you feel curious about the features you have noticed and can you make sense of them? There are three striking features. Let us consider them in turn.

1   The most obvious feature of the eleven conversion rates is that they are all expressed in decimal numbers. This gives them a kind of uniformity and provides a simple basis for calculations about transactions involving the rates. Whether or not the eleven currencies are decimal systems of money cannot be inferred from their conversion rates being expressed in decimal.

2   The next feature you may have noticed is that the rates vary in the number of digits to the right of the decimal point. The Italian lire rate is expressed to two decimal places, whilst the rate for the Irish pound is expressed to six decimal places. The numbers in the conversion list, in descending order of magnitude, giving the integer part only and the number of decimal places in brackets afterwards are as follows:

1936(2), 200(3), 166(3), 40(4), 40(4), 13(4), 6(5), 5(5), 2(5), 1(5), 0(6).

Notice that the number of decimal places turns out to be in ascending order with the integer parts in descending order.

3   The most curious feature of the conversion rates, however, is that all the rates are expressed to six significant figures. The first significant figure in a decimal number is the first non-zero digit in the number as you look at it from left to right. So the first significant figure in the rate for the Irish pound is the 7 to the immediate right of the decimal point.

The reason for the six significant figure accuracy, rather than a uniform number of decimal places, is connected with the notion of error in computation and will be dealt with in Chapter 5 where the notions of measure, accuracy, uncertainty and error will be considered in some detail.

The four operations of addition, subtraction, multiplication and division will now be discussed so as to gain some understanding of an algorithm for performing each operation.

Addition of decimal numbers

The algorithm for performing addition on decimal numbers, on paper, is essentially the same as that for the addition of whole numbers. The vertical alignment of the decimal points of the numbers to be added guarantees the vertical alignment of all other digits of corresponding place value. The twin processes of decomposition and carrying then form the basis of the algorithm for addition, just as for the addition of integers. The place values providing the framework for the addition of decimals are: …10 000, 1000, 100, 10, 1, 1/10, 1/100, 1/1000, 1/10 000 …

The three points on the left and right indicate that the place values continue indefinitely to the left and right according to the two principles.

Reminders

1   *The 'decomposition' process involves reducing the digit in one position by 1 and decomposing it into ten of the place value to its right.*

2 *'Carrying' involves transferring 10, or a multiple of 10, of the place value in one position to the position on the left, adding to the digit in that position the multiple of 10 concerned.*

The example of the addition of 157.68, 68.87 and 476.29 is given below as an illustration of the *alignment, decomposition and carrying* involved.

```
  1  5  7  .  6  8
     6  8  .  8  7
  4  7  6  .  2  9
  ─────────────────
  7  0  2  .  8  4
  ─────────────────
  2  2  1     2
```

Notice that the multiples of ten of the place values in any column are written under 'the answer digit' of the next column.

The 2 carried into the tenths column arises from 8, 7 and 9 having a sum of 24.

What is carried is the multiple of ten; what is written down as part of the sum (the total or answer) is the remainder after the extraction of as many tens as possible. Similarly, 1 is carried into the units column, 2 into the tens column and 2 into the hundreds column.

Have you spotted the absence of decomposition in the application of the algorithm for addition? This is due to the requirement of the algorithm to proceed from right to left only.

Addition involves alignment, carrying but no decomposition.

Subtraction of decimal numbers

The algorithm for the subtraction of decimal numbers also incorporates the same principles governing the subtraction of integers. The vertical alignment of the decimal points of the numbers involved in the subtraction guarantees the alignment of all the other digits of the same place value.

Let us consider the roles of alignment, decomposition and carrying in the processes of subtraction of one decimal number from another by taking the example of 38.9 subtracted from 124.3.

Here there is decomposition and no carrying, because the algorithm requires some processes from left to right even though the procedure focuses on the digits of the numbers from right to left, in increasing order of place value.

The subtraction, on paper, of 38.9 from 124.3 shown below illustrates the alignment and decomposition involved; the lack of any role for carrying should be carefully noted.

```
  ⁰1̶  ¹2̶  ³4̶  .  ¹3
  ─  3  8  .  9
  ─────────────────
     8  5  .  4
  ─────────────────
```

Notice that the 3/10 must become 13/10 by the decomposition of one of the 4 units, making the 124.3 into 123 + 13/10. When subtracting the units the 3 must be changed into 13 by the decomposition of one of the 2 tens, making the 123 into 110 + 13. Finally, when the tens are being subtracted the 1, in the tens position, must become 11 by the decomposition of the 1 hundred into 10 tens, making the 110 into 0 hundreds and 11 tens.

Subtraction involves alignment and decomposition, but no carrying.

Multiplication of decimal numbers

The algorithm for the multiplication of decimal numbers is essentially the same as that for the multiplication of integers, with an extension to take account of the digits to the right of the decimal points. Many people use a learnt rule (not always understood) for multiplying decimal numbers. Here is an explanation as to how the rule works.

Before starting the actual multiplication, it is advisable to decide the place values of the rightmost digits and multiply them as fractions to determine the number of digits to the right of the decimal point in the product.

Consider the example of the product of 251.6 and 43.7 set out on paper as below.

$$
\begin{array}{r}
2\ 5\ 1\ .\ 6 \\
\times\qquad 4\ 3\ .\ 7 \\
\hline
1\ 0\ 9\ 9\ 4\ .\ 9\ 2
\end{array}
$$

The rightmost digits, 6 and 7, represent 6/10 and 7/10 and give 42/100 on multiplication. Can you extract a rule for positioning the decimal point in the final product?

The final product of 10994.92 is expressed to two decimal places. Both of the numbers multiplied to give that product, 251.6 and 43.7, are given to one decimal place. There is a rule suggested by this:

The first number has one digit to the right of the point.

The second number has one digit to the right of the point.

1 + 1 = 2, so the product of the two numbers must have two digits to the right of the point.

Let us test this suggested rule before describing the algorithm for multiplication.

Consider the product of 63.728 and 8.14. The first of these numbers is given to three decimal places and the second is given to two decimal places. Since 3 + 2 = 5, the product must have five digits to the right of the point. Is this what is indicated by an examination of the rightmost digits of the numbers to be multiplied?

The 8 of 63.728 represents 8/1000 and the 4 of 8.14 represents 4/100. The product of those digits is, therefore, 32/100000. The place value of one hundred thousandths is occupied by the digit in the fifth position to the right of the decimal point. (The 5 zeros correspond to the position.) So the product may then be found by setting things out as follows:

$$
\begin{array}{r}
6\ 3\ .\ 7\ 2\ 8 \qquad (3) \\
\times\qquad 8\ .\ 1\ 4 \qquad (2) \\
\hline
5\ 0\ 9\ 8\ 2\ 4\ 0\ 0 \\
6\ 3\ 7\ 2\ 8\ 0 \\
2\ 5\ 4\ 9\ 1\ 2 \\
\hline
5\ 1\ 8\ .\ 7\ 4\ 5\ 9\ 2
\end{array}
$$

The final product is, therefore, 518.74592 which is a number to 5 decimal places.

The algorithm for the multiplication of decimal numbers may now be described as a three-step procedure.

1   *Write down the numbers to be multiplied one under the other. It is not really necessary to align the decimal points and the digits of the same place value, but such an alignment may improve the presentation.*
2   *Count the number of digits to the right of the point in each of the decimal numbers and add those two numbers together. Their sum is the number of digits to the right of the point in the product.*
3   *Ignore the decimal points in the two given numbers and just multiply them as though they were integers. In other words, apply the algorithm for the multiplication of two integers. Insert the decimal point in the position determined by step 2.*

Have you noticed one important feature of multiplication which is not shared by either addition or subtraction?

If you cannot think of anything, look back at the previous examples. Compare the accuracy of the 'answer' with the accuracy of the numbers added or subtracted. You should find that the accuracy of the most accurate of the numbers involved in the addition or subtraction is the same as the accuracy of the 'answer'. So, if a number to 2 decimal places is added to a number to 3 decimal places the sum of the two numbers is to 3 decimal places.

The number of decimal places in the product of two numbers is always at least twice the accuracy of the least accurate of the numbers multiplied. The accuracy (the number of decimal places) may be given by the algorithm, but in a practical situation it is sensible to raise the question:

Is the accuracy of the result of a computation greater than is justified by the accuracy of the data used in the computation?

Is there any advantage in considering the multiplication of decimal numbers as repeated addition? You could do, but it would be rather tedious. The example of 251.6 times 43.7 could be done by writing down 251.6 forty-three times, and adding them to get 10818.8. Then you would need to find 0.7 of 251.6, which is 176.12, and add that to 10818.8 to finally obtain the 'product' of 10994.92. How much wiser to know the algorithm for multiplication!

Let us now consider what may well be the most difficult of the binary operations on decimal numbers.

Division of decimal numbers

What is involved in the division of decimals may be better understood by recalling two notions dealt with in earlier sections:

- the notion of division being thought of as repeated subtraction; and
- the notion of a fraction being thought of as the numerator divided by the denominator.

Let us take the first of these notions and consider it in relation to the division of 3.4 by 0.2.

To understand how this may be thought of as 'the repeated subtraction of 0.2 from 3.4', take a look at the representation of 3.4 in the diagram below. To see how the repeated subtraction may be performed, use is made of the equivalence of 0.2, 2/10 and 1/5.

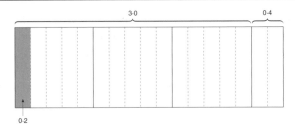

The shaded rectangle representing 0.2 fits into the square representing 1 five times, so there are fifteen 0.2s in 3.0. Add to that the two 0.2s which fit into the 0.4 and you obtain the total of 17. You have arrived at the result:

$$3.4 \div 0.2 = 17$$

or 17.0 to the same degree of accuracy as the numbers involved in the division.

This example of the division of decimal numbers was carefully chosen because of its simplicity. What makes it simple? There is no remainder. The decimal result, or quotient as it is called, terminates. The quotient is 17.0 exactly. Before considering a decimal division which does not terminate, let us look at the second notion referred to – that of a fraction being thought of in terms of division.

Consider the division of 6.072 by 1.32 and represent this as a fraction.

If $6.072 \div 1.32$ is written as 6.072/1.32, an unusual feature of the fraction is that both the numerator and denominator are not integers. Recalling that division may be thought of as repeated subtraction and deciding that 1.32 times 4 gives 5.28 the fraction may be re-written as:

$$6.072/1.32 = 5.28/1.32 + 0.792/1.32$$
$$= 4 \qquad + 0.792/1.32$$

Now recall that any number multiplied by the mutiplicative identity, 1, retains the same value. Multiplying the fraction by 1000/1000 changes both the numerator and denominator into 792/1320, a fraction with integer numerator and denominator. The algorithm for the division of integers may be applied to convert this fraction into a decimal number by setting the division out as shown below:

$$
\begin{array}{r}
0\ .\ 6 \\
1\ 3\ 2\ 0\ \overline{\smash{)}\ 7\ 9\ 2\ .\ 0} \\
7\ 9\ 2\ .\ 0
\end{array}
$$

This is the long-division procedure extended to decimals, to give a quotient of 0.6. It is a procedure which requires some justification. Think again of the division in terms of a fraction and of a multiplicative identity in the form of 10/10, so that:

$$
\begin{aligned}
792/1320 &= 792/1320 \times 10/10 \\
&= 7920/1320 \times 1/10 \\
&= 6 \times 1/10 \\
&= 6/10 \\
&= 0.6
\end{aligned}
$$

This provides the justification of ignoring the point in 792.0 and the division of 7920 by 1320 to get the 6 to the right of the point in the quotient.

Again the division terminates. The quotient is 4.6 exactly. The actual, complete division is carried out as shown below with 6.072 divided by 1.32 changed into 607.2 divided by 132. (6072 divided by 1320 would give exactly the same result. Why choose one form rather than the other?)

```
                    4 . 6
          ┌─────────────
      132 │   6 0 7 . 2
              - 5 2 8    ↓
              ─────────
                  7 9   2
                - 7 9   2
                ─────────
                        0
```

The procedure to adopt when the division does not terminate is best illustrated by means of an example.

Consider the division of 52.6 by 8.32. This works out to be 6.322115385, way beyond the accuracy of the two numbers involved in the division. (The *dividend* and *divisor* for those who may be interested in the terminology.) In cases where the division produces either a non-terminating quotient or a quotient with a lot of digits to the right of the point, a ecision has to be made at the outset as to how many decimal places are required in the quotient. How this decision is made will be dealt with in Chapter 5. If a decision is made in advance that the quotient is to be worked out to 2 decimal places, then the division would be set out as:

```
                    6 . 3 2
          ┌──────────────────
      832 │   5 2 6 0 . 0 0
              - 4 9 9 2
              ─────────
                  2 6 8   0
                - 2 4 9   6
                ─────────
                    1 8   4 0
                  - 1 6   6 4
                  ─────────
                      1 7   6
```

The presentation of division involved some references to changing a fraction into decimal form. This kind of transformation needs to be dealt with more generally.

The conversion of fractions into decimal form

Any fraction may be expressed in decimal form just by dividing its numerator by its denominator. The decimal may be exactly equal to the fraction or be approximately equal to it. Let us consider each case in turn.

The fraction 7/8, changed into a decimal by dividing 7 by 8, is found to equal 0.875.

This means that $7/8 = 8/10 + 7/100 + 5/1000$ exactly.

However, when the same is tried with 4/7 the decimal obtained is 0.571428571...

The decimal does not terminate. In such a case you could opt for a chosen degree of accuracy, of say 2 decimal places, and write:

$$4/7 = 0.57 \text{ (2DP) because } 4/7 \approx 5/10 + 7/100.$$

(The symbol $\approx$ means 'is approximately equal to'.)

Alternatively, if you realise that the digits 571428 keep repeating in the decimal expansion when you persist with the division process, you could indicate the recurring digits by placing a dot above the first and last digits in the repeating group and write:

$$4/7 = 0.\dot{5}7142\dot{8}$$

One final aspect of the structure of the decimal system of numbers is worth making explicit at this stage. Recall that the place values have an apparent pattern of multiplying by 10 as positions move to the left away from the point and multiplying by 1/10 as positions move to the right away from the point. There is an alternative way of describing this pattern.

Consider the positions to the left of the point.

First there is 10.

Second there is 100. This can be thought of as 10×10 and written as 10^2.

Third there is 1000. This can be thought of as $10 \times 10 \times 10$ and written as 10^3. The small digit to the top right of the 10 is called an index number. (The plural of index is indices.) So the next place value would be 10^4 and it would be read as 'ten to the power of four'.

Now think of those same powers from left to right: 4, 3 and 2. What is the pattern in this sequence of powers? They are decreasing by 1 each time. How, then, would you expect the sequence to continue?

After 2 comes 1 and then 0. 1 less than 0 is –1. 1 less than –1 is –2 and so on.

The sequence of place values may, therefore, be written as:

$$\ldots 10^4, 10^3, 10^2, 10^1, 10^0, 10^{-1}, 10^{-2} \ldots$$

Comparing this list with the previous way of expressing the place values yields the following equivalent expressions:

$$10^4 = 10\,000$$
$$10^3 = 1000$$
$$10^2 = 100$$
$$10^1 = 10$$
$$10^0 = 1$$
$$10^{-1} = \tfrac{1}{10}$$
$$10^{-2} = \tfrac{1}{100}$$

Key Issues in teaching decimals

Research has highlighted that children find the concept of decimals difficult. A robust understanding of the place value of whole numbers and reinforcement of the relationship between columns – each column to the left is ten times larger – is a good basis for understanding that the values get ten times smaller to the right.

As in the case of teaching of whole numbers, it is useful to demonstrate the concept of decimals using concrete apparatus and discussion. Some of the common mistakes made by children such as ordering decimal numbers according to the number of digits regardless of the position of the decimal point and the use of zeros can be avoided if children are encouraged to discuss the role of the point and its role in determining the size of numbers. You can read more on this in the chapter on children's misconceptions in Section C of this book. The section on teaching and assessing of decimals in the SCAA publication (SCAA, 1997) provides much support for considering issues regarding the teaching of decimals.

3.3 Indices

The place value system of numbers – both whole numbers and decimals – is based on powers of ten. In this section we will broaden the discussion of powers to include powers of any integer. The index notation is used to represent, in a compact way, the product of a number by itself many times.

Consider 10^3.

The three above the 10 is called a 'power' and the ten is called the 'base'. The power indicates the number of times the base is multiplied by itself. This is sometimes thought of as 'three tens multiplied together', so that $10^3 = 10 \times 10 \times 10$. When verbalising it this way, children may mistake this to mean '3 times 10'. Thinking of 10 as 'three tens multiplied together' can lead someone to ask the question about 10^0:

How can you have zero tens multiplied together and get $10^0 = 1$

To understand how this question is misguided, the notion of the multiplicative identity needs to be reviewed. Let us do this in two stages.

First, let us look into the way in which the operation of multiplication works with numbers expressed as powers of a base number.

Consider the product of 4 and 8.

$4 \times 8 = 32$

$4 = 2 \times 2$, so 4 can be written as 2^2

$8 = 2 \times 2 \times 2$, so 8 can be written as 2^3

$32 = 2 \times 2 \times 2 \times 2 \times 2$, so 32 can be written as 2^5.

Now look at the same product, with the three numbers written as powers of 2.

$$2^2 \times 2^3 = 2^5.$$

Focus on the indices and notice that $2 + 3 = 5$. This gives a rule for multiplying powers of the same base number:

When multiplying powers of the same base number, just add the indices to obtain the product.

Multiplying in this format can be much easier than applying the multiplication algorithm to integers. Which would you prefer to do? $27 \times 81 = 2187$ or $3^3 \times 3^4 = 3^7$?

3 + 4 = 7 is much easier provided, of course, you know which powers of 3 equal the numbers to be multiplied (i.e. that $27 = 3^3$, $81 = 3^4$).

Second, consider the rule for adding index numbers in relation to the multiplicative identity, 1.

$125 \times 1 = 125$ because you are multiplying by the identity, 1. Can this be written in index form? $125 = 5 \times 5 \times 5$, so 125 can be written as 5^3. If 1 can be written as a power of 5 and the rule for adding indices applied to give the same power of 5, what power of 5 must be used to represent 1? Zero. That makes it possible to write $125 \times 1 = 125$ in the form $5^3 \times 5^0 = 53$.

The same kind of argument can be used to justify any integer to the power of zero being acceptable as a representation of 1.

Suppose you want to divide two numbers with the same base, perhaps with different powers; here you can subtract the indices.

For example, $4^5 \div 4^2 = 4^3$

Check that $4^5 = 1024$, $4^2 = 16$, $4^3 = 64$ and $1024 \div 16 = 64$.

3.4 Standard index form

If the unit of measurement has been fixed, a measurement in terms of that unit can sometimes be an extremely large number. Sometimes a measurement can be an extremely small number. In either case, only a few digits of the measurement may be reliable. With such measurements, the standard index form of numbers can have considerable advantages. Let us consider a few very small and a few very large numbers.

An electron, one of the twelve elementary particles of modern physics, has a mass of 9.1×10^{-31} kg. Why should such a small mass be measured in kilograms? (1kg is equivalent to about two and a quarter pounds). The smallest bacteria are about 400 nanometres in size. (1 nanometre equals 10^{-9} metres.) The mass of an electron was given in standard index form. The information was given in two parts. The first part consisted of a number from 1 and up to 10; the second part consisted of a power of 10. The size of the smallest bacteria can be changed into standard index form as follows:

$$400 \times 10^{-9} \text{ m} = 4.0 \times 100 \times 10^{-9} \text{ m}.$$
$$= 4.0 \times 10^2 \times 10^{-9} \text{ m}.$$
$$= 4.0 \times 10^{-7} \text{ m}.$$

Some large measurements are the mass of the Sun, 1.989×10^{33} gm, and the mass of our planet Earth, 5.977×10^{27} gm.

How much greater than the mass of Earth is the mass of the Sun? Thinking of the mass of the Sun divided by the mass of Earth in the form of a fraction:

$$\frac{1.989 \times 10^{33}}{5.977 \times 10^{27}} = \frac{1.989 \times 10^{33}}{5.977 \times 10^{27}}$$
$$= 0.333 \times 10^6 \text{ or } 3.33 \times 10^5 \text{ in standard index form.}$$

So the mass of the Sun is about three hundred thousand times greater than the mass of the Earth.

So, how do you write numbers in standard index form?

The standard form for
$$2000 = 2.0 \times 10^{3}$$
$$160 = 1.6 \times 10^{2}$$
$$0.0005 = 5.0 \times 10^{-4}$$

Try representing 0.00000000678 in standard form. It is 6.78×10^{-9}; now you see how it simplifies reading that number.

3.5 Percentages

Have you noticed on a semi-skimmed milk carton, perhaps on the top, 1.7% fat?

Have you noticed, on a packet of corn flakes, the information that the contents contain 2.2 g of fat per 100 g of the cereal? Both items of information refer to 100. 'One hundred' is of considerable cultural importance. The notion of a century, the subdivisions of units of money, length and volume used in many countries, all relate to the number 100.

Have you noticed any differences in the two bits of information? The cereal information is definitely about weight; it contains two weights, both in grams. Since 2.2 g out of 100 consists of fat, it can also be said that 2.2% of the cereal consists of fat. What about the information concerning milk? Is that relating to weight or volume? The milk is sold by volume. The 1.7% which is fat is of a different density to the rest of the contents of the milk. So, whether the fat content is 1.7% by weight or by volume does make a difference. This highlights one of the greatest sources of confusion when considering percentages. What is the percentage a percentage of? Failure to be clear about the answer to this question, or failure to even ask the question, can lead to either misunderstanding or misrepresentation becoming possible.

Of course, not all information starts out as a percentage. A student who has scored 17 out of 20 in a test after previously scoring 41 out of 50 may be interested in judging whether there has been any improvement in performance. One way of comparing the two scores is to convert them both into equivalent scores out of 100.

If each of the scores is thought of as a fraction of the total marks available then each can be multiplied by the multiplicative identity, expressed in an appropriate form.

So the first score can be converted into an equivalent score out of 100 as follows:

$$17/20 \times 5/5 = 85/100.$$

5/5 is the chosen form because 20 needs to be multiplied by 5 to give the result of 100. This enables the score in the first test to be described as 85%.

The second score can be converted into an equivalent score out of 100 by choosing 2/2 as the identity, since 50 needs to be multiplied by 2 to give the result 100. This produces:

$$41/50 \times 2/2 = 82/100.$$

This may be expressed as 82%, a relatively lower score than in the first test.

These two examples of converting fractions into percentages were quite easy because their denominators were factors of 100. What if 100 is not a multiple of a fraction's denominator? Take the case of a class of 28 having 3 pupils absent. What is the percentage of the class which is absent? Is the absenteeism worse than in another class of 25 with 2 pupils absent?

The fraction of pupils absent in the first class is 3/28. To change this into a percentage, an appropriate form of the identity is required.

28 times what equals 100? 28 times 100/28 equals 100.

This gives the numerator and denominator of the appropriate form of the identity:

$$3/28 \times (100/28) / (100/28).$$

The denominator of the result is, of course, 100.

What is the numerator?

It is $3 \times (100/28)$, which is 300/28. Cancelling 4 into the numerator and denominator of this yields 75/7 and this approximates to 10.71.

The percentage of pupils absent in the first class is, therefore, 10.71% and is greater than the 8% absent in the second class. The second was much easier to work out as:

$$2/25 \times 4/4 = 8/100.$$

A major advantage of the notion of percentages is that it provides a common standard for comparisons. Different amounts out of different totals, expressed as equivalent amounts out of totals of 100, can then be compared. A salary increase of £1500 per annum, for someone earning £15 000 p.a. is an increase of 10%. The same increase, for someone earning £20 000 p.a., is an increase of 7.5%.

This advantage of percentages for comparing quantities is very useful for many situations. When, however, the numbers involved are very small or very large there is another strategy for making comparisons. This strategy requires the two numbers to be compared to be expressed as a decimal times the same power of 10. For example, the mass of the Sun is 1.989×10^{33} gm, the mass of the Earth is 5.977×10^{27} gm. What is the comparison of the two masses? The answer could be obtained using two strategies.

$$\frac{\text{Mass of Sun}}{\text{Mass of Earth}} = \frac{1.989 \times 10^{33}}{5.977 \times 10^{27}}$$

$$= \frac{1.989}{5.977} \times 10^{6}$$

$$= 0.333 \times 10^{6}$$

$$= 3.33 \times 10^{5} \text{ in standard index form.}$$

Alternatively, the strategy used could be: $1.989 \times 10^{33} = 1.989 \times 10^{6} \times 10^{27}$, so

$$\frac{\text{Mass of Sun}}{\text{Mass of Earth}} = \frac{1989000 \times 10^{27}}{5.977 \times 10^{27}}$$

$$= \frac{1989000}{5.977}$$

$$= 332775.64$$

$$= 3.33 \times 10^{5} \text{ in standard index form.}$$

Tasks relating to the classroom

1 Ask a few children to order the fractions: 1/3, 1/16, and 1/20 and explain how they decided the order.

2 The following mistakes were collected from a Year 6 class of children. For each of the mistakes, consider what may be the reason why a child makes this mistake and how you would be pro-active and address this at the teaching stage?

a) $3 - 2.31 \rightarrow \begin{array}{r} 2.31 \\ -\ \ 3 \\ \hline 2.01 \end{array}$

b) $\dfrac{3}{5}$ of £1.80 = £3.00

c) $5^3 = 15$

d)   £47.37 −27p. Used a calculator and got £20.37

e) $\dfrac{3}{5} + \dfrac{1}{3} = \dfrac{4}{8}$

3 A child ordered the following numbers, from the smallest to the largest, and brought it to you to be marked. What action would you take?

111, 1001, 11.01, 111.11

Tasks for self-study

1 Do the following fractions and decimal sums. Estimate the solutions before you do them.

a) $\dfrac{3}{4} + \dfrac{11}{12} =$

b) $\dfrac{7}{8} = \dfrac{?}{16}$

c) $2.11 + 41.42 + 0.08 =$

d) $19.3 - 14.27 =$

2 Put > or < between the pairs of numbers:

a) $\dfrac{3}{5} \quad \dfrac{4}{7}$

b) $\dfrac{2}{3} \quad \dfrac{4}{5}$

c)   1.901   1.222

3 What is 15% of £180?

Find out how you would do this calculation using a calculator?

4   Complete the chart :

Fraction	Decimal	Percentage
$\dfrac{1}{2}$		
	0.6	
$\dfrac{2}{5}$		
	0.25	
		75%
$\dfrac{1}{20}$		
		20% .

5   Express the following in index form:

a)   5 =

b)   25 =

c)   125 =

d)   625 =

e)   3125 =

f)   1 =

g) $\dfrac{1}{5}$ =

h) $\dfrac{1}{25}$ =

i) $\dfrac{1}{125}$ =

6   Write the following numbers in standard index form:
Example: $0.006043 = \mathbf{6.043} \times \mathbf{10}^{-3}$

a)   0.025 =

b)   0.25 =

c)   0.79 =

d) 0.0079 =

e) 0.926 =

f) 0.0805 =

g) 0.000018 =

h) 0.0000000062 =

i) 36 =

j) 84=

Chapter 4

Number patterns and sequences

Objectives

This chapter focuses on:

4.1 Sequences
4.2 Series
4.3 Generalised arithmetic
4.4 Functions
4.5 Identities and equations
4.6 Equations
4.7 Inequalities

4.1 Sequences

Some collections of numbers exhibit a kind of pattern whereas other collections, even when arranged in different ways, seem to have no regular feature of any kind. Look at the following collection of numbers arranged in a list:

$$31, 28, 31, 30, 31, 30, 31, 31, 30, 31, 30, 31.$$

What do you make of the list? It is, in fact, the list of the number of days of the months in 1999. Mathematically, it is a *sequence* of twelve terms; each term in the sequence has a position and a value. The term relating to April, for example, has the fourth position in the list. Its value is 30; the fourth term in the sequence is 30. What is the tenth term in the sequence? It is 31 and it relates to the month of October. Not all sequences have an obvious practical interpretation, like the months of the year. Not all sequences are finite; some are infinite – they carry on so that there is no such thing as a last term. The sequence consisting of the squares of the integers is an infinite sequence:

$$1, 4, 9, 16, 25, \ldots$$

The fourth term of this sequence, four squared, is 16. The three dots following the 25 indicate that the terms continue indefinitely. The two sequences of days and of square numbers differ in two respects. One is finite and one is infinite. The other difference concerns the connection between the position of the term in the sequence and the value of the term. If you have 'seen' the pattern in the sequence of squares of the integers, you should be able to give the seventh term in the sequence. You take the 7 and square it to obtain 49. There is a rule which connects the position of the term and its value. There is no rule which connects the number of the month and the number of the days in the month. For October, the tenth month, there is not a rule which enables you to obtain 31 so that applying the same rule in the same way to 6, for June, you can obtain 30. Of course, there is a constancy in the list of days in the months of the year; only the number for the second month varies and most people know of the constancy. But the constancy is not a rule in the way that a rule applies to the sequence of squares. Sequences which can be generated by a rule are of more interest to mathematicians than sequences of numbers which are not generated by a rule. The latter type of sequence is really just a list; it could be a list of data items obtained in an experiment or even a list of random numbers for use on a Lottery ticket.

Working out sequences

There are two skills associated with sequences governed by a rule:

1   The skill which enables someone, given the rule, to find terms of the sequence specified by the position number of the terms. For example, 4, 8, 12, 16, … ; here the number that fits into blank space is 20 which is the fifth in the sequence. This is obtained by multiplying $5 \times 4 = 20$, the 20th term will be 20×4 and following this rule the nth term will be $n \times 4$ or $4n$.
2   The skill which enables someone, given at least three consecutive terms of the sequence, to discover the rule for the sequence so that further terms can be generated.

Perhaps the simplest of rules is 'add 1 to each term to obtain the next term'. Following this rule enables someone to count on from any starting number. Beginning with 1, using the rule generates 2, 3, 4, 5 and so on. Starting with 78, the rule enables you to follow on with 79, 80, 81 and so on.

This kind of rule links each term with one, or more, previous terms. A rule which links each term with two previous terms is 'add two consecutive terms to get the next term'. So starting with 1, 2 the next term is 3; continuing to follow the rule generates the sequence:

$$1, 2, 3, 5, 8, 13 \text{ and so on.}$$

Can you think of a shortcoming of this type of rule which expresses each term of a sequence as obtainable from previous terms?

Focus on the sequence given by the first two terms 4, 7 and the rule, applicable to the third term onwards, 'square the previous term and add the term before that to the result to get the next term'. The third, fourth and fifth terms of this sequence are: 7 squared plus 4, which is $49 + 4 = 53$; 53 squared plus 7, which is $2809 + 7 = 2816$; 2816 squared plus 53, which is $7929856 + 53 = 7929909$. So the first five terms of the sequence are:

$$4, 7, 53, 2816, 7929909.$$

Can you jump ahead to find the twentieth term of this sequence without finding all the intermediate terms from the sixth to the nineteenth? No! There is another kind of sequence which enables such jumping ahead to be made quite easily. The sequence of cubes of integers is an example of this kind. The first three terms are 1, 8, 27. What is the twentieth term of this sequence? Well, the first term is 1 cubed, the second term is 2 cubed and the third term is 3 cubed. So the twentieth term is 20 cubed which is 8000. The rule for this sequence takes the form of a process related to the position of the term required. The rule is 'cube the position of the term to get the term'. There is no reference to previous terms in this rule, so knowledge of previous terms is not needed.

The difficulty with this kind of sequence is detecting the rule for its generation on being given just the first three terms. Consider the first three terms 6, 9 and 14. What is the twentieth term of the sequence?

Can you spot that 6 is 1 squared plus 5, 9 is 2 squared plus 5 and 14 is 3 squared plus 5? Check that the rule 'square the position number and add 5' gives the first three terms. A simple application of the rule gives a twentieth term of 20 squared plus 5, which is $400 + 5 = 405$.

So sequences can be thought of as being of two kinds, depending on the type of rule determining the sequence. There are occasions when adding the terms of a sequence is required, perhaps to solve a particular problem. Such a procedure involves the notion of a series.

4.2 Series

A series is simply the addition of the terms of a sequence. The *sum* of a series is the result of adding the terms.

Take the sequence 1, 4, 9, 16, 25, 36. The series obtained from this sequence is:

$$1 + 4 + 9 + 16 + 25 + 36.$$

The sum of this series of six terms is 91.

If the number of terms to be added is quite large, it could be very laborious adding on the terms one by one. Some kind of short-cut could save a lot of time.

Let us consider a situation in which the sum of a series needs to be found.

Imagine that someone is organising a tournament in which six teams have to play each other just once. How many games have to be arranged?

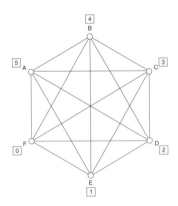

Call the six teams A, B, C, D, E and F, since their actual names do not matter.

Consider the games arranged for each team in turn.

Team A has to play B, C, D, E and F; that is five games to be arranged.

Team B has one of its games already arranged; it also has to play C, D, E and F – a further four games.

Team C has two of its games already arranged; it also has to play D, E and F – a further three games.

Team D has three of its games already arranged; it also has to play E and F – a further two games.

Team E has four of its games already arranged; it also has to play F – one further game.

Team F has all of its games arranged. There are no further games to arrange.

So the total number of games which have to be arranged and played is:

$$1 + 2 + 3 + 4 + 5.$$

This is not difficult to work out. But what if the tournament involved sixty teams rather than six? Then a short-cut way of adding the integers 1 to 60 would surely be useful. So, let us find a short-cut by taking the easier example with six teams. Look at the series. Reverse the terms to get another series:

$$5 + 4 + 3 + 2 + 1.$$

Add 1 and 5 (the first terms of the original series and the new one), then the second terms of both series and so on. Each time you get a result of 6. The total is 5×6. This is twice the sum of the original series, so the sum of the series $1 + 2 + 3 + 4 + 5$ is $1/2 \times 5 \times 6$. A half of thirty is fifteen, which is the correct total. Can you jump ahead and decide how many games would need to be arranged for a tournament involving sixty teams in which each team has to play every other team once? The number of games needed in the tournament would be:

$1 + 2 + 3 + \cdots + 59$. On the basis of the result for the sum of the integers from 1 to 5, the sum of the integers from 1 to 59 is $1/2 \times 59 \times 60 = 1770$. How much simpler this is than laboriously adding the fifty-nine integers together by repeated addition!

This illustration of a short-cut, saving time and energy in obtaining a required result, is just one of the means by which conciseness is provided in mathematics. Other devices include the use of symbols (for operations) and letters (as place-holders for numbers). Five operations and their associated symbols have already been considered, so some attention can now be given to the role of letters.

4.3 Generalised arithmetic

If you think back to the series of squares of the integers, the question of 'jumping ahead' to find terms such as the tenth can be generalised so that it is meaningful to ask about the nth, where n can stand for any integer.

The nth term of that series is n^2 (n squared written using an index number). A very useful and concise symbol – for a term of a sequence or series – is u_n, where the n written as a subscript indicates the term being referred to. Using this notation, the series of the squares of integers can be shown as:

$$u_1 = 1; \; u_2 = 4; \; u_3 = 9; \; \ldots \; ; \; u_n = n^2 \text{ and so on (the } n\text{th term is equal to } n^2).$$

This notation is useful for describing sequences and series in which a term is given as connected to previous terms.

Remember the sequence : 4, 7, 53, 2816, … This can be described as:

$$u_1 = 4; \quad u_2 = 7; \quad u_n = u_{n-1}^2 + u_{n-2}$$

Since the general term, the nth term, is expressed as connected to the two previous terms, the first two terms must be given specific numerical values. Any particular term can then be found by substituting the appropriate integer value for n in the expression for the general term. If, for example, the fiftieth term is needed, just replace n by 50 to get:

$$u_{50} = u_{49}^2 + u_{48}$$

Of course, without actual numerical values for the forty-ninth and the forty-eighth terms, that is as far as you can take it.

Nevertheless, the expression is far more compact than the statement:

The fiftieth term equals the forty-ninth term squared plus the forty-eighth term.

How can this sequence be described using the notation just given?

$$7, 11, 15, \ldots$$

$$u_1 = 7 = 4 \times 1 + 3; \qquad u_2 = 11 = 4 \times 2 + 3; \qquad u_3 = 15 = 4 \times 3 + 3.$$

Looking at what is constant and what is varying, the nth term can be expressed as:
$u_n = 4n + 3$. (Note that $4n$ is a compact way of writing $4 \times n$.)
Can you find the nth term of the sequence : 3, 8, 13, ...?

$$u_1 = 3 = 5 \times 1 - 2; \qquad u_2 = 8 = 5 \times 2 - 2; \qquad u_3 = 13 = 5 \times 3 - 2.$$

Again, looking at what is constant and what is varying, the expression for the nth term is:

$$u_n = 5n - 2.$$

Before further consideration of how to find general expressions, let us recall the properties of the binary operations and express them as generalisations.

'Addition is commutative' can be stated as : $x + y = y + x$. (Any numbers can be substituted for x and y.)

'Addition is associative' can be stated as: $(x + y) + z = x + (y + z)$. This is true for any numbers x, y and z.

'Multiplication is commutative' can be expressed as $x \times y = y \times x$, for all values of x and y.

'Multiplication is associative' can be stated as $(x \times y) \times z = x \times (y \times z)$, for all x, y and z.

A property linking addition and multiplication is, expressed in words:

'Multiplication is distributive over addition'. The influence of $\times$ is distributed over $+$. In general, in symbolic form this is stated as: $(x(y + z) = xy + xz$. Notice that $\times$ has been dispensed with three times – between the x and the left bracket and, on the right of the equals sign, between the x and the y and also between the x and the z. A diagram illustrates this distributive property and, in a way, makes it acceptable.

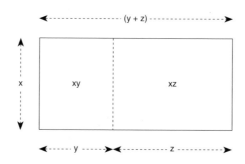

An expression for the area of the whole rectangle is $x \times (y + z)$ or $x(y + z)$. This is the sum of the areas of the two smaller rectangles: xy and xz.

So, from the diagram, $x(y + z) = xy + xz$

The additive identity and the additive inverse can be similarly stated as:

$$x + 0 = x \text{ and } x + (-x) = 0.$$

The multiplicative identity and the multiplicative inverse can also be stated in general form:

$$x \times 1 = x \text{ and } x \times 1/x = 1$$

There is a slight snag with the last of these statements, but the previous three are true for all values of x. What is the snag? Remember that a fraction can be thought of as 'the numerator divided by the denominator'. Division by 0 is not possible, so $x \times 1/x$ is true for all values of x except zero.

With these generalisations in mind, we can return to consider a few more series, rather better equipped.

The 'rich aunt' generalisation

Imagine a child with an affluent aunt who wants to encourage the child to be thrifty. She strikes a bargain with the child and undertakes to give the child £3 more each month than the previous month, provided the child saves £20 each month out of the generous pocket-money given by the parents. The agreement is for one year. By sticking to the agreement, how much money will the child have accumulated by the end of the year?

Let u represent the amount added to the total in the nth month.

In the first month, the child saves £20 and the aunt gives nothing.

So $u_1 = 20$.

In the second month, the child again saves £20 and the aunt gives £3.

So $u_2 = 20 + 1 \times 3$.

In the third month, the aunt adds £6 to the child's £20.

So $u_3 = 20 + 2 \times 3$.

Continuing in this way, at the end of the twelfth month the aunt gives £33 to add to the child's £20.

So $u_{12} = 20 + 11 \times 3$.

The twelve monthly amounts can be thought of as twelve terms of a series. The amount the child has accumulated by the end of the year can be thought of as the sum of the twelve terms of that series. Is there a short-cut method of finding the sum, which could then be extended to finding the sum of more terms of the same series or applied to other series of the same type?

Remember what was done to find the sum of the first n integers. Using the same technique, write down the terms of the series twice as shown below:

20 ,	$20 + 1 \times 3$,	$20 + 2 \times 3$,	... ,	$20 + 11 \times 3$
$20 + 11 \times 3$,	$20 + 10 \times 3$,	$20 + 9 \times 3$,	... ,	20

Adding the first terms of the two series together, then adding the second terms, then the third and so on, you get '$2 \times 20 + 11 \times 3$' each time. In all, this result is obtained twelve times and gives twice the required total of the series. So the sum of the series, the amount the child will have accumulated by the end of the year, is a half of 12 $(2 \times 20 + 11 \times 3)$. This comes to £438.

Arithmetic progressions

The example above has been an illustration of the type of series called *arithmetic progressions*. To generalise what was done with the particular case of the aunt and child so as to find a way of getting the sum of any arithmetic progression, we need to focus on what was fixed and what varied in the particular case. Two things were fixed – the 20 and the 3. 20 was the actual first term; it is customary to represent the first term of an arithmetic progression by the letter *a*. The aunt could have asked the child to save a different amount each month; *a* could have been given a different value. 3 was the extra, compared with the previous month, given by the aunt. It was the difference between the terms, the difference between the total accumulated in a month compared with the previous month. It is customary to represent this common difference in arithmetic progressions by the letter *d*. What varied from month to month was the number of ds connected to each month, but it varied from 0, for the first month, to 11 for the twelfth month. These 'month' numbers are connected to the total 12, the number of terms of the series. It is customary to use the letter *n*, in arithmetic progressions, to represent the number of terms of the arithmetic progression involved in the sum. It is also customary to use *S*, for sum, with a subscript *n* to indicate the number of terms, to represent the sum of *n* terms of an arithmetic progression. Looking back at the total accumulated by the child, 1/2 of 12$(2 \times 20 + 11 \times 3)$ and replacing 20 by *a*, 3 by *d* and 12 by *n*, with 11 replaced by $(n - 1)$, a formula for the sum of *n* terms of an arithmetic progression is obtained:

$$S_n = n/2[2a + (n-1)d].$$

Using a formula saves time and energy, but it is better for your understanding and mathematical development if you have some appreciation of how any particular formula has been established.

Just as a check on your skill in using this formula, suppose that the agreement between the aunt and child had been for three years, that the child was required to save £12 each month and that the aunt undertook to give £5 more each month rather than £3. How much would the child have accumulated by the end of the three years?

To use the formula, just substitute 36 for *n*, so that $n - 1$ is replaced by 35. Then substitute 12 for *a* and 5 for *d*. This produces:

$$S_{36} = 36/2[2 \times 12 + 35 \times 5]$$
$$= 18[24 + 175]$$
$$= 18 \times 199$$
$$= 3582$$

How much easier is the use of the formula than adding 36 numbers and how much wiser it would have been for the money to have been deposited in a bank! (Calculating the interest involves the use of yet another formula.)

Geometric progression

Let us now turn to a different kind of series. In biology, populations of many kinds are studied. There are populations of people, of animals, of cells and trees; there are even populations of bacteria and viruses. How they grow or decline is of great importance. It is now quite common to try to create a model, which is a mathematical formula, to describe, predict and perhaps control a specific population. A simple type of model takes the form of a *geometric progression*. Let us explore this idea by considering an imaginary population of bacteria which increases in size every minute by doubling the increase in size of the previous minute.

Consider the growth of these bacteria over a period of n minutes. Assume that the starting size of the bacterium population is a. By the end of the first minute there will be an increase in the population of $2a$ bacteria; so the total population at the end of 1 minute is $3a$. ($a + 2a = 3a$). By the end of second minute there will be a further increase in size of $4a$ bacteria. This makes the total population at the end of the second minute $7a$ bacteria ($3a + 4a = 7a$). By the end of the third minute there will be an increase of size of $8a$ bacteria making the total population at the end of 3 minutes $15a$ and so on. What will be the increase in population size in the sixtieth minute?

Two to the power of sixty (2^{60}): the size of the bacterium population after n minutes is the sum of n terms of the geometric progression, given by:

$$S_n = a + 2a + 4a + 8a + \ldots + 2^{n-2} a + 2^{n-1} a \tag{1}$$

If two things are equal, then double the two things will also be equal.
Doubling both sides of the equals sign produces:

$$2S_n = 2a + 4a + 8a + \ldots + 2^{n-1} a + 2^n a \tag{2}$$

Subtracting (1) from (2) gives:

$$S_n = 2^n a - a$$
$$= a(2^n - 1) \text{ taking out } a \text{ as a common factor.}$$

Now suppose that instead of doubling, the population increase compared with the increase of the previous minute is a multiple r.

So, just replace 2 by r in (1) and (2) above. This produces the following:

$$S_n = a + ar + ar^2 + ar^3 + \ldots + ar^{n-2} + ar^{n-1} \tag{3}$$

Multiplying both sides by r:

$$rS_n = ar + ar^2 + ar^3 + ar^4 + \ldots + ar^{n-1} + ar^n \tag{4}$$

Subtracting (4) from (3) gives:

$$S_n(1-r) = a - ar^n, \text{ so that } S_n = a(1-r^n)/(1-r)$$

When $r = 2$ the population was increasing, by greater and greater amounts. What if r had a fractional value, between 0 and 1? Would the population be decreasing? No. It would still be increasing, but by smaller and smaller amounts. What if r had the value 1? The population would be increasing by the same amount each minute.

What has been taken for granted throughout the discussion of the population model? That no bacteria die! That is hardly realistic, but to take account of the death of the bacteria would require a more complicated model – which could kill off your enthusiasm.

What has been considered in this chapter are various cases of something being connected to something else. Let us now take a closer look at this process of connecting things.

4.4 Functions

'Think of a number and double it' is an invitation to think of a particular *function*. If you think of 5 and double it you get 10. If you think of 17 and double it you get 34. These are just two possibilities selected from the infinite collection of integers. The result of the doubling process depends on the number thought of. In mathematical language, it is said that the result of the doubling process is a *function* of the number thought of. The number thought of is represented by the letter n, where n can be any number; strictly speaking the kind of number should be specified – integer, rational or real. The doubling function can then be represented as:

$$f(n) = 2n$$

This should be read as 'f of n equals two n'. So, if 14 is the number thought of, the value to be substituted for n is 14 giving:

$$f(14) = 2 \times 14$$
$$= 28$$

There are two aspects of functions to consider:

- given the function, the process of finding values of the function;
- given pairs of numbers, values of the function corresponding to chosen 'starting numbers', the process of deciding the algebraic description of the function.

Let us consider each aspect in turn.

Take as an example, the function defined by:

$f(x) = 4x + 5$, with x restricted to values from 1 to 10 inclusive. Substituting the integer values for x in turn produces:

$f(1) = 4 \times 1 + 5 = 9$; $\quad f(2) = 4 \times 2 + 5 = 13$; $\quad f(3) = 17$; $\quad f(4) = 21$; $\quad f(5) = 25$;
$f(6) = 29$; $\quad f(7) = 33$; $\quad f(8) = 37$; $\quad f(9) = 41$; $\quad f(10) = 45$.

Of course, the values chosen for x are quite arbitrary, but for the chosen values the function is just as well described by the pairs of values:

(1,9), (2,13), (3,17), (4,21), (5,25), (6,29), (7,33), (8,37), (9,41), (10,45).

The first number in each pair is the value of x; the letter x is called the *variable*. x is a place-holder; it holds a place until it is filled by a number which is substituted for it.

The second number in each pair is the value of the function for the value, or number, substituted for x. It is the second aspect of functions which can, sometimes, be more difficult. Consider the following pairs of numbers:

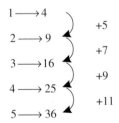

Can you find the connection between the numbers in each pair?

When looking for the connection, some people focus on the values of the function – the second numbers. They see the list 4, 9, 16, 25, 36 as increasing by 5, from 4 to 9, then by 7 from 9 to 16, then by 9, from 16 to 25, then by 11, from 25 to 36. The second numbers go up by 2 more each time. So the next increase after 11 will be 13 giving the next pair (6,49). Realising this does not amount to spotting the connection between the first and second numbers in the pairs so that you can jump ahead and give the second number paired with 50, for example.

Let us examine the first three pairs.

          1 is linked with 4 = 2 squared.

          2 is linked with 9 = 3 squared.

          3 is linked with 16 = 4 squared.

Looked at this way, you should see that the number which is squared is 1 more than the value being considered. So 4 is linked with (4 +1) squared; (4,25) is in the list describing the function.

How can the function be described algebraically? If n is used to represent the value being considered, it is linked with $(n+1)$ squared, so the function can be described algebraically as:

$$f(n) = (n+1)^2$$

Note that there is nothing special about the letter n which was selected. Any other letter could have been chosen. The function described by $f(x) = (x+1)^2$ is exactly the same function as $f(n) = (n+1)^2$. Having got what you think is the function in algebraic form, it is wise to check it using specific numbers. What is $f(5)$, using the expression $(n+1)^2$? It is 6 squared, which is 36. Correct!

Spotting the connection and describing it in algebraic form takes skill and patience.

Try to find the connection between the numbers in the following pairs, describe the function algebraically and then find $f(20)$.

$$1 \longrightarrow 10$$

$$2 \longrightarrow 17$$

$$3 \longrightarrow 24$$

If you focused on the list of second numbers, 10, 17, 24, and noticed that they go up in sevens, then it takes too long to find the number which pairs with 20.

What you need to find is what you can do to 1 to get 10 so that when you do the same to 2 you get 17 and when you do it to 3 you get 24. Not all that easy! There is 'trial and error' involved.

Here is one way of finding the connection between the pairs of numbers, still using the fact that the second numbers go up in sevens – though relating the sevens to the first numbers.

$$1 \longrightarrow 10$$

$$2 \longrightarrow 10+7$$

$$3 \longrightarrow 10+14$$

Writing the 10, 17 and 24 in this way helps to reveal what is being done to the 1, 2 and 3. The number of 7s being added to the 10 is increasing by 1, so the three pairs of numbers can be shown as:

$$1 \longrightarrow 10 + 0 \times 7$$
$$2 \longrightarrow 10 + 1 \times 7$$
$$3 \longrightarrow 10 + 2 \times 7$$

What is wanted is $f(x)$ equal to some expression containing x. The number of 7s being added is 1 less than x each time; 1 less than x can be written as $(x - 1)$. The connection between the pairs, therefore, is revealed as:

$$x \longrightarrow 10 + (x - 1)7$$

Remember that multiplication is commutative. This justifies changing the order, giving $7(x-1)$ instead of $(x-1)7$. So the connection can be written as:

$$x \longrightarrow 10 + 7(x - 1)$$

Remember also that the multiplication sign 'exists' to the right of the 7 and that multiplication is distributive over addition so that $7(x - 1) = 7x - 7$, giving:

$$x \longrightarrow 10 + 7x - 7 = 7x + (10 - 7)$$

both the commutative and associative properties of addition are involved here. The required description of the function, f, simplifies to:

$$f(x) = 7x + 3 \quad \text{because } 10 - 7 = 3$$

$f(20)$ can then be found, skipping out values from $f(4)$ to $f(19)$

$$f(20) = 7 \times 20 + 3$$
$$= 143$$

A somewhat harder example is the following three pairs:
$(1,-1)$, $(2,6)$, $(3,25)$. Can you find the description of the function, f, which changes the first numbers into the second numbers?

Focusing on the list of second numbers does not seem to be helpful this time.

$-1, 6, 25$ shows successive increases of 7 and 19. Not obviously helpful! In this kind of situation, you could just give up. Learning mathematics, however, needs patience and the willingness to try conjectures. So look at the first pair and try to come up with some possibilities.

$1 \to -1$. How can 1 be changed into 'minus 1'? Multiplying by 'minus 1' would do it, but multiplying 2 and 3 by 'minus 1' does not produce 6 and 25. How else can it be done? By subtracting 2! Trying that with 2 and 3, as well as with 1, gives:

$$1 \longrightarrow 1 - 2 = -1$$
$$2 \longrightarrow 2 - 2 = 0, \text{ not } 6$$
$$3 \longrightarrow 3 - 2 = 1, \text{ not } 25$$

Either you scrap the idea of subtracting 2 or you pursue the conjecture:
What numbers, when 2 is subtracted from them, give -1, 6 and 25 in turn?

Those numbers are 1, 8 and 27. Take a look at another way of showing the pairs, bearing in mind that 1, 8 and 27 are the cubes of 1, 2 and 3.

$$1 \longrightarrow 1 \text{ cubed minus 2, which gives } -1$$

$$2 \longrightarrow 2 \text{ cubed minus 2, which gives } 6$$

$$3 \longrightarrow 3 \text{ cubed minus 2, which gives } 25$$

So, if n represents the number you start with, the required description of the function, f, is given by:

$$f(n) = n^3 - 2$$

This enables you to find $f(20)$ without finding the value of the function for all the values from 4 to 19, even if you had a way of doing that.

$$f(20) = 20 \text{ cubed, take away } 2$$
$$= 7998$$

When given a function described algebraically, such as $f(x) = 4x + 7$, does it make sense to ask whether it is true or false? Not really. It is just a rule by which pairs of numbers are connected which enables you to find the second number when the decision has been made as to what number is to be substituted for x. The *expression* $4x + 7$ has a numerical value, not a truth value. That numerical value may be correct or incorrect for the particular value of x being considered. 31 is correct for x equal to 6 and incorrect for x equal to 5. Although $f(x) = 4x + 7$ is neither true nor false, it is a rule for finding the value of the function for each chosen value of x: $f(6) = 31$ is true and $f(5) = 31$ is false. This is because 31 is the correct value of $4x + 7$ when x is 6 and incorrect when x is 5. To explore further situations in which some values of x, or some other variable, produce true statements and other values of the variable produce false statements, attention must now turn to the next topic.

4.5 Identities and equations

Recall some of the properties of addition and multiplication.

'Addition is commutative.' In algebraic symbols this was written as: $x + y = y + x$. Is it true or false that $x + y = y + x$? It is true. For what values of x and y is it true? For all values of x and y.

'Multiplication is distributive over addition.' In algebraic symbols this was written as: $x(y + z) = xy + xz$. Is it true or false that $x(y + z) = xy + xz$? It is true. For what values of x, y and z is it true? For all values of x, y and z. The two algebraic statements just considered are examples of identities.

Identities are always true.

When learning to change algebraic expressions into other expressions you are really engaged in finding identities. Using the distributive property just referred to, you can change $5(2x + 7)$ into $10x + 35$. In doing so you have produced an identity:

$$5(2x + 7) = 10x + 35.$$

This is true for all values of x. Try some!

$$\text{For } x = 6, \quad 5(2x+7) = 5(2 \times 6 + 7)$$
$$= 5 \times 19$$
$$= 95$$

The distinction between algebraic statements which are always true and algebraic statements which are sometimes true, and sometimes false, is fundamental in mathematics. There are occasions when it is necessary or helpful to indicate which is the case – sometimes true or always true. To make it quite clear which is meant to be the case, mathematicians use special symbols called quantifiers. There are two of them: a *universal* and an *existential* quantifier. Let us consider each in turn.

When multiplying a number by 17 you can do so in two stages. You can multiply the number first by 10 and then by 7; then you add the two results obtained. Expressed with the aid of algebraic symbols, this process is put in general form as:

$$17x = (10+7)x$$
$$= 10x + 7x$$

Note the reliance on distributive and commutative properties.

To emphasise that this is true for all x you could say:

For all x, $17x = 10x + 7x$.

Alternatively, you could write the universal quantifier symbol, $\forall_x$, with a subscript showing the letter it applies to, x in this case. The symbol is just an upside down A and $\forall_x$ is read as 'for all x'. So the algebraic statement may be written as:

$$\forall_x \; 17x = 10x + 7x$$

Substitute any number for x and you will get a true statement. Try it with $x = 2.3$: $17 \times 2.3 = 39.1$; $10 \times 2.3 = 23.0$ and $7 \times 2.3 = 16.1$. Since 39.1 is the sum of 23.0 and 16.1, it has been shown that $17x = 10x + 7x$ is true for x equal to 2.3.

The other quantifier is used with a different kind of algebraic statement which must now receive some attention.

4.6 Equations

Have you witnessed children playing 'number games'? This can be suggested by a child wanting to show off competence with numbers. The 'show off' says:

Think of a number, multiply it by 2 and then add 5. What is your answer?

The show off's 'victim' replies 73. Almost immediately the 'victim' is told that the number thought of had been 34. The 'victim' is very impressed and does not know that the 'show off' has learned to solve a particular kind of equation. Let us go through the process of solving an equation.

First, the equation has to be written down. The number thought of can be represented by x, because the value of x is unknown. The instruction to multiply it by 2 must be translated into $2x$. The instruction to add 5 to that produces $2x + 5$. Showing that the result is 73, gives the equation: $2x + 5 = 73$.

This is true for only one value of x. To show that it is true for some value of x (that is, for at least one value) mathematicians use the existential quantifier symbol, $\exists$. It is just like a back-to-front E and is read as 'for some'. So the above equation may be written as:

$$\exists_x \; 2x + 5 = 73$$

It is easy enough to check whether that value is indeed 34. You just substitute 34 for x in the equation. $2 \times 34 + 5 = 68 + 5 = 73$. Correct!

There are rules for operating on the parts of an equation. Following the rules will lead to the solution of the equation, i.e. the required value of x. If, however, you want to understand why those rules work, there are two ways of gaining that understanding. Some prefer one way. Some prefer the other way. Try both. Have patience. When you have understood the rules, remembering them is much easier and applying them should be quite straightforward.

Each way depends on representing an equation by a diagram. The first way shows the equation as a balance. The second way shows the equation as a flow diagram.

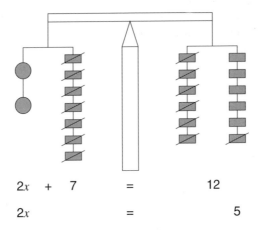

$$2x \quad + \quad 7 \quad\quad = \quad\quad 12$$

$$2x \quad\quad\quad\quad\quad = \quad\quad 5$$

A balance diagram relies on the idea of a weighing scale or balance. At all times, both sides of the balancing point (the fulcrum) must be equal so that the scale remains in equilibrium. Let us first see how to load the weighing scale. You need to imagine that you have a supply of weights which all weigh the same and that you do not know what that weight is, so you call that weight x. You must also imagine that you have a stock of 1lb weights. (Be metric if you prefer.) Consider the equation:

$$2x + 7 = 12$$

Load up, using 2 of the unknown weights on the left, as well as 7 singles. On the right you need to load 12 singles.

Each equation under the diagram describes the state of affairs at each stage of the solution. The first equation describes the scale when it is first loaded. At the next stage, 7 single weights need to be removed from the left-hand side of the scale. To keep the two sides balancing 7 singles must also be taken off the right-hand side. The second equation shows the result of this process, with $2x$ remaining on the left and 5 remaining on the right. A procedure for doing this, without the aid of a diagram, could be derived in two ways. Some like to work with rules as soon as possible. To extract a rule, consider the first equation under the diagram:

$$2x + 7 = 12$$

This can be thought of as consisting of three *terms*. The terms of an equation are just the parts separated by one of the binary operations of addition or subtraction. So the 5 on the right-hand side of the second equation under the diagram, can be thought of as obtained by following the rule:

If you move a term from one side of an equation to the other the sign in front of it must be changed.

Accordingly, the + 7 becomes – 7 and the 12 – 7 gives the 5.

The second way of obtaining the 5 is to add the additive inverse of 7 to both sides of the first equation to get:

$$2x + 7 + (-7) = 12 + (-7)$$

Then you use what you have learned about associativity and the additive identity to obtain:

$$2x + 0 = 12 - 7$$
$$2x = 5$$

The last stage you can think of as either dividing both sides by 2 or multiplying both sides by 1/2, the multiplicative inverse of 2.

The solution of the equation is, therefore, $x = 5/2$ or $2\frac{1}{2}$.

This may be checked by substituting $2\frac{1}{2}$ for x in the original equation:

$$2 \times 2\frac{1}{2} + 7 = 5 + 7$$
$$= 12$$

The equation has become a true statement so the obtained solution is correct.

Instead of using the weighing-scale diagram to extract a method of solving an equation, a flow diagram could be used. Some prefer this strategy. The basis of this approach is to start with the unknown number, x, and change it in stages to the value 12 on the right.

$$x \xrightarrow{\times 2} 2x \xrightarrow{+7} 2x + 7.$$

Then you work backwards from the 12, the value of $2x + 7$

$$x = 5/2 \xleftarrow{\div 2} 5 \xleftarrow{-7} 12$$

Note that above the arrows is written what has been done to bring about the change corresponding to the arrow and its direction. Compare the two lines of the flow diagram and you will see that we have made use of the following:

The reverse of adding 7 is subtracting 7.

The reverse of multiplying by 2 is multiplying by 1/2.

Are you beginning to appreciate the usefulness of knowing about additive and multiplicative inverses?

Let us now move on to consider a different equation and explore the ways of finding its solution using the same two methods – involving the balance diagram and the flow diagram.

The equation to be considered is:

$$2(3x - 4) + 5 = 9$$

First, let this be represented by a weighing-scale diagram.

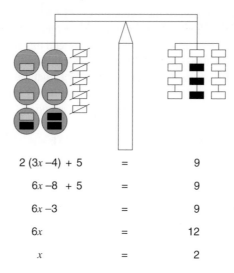

2 (3x −4) + 5	=	9
6x −8 + 5	=	9
6x −3	=	9
6x	=	12
x	=	2

x is represented by the shaded circular disc.

Notice that there are two lots of $(3x - 4)$ and that the 'minus 4' is shown as 4 holes punched out of the three xs; each hole can be thought of as '1 lb missing'.

Then you can proceed to use the distributivity of × over + to get $(6x - 8)$. After that, you need to plug the holes with 1lb weights. You can either do this by using the 5 to plug five of the holes and then add 3 to both sides, or you could add 8 to the left-hand side and the right- hand side to keep the two sides balancing. The solution of $x = 2$ should be checked to make sure that substituting 2 for x in the equation changes it into a true statement.

$$2 \times (3 \times 2 - 4) + 5 = 2 \times (6 - 4) + 5$$
$$= 2 \times 2 + 5$$
$$= 9$$

The flow diagram method would be as follows:

$$x \xrightarrow{\times 3} 3x \xrightarrow{-4} 3x - 4 \xrightarrow{\times 2} 2(3x - 4) \xrightarrow{+5} 2(3x - 4) + 5$$
$$2 \xleftarrow{\times \frac{1}{3}} 6 \xleftarrow{+4} 2 \xleftarrow{\times \frac{1}{2}} 4 \xleftarrow{-5} 9$$

Whether you try to solve an equation using rules based on principles of a balanced scale or a flow-diagram method, there are equations for which the techniques illustrated so far will not work.

Even the simple-looking equation $x^3 = 12$ cannot be solved using the ideas presented so far. It is, however, possible to guess the solution approximately. Knowing that 2 cubed is 8 enables you to guess that x must be greater than 2. Knowing that 3 cubed is 27 enables you to guess that x must be less than 3. The solution of the equation is not an integer, but it has a value somewhere between 2 and 3. To explore what is involved here a little further a new idea needs to be introduced.

4.7 Inequalities

When it was said that the solution of the equation $x^3 = 12$ was greater than 2, it could have been more concisely expressed, using the mathematical symbol, >, which is read as 'is greater than'. If $x^3 = 12$, then $x > 2$. In a similar way, when it was said that the solution of the equation was less than 3, the mathematical symbol, <, could have been used; it is read as 'is less than'. So, if $x^3 = 12$, then $x < 3$. Of course, part of the difficulty is that the solution is not an integer. With patience and trial and error a better approximation could be obtained. Calculating that 2.1 cubed is 9.261, that 2.2 cubed is 10.648 and that 2.3 cubed is 12.167, establishes that the solution is between 2.2 and 2.3.

This can be stated quite succinctly as $2.2 < x < 2.3$ This is a short way of writing two inequalities $2.2 < x$ and $x < 2.3$

The original can be read as 2.2 is less than x which, in turn, is less than 2.3 or even better, as x is between 2.2 and 2.3. Some find it helpful to have such inequalities illustrated by a diagram. Such a diagram is based on the notion of representing the real numbers by a straight line. As soon as a point is arbitrarily chosen to represent 0 and an arbitrary length is chosen to locate the integer 1 to the right of 0 the real line is established.

Every point on the line corresponds to a real number and every real number is represented by a point on the real line.

Using this form of representation, what was said about the solution of the equation $x^3 = 12$ can be illustrated by the diagram:

Notice that the points corresponding to 2.2 and 2.3 are shown as circled, but with the circles not filled in; this shows that the numbers 2.2 and 2.3 are not included in the inequality.

Finally, let us briefly consider a common situation – boiling a kettle of water – which can be partly described using inequalities.

Let the letter t represent the temperature of the water in degrees Celsius.

Since it has been possible to pour the water into the kettle, it must be true that $t > 0$, the freezing temperature of water. Before the water boils it is true to say that $t < 100$, the boiling temperature of water. Suppose the water, when poured into the kettle, is at a temperature of 20 degrees Celsius. What is true of the water's temperature before it boils can be shown both by an inequality and by a diagram. (To show how the temperature changes over time requires a different kind of diagram, called a graph. Such diagrams will be considered in Chapter 5.)

As an inequality, the temperature can be shown to be in the range represented by the inequality:

$$20 \leq t < 100$$

This is read as '20 is less than or equal to t which, in turn, is less than 100'. The 20 is included in the interval.

As a diagram, the range of possible temperatures is illustrated by:

20   100

Notice that the 20 is shown as a filled-in circle because 20 is included whilst 100 is shown as a circle, but not filled-in because 100 is not included.

The notion of an inequality is particularly useful when considering inaccuracies and uncertainties associated with numbers representing measurements.

Key issues in teaching number patterns and sequences

Developing children's 'number sense' is a key objective of the National Numeracy Strategy. Many of the mathematical ideas explored in this chapter can be used as the basis of classroom activities to help children to develop a 'feel' for number, which in turn should enhance their accuracy, speed and confidence in numerical work. By encouraging children to verbalise the strategies they use for predicting patterns, sequences and generalisations they will undoubtedly develop their 'at homeness' with number and reasoning abilities which play an important part in raising achievement.

Many of the teaching points included in the section entitled 'Laying the foundation for Algebra' in the *Framework for teaching mathematics* (DfEE, 1999) for the National Numeracy Strategy are introduced and explained in this chapter. The ideas included in this chapter should also support in the teaching of 'properties of number' in the *Framework*. Working with number patterns is an excellent way to engage children in a variety of numerical calculations. The following ideas have been found useful by teachers to get children to think about properties of number. These activities also provide effective contexts for whole-class discussions.

At a simple level, even very young children can count in 2s and 3s using a number line, progressing to 'counting on and back' in different sized jumps to 10 and beyond in later stages. Asking children to predict the 'next two numbers' in the series or sequences of whole numbers, fractions, decimals or negative numbers and then explaining the reasons for their solutions should be a regular feature of the daily mathematics lesson. This kind of activity involves both mental and oral mathematics and could form the introductory part of the daily mathematics lesson.

As children gain confidence, they can be introduced to more complex number sequences such as 'square' numbers: 1, 4, 9, 16, 25, 'triangular' numbers: 1, 3, 6, 10, 15 and 'cube' numbers: 1, 8, 27, 64 and so on. Children often enjoy the challenge of predicting number sequences and learning about number sequences such as the Fibonacci series: 1, 2, 3, 5, 8, 13, … where you add the previous two terms to obtain the 'next' number. Familiarity with 'factors' and 'prime' numbers also adds to children's understanding of how numbers behave.

One activity which many teachers have found useful is 'what is my secret number?'. The teacher or child selects a number and others ask questions about the properties of the secret number in order to guess the right one. The person who holds the secret number only responds by saying 'yes', or 'no'. Only after a reasonable number of questions, the number can be 'guessed'. For example, the type of questions that could be asked include:

Is it an odd number?
Is it a multiple of ...?
Has it got more than 2 factors?
Is it a prime number?
Is it a whole number?

Activities such as 'guess my number' offer opportunities for children to use number lines and number squares meaningfully, to analyse the properties of number, and to become familiar with correct mathematical vocabulary. Similarly, introducing children to tests of divisibility reinforces number operations as well as the concepts of multiples and factors.

For those who are not familiar with the divisibility tests, a whole number is:

- divisible by 2 if the last digit is 0, 2, 4, 6, or 8
- divisible by 3 if the sum of the digits is divisible by 3
- divisible by 4 if the last two digits are divisible by 4
- divisible by 5 if the last digit is 0 or 5
- divisible by 6 if it is an even number and also divisible by 3
- divisible by 8 if half of it or the last three digits are divisible by 8
- divisible by 9 if the sum of the digits is divisible by 9.

Encouraging children to make hypotheses, test them and make generalisations also helps them to develop their skills of estimation and checking the reasonableness of answers. These generalisations can range from simple statements to more complex ones.

- After number 1, every other number is odd.
- The sum of three consecutive numbers is odd if your starting number is even.
- The product of an even and an odd number is always even.
- An odd number can be expressed as double a number plus one, e.g. $2 \times 3 + 1 = 7$.
- The total of numbers 1 to 10 can be expressed as 10×11 divided by 2; 0 to 100 as 100×101 divided by 2 and so on.

Forming and solving equations can be introduced at all levels in a primary classroom. Asking children to record $16 + 3 = 19$ on the board provides opportunities for introducing the concept of equals. From an early age children can be engaged in solving the unknown number in the box: $4 + \square = 9$ or two unknown numbers: $\square + \Delta = 19$. They can also work out questions such as: I am thinking of a number, then I double it and add 4 to it, the answer is 12, what is my number? The idea of inequalities like $3 < \square < 7$ can help children to see that the unknown numbers are not always fixed. The ideas in this chapter reinforces the three concepts – commutative, associative and distributive – properties which were introduced previously.

Tasks relating to the classroom

1   Ask the children to make, using matchsticks or cubes, the first three terms of a number sequence and ask their classmates to predict what the next two terms are.

2   Build a table for sequences and complete:

Sequence	10th term	50th term	Rule (in words will do)
1, 4, 9, 16, …			
5, 8, 11, 14, …			
6, 10, 14, 18, …			
1, 4, 7, 10 …			

3   Write a rule which can be used to find the perimeter of any rectangle from the following examples?

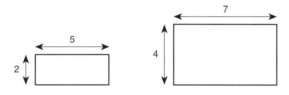

Tasks for self-study

1   Suppose you are given an allowance of £2.00 in the first week of the term to spend on aromatherapy or some other stress-reducing item. The amount is trebled each week. How long will it be before you get £100.00 a week? Try to find out using a geometric progression explained in this chapter.

2   I am thinking of a number. I double it, and add 8 to it. The answer is 40. What is my number? Try to work this out using a flow chart and work backwards. Think of more 'thinking of a number' type questions and make up equations for them.

3   How would you interpret the following inequalities? Draw a diagram for each one.

$$1.8 < t < 3.2$$

$$5.0 \leq d < 9.5$$

$$3.5 \leq s \leq 8.5$$

4   Look at the following pattern:

1	= 1	= 1 × 1
1 + 3	= 4	= 2 × 2
1 + 3 + 5	= 9	= 3 × 3
1 + 3 + 5 + 7	= 16	= 4 × 4

Try and write down:

(a)   the total of the first 10 odd numbers without adding them up

(b)   the total of the first 30 odd numbers

(c)   the total of the first n odd numbers

5   Find out how the constant key on a calculator works and write down three questions you can explore with children using it.

6   How many diagonals can you draw for
    (a)   a six sided shape?
    (b)   a 20 sided shape?
    (c)   an n-sided shape?

7   Design a function game for a group of children using input and output cards and a list of functions using whole numbers and fractions.

Chapter 5

Measures

Objectives

This chapter focuses on:

The task of understanding our surroundings and the world in which we live sometimes involves trying to gauge how much or how little of various things are in existence. Systems of counting and ways of writing numbers are indispensable foundations for such assessments. As the concept of number grew from integer to real number, so did the refinement of the gauging procedures and the need for measuring instruments. The need for greater and greater accuracy has challenged the inventiveness of those who design and make instruments. Yet more accurate instruments would not be possible if the real number system did not exist. The possibility of measuring something more accurately depends on the possibility of expressing a number to more decimal places. It is as though numbers reached maturity when they acquired decimal form. Let us explore this partnership between the maturity of numbers and the refinement of measurement.

5.1 The concept of measure

Anything which is measured is really being compared to some particular unit of measurement. The units in most common use nowadays are from the International System of Units; it is referred to as the *SI system*, in accordance with its French name. The units are also frequently called metric units. Multiples and subdivisions of metric units involve powers of ten. It may be of interest to know that the UK is being allowed to delay its abandonment of imperial units for another ten years. This is apparently due to EU concern over the need to avoid difficulties in economic relations with the USA where metric conversion has also not been complete.

In the following development of the various aspects of 'measures' there are two strands providing an underlying framework:

- the distinction between basic and derived units;
- the role of 10 in metric measures and the role of 12 in non-metric measures.

(A basic unit for measuring length is the mile and a basic unit for measuring time is the hour. A derived unit for measuring speed is miles per hour.)

(Basic *metric* units for measuring length are the centimetre, equal to 10 millimetres, and the metre equal to 100 centimetres. We have a 24 hour day, 12 times 2 equals 24.)

You have probably heard it said that we live in a three-dimensional world. A two-dimensional world would be flat! Assuming that is a reasonable basis of a sound outlook on our world, let us now turn our attention to the various aspects of our world which we try to understand by means of measurement. The three dimensions will be approached in stages – first one, then two and then three.

5.2 Length

Length is a one-dimensional concept in the sense that the straight line which corresponds to the length of a thing is one-dimensional. The reference to a straight line is hardly surprising since common instruments of measurement, such as a tape or a ruler have straight edges.

There are tape-measures, one metre long and marked only at every centimetre, with each centimetre not subdivided into millimetres. This has an implication for the accuracy which is possible when measuring with such a tape-measure. Suppose you are measuring a length of cloth to make sure you have enough to make one part of a garment. You place one end of the tape at the edge of one end of the cloth, and straighten out the tape so that the other end of the tape goes beyond the other edge of the cloth. You then look to see where that other edge 'crosses' the tape. It crosses between the 52 and the 53 cm marks. How long is the piece of cloth? It is somewhere between 52 and 53 cm long. With this tape-measure you cannot measure more accurately than to the nearest centimetre. Being mathematical, you could say that if l represents the accurate length of the cloth then:

$$52 < l < 53$$

Being an amateur garment maker you would not be inclined to bother with inequalities. Not formally, anyhow. Practically you would be thinking in terms of both inequalities and estimation. Your interest is not likely to be with the right-hand end of the interval, in this situation – unless you needed at least 53 cm of the cloth. You are more likely to be interested in whether you have at least 52 cm or even 50 cm. Let us now take a look at a case in which both ends of the interval are of importance.

Imagine a manufacturing company needing a component which it has to order from a smaller firm – its supplier. The component it needs is cylindrical carbon rods. It needs thousands of them each month. When the company places the order with its supplier, it must provide specifications. The rods are required to be of length 7.5 cm. The ordering company realises that the production process of the supplier cannot guarantee that all the rods will be 7.5 cm long or even very close to that. So the company, when placing its order, provides tolerance limits. It indicates that it will accept rods which are within 2 mm of the required length. The tolerance limits could be given in the form:

$$7.5 \pm 0.2 \text{ cm}$$

This is a compact way of specifying the acceptable interval:

$$7.3 \text{ cm} < \text{rod length} < 7.7 \text{ cm}$$

Of course, the company will ensure that the rods delivered by the supplier are within the limits of tolerance by taking a random sample from each delivery.

Apart from tolerances dictated by companies, there are deviations from what may seem to by an exact measurement because of inherent inaccuracies. A tape-measure with markings at every centimetre is simply not designed for measurement to the nearest millimetre. There are, in fact, two sources of inaccuracy:

1   The measuring instrument is so designed as to impose a limit on the accuracy which is possible with its use. A ruler with markings at every millimetre is designed to offer no more than accuracy to the nearest millimetre.

2   The observer, the person reading the instrument, has limitations imposed by the quality of eye-sight.

If the end of a line being measured seems to fall between the 7.6 cm and the 7.7 cm markings, a decision has to be made by the reader of the instrument as to whether the length of the line is nearer to one than the other. Faced with the inequality:

$$7.6 < \text{length} < 7.7$$

the reader's eyes must arbitrate and judge whether the end of the line satisfies another inequality:

$$7.60 < \text{end of line} < 7.65$$

If the end of the line is judged to satisfy the inequality, then the length of the line must be declared to be 7.6 cm to the nearest millimetre. If, on the other hand, the end of the line is judged to satisfy the interval:

$$7.65 < \text{end of line} < 7.70$$

then the length of the line must be declared to be 7.7 cm, to the nearest millimetre.

Conversions

If the supplying firm uses imperial measures then any order it receives in metric units will need to be converted. Let us consider this conversion aspect of measures because it is of considerable practical importance. Although we don't need to think about the mathematical principles involved every time when we are converting measures, it is useful to know what we are actually doing.

In a book of conversion factors you could see the information that 1 inch is equivalent to about 2.54 centimetres (to two decimal places). How could the previous rod measurement be converted to inches?

Remember the notion of the multiplicative identity. You want to be able to give 7.5 cm in inches. Form a fraction which is equal to 1, the multiplicative identity. Such a fraction is 1 inch / 2.54 cm. Remember the cancelling technique of dividing the numerator and the denominator of a fraction by the same thing. Assume this can be done with units of measurement just as much as with numerical factors. This enables you to state that:

$$7.5 \text{ cm} = 7.5 \text{ cm} \times 1 \text{ inch} / 2.54 \text{ cm}$$
$$= 7.5 \times 1 \text{ inch} / 2.54 \text{ because the cm cancels}$$
$$= 7.5 / 2.54 \text{ inches}$$
$$= 2.95 \text{ inches}$$

Check that using two rulers – one metric and one imperial.

Of course, it is sometimes necessary to make conversions from one metric unit to another metric unit. Some conversion factors in metric are:

$$100 \text{ centimetres} = 1 \text{ metre. } 1000 \text{ metres} = 1 \text{ kilometre.}$$

The same conversion technique used above can still be used when these factors are involved.

What would 6.83 km be in metres? You need to cancel the km, so the form of multiplicative identity you use must contain km in the denominator and, since you need the final result in metres, the numerator must contain m. So, using the appropriate form of the multiplicative identity, the required conversion becomes:

$$6.83 \text{km} \times 1000 \text{m}/1 \text{km} = 6.83 \times 1000 \text{m}/1$$
$$= 6830 \text{m}$$

(Multiplying a decimal number by 1000 shifts the decimal point 3 places to the right.)

Now try converting 759 cm to metres. This time you need to cancel the cm so you need a form of the multiplicative identity containing cm in the denominator. Since you want the final result to be in metres you need to have m in the numerator. The required conversion is, therefore, given by:

$$759 \text{ cm} \times 1 \text{ m} / 100 \text{ cm} = 759 \times 1 \text{ m} / 100$$
$$= (759 / 100) \text{ m}$$
$$= 7.59 \text{ m}$$

(Dividing a decimal number by 100 shifts the decimal point 2 places to the left.)

Let us now move on to thinking about things which exist in two-dimensions.

5.3 Area

Area is a two-dimensional concept. The measurement of area relies on comparison with a square. In metric measurement, the square used for comparison has sides which are each 1 metre in length. The area of such a square is 1 square metre; this is written as 1 sq m or 1 m^2. Of course, subdivisions and multiples are also used to give units such as square centimetre and square kilometre.

Shapes bounded by straight lines – squares, rectangles, parallelograms and so on – can be compared with a unit square by deciding how many such squares fit into the shape. Shapes bounded by curved lines require estimates of the number of squares which will fit into them.

(More advanced mathematics can be used provided you have an equation for the boundary curve.)

Let us now consider the sources of inaccuracies in area measurement.

If the shape being considered is a rectangle, for example, then the length of each of its sides needs to be measured. Each of those measurements involves some lack of accuracy.

Conceptually, by looking at the diagrams below, you can 'see' how 15 squares fit into the 5 by 3 rectangle. Visually, you can also see how the right-angled triangle within the parallelogram can be sliced off and fitted to the left-hand part to show that the parallelogram has the same area as the rectangle.

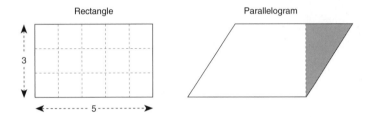

How well you can judge the accuracy of a measurement depends on whether you have done the measuring yourself or it has been done by somebody else. Suppose you have been given the length and breadth of a rectangle as 3.0 cm and 5.0 cm. With only the numbers to go on, you have to assume that each measurement is accurate to the nearest millimetre. Each measurement, therefore, has a 'true' value somewhere within an interval of 1 mm, since $2.95 < 3.0 < 3.05$ and $4.95 < 5.0 < 5.05$. What does this indicate about the true or correct value of the rectangle's area? Its least possible value is given by 2.95 times 4.95, which is 14.60 to two decimal places, and its greatest possible value is given by 3.05 times 5.05, which is 15.40 to two decimal places. The maximum error resulting from taking 15.0 as the area is 0.40. As a percentage of 15.0 this error works out as 2.7%. Check it!

The second source of inaccuracy in judging the area of a shape arises from having to estimate it because the shape is bounded. Try estimating the area of each of the shapes in the diagram below. Get a few other people to do so and compare the results.

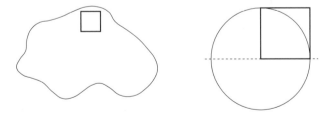

For the shape on the left, see how many whole squares you can fit in – and then estimate how many squares could be made from the bits left on the outside.

Compare your estimate of the area of the circle with that of the square resting on the radius. You should find that it is about 3.14 times greater in area than the square. (3.14 is the value of π to two decimal places.)

Using a formula

A formula is a very convenient instrument for finding the value of some quantity. You just substitute numbers for all but one of the letters to find the value determined for the remaining letter or variable. There are three things about the use of any formula which should be borne in mind:

1   Try, if possible, to get some understanding of how the formula was derived.
2   Try to remember that the formula is only as good as the data that is put into it; no formula can compensate for the inaccuracies of the values substituted for the letters it contains.
3   Have a stock of techniques to enable you to 'change the subject of the formula'; this merely involves changing the formula so that a different letter is on the left-hand side of the equals sign.

As an example of a problem needing the use of a change of subject of a formula, imagine a manufacturer with a contract to produce circular, metal plates of area 314 square centimetres. If each plate is to be cut from a sheet of square metal, what size of square metal sheet must the manufacturer use to make each circular plate? This amounts to deciding the required radius of the circular plate.

The formula for the area of a circle is $A = 3.14 \times r^2$

If the area, A, has to be 314, then $3.14 \times r^2 = 314$.

You could then proceed to divide both sides by 3.14 to obtain $r^2 = 100$. From this the required radius is obtained by taking the square root of 100. So $r = 10$. Using a sheet of metal 10 cm square enables the manufacturer to produce the circular plates of area 314 sq cm because they have a radius of 10 cm.

(You could also think of changing the subject of the formula for the area of the circle in terms of multiplicative inverses. To isolate the r^2 you need to remove the 3.14. This can be done by multiplying both sides of the equation by the multiplicative inverse of 3.14. This changes the formula to $\frac{1}{3.14} A = 1 \times r^2$.)

The same concerns about measurement and estimates apply to volumes of objects in three dimensions as applied to areas of shapes in two dimensions.

5.4 Volume

Volume is a three-dimensional concept. It concerns the amount of space occupied by an object which is not flat. Objects can be thought of as solid or as empty. When buying shoes your feet are to be thought of as solid objects. The volume of each foot must be slightly less than the volume enclosed by the shoe; the shoe, in turn, must enclose that volume by being of the right shape. The number of people that can comfortably sit on the back seat of a car depends on their bulk; their bulkiness is related to their volume.

How much you can pack into a suitcase, how much you can put into the boot of a car or store in a cupboard depends on the *volume* of the suitcase, the car boot or the cupboard.

When buying a freezer you are told the capacity of the freezer – in other words, its volume. Is it easy to check that information by measuring?

When buying a car you are told the capacity of the boot. Is it easy to check the size of the boot by measuring?

It is not likely that you should ever need to know the volume of your foot, but why would it be more difficult to find its volume than the volume of a freezer?

The volume of an object is a comparison of the amount of space it occupies compared with a standard cube. In metric measurement a unit cube has a volume of 1 cubic metre. So volume, like area, is measured in a derived unit; cubic metres are derived from the basic unit metres.

Some objects can be compared with the unit cube quite easily, because cubes can be imagined to fit into them.

Think of sugar cubes packed into a box so that they can be offered for sale in a supermarket. Boxes with square or rectangular faces can be dealt with in that way; just multiply the length by the width and then by the height. So, a box which is 8 cm long, 5 cm wide and 3 cm high is 120 cubic centimetres in volume.

$$V = \text{length} \times \text{width} \times \text{height}$$
$$= l \times w \times h$$

If the object is an irregular shape, for example a lump of plasticine, it could be placed in a liquid to see the rise in height of the liquid caused by the immersion of the object. Measuring cylinders used in laboratories or in kitchens operate on this principle, first discovered by Archimedes. If water in a measuring cylinder shows a level of 25 ml (millilitres) and dropping a piece of plasticine into the water raises its level to 28 ml then the volume of the plasticine must be 3 ml. Should you ever wish to find the volume of your feet you should now understand how to go about it!

5.5 Weight

The common, everyday use of the term 'weight' is scientifically incorrect. There is a difference between the *mass* of an object, which is the amount of matter it contains, and the weight of the object, which is the force exerted on it by gravity. However, the common practice is so deeply entrenched that there is no point in being pedantic about it; in any case, there is no significant variation in the amount of gravity on Earth. So, the S.I. unit for 'weight' is the kilogramme.

Due to the lack of conversion to metric units, interchanging with imperial units is still sometimes a requirement. Let us take a brief look at a few examples.

Using the approximate equivalence of 1 kg equal to 2.25 lb, find the equivalent of 16 lb in kg.

You need to get rid of lb in the numerator, so the version of the multiplicative inverse used must have lb in the denominator. Since kg are required, the numerator of the inverse must have kg. Therefore,

$$16 \text{ lb} = 16 \text{ lb} \times 1 \text{ kg} / 2.25 \text{ lb}$$
$$= 16 \times (1 / 2.25) \text{ kg}$$
$$= 7.11 \text{ kg to two decimal places}$$

Another source of confusion about weight concerns the notion of bulk. When someone is worried about putting on weight, it is the effect on their appearance which tends to matter. It is their increase in bulk or volume which creates the anxiety. The link between 'weight' and 'volume' is provided by the concept of *density*. This is defined as follows:

$$\text{density} = \text{mass} \div \text{volume}$$

Bearing in mind that the mass of your body is the amount of matter it contains so that the mass is proportional to your weight and assuming the density of your body remains constant, near enough, then an increase in mass or weight must be accompanied by an increase in volume. Putting on weight means increasing your volume, because your density remains about the same!

Why is iron said to be heavier than wood? Because the density of iron is greater than that of wood; the same volumes of iron and wood contain different masses of the two. The mass of iron is greater than the mass of wood and so the iron is heavier; the weight of the iron is greater than the weight of the same volume of wood.

5.6 Time

The most significant thing about time measurement is that it is not metric; this causes difficulties for children when calculating and converting units of time. There are 24 hours in a day, 60 minutes in an hour, 60 seconds in a minute. All are multiples of 12, the same as the number of signs of the zodiac. Why mention astrology? Because Babylonian astrologers thought there were 360 days in a year and produced their astrological charts accordingly. Although astrology is not considered to be scientific by many people, the connection between our time system and astronomical movements is not in dispute. Our day, consisting of 24 hours, is the time it takes the moon to spin around its axis once. Our year, consisting of $365\frac{1}{4}$ days, is the time it takes the planet Earth to orbit around the Sun.

5.7 Angles

The measurement of angles is also not metric. There are 360 degrees in one complete turn; the more mathematical word for a turn is a *revolution*. The connection with the Babylonian estimate of the number of days in a year is obvious. To explore the way in which angles and time are connected think of a clock face with a minute and an hour hand. The clock face is split into twelve parts – the same as the signs of the zodiac – with the numbers 1 to 12 marked off at equal intervals around the edge. In one hour the minute hand moves through one complete revolution, that is through 360 degrees. In that hour, the hour hand moves through one-twelfth of a turn, that is through 30 degrees. In this way angles can be thought of as related to motion or rotation. An angle can also be thought of as a measure of how two fixed lines are related. At a particular time the two hands of a clock face have a particular angle between them. What, for example, is the angle between the hands of a clock when the time is 3:25? Look at the diagram.

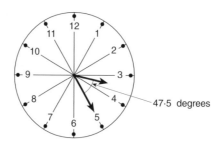

The minute hand is exactly opposite the dot corresponding to 5. The hour hand, however, is not exactly opposite the number 3. Why? Because it has been moving away from the 3 for 25 minutes. Between the 3 and the 5 positions is an angle of 60 degrees. What is the angle through which the hour hand moves in 25 minutes? The hour hand moves through 1/12 of 360 degrees in 60 minutes, which is 30 degrees. In one minute it moves through 1/60 of 30 degrees; in 25 minutes, therefore, the hour hand moves through 25/60 of 30 degrees. This works out to be $12\frac{1}{2}$ degrees. The angle between the hands of the clock face at 3.25 is obtained by subtracting this amount from 60 degrees. This, of course, is $47\frac{1}{2}$ degrees.

Of all the angles which are of special practical importance, perhaps, the right angle deserves to be singled out. *Right angle* is the name given to an angle of 90 degrees. Just look at any building and see the abundance of right angles.The ordinary words 'upright' and 'vertical' make reference to something which is perpendicular and, therefore, a right angle.

5.8 The use of scales

The use of scales in making maps and three-dimensional models of planned buildings or machines is a major application of the notion of the non-isometric transformation of enlargement. What does this mean? 'Transformation' means change. 'Isometric' means the same measurements. An isometric transformation of a shape leaves its shape and measurements unchanged. Isometric transformations include rotation, translation and reflection. These transformations are dealt with in Chapter 6. Enlargement is non-isometric because it changes lengths – although it does not change shape.

Representing portions of the planet Earth's surface on flat sheets of paper is a particularly impressive achievement, considering that the Earth is approximately a sphere. Small parts of the Earth's surface, however, can quite reasonably be thought of as flat. It is this together with the idea of a scale which makes the drawing of a map possible.

Suppose the scale of a map is given as 1 to 10000 (sometimes written as 1:10000). This means that two points on the map which are 1 cm apart are actually 10000 cm apart on the Earth's surface. Since there are 100 cm in a metre and 1000 m in a kilometre, the scale of the map could be described as 1 cm to 1 km. The basic unit for the map is the unit of length. The unit chosen by the reader of the map could be any unit of length. So, if the scale was given as 1 to 10000 and the map reader was uneasy about metric measurements of length the reader could actually take two small buildings on the map which are 1 inch apart and think of them as really being 10000 inches apart. Possible, justifiable, but not, perhaps, very sensible.

A plot of land on the map which was rectangular and measuring 5 cm by 4 cm would represent an area of 5 km by 4 km or 20 square kilometres. The connection between the rectangle on the map and the actual land it represents, in mathematical terms, is that the land is an enlargement of the portion of the map with a scale factor of 10000.

Scales are also used by professional people such as architects. If a scale model of a building is made by an architect, with a used scale of 1 to 100, so the designed building can be shown to a client before it is built then the client can interpret the scale to mean 1cm represents 1m. The client can then continue to examine the model of the building taking every length of 1cm to be 1m; every area of 1 sq cm to be 1 sq m and every 1 cubic centimetre of the model to show 1 cubic metre of the proposed building.

Units of measurement

Length

mm, cm, m, km
10 mm = 1 cm
100 cm = 1 m
1000 m = 1 km
2.54 cm = 1 inch
1609 m = 1 mile

Area

cm^2, m^2

Volume

cm^3, m^3

Weight

1000 g = 1 kg
1 lb = 454 g
1 oz = 0.28 g

Time

60 seconds = 1 minute
60 minutes = 1 hour
24 hours = 1 day

Key issues in teaching measures to children

Most of the 'measuring work' undertaken by primary school children involves working with discrete data. These are separate, distinct amounts which are sometimes approximations, as opposed to continuous data. When measuring time – to find out how long I took to write a page – it is measured as an approximation rounded off to a discrete number; in this case it may be described as 32 minutes and 30 seconds. This is true of all measuring activities and it makes calculations easier.

In the primary school, children are taught to measure length, weight, capacity and volume, area and time. Although children may not learn mathematics in any special order, many teachers follow a sequence of teaching points for teaching measures. They are:

* Activities which introduce the appropriate language related to a particular measurement. Long, short, thick, width in the context of length.
* Comparing two objects: heavier and lighter.
* Ordering three or more objects according to capacity or weight.

- Using non-standard units to measure: handspans and straws to measure objects.
- Learning about standard units of measure.
- Interrelationships between units: 1 hour = 60 minutes; 1 minute = 60 seconds and so on.
- As we still use imperial measures it is also useful to establish the relationship between units of imperial and metric measures.

When 'measures' are taught to children, it is useful to stress the need for standard units in order to have a consistent unit for communication with other people. The need for estimating and aiming for the highest amount of accuracy should be pointed out.

Most of the work carried out in 'measuring' lessons will be working with numbers; this provides useful and meaningful contexts for using whole numbers and decimal numbers and for solving word problems.

As children get older, they can be introduced to scale drawings which not only help to reinforce the idea of measuring length as useful in real contexts, it also helps them to see the relationships between units of measurement. For example, when a decision is made that every centimetre on paper represents a metre of the classroom floor or when a map drawn to scale is read, children should make conceptual links about units of measures and their uses in real life.

Tasks relating to the classroom

1   Think of some stories you can tell children to convince them of the need for standard units of measure. For example, you go to a carpet shop and ask for 'enough' carpet for your lounge or asking the butcher for a joint for your Sunday lunch.
2   Plan how you would encourage children to make up a personal book of units of measures and relationships between units.
3   Make up some more 'likely or unlikely' statements for class discussion:
    (a) Your maths book weighs 3 kg.
    (b) The distance between the classroom and hall is 20 metres.
    (c) I can drink 20 litres of lemonade in one swallow.
    (d) You have been alive for 1 million minutes.
4   Plan a trip to the nearest beach, show using a scale map that it is the nearest to you.
5   Study the following mistakes and think about ways of helping children to avoid them.
    (a)

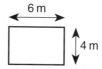

Child's answer: area = 24 m, perimeter = 24 m
    (b)

Weeks	Days
12	6
2	6
1	6
16	8

(c) A pantomime starts at 10:15 and finishes at 12:55. How long does it last? Child's answer: 3 hours 40 minutes.

(d) What are the actual measurements of this field? Scale: 10 m = 1 cm. Child's answer 3 m × 1.5 cm.

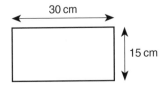

Tasks for self-study

1   How many rectangular tiles measuring 9 cm by 5 cm do you need to cover a narrow section of floor space which is 18 m by 1.5 m?

2   Find the area of these shapes:

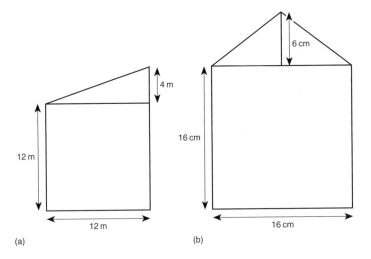

(a)   (b)

3   How many 1 cm cubes will fit into a box with the measurements shown?

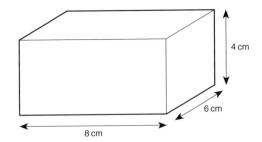

4   This drawing shows a plan of the playground.

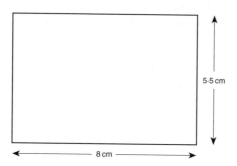

5·5 cm

8 cm

Scale 1cm = 50 m Find
(a) the real length of each of the sides
(b) the perimeter of the playground

5   The following are pictures of tiles fitting together. Find the angles marked *a*.
(a)

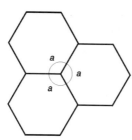

(b)

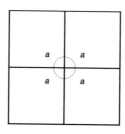

(c)

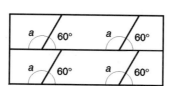

Chapter 6

Shape and space

Objectives

This chapter focuses on:

6.1 Coordinates
6.2 Transformations
6.3 Enlargement

Knowing where things are in our surroundings is an important aspect of our lives and knowing where to find things when we need them can be vital.

In mathematics, the location of something is indicated by one, two or three numbers – depending on whether the item under consideration is to be thought of as being in one, two or three dimensions.

There are things which move in a straight line. Children who play marbles or adults who go bowling are basically concerned with trying to roll a spherical object along a straight line; the path of the motion is one-dimensional. When considering the role of mathematics in providing an increased understanding of the physical aspects of the world, you should bear in mind the distinction between the static view of things – in which the position of things is receiving emphasis – and the dynamic view of things concerned with changes in the position of things over a period of time.

Let us begin by focusing on the static view and the mathematical way of describing position by means of numbers playing the role of coordinates.

6.1 Coordinates

In the mathematical one-dimensional world, the things which exist are points. Even if the position of a child on a straight line is being considered for the purpose of illustration, the child is represented by a point. That is the approximation and simplification technique of mathematics!

One-dimensional coordinates

The line below is a representation of that one-dimensional world. Its important features are the arbitrary choice of two fixed points.

One point is called the origin; it is labelled O. It is pronounced as though it is a letter of the alphabet. Anything at the position O has coordinate 0 (zero), meaning that its position from the origin is a 'distance' of zero away. The second of the fixed points is chosen to be at a selected 'distance' to the right of the origin and is labelled 1. This sets the standard, the unit of distance, enabling further points to be marked off at equal distances to the right of 1 (and marked 2, 3, 4 and so on) as well as to the left of the origin (and marked -1, -2 and so on). The $-$ in front of the 2, for example, indicates two units to the left of the O; it should not be confused with $-$ used to mean the symbol for subtraction. In this one-dimensional world two things are possible:

- a particular point may have a non-integer coordinate;
- two points may have a non-zero distance between them.

Both possibilities need some explanation and clarification. Take a look at the points labelled A, B, C and D in the diagram below.

Point B has a coordinate of $\frac{1}{2}$ and point C has a coordinate of $1\frac{3}{4}$. (The decimal form of the numbers could have been used.) The distance of D from A is $5\frac{1}{2}$. Note that the word 'distance' is being used without reference to any unit of measurement. This is quite legitimate. The unit is the standard provided by the 'distance' from 0 to 1.

Two-dimensional coordinates

Let us now expand the world being considered from the one-dimensional straight line to the two-dimensional flat surface. The mathematical term for a flat surface is a *plane*. Again, the basic things in this two-dimensional world are points. Just as one number is needed to give the position of a point in the one-dimensional world of the straight line, so two numbers are needed to give the position of a point in the two-dimensional world of the plane. The usual method of establishing the coordinate system for a plane is to impose two arbitrary straight lines on it which cross each other at right angles at a point; that point becomes the origin of the *Cartesian coordinate system*. (The adjective Cartesian acknowledges Descartes, the originator of the system.) The two straight lines are referred to as *axes*. The axis drawn horizontally is called the x-axis and the line drawn up the page is called the y-axis. The axes act as base lines, so that the coordinates of any point in the plane are really the distances of the point from each of the axes. Look at the diagram below and note, particularly, how points below the *x*-axis are assigned negative *y*-coordinates. To see how the system works, just check the coordinates of the points P, Q, R and S which are written as pairs near the letter labelling the point.

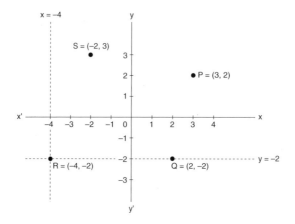

Notice the order in which the coordinates are listed; the *x* coordinate is given first and the *y* coordinate second, separated by a comma and both enclosed in parentheses. The Cartesian system can be thought of as a grid composed of two sets of parallel lines – one parallel to the *y*-axis and the other parallel to the *x*-axis. The point R, for instance, can then be thought of as the point of intersection of two lines of this grid. The line $x = -4$ is parallel to the *y*-axis and cuts the *x*-axis at -4 and the line $y = -2$ is parallel to the *x*-axis and cuts the *y*-axis at -2.

Three-dimensional coordinates

Positions of points in the three-dimensional world, by extension of the systems for one and two dimensions, require three axes as a basis of reference. Again, the three straight lines intersect at a point which becomes the origin of the system and the lines, considered in pairs, are at right angles to each other. Take a look at the diagram below.

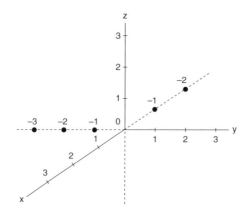

Each of the axes has a negative half. Focus, for a moment, on the positive parts of the three axes so as to see that they form what is called a right-hand system. To understand what this means, imagine your right hand holding the positive part of the z-axis and turning it as though it was a corkscrew, from the x-axis towards the y-axis. The direction in which the corkscrew would move would be in the direction in which your thumb is pointing; that confirms the positive direction of the z-axis.

Now try to imagine the diagram showing three planes, each perpendicular to the other two. This is just like the two walls and floor of a room meeting in a corner. To appreciate this, you may well need names for the planes. Focus on the x- and y-axes. Imagine the plane containing them to be horizontal. It is reasonable to call that plane the xy-plane. This is similar to the floor of the room. Now focus on the x- and z-axes. Imagine that plane coming out of the paper, at right angles to it. It is reasonable to call that plane the xz-plane. This is like one of the walls. Finally, focus on the y- and z-axes. Imagine the plane containing them to coincide with the paper. It is reasonable to call that plane the yz-plane. This is like the other wall of the room.

Think back to the two-dimensional case. The axes split the plane into four sections.

The three planes just considered split the three-dimensional space, in which we think of ourselves as living, into eight sections. Think of four rooms upstairs, four rooms downstairs with the ceiling of the downstairs rooms and the floors of the upstairs rooms being the xy-plane.

Just as the two axes, in the two-dimensional coordinate system, each had an infinite number of lines parallel to it, so each of the planes, the xy, the xz and the yz, in the three-dimensional system has an infinite number of planes parallel to it. The coordinates of any point in space on which a three-dimensional Cartesian system has been imposed can be thought of as the point of intersection of three planes. Look at the diagram of the 'block' resting on the xy-plane, with one vertex, A, at a point on the x-axis, the edge AE resting along the x-axis (with E at the origin), the edge EF resting along the y-axis and the edge EH resting along the z-axis.

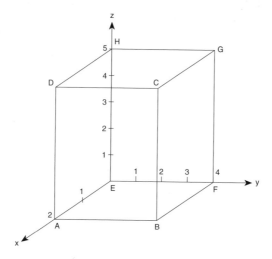

Focus on the vertex of the block called C. What are its coordinates?

To understand the answer to that, first think of the block as having 6 faces. The bottom face, *ABFE*, rests on the *xy*-plane. $z = 0$ at all points on that face. So the equation of the face *ABFE* is $z = 0$. Similarly, the top face *DCGH* has equation $z = 5$; the front face *ABCD* has equation $x = 2$; the back face *EFGH* has equation $x = 0$; the left face *AEHD* has equation $y = 0$ and the right face *BFGC* has equation $y = 4$. Check that the point C is where the planes $x = 2$, $y = 4$ and $z = 5$ intersect, so the coordinates of C are $(2,4,5)$. Now make sure you agree that the other vertices are given by:

$B = (2,4,0)$, $D = (2,0,5)$, $A = (2,0,0)$, $E = (0,0,0)$, $F = (0,4,0)$, $G = (0,4,5)$ and $H = (0,0,5)$.

That concludes the description of the static aspect of shapes and the method of determining the position of a point in one- two- or three-dimensional space by one, two or three coordinates. Let us now take a look at changes in position and the possibility of a framework for describing such changes.

6.2 Transformations

Just as the static aspect of shapes and the description of positions progressed through one, then two and then three dimensions, so will the description of changes in position – the dynamic aspect – be considered in stages.

So, it is back to points in the one-dimensional world of the straight line.

Only one point needs to be studied. We may as well call it *P*.

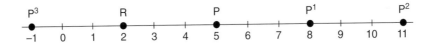

Assume that it starts at the point 5 units to the right of the origin. What kind of position changes can it be subjected to? It could be moved 3 places to the right of its starting position. Starting at 5, it could be move to P^1, at 8. Starting at 8, it could be moved to P^2, at 11. (P^2 does not mean P squared, it is read as 'P two' a second position.)

This kind of change is called a *translation*. This translation could be described as 'move to the right 3 places'.

Point, *P*, could also be moved to the other side of the point R the same distance as it is from R in the first place. So P would finish up at the point corresponding to -1 on the line, that is at P^3. This kind of change of position is called a reflection. This reflection could be described as 'a reflection in the point R, at 2 on the line'.

In the two-dimensional world of the plane there is one more possible type of change of position. Let us consider that first before applying translation and reflection to two dimensions.

Start with a right-angled triangle *ABC* with coordinates for its vertices given by: $A = (3,1)$, $B = (5,1)$, $C = (5,2)$.

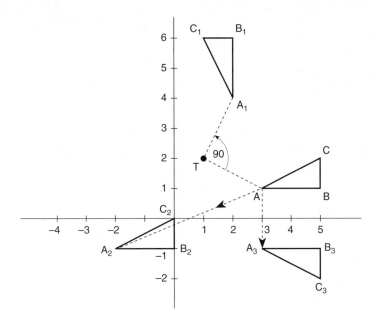

The point $T = (1,2)$ has been selected as the centre of rotation. The angle of rotation selected is 90 degrees. In mathematics the direction of positive rotation is anti-clockwise. The triangle *ABC* is, therefore, to be rotated through 90 degrees about *T*. It finishes up at $A_1B_1C_1$ with coordinates given by $A_1 = (2,4)$, $B_1 = (2,6)$, $C_1 = (1,6)$.

As an example of translating a shape in two-dimensional space, let us try translating triangle *ABC* in a direction 5 units to the left and 2 units down. The resulting position of the triangle is $A_2 B_2 C_2$.

The coordinates of its vertices are: $A_2 = (-2,-1)$, $B_2 = (0,-1)$, $C_2 = (0,0)$.

Comparing the original triangle *ABC* with each of its three new positions, in turn, two common features are evident, looking at $A_1B_1C_1$ and $A_2B_2C_2$:

- Each of the 'new' triangles has its vertices labelled using the same letters that were used for the original triangle: A, B and C.
- The letter labels of the new triangle have the same subscripts attached to them.

What are the reasons for these two conventions?

Let us explain the conventions by focusing on another of the position changes, that of ABC being reflected in the *x*-axis. The new position of the triangle is named using the same letters to emphasise that the new triangle has been obtained from the old one. The common subscript, 3, merely indicates that it was the third change considered – any other common subscript could have been used. Further, the naming of each new vertex indicates which point of the original triangle was its starting position. So, the naming is a succinct way of showing the following connections:

$$A \rightarrow A_3, B \rightarrow B_3, C \rightarrow C_3$$

Just three examples of change of position have been given, so some justification needs to be given for the choice. Before that justification is offered, let us look at some essential vocabulary in order to make the discussion more precise.

Whenever a change of position of a shape is to be described, the shape in its starting position is called the *object*. In the previously described examples the triangle *ABC* was the object. When the traingle is moved to its new position, the triangle in the new position is called the *image*. When the triangle *ABC* was reflected in the *x*-axis the image was the triangle $A_3B_3C_3$.

What do the three images of the three changes in position previously described have in common, even though they are in different places? They are all the same shape and size as each other; in mathematical language they are *congruent*. So each of the three images is congruent to their common object – the triangle *ABC*.

The three kinds of change of position are, in mathematical language, referred to as *transformations*. There are many other transformations dealt with in mathematics, but the three considered so far in this chapter are:

1   translation (to produce $A_2B_2C_2$)
2   rotation (to produce $A_1B_1C_1$)
3   reflection (to produce $A_3B_3C_3$)

So far, what has been extracted as a common feature of these three transformations is that the object and image associated with them are congruent. This common feature makes these transformations *isometric*; object and image have the same measurements. So, it is hoped that this new terminology will make a more detailed analysis of the three isometric transformations easier. Let us consider them in turn.

Translation

To specify a translation two things need to be indicated:

1   the direction of the translation, and
2   the size of the translation.

Start with an object which is a triangle PQR, with coordinates given by:

$$P = (1,2), Q = (3,3), R = (5,1)$$

For the moment, let the translation be specified by: 'Move each point of the object 3 units to the right and 4 units up'.

The object and image are shown on the diagram below.

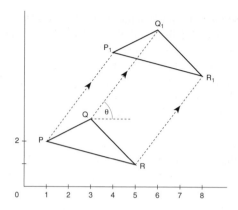

Consider how the object became the image.

Each point could have been moved in two stages, in accordance with the description of the translation. The points of the object could, in fact, have moved along all sorts of paths to get to their final positions. They could also have moved along the dotted lines as shown in the diagram. Those lines have a definite advantage over all the other possibilities – they are parallel to each other and are all of the same length.

There are two things which require emphasis to avoid confusion. Firstly, the transformation of translation *is* a movement of *all* points of an object the same distance along parallel lines. Secondly, although a shape may not have, in fact, arrived at its final position by translation, the relation between the object and image may still be described as a translation if the description fits the final position of the image relative to the object. In such a case you could say that the object arrived at the image as though it had been translated. This second possibility is an interesting study; but it is not considered here.

If the above translation was to be specified in accordance with the two items 1 and 2 mentioned above, both the angle θ (pronounced 'theta') should be given – for the direction – and the distance from P to P_1 for the amount of translation. It happened to be easier to describe the particular translation in the equivalent form of '3 to the right and 4 up'. The required distance of 5 could be worked out by Pythagoras' theorem; this will be dealt with in Chapter 8. The angle θ is approximately 53 degrees.

Let us now move on to consider the second of the isometric transformations.

Rotation

There are two things, again, which need to be considered in order to specify a rotation:

1   an angle of rotation; and
2   a centre of rotation.

Start with an object triangle *LMN*, with coordinates given by:

$$L = (3,1), \ M = (6,1), \ N = (5,6)$$

Let *LMN* be rotated about the point $C = (2,-2)$ through an angle of 90 degrees. Study the diagram below. With a compass point at *C*, the pencil point of the compass can be opened out to the vertices of the triangle *L*, *M* and *N* in turn and swung around through 90 degrees so the pencil point reaches L_1, M_1 and N_1. The arcs of the circles shown can be thought of as the actual paths taken by the vertices of the object to arrive at their corresponding positions on the image

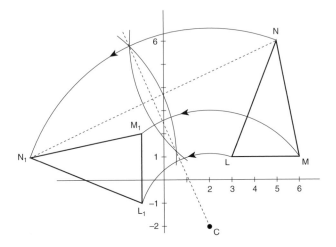

Now try to imagine that you are given a diagram showing only the object, the triangle *LMN* and its image, $L_1M_1N_1$. How could you check whether the transformation which produced the image was a rotation? Here is the procedure to follow:

1   Join two corresponding vertices, such as *N* and N_1, with a straight line.
2   Draw the perpendicular bisector of that line, using a compass and ruler. (This construction is shown in the diagram.) Do the same for two other corresponding points on the object and image. The second perpendicular bisector will intersect the first one at the point which is the centre of rotation.
3   To get the angle of rotation join, say, *N* and N_1 to the centre *C* and measure the angle formed (angle NCN_1).

Before turning to the third of the isometric transformations, it should be remembered that the angle of rotation could have any value. Is there any purpose in making the angle more than 360 degrees? What if wheels could not rotate more than 360 degrees?

Reflection

Only one item needs to be specified to determine a reflection: the line of reflection (sometimes called the mirror-line).

Take as the object this time the triangle *UVW*, with coordinates given by:

$$U = (2,1), \ V = (5,4), \ W = (3,5)$$

Take as the line of reflection the vertical line with equation $x = 1$.

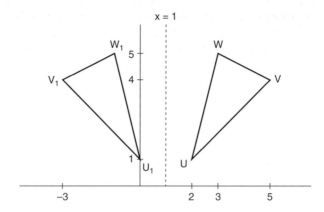

Look at the connection between the object and image. The lines joining object points to their image points cross the line of reflection at right angles (90 degrees) and are bisected by that line. In other words, each image point is as far behind the line of reflection as the object point is in front of it – hence the alternative name of 'mirror line' for the line of reflection.

Note that the line of reflection may be anywhere in the plane and does not have to be parallel to either of the axes.

So, now you should know the essentials of isometric transformations. Why are they of any importance? The short answer to that is that any movement from one position to another can be described, or even accounted for, in terms of a succession of transformations; the first is applied to the original object and then the others are subsequently applied to the intermediate images until the final position is occupied by the final image. It can get a bit complicated!

Apart from describing movements from one position to another as a succession of isometric transformations, do such transformations help to make sense of any other phenomena?

Symmetry

Let us try linking each of the three with one thing.

What about the notion of *symmetry*? Think of a butterfly with its wings open.

This is a special case of the transformation of reflection; the line of reflection is down the middle of the body of the butterfly.

What about the notion of rotational symmetry? This is a special case of rotation. The regular polygons are very good examples of this. Any such polygon, if made out of card, will have a balancing point or centroid. Each of the regular polygons shown in the diagram has its centroid marked as *C*.

In each, the point *C* can be thought of as the centre of rotation. Each of the polygons could be produced by a repeated application of a rotation about *C* of just a fraction of the polygon. In the case of the square, start with one of the four triangles and rotate it about *C* four times through 90 degrees and it will finish up where it started. The same can be done with the other two polygons. The pentagon can be produced by taking one-fifth of it and rotating it about *C* through 72 degrees repeatedly. The angle of rotation for the hexagon is, of course, 60 degrees.

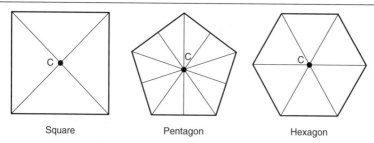

Square   Pentagon   Hexagon

How dull the world would be if all transformations were isometric. Things do change in shape and in size.

In the two-dimensional world, an interesting non-isometric transformation is that of enlargement. Let us now consider that and how it can contribute to our understanding of some changes.

6.3 Enlargement

The basic notion of an enlargement, as when a photograph is enlarged, involves every part of a thing increasing in the same proportion. What does that mean? Consider something much simpler than a photograph – a rectangular shape. Let us put one on a diagram and enlarge it. Call the shape *ABCD* and make the coordinates:

$$A = (2,1), \ B = (5,1), \ C = (5,3), \ D = (2,3)$$

Look at how the rectangle has been enlarged so that each of its sides has become 3 times longer. The usual conventions have been used in naming the image of *ABCD* as $A_1B_1C_1D_1$.

Take a good look at the object and image in the diagram and try to spot something about the way they are related to each other.

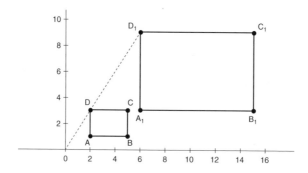

If you draw lines connecting image points to their corresponding object points, (D_1 to D and so on), something quite curious happens if you extend those lines backwards. The four lines meet at the point (0,0). This is called the centre of enlargement. So, enlargement is a *non-isometric transformation* which requires two things to be specified in its description:

1   the centre of enlargement (this does not have to be the origin); and

2   the scale factor of the enlargement (this is the number by which each length of the object is multiplied to produce the corresponding length on the image).

In the above example the scale factor was 3. How does the size of the scale factor affect the area of the image relative to the area of the object?

Since both object and image are rectangles, their areas can be obtained by multiplying the length by the breadth. The area of the object is, therefore, 6 units and that of the image is 54 units. The area of the image is 9 times larger than that of the object.

Length has been multiplied by 3; area has been multiplied by 9.

9 is 3 squared.

If the lengths of the object had been multiplied by 4, what would have happened to the area? The area of the image would have been 16 times bigger than that of the object because 4 squared is 16.

Does this relationship between the scale factor of enlargement of length and the scale factor of enlargement of area hold for three-dimensional objects as well? Let us take two basic objects, shown in the diagram below.

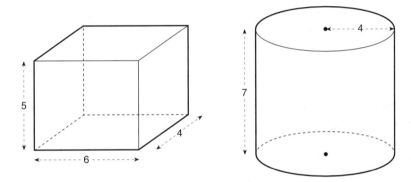

The outer surface area of the box is the total area of its six faces.

Those faces can be thought of as three pairs. The total surface area of the box works out as $2(30 + 20 + 24) = 148$ units. Suppose the box is enlarged so that each of its edges is multiplied by a factor of 10. Its total surface area then would be $2(3000 + 2000 + 2400) = 14800$. The surface area has increased by a factor of 100 which is 10 squared.

What about the cylinder? The original cylinder, the object, has a curved surface area of $2\pi rh$, with $r = 4$ and $h = 7$. So its curved surface area is 56π units. Since π is an irrational number we will avoid replacing it with an approximate value. There are also two circular faces. Their total area is $2\pi r^2$ which works out at 32π. That makes the whole surface area of the cylinder 88π units. Now suppose that its radius and its height are multiplied by a factor of 10. What is the new surface area – of the image?

(Have you noticed that the centre of enlargement is being ignored? It is not that three-dimensional enlargements do not have a centre, it is just that the centre has no role in the calculations being investigated.)

The curved surface area becomes $2\pi rh$ with $r = 40$ and $h = 70$. This works out to be 5600π units and the new circular ends have a combined area of 3200π units, making the total surface area of the new cylinder 8800π units, 100 times larger than the original.

The connection between increases in length, area and volume seems to apply equally well to both two- and three-dimensional objects.

Key issues in teaching shape and space to children

This chapter so far has dealt with some underlying principles of working with 'Shape and Space' at your level. It is assumed that you have the basic knowledge of names of angles and shapes. 'Shape and Space' is listed as one of the five strands to be taught to children as part of the National Numeracy strategy and the National Curriculum. This is a welcome suggestion, as we often find this area of mathematics receiving less attention than other topics involving numerical work. Many teachers feel that both 'Measures' and 'Handling Data' can be incorporated into the 'Number' section of the scheme, whereas they feel less comfortable teaching 'Shape and Space' as part of the work done within the 'Number' section.

One question often asked by teachers is whether to start teaching two-dimensional shapes or three-dimensional shapes. It probably makes sense for children to start exploring three-dimensional shapes first as most of their early experiences are relating to three-dimensional objects. Their first experiences are likely to be building blocks and construction toys. This does not imply teaching very young children complex names of shapes at this stage. From this starting point two-dimensional shapes can be introduced.

In the teaching of 'Shape and Space' to children the following are useful points to remember:

*   Children need plenty of practical experiences; many of the concepts are abstract and need personalising.
*   Any practical work should be accompanied by discussion of properties and correct names of shapes.
*   Children often feel confused about the names of shapes and need reinforcement. Encouraging children to make word-books on terms relating to names and properties of shapes has been found useful.
*   The use of Floor Turtles and Logo helps children to understand the concept of angle.
*   Making patterns involving symmetry and tessellations are useful experiences. They should be accompanied by discussions which involve thinking in depth about geometrical ideas.

Tasks relating to the classroom

1   Children often get confused about names and properties of shapes. For example they refuse to accept that a three-sided shape is a triangle if it is presented in a different orientation to the one they are used to, such as:

Make up a snap game presenting varied presentations of two-dimensional shapes.
2   Ask children to create their own glossary of the following words and illustrate them: angle, acute, right, obtuse angles, reflex angles, quadrilateral.

3   Make up a display of polygons and capital letters of the alphabet and mark all the lines of symmetry.
4   Enlarge a pin-person from a given picture and squared paper.

Tasks for self-study

1   Draw diagrams to show examples of reflection, translation, rotation and enlargement.
2   Design a mystery picture for children to work out using coordinates, both negative and positive.
3   Make a card folder for reference with names and properties of three-dimensional shapes.

Chapter 7

Probability and statistics

Objectives

This chapter focuses on :

7.1 Probability
7.2 Statistics

7.1 Probability

In a world of much uncertainty, in which luck and chance events can have major influences on our lives, it should not be surprising that mathematics has been used to explore the possibility of some things happening so that plans can be drawn up to avoid their consequences. Knowing in advance that there is a 60% chance of rain tomorrow, you will take an umbrella with you when go out to avoid getting wet. Being told the probability of someone in your occupation dying of respiratory disease before the age of 60, you can make financial plans for the protection of your family. In spite of being told that the chance of winning the Lottery is very small, you go ahead and buy a ticket anyway! The mathematics of an event does not have to kill off hope of better things to come. What sense can be made of these references to a 60% chance of rain, to the probability of dying by the age of 60 and to the millions-to-one chance of picking the lucky numbers for the Lottery? These questions and others with serious, wide-ranging consequences are the province of the mathematical science of statistics which is ultimately founded on the concept of probability.

Let us now turn to practical situations involving luck, chance and probability which is little more than a formalisation of those uncertain aspects of life.

Probability and relative frequency

Heads or tails

Some sporting events start with the tossing of a coin. In a series of five Test matches in cricket, the coin tossed before the start of the match – to allow one of the captains to decide whether to bat or to field first – may come down tails twice and come down heads three times. The relative frequency with which the coin has come down tails is two times out of five. Another way of expressing this is to say that the coin came down tails two-fifths of the time. If this is all the evidence you can have about the behaviour of the coin, the best you can do is judge that the relative frequency with which the coin produces a tails is two-fifths. It is expressed as a fraction, 2/5, and gives one form in which probabilities can be expressed. If you say that the probability of getting tails with one toss of the particular coin used is 2/5, then you are claiming two things:

1   The probability is based on practical evidence – the relative frequency with which the coin came down tails in five trials.
2   The probability, expressed as a fraction, asserts that if the same coin was tossed a very large number of times then it would come down tails a number of times equal to two-fifths of the number of tosses.

Of course, this particular probability measure is open to criticism, partly because it is based on very little practical evidence and partly because it relates to one particular coin and not to all coins. However, the purpose of the illustration has been to demonstrate the way in which the probability of something happening can be assessed by practical evidence which produces a relative frequency. Relative frequency estimates of probabilities are quite common in practical applications; the evidence of repeated trials gives you the best estimates you can get. In such circumstances there is no such thing as the absolutely correct value or the exact value of the probability.

Probability tables

When taking out life insurance, the premium you have to pay will depend on an actuary's assessment of your life expectancy. This is related to what is called a mortality table. An imaginary entry in such a table could indicate 'a probability of 0.73 that you will die by the age of 70'. This entry in the mortality table is really just another relative frequency. It means that people of your present age and circumstances have been studied and that it has been found that 73 out of every 100 in such groups studied have died by the age of 70. If future evidence suggests that the mortality rate of 0.73 used by the actuary was seriously inaccurate, then the probability would need to be revised, somehow. The profitability of the insurance business would demand it. Take note that the probability in the actuarial example was expressed as a decimal. This is just an alternative form. It could just as well have been given as the equivalent fraction, 73/100.

A comment on the two cases so far considered is required at this stage. Both gave probabilities of something happening. What about the events referred to not happening?

If the coin did not come down tails, it came down heads. The relative frequency with which it came down heads – the probability of getting heads – was 3/5, using the fraction form. What have you noticed? The two fractions, 2/5 and 3/5, add up to 1. This is because the two events of 'getting tails' and 'getting heads' are *mutually exclusive*. This means that they cannot both occur. The total of 1 also means that 'getting tails' and 'getting heads' are *exhaustive*; at least one of them must occur.

A general principle has emerged which can be summarised in a formula.

Let P represent a probability function, so values of the function can range from 0 to 1. Then let A represent an event, such as 'getting tails', and B represent another event, such as 'getting heads'. If A and B are mutually exclusive and exhaustive then:

$$P(A) + P(B) = 1$$

If your interest is in the probability of *A*, but your information is only about *B*, then you can find what you want, simply by adjusting the formula to obtain:

$$P(A) = 1 - P(B)$$

So, in accordance with the two previous examples, two further probabilities become available. Since a coin comes down heads or tails, the probability of 'getting heads' with that particular coin is 3/5, obtained by subtracting 2/5 from 1. Since you will be alive at 70 if you have not died before 70, the probability of you being alive at 70 is 0.27.

Weather forecasts

Another form in which probabilities can be expressed is used within some weather forecasts. A 60% chance of rain tomorrow is a probability statement. The forecaster is claiming that when the meteorological conditions expected tomorrow have occurred in the past, then 60% of those days in the past had rainfall. It is another case of a relative frequency, obtained from practical evidence, giving the best possible estimate of the probability. Note that the percentage version of the probability could equally have been given as either a fraction, 6/10 or 3/5, or a decimal, 0.6. What is the probability of it not raining tomorrow? 40%, since it must either rain or not rain.

Now for a different way of producing probabilities. Gaining practical evidence in support of each probability is popular with some and unpopular with others.

Winning the National Lottery

When buying a National Lottery ticket, the six numbers, from 1 to 49, may be selected in 49 times 48 times 47 times 46 times 45 times 44 ways. This comes to $1.006834752 \times 10^{10}$. Ignoring the order in which you selected the numbers, your choice could have been made in one of 1.3983816×10^{7} ways. So your chance of winning with your six numbers is about 1 in 14 million. Here we have another use for standard index form. The mechanism for producing each number at the time of the draw is designed to give each of the 49 numbers an equal chance of coming out. 'One chance in 14 million' is a fourth way of expressing a probability. This time the probability is determined by the design of the machine. Each of the numbers is selected *randomly*. A random number is one which has an equal chance of being selected, along with all other possible numbers. The relative frequency notion is involved in this sense. Consider the six particular numbers you have selected. If the Lottery draw was repeated many, many times – say 14 million times – then you could be sure of winning once because of the relative frequency with which your selected numbers will come up.

A similar line of reasoning would determine your chances of winning something with a Premium Bond. This time you would need to know the number of bonds in the draw. Call that unknown number *x*. The probability of you winning anything with your one Premium Bond in any particular draw will be 1/*x*. This is because the computer, Ernie, has been designed to select the bond numbers at random – giving each bond an equal chance of being selected.

Should you care to visit a casino, a similar case will be observable at the roulette table. There are 36 numbers on the roulette wheel, 1 to 36. The wheel has to be designed so that a bet placed on one of the numbers, with one spin of the wheel, has an equal chance of success as a bet placed on any of the other numbers. Place your bet on 17, for example, and the probability of you winning will be 1/36.

The three cases of equal probabilities have been dependent on random selection of a number by a machine carefully designed to make such a selection. Let us now turn to situations in which equal probabilities emerge for a different reason.

A priori probability

In situations where evidence of relative frequency is impossible, very expensive or unimportant the strategy of a priori probability is adopted. It simply involves assuming equal probabilities for all possible events. In the case of tossing a coin it is usually assumed that heads and tails are equally likely outcomes, so that the probability of getting heads on any toss, with any coin, is 1/2. Even a quite large number of tosses will not come out 'heads' half of the time, but the assumption of a probability of 1/2 is still adhered to, partly because of simplicity and partly because it is believed that, in the long run, the coin will produce heads in half the number of tosses.

The fact that there are just two possible outcomes is not a good enough reason for assuming equal probabilities. Dice should produce random results so that the probability of one die when rolled giving 5 is 1/6. If the die is loaded it will have a bias towards one or more numbers. The only way to check whether a particular die is loaded is to investigate the relative frequencies with which each of the six numbers turns up when the die is rolled a very large number of times.

When a child is born it may be a boy or a girl. That does not imply that the probability that a woman will give birth to a girl is 1/2. In the absence of birth records you may assume equal probabilities of 1/2 for 'boy' and 'girl', but where records are available over many years a bias towards 'girl' produces an imbalance of the sexes which may causes anxiety in some cultures and countries.

7.2 Statistics

An enquiry into any aspect of our surroundings for the purpose of trying to increase our knowledge and improve our understanding will, at some stage, require the collection and interpretation of *data*. There is a distinction between data and information, data being regarded as the raw material out of which information is developed. Any enquiry can accumulate a great deal of data, but if that data is not analysed to provide an enhanced understanding of some situation or to suggest a possible solution to a problem then the gathering of that data has served little purpose.

Data which has been collected may be either *numeric* or *non-numeric*. The number of pupils on a roll in a particular school is an item of numeric data. The age and annual salary of an adult are two items of numeric data. The colour of a child's eyes is an item of non-numeric data. The occupation and marital status of an adult are two items of non-numeric data. Much of the non-numeric data collected relies on the classification of a group of things into just two sub-groups or classes. The children in a class may be classed as 'boy' or 'girl'. Adults may be classed as 'earning £20,000 per annum or more' or 'earning less than £20,000 per annum'. After non-numeric data have been collected, however, it tends to be referred to by a numeric code for the purpose of analysis and the production of information. If the employees of a company have been the subject of a statistical enquiry and their job descriptions have placed them in the categories of 'management staff', 'office staff', 'factory staff', then there may be some advantages in assigning the job categories the numbers 1, 2 and 3 respectively. This would be simply to speed up the recording of employee data and facilitate its analysis. The assigned numbers do not have to imply any kind of ranking of the employees.

The splitting of a group into two classes is sometimes arbitrary, but considering the advantages of simplifying things by forming categories can justify such a move. Analysis without some assumptions is not an option. Evaluating the results of analysis without concern for what the assumptions may have been can certainly devalue those results.

Discrete and continuous data

In order to consider the distinction between discrete and continuous numeric data, it is useful to remember rational and irrational numbers. Remind yourself that a rational number is a number which can be expressed exactly as a fraction, whilst an irrational number cannot be expressed exactly as a fraction – only as a decimal, approximately, to a required number of decimal places. For a common illustration of the distinction between discrete and continuous data, consider what has happened to watches and clocks over recent years. A digital watch, worn on the wrist, and a digital clock on a video recorder have something in common – the time they show changes discretely. If you look at such a clock and the time it shows is 3:37 the next time it will show will be 3:38. Times between those two times are not indicated; the watch or clock 'jumps' every minute. But in reality, there are many intermediate values possible between 3:37 and 3:38. The data here can take any value between 3:37 and 3:38. When we talk about a litre of milk, we are referring to a value between 0 and 2 litres; of course it is nearer to 1 litre. When data can be expressed within a specified range it is called continuous data; the accuracy can, theoretically, be increased to more and more decimal places.

Now consider data referring to the number of car accidents in a month or the number of children in families. The data can only be expressed as a specific set of numbers; you cannot have half or quarter people or accidents. This is referred to as discrete data.

Time, length, weight and angle are basic quantities. They are all continuous variables. Quantities derived from them are also continuous variables. Area and volume are derived from length. They are measured to an accuracy determined either by the limitations of the measuring instrument or by the requirements of a practical situation. In athletics the requirement for greater and greater accuracy has increased greatly because of international competitions and the status associated with winning them. Take the example of the 100-metres race. The phenomenon of the 'dead heat' has required better and better measuring systems so that nowadays the time a runner takes to run 100 metres can be measured to two decimal places – that is, to the nearest one-hundredth of a second. So far this seems to be sufficient accuracy to tell two finishing times apart.

One major advantage of statistical enquiry is that it enables a simplified, and hence more understandable, view of a large amount of numerical data to be created. A basic concept used for that purpose is that of the average. Let us now turn to that.

Averages – mean, median and mode

The term 'average' is usually used to refer to the mean, although the mean is just one of the three main averages available to summarise data.

The mean of a collection of numbers is the total of the numbers divided by how many there are.

The mean of 8, 12, 15 and 45 is 80/4 = 20. The mean does not have to be one of the numbers in the collection it is summarising.

Note that the mean times 'how many there are' equals the total of the numbers.

The extent to which the mean gives a reasonable summary of the collection can be distorted by the presence of either a very large or a very small value – compared with the rest of the collection. If the 45 in the previous example was replaced be 345, then the mean would become 95. The 95 is less typical of this collection than was the 20 for the previous collection. It is because of this kind of distortion that one of the other averages is sometimes used.

The median of a collection of numbers is defined as the middle value.

The median of the numbers 8, 12, 15, 45 and 345 is 15. The list of numbers needs to be arranged in ascending or descending order to facilitate spotting the middle one. If the 345 was removed from the list there would be just four numbers, with no middle one. The convention in such a case is to take the mean of the two 'middle' values. In the list being considered those middle numbers are 12 and 15. Their mean is 13·5 and that becomes the median of the four numbers 8, 12, 15 and 45.

The mean and the median of a collection of numbers always exist.

The mode, being defined as the most frequently occurring value, need not exist in all cases. In the list 4, 7, 34, 34, 45, 67, 78, 93 the mode is 34 because it appears twice when all the other numbers appear only once. Remove one of the 34s from the list and there is no longer a mode; all the numbers appear with the same frequency. Add a 78 to the list and there are two modes are in the list: 34 and 78.

Of course, none of these averages gives any indication of how the numbers in a list are spread out. The amount of spread does have an influence which is worth briefly considering.

The effect of spread on the location of the median

Suppose the list is 8, 12, 15, 45, 220.

The mean is 60 and the median is 15.

If the list is changed to 8, 12, 15, 45, 60, then the mean becomes 28 and the median is still 15. The first list is more spread out; the mean has been pulled to a position between the fourth and the fifth in the list. In the second list the numbers are less spread out and the mean has moved closer to the median. Experiment with different collections of numbers to really appreciate how the mean and median change their relative positions as the amount of spread changes.

Displaying data

Data are usually presented in the form of tables, graphs and charts which make the information more readily accessible.

Frequency charts

Say, you want to represent the following information on 20 pupils' test scores, out of 10, in mathematics: 6, 5, 4, 4, 7, 8, 9, 6, 3, 5, 7, 5, 8, 6, 8, 5, 5, 4, 5, 6.

This information can be represented by tallying the data on a frequency chart as shown in Figure 7.1.

Marks	Frequency
0	
1	
2	
3	I
4	III
5	⊞ I
6	IIII
7	II
8	III
9	I
10	

Figure 7.1 Pupils' test scores

The total of the frequencies is 20; this can be used as a check of your tallying method.

Bar charts

Using the information from a frequency chart, a bar chart can be constructed. The lengths of the bars correspond to the frequency. In Figure 7. 2 a bar chart shows the hobbies of 40 pupils.

Hobby	FREQUENCY Children with the hobby in Class 3R	RELATIVE FREQUENCY Children with the hobby in Class 3R
Collecting stamps	6	0·150
Reading Science fiction	5	0·125
Making model aeroplanes	3	0·075
Collecting Spice Girl cards	12	0·300
Making a Manchester United scrap book	14	0·350

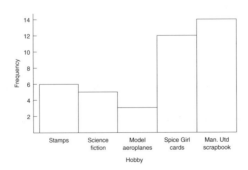

Figure 7.2 Bar chart

Histograms

The type of diagram called a histogram, as shown in Figure 7.3, can be scaled so that it consists of the relative frequency with which items of the group occur.

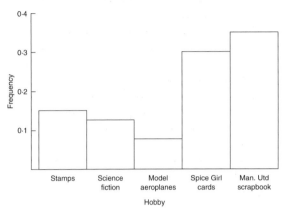

Figure 7.3 Histogram

Pictograms

The pictogram is used to represent data in a visual way. The pictogram in Figure 7.4 represents car sales over a year.

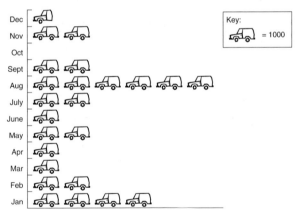

Figure 7.4 Pictogram

Pie charts

A pie chart, as can be seen in Figure 7.5, is a circular representation of the whole of the data. A sector of the circle containing an angle of 1 degree represents 1/360 of the whole collection of data. The relative sizes of the sectors indicate the relative prominence of the corresponding groups in the collection of data.

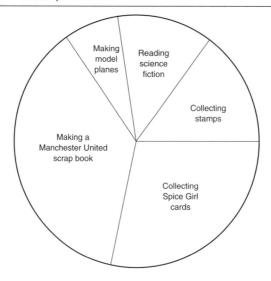

Figure 7.5 Pie chart

Samples and populations

If the whole population of items could be studied within a reasonable time and at reasonable cost there would be no need to consider a sample. The important thing to bear in mind when trying to make sense of a large amount of numerical data is that there has to be an element of simplification and approximation to make understanding possible. Exact numerical data is not always possible or necessary. The competence to produce exact numerical results of computation is, however, vital. Skill with exact numerical data is an indispensable prerequisite for appreciating approximation procedures.

Sorting data

Venn diagrams and Caroll diagrams can be used to sort data. In the following example, numbers 1 to 20 are sorted using two attributes.

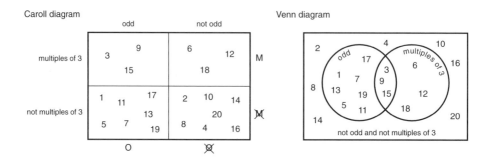

Key issues in teaching probability

A few years ago probability was included in the Key Stage 1 scheme of work, now it appears in the content of mathematics taught at Key Stage 2. Regardless of where the topic of probability appears in the National Curriculum, exploring probabilities can lead to some lively discussions. Children enjoy these discussions and for the teacher they provide an opportunity to encourage communication and reasoning.

Discussing the likelihood of the following statements being 'certain' or 'fairly certain' or having 'very little' chance of happening makes children think and reason:

- It will rain tomorrow.
- An actor will appear in the school playground this afternoon.
- I will have chips for dinner today.
- A lion will walk into the classroom.
- Your teacher is going to the moon.
- A coin will land as either a head or a tail.

Ideas of probability and randomness have gained more meaning for more people with the introduction of the Lottery which provides a good context for teaching probability.

Children start handling data from a very early age. Although sophistication of terminology and methods of representation change as they get older, the purpose of handling data remains the same and will follow the pattern: posing the question for the inquiry, planning and collecting information, processing and representing the information and finally interpreting the information in order to make conclusions – this may lead to a fresh inquiry.

With Information Communication Technology providing data handling packages such as Databases and Spreadsheets children can carry out projects which involve substantial amounts of numerical data which should enhance their understanding of the use and applications of number.

Tasks relating to the classroom

1   Study the probability scale below, marked impossible to certain, and show where the following statements will fit.
     (a) A mouse will fly.
     (b) When you flip a British coin, it will come down heads.
     (c) It will rain somewhere in the world today.
     (d) Your favourite film star will walk into your room this week.
     Now make up a scale on an OHT and some more statements for classroom discussion.

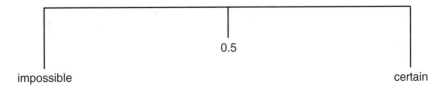

2   Ask some children:
   (a) When I throw a fair die, what is the probability that I will get a 5? What is the probability that I will get an even number?
   (b) When you toss a fair coin what is the probability that it will land as tails?
3   How many possibilities are there for throwing 2 coins? Record all possibilities to prove your answer. Try this with 3 coins.
4   Collect data from 10 children in Year 5 about how much time they spend doing different things in a day. Present it on a pie chart to see if the rumour that most children in Year 5 watch television for over 6 hours a day and read only for 1 hour a day is true.

Tasks for self-study

1   Children often think that when you throw 2 one to six dice there are only 12 possible outcomes. Is this true? Draw a table and show all the outcomes of the throws. In order to distinguish the two dice call one red and the other blue. Now try to answer the following questions:
   (a) How many possible outcomes are there?
   (b) What is the probability of throwing a double: 3,3 or 4,4 and so on?
   (c) What is the probability of getting a total of 7?
   (d) Is it true that 6 is the easiest total score to get?
2   How will you organise an experiment to find the experimental probabilities for (a) tossing a coin? (b) rolling two dice? Think of the aspects of recording.
3   What is the mean of these daily wages: £80, £67, £72, £85 and £91?
4   Rearrange the following numbers and write down the median:
   25, 6, 22, 5, 22, 23, 1, 18, 22, 25.
5   The set of marks, out of 30, for 10 children in a mental arithmetic test, is as follows: 26, 23, 25, 27, 27, 19, 22, 29, 22, 19. What is the mode?
6   You are planning to teach children about handling data. For each of the following ideas, think about what you would need to prepare to teach it effectively.
   (a) The number of pencils lost in each class during the month of June.
   (b) Investigating if there is any truth in the statement that your headband length is a third of your height.
   (c) Channel 4 is the most informative television channel for international news.
   (d) The most frequent letter used in a paragraph, based on a newspaper extract.
   (e) Ways in which children spend their pocket money.

Chapter 8

Mathematical proof

In the previous chapter the distinction was made between a sample and a population. A central problem for statisticians is that of devising ways of thinking which guard against 'jumping to conclusions' and attributing to a whole population what has been found out about a sample, without a scientific word of caution about the confidence you can legitimately have in such conclusions. In many respects, this is also a central, and much neglected, concern within mathematics. Remember the definitions of the universal and existential quantifiers in Chapter 4, Section 5. Their use is in emphasising the difference between cases of something being true for all possibilities and something being true for just some possibilities. In this chapter the notion and strategies of *proof* will be explored. The appreciation of what is involved in designing your own proofs and following the proofs of others will, it is hoped, be enhanced by contrasting proof with strategies of provision of partial evidence for generalisations. The citing of particular examples, the use of diagrams to support general arguments, the contrast between deduction and induction and the process of searching for exceptions to either disprove a generalisation or impose a limitation on it will provide the backdrop to the presentation of mathematical proof.

8.1 The role of induction

The phrase 'jumping to conclusions' suggests the procedure of concluding that something is true of a large group of things on the basis of believing it is true of a smaller group of things and that such a procedure is flawed or unjustified. Before considering mathematical examples, let us reflect on what is involved in a few non-mathematical cases of our beliefs.

'Night follows day' is something we believe because of our past experience of days of living. The fact that we have not experienced future days to confirm that day will be followed by night does not undermine our belief. We are justified in our belief because our thinking conforms to the process of *induction*. Someone who did not share our belief would be thought of as rather peculiar, to say the least. Learning from science that our planet Earth rotates on its axis once every twenty-four hours explains how the position where we live is exposed to sunlight for part of the day and cut off from sunlight for part of the day. This scientific knowledge supports our belief that 'night follows day'; it justifies our inductive step in saying something about days we have not lived on the basis of our experience of days we have lived through. In mathematical language, the illustration just considered amounts to making a statement beginning with 'for all' on the basis of a statement beginning with 'for some'. Remind yourselves about the use of the universal quantifier, $\forall$, and the existential quantifier, $\exists$. However, a statement containing these quantifiers, with 'x' replaced by 'days' would not be appropriate. The statement about night and day has not been proved by mathematical logic. Induction, supported by well-established scientific theory and observation, has been the justification of our belief that 'night follows day' – not logic and proof.

Another illustration should re-enforce our understanding of the distinction between a justifiable process of induction and a proof in the mathematical sense. Someone with experience of playing snooker will eventually realise that the angle with which a ball bounces off the cushion of the snooker table – ignoring spin – is equal to the angle with which the ball has just hit the cushion. Many future shots in snooker games will take this belief into account. If, at some later time, the player acquires the scientific knowledge about rays of light being reflected by a plane mirror so that 'the angle of incidence equals the angle of reflection', then the scientific knowledge about rays of light has re-enforced his belief about the behaviour of snooker balls. His induction has been supported. He has not jumped to conclusions about balls on the snooker table. Nevertheless, his belief has not been proved.

Suppose, now, that a male driver has several bad experiences with female drivers on the road. He has witnessed them doing daft and dangerous things and decides, on the basis of his experience, that 'women are bad drivers'. This is not induction; experience providing evidence 'for some' does not justify the statement concerning 'for all'. The male driver certainly has not proved his belief about female drivers. There is plenty of evidence available to him to show that a very large number of women are very good drivers. The male driver has 'jumped to a conclusion', without justification; he has not produced an induction. He has ignored evidence indicating that his belief that 'women are bad drivers' is wrong.

8.2 Proof by induction

This brings us to the question of whether induction plays a part in mathematical reasoning and what safeguards there are, in mathematics, against jumping to conclusions. There is a method of proof called 'proof by induction' which imposes an ingenious control over the process of making statements about populations on the basis of statements about samples. If a way can be found to establish that something which is true of a sample of things of a general, but unspecified, size n is inevitably also true of a sample of size $(n + 1)$ then that something will be true of the whole population – provided it can be separately shown that the statement in question is true of a sample of a specific size.

To illustrate this type of proof, let us consider the formula for the sum of the first n integers:

$$S(n) = (n / 2)(n + 1)$$

Assuming that this formula is true amounts to thinking of it giving an accurate expression for the sum of the first n integers – that is, assuming it is true for a sample of n integers:

$$1, 2, 3, \ldots, n.$$

Assume that the formula $S(n) = (n / 2)(n + 1)$ is true for $n =$ some definite number (k). So, $S(k) = 1 + 2 + 3 + \ldots + k$ becomes equal to $\frac{k}{2}(k + 1)$.

Now add $(k + 1)$ to both sides. Note that $(k + 1)$ is the next term in the series and that adding it to both sides will leave both sides still equal. What we have then is:

$$1 + 2 + 3 + \ldots + k + (k + 1) = \frac{k}{2}(k + 1) + (k + 1)$$

The left-hand side is the expanded form of $S(k + 1)$.

$(k + 1)$ is a common factor of the two expressions on the right-hand side. Taking out this common factor gives:

$$\tfrac{k}{2}(k+1)+(k+1) = (k+1)[k/2+1]$$
$$= (k+1)[k+2]/2$$
$$= ((k+1)/2)[(k+1)+1]$$

The final expression has been written in the way that it has, so as to make it easier to spot that it equals $S(k+1)$. What has been established, therefore, is that the formula must also be true for the value $k+1$ if it is true for the value of k.

Start by taking the value of k to be 1. So

$$S(1) = (1/2)(1+1)$$
$$= (1/2) \times 2$$
$$= 1$$

This is certainly true. So, on the basis of what has just been established, the formula must be true for $k=2$, so $S(2) = (2/2)(2+1)$. It must then be true for $k=3$, so $S(3) = (3/2)(3+1)$ is true and so on. In other words, the formula is true for the whole population of integers. The proof by induction has established that the formula: $S(n) = (n/2)(n+1)$ gives the sum of the first n integers for all values of n.

Jumping to conclusions in mathematics can be guarded against in a variety of ways – by trying to produce some kind of proof of your statements, by understanding the distinction between a conjecture and a proved generalisation and by getting into the habit of looking for exceptions. These aspects of reasoning in mathematics will be dealt with in turn in the next three sections.

8.3 Deductions and arguments

The notion of an argument in mathematics is quite distinct from the notion of a disagreement in everyday life. The notion concerns the deduction of a conclusion from assumptions called premises.

The notion has a very long history going back to the time of Aristotle who devised forms of valid reasoning called syllogisms. An example of a mathematical syllogism would be:

- All triangles have three angles which sum to 180 degrees.
- ABC is a triangle.
- ABC has three angles which sum to 180 degrees.

The first two statements form the premises, whilst the third statement is the conclusion which follows from the premises; it can be validly deduced from the two premises taken together. If the two premises are true, then the third statement must be true; it is a conclusion which someone is justified in deducing from the premises.

To indicate quite explicitly that one statement follows from another in mathematics, the special symbol, $\Rightarrow$, is used. It is called the implication symbol and is read as either 'implies' or as 'if … then …'. So, in the illustration of the method of proof by induction, it was established that $S(n) = (n/2)(n+1) \Rightarrow S(n+1) = ((n+1)/2)(n+2)$.

Some examples of the use of the implication symbol ($\Rightarrow$) are:

$$2x + 5 = 11 \Rightarrow x = 3$$
$$5x - 7 > 3 \Rightarrow x > 2$$

The right-hand side follows from the left-hand side.

Take a good look at the next example and try to decide whether it is in any way different to the previous two examples.

ABC is an equilateral triangle $\Rightarrow$ the angles of triangle ABC each measure 60 degrees.

Does the statement to the right of the implication sign follow from the statement to the left of it? Yes. If the right-hand statement is true, does it follow that the left-hand statement is true? Yes. So the implication works both ways. To show that this is the case, an equivalence sign, $\Leftrightarrow$, is used instead of an implication sign. (Imagine $\Leftrightarrow$ being the result of fitting together the two signs, $\Rightarrow$ and $\Leftarrow$). It should be stressed that arguments and deductions in mathematics involve the use of the implication sign. The equivalence sign is more appropriate for indicating that two statements are both true or both false, because in either case they are equivalent.

Look at the following examples:

$$y = 4(3x + 7) \Leftrightarrow y = 12x + 28$$

The implication from left to right requires the use of 'multiplication is distributive over addition'. The implication from right to left involves taking out the highest common factor of $12x$ and 28, which is 4. To test the equivalence of the two sides, just substitute a selection of pairs of numbers for x and y. For $x = 2$ and $y = 52$ you get:

The left-hand side becomes $52 = 4 \times 13$, which is true.

The right-hand side becomes $52 = 24 + 28$, which is true.

Both sides being true for the same pair of values confirms their equivalence.

Now try $y = 15$ and $x = 1$.

The left-hand side becomes $15 = 4 \times 10$, which is false.

The right-hand side becomes $15 = 12 + 28$, which is false.

Both sides being false for the same pair of values again confirms their equivalence.

Discussion can be made easier by introducing the notion of a propositional variable. Just as the letters x and y, in the example above, could be replaced by numbers, so propositional variables p and q may be replaced by propositions, or statements.

Let p represent the proposition 'A polygon has five equal sides', so p can be replaced by the proposition. Similarly, let q represent the proposition 'A polygon has five equal angles'. Then $p \Leftrightarrow q$ is an equivalence because either p or q can be used as a definition of a regular pentagon. The equivalence symbol, $\Leftrightarrow$, is an appropriate symbol to use when defining things in mathematics. So much so that an alternative way of reading '$p \Leftrightarrow q$' is 'p if and only if q'.

All the illustrations of implications and equivalences could have had the universal quantifier attached to them. For example, $y = 4(3x + 7) \Leftrightarrow y = 12x + 28$ could have been written more thoroughly as:

$$\forall_x \quad 4(3x + 7) = 12x + 28$$

In practice, it is quite common to leave out the universal quantifier, the meaning of its presence being understood.

Of course, trying to develop an argument or make a deduction requires either a purpose for the argument or some basis, some premises, from which to extract the deduction.

Let us now move on to consider the second of these aspects – the premises – and explore ways in which starting points may be generated to provide the basis for mathematical enquiry.

8.4 Conjectures and supporting evidence

Generating conjectures involves looking at collections of mathematical facts in innovative ways. It requires patience and experience. Start by taking some relatively easy examples, such as consecutive numbers. Selections of three consecutive numbers are: 3, 4, 5 and 9, 10, 11. Try adding each batch to see if anything of interest crops up.

$$3 + 4 + 5 = 12 \text{ and } 12 = 4 \times 3$$
$$9 + 10 + 11 = 30 \text{ and } 30 = 10 \times 3$$

Just these two cases are sufficient to make possible a conjecture:
The sum of three consecutive numbers is three times the middle number.

This may be further explored by taking other selections to see whether adding them provides supporting evidence. It is better to spend a little time on this track, rather than searching for some way to prove the general case too early – even if the proof turns out to be quite easy for you.

8.5 Looking for exceptions

A further aspect of the search for further evidence relating to a conjecture which you may hope will support it, is the testing of the conjecture with a fact or statement which may turn out to be an exception. This is also a wise step to take so as to avoid substantial wasted effort in looking for a proof of something which is not entirely true.

Consider an enquiry suggested by special cases of Pythagoras' theorem. $3^2 + 4^2 = 5^2$ and $5^2 + 12^2 = 13^2$ could suggest the possibility of going the other way – starting with one square number and trying to express it as the sum of squares of other numbers. Being systematic in your enquiry, you decide to investigate the square numbers in ascending order. This produces the following:

$$1^2 = 1$$
$$2^2 = 2^2$$
$$3^2 = 2^2 + 2^2 + 1^2$$
$$4^2 = 2^2 + 2^2 + 2^2 + 2^2$$
$$5^2 = 2^2 + 2^2 + 2^2 + 2^2 + 3^2$$

This gives rise to the following conjecture: n^2 can be expressed as the sum of n square numbers with the last being $(n-2)^2$. It is assumed that $n \geq 3$.

Supporting evidence for this conjecture is provided by the square number, 36, expressed as:

$$6^2 = 2^2 + 2^2 + 2^2 + 2^2 + 2^2 + 4^2$$

The square of six has been shown to equal the sum of six square numbers, the last of which is the square of four – two less than six.

From this evidence you could pursue your enquiry in two directions. You could search for a general proof of the conjecture or you could try to find an exception so as to make the search for a proof redundant. Would you care to make your choice?

The difficulty in making the choice is that you cannot know in advance which is the wise choice.

We will shortly return to the theorem of Pythagoras which expresses a square number as the sum of two square numbers. Before considering an algebraic proof of that theorem which some readers may find too abstract for their taste, a useful stepping stone for convincing someone of the truth of a mathematical statement will be illustrated. This involves using a cut-out diagram to demonstrate the statement.

'Proof' by cut-out diagram

Two illustrations of this technique should suffice before using it to demonstrate the theorem of Pythagoras.

For the first illustration, let us take the mathematical statement:

The sum of the interior angles of a triangle is two right angles (180 degrees).

A demonstration of this can be provided in four stages.

1   Draw a triangle on paper and mark the interior (inside) angles with three letters, say *a, b* and *c*. These letters stand for the sizes of the angles in degrees, although the actual sizes are not required.
2   Cut out the triangle.
3   Tear off the three angles.
4   Place the three angles next to each other to show that they lie along a straight line.

The angles lying on a straight line indicates that their sum is 180 degrees or two right angles. A line which has rotated through half a turn has moved through 180 degrees.

The results of the sequence of four steps are shown in the two diagrams below.

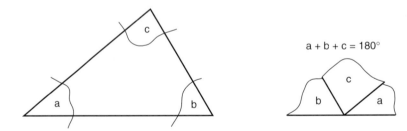

For the second illustration let us take the mathematical statement:

The sum of the four interior angles of a quadrilateral is four right angles (360 degrees).

A demonstration of this can also be provided in four stages.

1   Draw a quadrilateral (a four-sided shape) on a sheet of paper and label its interior angles with letters – say *p, q, r* and *s*. Again the letters stand for the sizes of the angles, although the actual sizes in degrees do not need to be known.
2   Cut out the quadrilateral.
3   Tear off the four angles.
4   Place the four angles together to show that they fit together 'in a circle'.

A line which rotates through one revolution about a fixed point has turned through 360 degrees or four right angles.

The results of the sequence of four steps are shown by the two diagrams below.

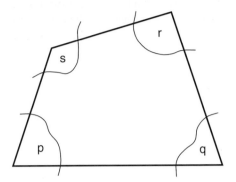

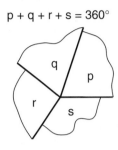

$p + q + r + s = 360°$

It should be emphasised, however, that the two demonstrations just described are merely designed to help convince somebody that two mathematical statements are true. The technique used is not what amounts to proof as mathematicians understand the word. Nevertheless, the technique is still very useful; using a piece of paper as a visual aid probably makes the mathematical statements more meaningful, especially to young children, than an abstract proof. 'Proof' by cut-out diagram may not strictly be proof, but it can provide a worthwhile stage in the developement of understanding of mathematical statements.

To further prepare you for the proof of Pythagoras' theorem, let us take a look at how an understanding of the statements 'proved' by the cut-out diagram method can be enhanced by formal proofs.

The first of the statements will now be re-stated as a theorem, since a theorem in mathematics is just a statement which is true. So the theorem is:

The three interior angles of a triangle sum to two right angles.

A statement may be true or false, but a theorem needs to be proved. The proof of the theorem is made much easier with the help of a diagram. The proof also makes use of three facts.

Fact 1:   Alternate angles are equal.
            Alternate angles are the pair of angles existing in a Z-shape, as shown in the diagram. The arrow heads are used to indicate that the two lines are parallel. This is an accepted convention in mathematics. The two angles marked by arcs in the Z are both 'a' degrees in size.

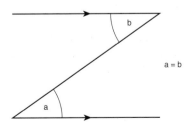

$a = b$

Fact 2:   Angles which can fit together on a straight line have a sum of 180 degrees.
This fact, as dealt with earlier, is based on half a turn being two right angles.

Fact 3:   Corresponding angles are equal.
The diagram below shows the angles marked 'a' and 'b' are corresponding equal angles. Notice the need for parallel lines and that there are three other pairs of corresponding angles in the diagram.

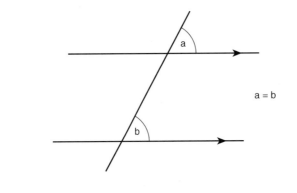

a = b

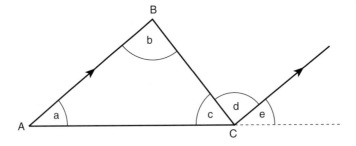

Proof.
The sum of the interior angles of triangle $ABC = a + b + c$
$c + d + e = 180$ (angles on a straight line).
$b = d$ (alternate angles).
$a = e$ (corresponding angles)
So $a + b + c = e + d + c$
$= c + d + e$
$= 180$
Therefore the sum of the interior angles of a triangle is 180 degrees.
End of proof.

The next theorem requiring a formal proof may be stated as:
The sum of the interior angles of a quadrilateral is 360 degrees.
The proof of this theorem is also made easier by a diagram and depends on two facts.

Fact 1:   The sum of the interior angles of a triangle is 180 degrees.

Fact 2 :   Angles which can be fitted together 'in a circle' must add up to 360 degrees.

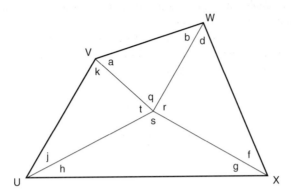

Proof
    The point P inside the quadrilateral is an arbitrary point.
    The sum of the angles at $P = q + r + s + t$
    $q + r + s + t = 360$ (angles fitting together at a point)
    The interior angles of $UVWX = (h + j) + (k + a) + (b + d) + (f + g)$
$$= h + g + f + d + b + a + k + j$$
$$= (h + g + s) + (f + d + r) + (b + a + q) + (k + j + t) - 360$$

(s, r, q and t have been added on so they must also be taken away)
$$= 180 + 180 + 180 + 180 - 360$$

(Each expression in brackets is the sum of the three angles of a triangle)
$$= 360$$

The sum of the interior angles of a quadrilateral is 360 degrees.
End of proof.

We finally come to the theorem of Pythagoras. It is stated as:
The square on the hypotenuse of a right-angled triangle equals the sum of the squares on the other two sides.
    The word 'hypotenuse' simply means 'the longest side'.
    The diagram illustrating the theorem shows a triangle with sides of length 'a' and 'b' so the squares drawn on them have areas of a squared and b squared respectively. The square drawn on the hypotenuse of length 'c' has an area of c squared. You could try drawing triangles with sides of 4 and 3 units to find that the hypotenuse will be of length 5 ($16 + 9 = 25$) and with sides of 12 and 5 to find that the hypotenuse is 13 units long ($144 + 25 = 169$). These would, however, merely supply two bits of evidence to support the theorem; they would in no way offer a proof that the theorem is always true of any right-angled triangle.
    Before presenting the proof let us look at how some use of the cut-out diagram method may be of help. If you were to draw the diagram below and cut it out, then cut out the shaded triangle at the vertex (corner) P you could check that it fits exactly over the triangles at the vertices Q, R and S. Each of those triangles has an area of 1/2 of a times b. The area of the square drawn on the hypotenuse of the shaded triangle is still c squared as in the previous

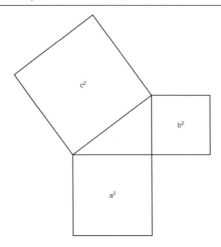

diagram. The length of each side of the square *PQRS* is $(a + b)$. The area of the square *PQRS* is, therefore, $(a + b)$ squared. To obtain a simplified expression for this area which is needed for the proof, study the diagram below. Focus on the way in which the square *PQRS* is split into four parts with areas of a squared, ab, b squared and ab.

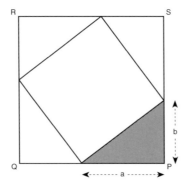

You should now be able to follow the formal proof of Pythagoras' theorem.

Proof

$$\text{The area of } PQRS = (a+b)^2$$ (1)
$$= a^2 + 2ab + b^2$$

If the area of *PQRS* is thought of as linked with four triangles identical with the shaded triangle at *P* and the square of area c squared, then:

$$\text{the area of } PQRS = c^2 + 4 \times 1/2ab$$ (2)
$$= c^2 + 2ab.$$

Equating the two expressions for the area of *PQRS* in (1) and (2) gives:

$$a^2 + 2ab + b^2 = b^2 + c^2 + 2ab.$$

Therefore, $a^2 + b^2 = c^2$ (subtracting $2ab$ from both sides).

So the square on the hypotenuse of a right-angled triangle equals the sum of the squares on the other two sides.

End of proof.

You should take note of the interchange in the above proof between the geometric notion of a square and the square of a number. You should also bear in mind that the numerical values of a, b and c may be any real numbers; their values need not be restricted to integers.

8.6 Proof by contradiction

A rather smart method of proving something sometimes is to assume the opposite and deduce that something false follows.

A very common illustration is the statement 'The square root of 2 is an irrational number'. Start by assuming that $\sqrt{2} = m/n$ where m and n are integers with no common factor. Square both sides to get $2 = \dfrac{m^2}{n^2}$. This implies that $m^2 = 2n^2$. This means that m^2 must be even, so m must also be even, and therefore, has a factor of 2. This contradicts the assumption which must, therefore, be false. Hence $\sqrt{2}$ cannot be expressed as a fraction and so must be irrational.

8.7 Generalisation and proof

The ultimate hope with any conjecture, for mathematicians, is to establish a proved generalisation. Here is a sample of one. The rest of the population is for you to explore.

Consider the lists of four consecutive numbers, with their sums written alongside.

2, 3, 4, 5 $14 = 2 \times 7$
3, 4, 5, 6 $18 = 2 \times 9$
4, 5, 6, 7 $22 = 2 \times 11$

Examining the sums leads to the conjecture:

The sum of four consecutive numbers is twice the sum of the middle two numbers.

The proof of this conjecture requires the numbers to be represented by n, $(n + 1)$, $(n + 2)$ and $(n + 3)$. Their sum is shown as follows:

$$n + (n+1) + (n+2) + (n+3) = 4n + 6$$
$$= 2(2n + 3)$$

$(2n + 3)$ is the sum of the two middle numbers: $(n+1)$ and $(n +2)$

Enjoy the remainder of the population.

Key issues in encouraging proof in mathematics teaching

The importance of developing mathematical processes of reasoning, making conjectures and proving have been highlighted in all official documents in the last few years. This is reflected in the Standard Assessment Tasks (SATs) where children are asked not only to find answers to tasks, but also to put forward reasons for their choices. The *Framework* for the National Numeracy Strategy also places a major focus on children being taught how to explain and reason. Being able to justify decisions helps children to gain confidence in their mathematical ability. During their explanations and mathematical communication – both in oral work and recording – the teacher can gain much insight into children's mathematical understanding and address any misconceptions.

From an early age, children can be encouraged to reason and justify what they are doing. Most mathematical topics provide opportunities for this. Giving explanations and offering proof does not have to involve the use of *letters*, verbal explanations will be sufficient which, in time, can lead to generalisations.

One of the ways in which 'proving' can be achieved is by asking children to examine statements to be 'true' or 'false'. In mathematics, statements can be true, false or 'sometimes' true. A simple example of this is the statement 'if you add three consecutive numbers, the answer is even'. This statement is true if you add 3 + 4 + 5 =12; but not true if you start with 4 and add 4 + 5 + 6 = 15. You need to qualify the statement to 'if you start with an odd number and add three consecutive numbers, the answer is even'.

Study the following statements to see the potential for discussion and reasoning:
- When you order numbers, you look at the number of digits to help you to decide.
- The exterior angle of a hexagon is 60 degrees.
- When you roll two dice together and total the scores, 7 will come up the most.
- All quadrilaterals tessellate.
- If you multiply two numbers, the answer will always be bigger than the two numbers you multiplied.

Examples of similar statements can be drawn from any topic in mathematics. These can contribute to lively and useful discussions in the classroom and are highly recommended.

Bibliography

Askew, M. (1997) *Teaching Primary Mathematics: A guide for newly qualified and student teachers,* London: Hodder & Stoughton.

Askew, M. and Wiliam, D. (1995) *Recent Research in Mathematics Education,* London: HMSO.

Askew, M., Brown, M., Rhodes, V., Wiliam, D. and Johnson, D. (1997*) Effective Teachers of Numeracy: A report of a study carried out for the Teacher Training Agency,* London: Kings College, University of London.

Brown, M. (1981) 'Place value and decimals' in Hart, K. (ed.) *Children's Understanding of Mathematics,* London: John Murray.

Burghes, D. (1999) 'Mathematics enhancement programme: Demonstration project' in *Mathematics in Schools*, May 1999, Mathematics Association.

Cockcroft, W. H. (1982) *Mathematics Counts: Report of the Committee of Inquiry into the Teaching of Mathematics in Schools*, London: HMSO.

DES (1991) *Mathematics in the National Curriculum*, London: HMSO.

DfEE (1995) *Mathematics in the National Curriculum*, London: HMSO

DfEE (1998) *The Implementation of the National Numeracy Strategy: The final report of the Numeracy Task Force,* London: Department for Education and Employment.

DfEE (1999) *The Framework for Teaching Mathematics*, London: Department for Education and Employment.

HMI (1985) *Mathematics 5–16: Curriculum Matters 3.*, London: HMSO.

Hughes, M. (1986) *Children and Number: Difficulties in Learning Mathematics,* Oxford: Basil Blackwell.

Koshy, V. (1988) *Place Value: An investigation of children's strategies and errors and an evaluation of a teaching programme,*. Unpublished M.Phil. Dissertation, Kings College, London.

Koshy, V. (1998) *Mental Maths Teachers' Book 9–11,* London: Collins.

Koshy, V. (1999) *Effective Teaching of Numeracy for the National Mathematics Framework,* London: Hodder & Stoughton.

Mitchell, C. and Koshy, V. (1995) *Effective Teacher Assessment: Looking at Children's Learning,* London: Hodder & Stoughton.

SCAA (1997) *The Teaching and Assessment of Number at Key Stages 1–3.* Discussion Paper No. 10, London: Schools Curriculum and Assessment Authority.

Self-assessment questions

The questions in this paper and in the multiple choice paper are designed to enable you to audit your subject knowledge and understanding of mathematics.

You can do this test in any order; solutions are provided in the appendix. Use the solutions in the appendix to mark your work and make notes on the aspects you need to work on. You may want to use the 'Record of Achievement' section in the appendix to plan what action you need to take.

1

Write down 2 examples for each of these:
(a) integer

(b) rational number

(c) irrational number

(d) negative number

(e) decimal number

(f) fraction

2

Study these decimal numbers and put them in order starting with the smallest:
4.2; 4.22; 0.422; 3.79; 4.10

3

How would you write 2300 metres as kilometres using decimal notation?

4

How much money will I save in 5 years if I save £556 a month?

5

Write two examples to show that addition and multiplication are commutative.

6

Do the following number operations and tick those you feel you are able to explain to children.
(a) 491 − 167
(b) 147 × 26
(c) 9 + 237 + 16
(d) 2346 divided by 25

7

Which of these numbers have the highest number of factors? 25, 88, 93 or 64?
List the factors to justify your answer.

8

(a) Complete two more terms in this sequence: 2, 4, 8, 16, … ; what is the 10th term in this sequence?

(b) 1, 4, 9 and 16 are the first four square numbers . What is the 8th term in this sequence? What is the nth term?

9

> To multiply a decimal number by another decimal number, for example,
> 23.65 × 1.45 = 34.2925, why do you count the number of decimal places to determine
> the position of the decimal point?

10

> If the following fractions represent parts of a cake, which piece would suit a glutton?
> 4/10   3/5   7/8   3/4   2/3
>
> How did you decide?

11

> The temperature in Boston in November changed from –9 to 6 degrees. Is this a rise or
> fall in temperature? By how many degrees did the temperature change?

12

> (a) What is 25% of £160.00? Show how you worked it out.
>
> (b) Convert the following to percentages:
> (i) 0.23
> (ii) a quarter
> (iii) 0.20
> (iv) 1/8

13

> Work out the following
> (a) 5^1 (f) 5^0
> (b) 5^2 (g) 5^{-1}
> (c) 5^3 (h) 5^{-2}
> (d) 5^4 (i) 5^{-3}
> (e) 5^5 (j) 5^{-4}

14

> Try these fraction calculations.
> (a) 3/4 × 2/3
> (b) 2/5 divided by 5/10
> (c) 2/5 + 1/10
> (d) 3/8 − 1/4

15

> Express the following in standard form:
> (a) 4000
> (b) 0.673
> (c) 0. 00000076

16

> Solve for x, $x + 3 = 8$

17

>
>
> What is the size of the angle a if the triangle is an equilateral triangle?

18

> 3/4 of an amount of money is £90.00, what is the whole amount of money?

19

> What is the probability of getting a total of 8 when two 1–6 dice are rolled together and the scores are added. Can you prove it? Use any method you like.

20

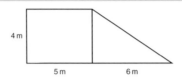

(a) What is the total area of this shape? (b) What is the perimeter of this shape?

21

Let $A = (2,-2)$, $B = (5\frac{1}{2},-4\frac{1}{2})$, $C = (4,1\frac{1}{2})$.
(a) The triangle ABC is reflected in the x-axis. Write down the coordinates of the image $A_1B_1C_1$

(b) If the triangle ABC is rotated through 180 degrees, write down the coordinates of of its image $A_2B_2C_2$

22

Draw a pie chart to show the grades obtained by 30 children in a class.
Grades
A   3
B   7
C   15
D   3
E   2

23

A school concert started at 09:25 and finished at 12:05. How long did it last?

24

8 books, priced the same, cost £28.60. How much does it cost to buy 18 books?

25

Estimate the value of $\dfrac{476 \times 81}{39}$

Multiple-choice mathematics

This test contains 20 questions, circle the correct option and check the solutions. Make a note of any action you may need to take.

1   The number divisible by 4 is?
    (a) 1409
    (b) 4588
    (c) 4542
    (d) 3002

2   Which of the following is an obtuse angle?
    (a) 260°
    (b) 300°
    (c) 92°
    (d) 185°

3   $3-(-4) =$
    (a) 1
    (b) 5
    (c) 7
    (d) −1

4   $4\frac{2}{5}-1\frac{3}{10} =$
    (a) $4\frac{1}{5}$
    (b) $3\frac{1}{10}$
    (c) $3\frac{1}{5}$
    (d) $-3\frac{2}{5}$

5   $4\frac{1}{3} \div \frac{1}{3} =$
    (a) $3\frac{1}{9}$
    (b) $4\frac{2}{9}$
    (c) 10
    (d) 13

6 The nearest number to 61 is?
   (a) 50.009
   (b) 60.23
   (c) 59.99
   (d) 61.07

7 For the numbers 1, 1, 2, 2, 3, 3, 3, 3, 5, 5, 5, 7 the median is?
   (a) 2
   (b) 3
   (c) 7
   (d) 1

8 The mode for the data in question 7 is?
   (a) 3
   (b) 4
   (c) 1
   (d) 7

9 The probability of getting a total of five, when two dice are thrown is?
   (a) $\frac{1}{36}$
   (b) $\frac{5}{12}$
   (c) $\frac{1}{5}$
   (d) $\frac{1}{9}$

10 1 kg 500 g is close to?
   (a) 3.4 lb
   (b) 2.44 lb
   (c) 4.2 lb
   (d) 1.30 lb

11 Which of the following has $x = 2$ as its solution?
   (a) $6x + 2 = 14$
   (b) $2x = \sqrt{4}$
   (c) $6 - x = 2$
   (d) $4x = 2 - x$

12 The interior angle of a hexagon is:
   (a) 120°
   (b) 110°
   (c) 60°
   (d) 30°

13 The rate of VAT is 15%. What amount will be added to a bill of £120.00?
   (a) £25.00
   (b) £15.75
   (c) £30.00
   (d) £18.00

14 When £600 is divided in the ratio of 1 : 5 the amounts in £s will be?
  (a) 320 : 180
  (b) 100 : 500
  (c) 250 : 150
  (d) 400 : 200

15 A bathroom floor to be tiled is rectangular in shape and measures 4 m × 6 m. The number of square tiles (25 cm) you need to buy is?
  (a) 384
  (b) 9600
  (c) 640
  (d) 240

16 $12\frac{1}{2}\%$ of 80 is?
  (a) £11.60
  (b) £20.00
  (c) £10.00
  (d) £9.60

Section C

The collection of papers in this section is centred around the theme of effective teaching and learning of mathematics. This is a crucial time in Britain for mathematics education. The Third International Mathematics and Science Survey (1997) highlighted deficiencies in British pupils' numerical skills and understanding. Schools and Local Education Authorities have set targets for achievements in mathematics in order to meet the government's targets for Key Stage 2 pupils. A National Numeracy Strategy is implemented from September 1999. It is a time when those who are engaged in teaching mathematics to children need guidance so as to productively reflect on the issues of *effectiveness of teaching* and *quality of learning*. All five papers are based on research – either carried out by the author as action research or through an externally funded project.

Margaret Brown offers a list of factors found to contribute to the effective teaching of numeracy. Based on research carried out by King's College, London, for the Teacher Training Agency, she highlights the importance of teachers' beliefs as well as their appreciation of the interconnections between mathematical topics. She provides the reader with some insight into the development in mathematics education which led to the introduction of the National Numeracy Strategy, before describing the three types of teaching styles observed by the research team and the possible effects of these styles on pupils' numerical achievement.

During their preparations for the implementation of the National Numeracy, one area which caused much concern among teachers was the introduction of mental and oral mathematics. Although, in the past, the teaching of mental arithmetic has been recommended in most official documents, it has not been given the importance it deserves. Most teachers – both practising and initial trainees – seem to have only memories of timed tests and chanting of tables without any real understanding. Jean Murray's paper addresses these anxieties which she has encountered during her work with both teachers and initial trainees. Enriched by her experience, she offers a framework for teaching mental and oral mathematics. The ideas explored in this paper, based on a redefined model of mental mathematics, are presented in an interactive style inviting the reader to carry out some small tasks.

Valsa Koshy, in her paper 'Children's Mistakes and Misconceptions', examines the common mistakes children make and why they may make them and shows how teachers can gain useful insights into children's thinking. The need to address children's misconceptions is emphasised very strongly both in the National Curriculum for Mathematics for trainee teachers and in the National Numeracy Framework. It is reasonable to assume that many children's mistakes and misconceptions can either be avoided or remedied if the teacher can analyse them early in the teaching programme.

The strategies suggested by Christine Mitchell and William Rawson for developing children's reasoning and communicating skills, using the idea of writing frames, offer much support in the implementation of these vital skills which are part of AT 1 – Using and Applying Mathematics. As the authors point out, with evidence to back up the claim, this is an area which is challenging to many practising teachers. Using examples from both key stages, the authors show how teachers can extend children's mathematical thinking.

In recent years the term 'differentiation' has been increasingly used in school inspection reports and reports on trainee teachers' planning records. There is little disagreement, amongst those involved in teaching, that effective differentiation is a key factor in raising achievement. With the introduction of the 'Numeracy Hour' in schools, issues of differentiation are on all teachers' minds. Lesley Jones and Barbara Allebone invite the reader, through examples, to consider factors which support differentiation in the classroom.

Chapter 9

Effective teaching of numeracy

Margaret Brown

Arithmetic, mathematics or numeracy?

The word *numeracy* has only recently been used in relation to primary education. Until about the 1960s, primary schools taught *arithmetic*, a subject which was mainly concerned with training pupils to do the calculations that they might need, either to pass the 11+ selection examinations to go to grammar school, or to enter employment at 13 or 14. Calculations which were needed had changed little from the previous century, and included mainly mental and written arithmetic, and imperial weights and measures. These would enable shop assistants to measure out quantities, calculate totals and give change, clerical assistants to do simple accounting and book-keeping for a variety of small firms, and local builders and merchants to estimate quantities and costs. For commercial reasons, a premium was justifiably placed on neatness and accuracy.

Arithmetic thus focused on performance; knowledge of addition facts and multiplication tables, standard 'tricks' of mental arithmetic, and the performance of the standard written calculation methods (algorithms) such as the 'borrowing and paying back' method for subtraction, long division, and techniques for conversion from one imperial unit to another. The standard methods to be taught were selected on the basis of their commercial efficiency, both in terms of speed and avoidance of error.

However, a sea-change began to happen in the 1950s, and by the mid-1980s it had affected all schools. This was a result of several converging factors. The work of Piaget and his successors suggested that many primary pupils had fundamental misconceptions about number, which was interpreted to demand more practical and diagrammatic activity as a basis for understanding. Following other, mainly continental, educational philosophers, there was also a growing tendency for the whole primary curriculum to become more child-centred and enquiry-based, centred round cross-curricular themes. Finally the 'modern mathematics' being introduced at secondary level, which included sets and logic, symmetry and geometrical transformations, statistics and probability, and computing, was beginning to filter down to the primary curriculum, mainly through the activities stimulated by the first Nuffield Mathematics Teaching Project.

Thus *mathematics* began to replace arithmetic in primary schools. This was a preparation not so much for employment, which was in any case now increasingly organised into large-scale manufacturing, commercial and retail operations, using computers, calculators and metric measures, but as a prelude to universal 5-year study of mathematics in the new comprehensive schools. It thus seemed logical to postpone the more difficult aspects of arithmetic, such as percentages and complex fraction operations, to the secondary school.

These could be replaced by the easier parts of geometry, statistics and number patterns, again shifting the emphasis from performance of techniques to achieving a basic conceptual understanding in all areas on which more could later be built.

The trends towards emphasising understanding were consolidated by the Cockcroft Report (DES/WO, Committee of Inquiry into the Teaching of Mathematics in Schools, 1982). Research among adults revealed that it was not want of techniques which seemed to be causing problems, but difficulties in knowing when to apply them, and a frequently incapacitating lack of confidence. The Report therefore encouraged more practical and everyday contexts at both primary and secondary level, the use of calculators for more complex calculations, and the introduction of investigations. The Cockcroft Report also proposed greater use of curricular differentiation, which was also intended to boost confidence.

However, towards the end of the 1980s and through the 1990s there has been a gradually increasing concern with the results of international surveys, which have showed English performance as consistently below international averages in the number area (although not necessarily in other areas, and certainly not in problem-solving where we have tended to do well). One cause was that international tests were still weighted towards performance of standard written techniques in arithmetic, which continued to form the major part of the curriculum in many countries. A second cause was a commonly adopted teaching method where pupils worked through textbooks on their own, an unintended result of the move towards greater curricular differentiation. This resulted in decreased emphasis on both mental and written methods of calculation; pupils working at their own pace were able to use any crude and slow methods of calculating as long as they mostly arrived at the correct answers.

The introduction of the national curriculum in 1988 was partly the result of a political attempt to improve national performance in number, although paradoxically the way it was implemented resulted finally in a greater weight being given to subjects other than mathematics and language in a broad curriculum, especially to science but also to history, geography, design technology and ICT. Within mathematics, the weightings put on the curriculum and assessment structure resulted in increasing priority being given to areas other than number.

National assessment did start to lead to greater emphasis on mental calculation, which was included from the beginning in the tests at Key Stage 1, and later also in Key Stages 2 and 3. Nevertheless, before the effect of these had had time to work through, there was political pressure in the latter years of the Conservative Government for a reduction in the breadth of the new curriculum and for more emphasis on basic skills. The movement, which had strong support from Her Majesty's Chief Inspector, favoured a renewed focus on what were now to be called 'literacy and numeracy', perhaps to acknowledge a broader interpretation than the Victorian 3 R's of 'reading, (w)riting and (a)rithmetic'.

Numeracy was a word first introduced in the Crowther Report (DES, 1959) with the very broad meaning of scientific literacy; it slowly then permeated into the language (although it was a long time before it was included in many dictionaries and spell-checks) with a more focused meaning concerned mainly with application of numbers in real life. The variety of current meanings encompass:

- arithmetical facility (knowledge of tables and facts, and mental and written calculation techniques);
- number sense, relating to a conceptual understanding of meanings of numbers and operations, including a sense of relative size;

- ability to solve real-life problems with a numerical component.

Both the Basic Skills Agency and the Labour Government, which prior to and after its election fully embraced the literacy and numeracy agenda of its predecessor, have tended to favour a traditional strongly arithmetical interpretation. For example the Secretary of State David Blunkett is quoted as saying in the White Paper *Excellence in Schools*: 'the first task of the education service is to ensure that every child is taught to read, write and add up' (DfEE, 1997, p. 9).

A slightly broader definition was used by the National Numeracy Project, which was set up by the Conservative Government in 1996 alongside the parallel literacy project. The aim of the Project was to improve numeracy performance in 13 low-attaining Local Education Authorities (LEAs). The same definition was later adapted for the National Numeracy Strategy (DfEE, 1998), which was formulated by a Government Numeracy Task Force to be implemented nationally starting in 1999. Because of early indications that the National Numeracy Project was proving successful in many schools, the decision was made to build the National Strategy on this, adopting its definition and many other features and publications.

The start of the general preamble at the beginning of the definition included something of all the three aspects of numeracy identified above:

> Numeracy at Key Stages 1 and 2 is a proficiency that involves a confidence and competence with numbers and measures. It requires an understanding of the number system, a repertoire of computational skills and an inclination and ability to solve number problems in a variety of contexts (DfEE, 1998, p. 11).

While this definition of numeracy included overtly all three aspects, including problem-solving and real-life applications, and goes on to encompass uses in other areas of mathematics such as measurement and data handling, the balance of emphasis became clear later in that seven of the ten detailed bullet points which followed related to abstract number skills rather than understanding and application.

This balance of about 70% on abstract number skills is not dissimilar to that in the various draft versions of the National Numeracy Project's curriculum framework, which was widely welcomed among project teachers and also widely disseminated well outside the project schools. The framework gave detailed objectives, with examples, for the numeracy curriculum in each year of the primary school, and in later versions suggested a detailed week-by-week scheme of work.

With few modifications (mainly the addition of a small section on properties of shapes) this framework became the *Framework for Teaching Mathematics from Reception to Year 6* (DfEE, 1999), which was circulated to all schools as a prelude to the introduction of what is popularly known as 'the numeracy hour' in September 1999.

The 1999/2000 revision of the national curriculum in mathematics was also based round this *Framework*, with the new programmes of study adopting the same headings and overall content.

Thus from 1999 onwards we have been in a situation in which primary *mathematics* is generally known as *numeracy*, and in fact includes very little mathematics which is not at least in the broad spirit of numeracy, if this is taken to include the application of number to data handling and measurement. In fact, probably at least 60% of the new curriculum is abstract *arithmetic*, closely related to the mental arithmetic and written algorithms which were taught in the 1950s, and indeed in Victorian times.

Few would argue about shifting the balance to reflect the importance of using mental calculation effectively, where this is a realistic strategy. Mental calculation is not only a useful skill in itself, but it can also help in the development of number sense, and is crucially needed for estimation, sometimes in order to check that calculator answers are roughly of the right order of magnitude. However, efficiency in the unthinking use of standard written methods such as fraction operations and long division and multiplication, including multiplication and division with decimal numbers, is more difficult to justify when for all practical purposes these can most speedily and accurately be done using a calculator.

It is not possible to tell yet whether there is sufficient attention in the *Framework* to the two aspects of numeracy which cannot be performed easily by machine, i.e. developing number sense and applying number ideas and skills to solving problems, whether these are mathematical problems or those set in real contexts. These two aspects are likely to become more and more important in relation to arithmetic as more of the population are likely to be required to interpret numbers and use computers as part of their work.

Although it is useful to identify the three aspects of numeracy, trying to separate them for teaching and assessment purposes, especially in order to emphasise skills over number sense and application, is likely to lead to problems. It is often assumed that children have to learn skills first before applying them, but in fact it tends to happen the other way round. Learning arithmetical skills is made easier by knowing about the conceptual meaning of numbers and operations, which itself often develops through application and problem-solving.

In the research and development work we have been doing at King's we have thus tried to integrate the three aspects by using the definition:

> Numeracy is the ability to process, communicate, and interpret numerical information in a variety of contexts.

The next section reports some findings of this research.

What makes an effective teacher of numeracy?

In 1995/6, Mike Askew, Valerie Rhodes, Dylan Wiliam, David Johnson and I carried out a 16-month study *Effective Teachers of Numeracy*, funded by the Teacher Training Agency. The detailed methods and results are given in the project report (Askew *et al.*, 1997).

The aims of the study were:

- to identify what it is that primary teachers know, understand and do which enables them to teach numeracy effectively;
- to suggest how the results can be used to help other teachers

We felt that it was important that the effectiveness of teachers was measured by the mean gains of their students over the year on specially designed tests, rather than by opinion (by Ofsted inspectors or other people) as to what constituted good practice. The 76 teachers of Year 2 to Year 6 in eight state and three independent schools formed the sample, with many of the schools explicitly chosen because previous evidence suggested they were highly effective in teaching numeracy. In each year-group the teachers were divided into three roughly equal groups ('highly effective', 'effective' and 'moderately effective') according to the size of the average numeracy gains made by their pupils. Sixteen teachers, distributed among these three groups and across different year-groups, were selected as case-study teachers, and were observed and interviewed on at least three occasions. The findings reported below draw on both the wider sample of 76 and the case-study sample of 16.

In the light of the very detailed guidance about lesson structure and the stress on whole-class teaching given in the National Numeracy Project and repeated in the National Numeracy Strategy (DfEE, 1998), it is interesting to note that no form of classroom organisation was common to all of the case-study teachers in the highly effective group. While some used a whole-class organisation, others used only group organisation; in the case of one highly effective teacher, pupils worked through textbooks entirely individually. (This lack of clear relationship is in line with other findings, as reported in a comprehensive review of the research literature relating to numeracy by Brown *et al.*, 1998.) Nor did setting seem to be a major factor.

What did seem to be common to the highly effective case-study teachers was not the organisation they used, but their educational orientations, which underlay their beliefs, priorities and styles of interacting with pupils, whatever the size of the group.

Three models of orientations emerged as important in understanding the approaches teachers took towards the teaching of numeracy:

- *connectionist* – beliefs and practices based around both valuing pupils' methods and teaching effective strategies based on pupils' understanding, with an emphasis on establishing connections within mathematics;
- *transmission* – beliefs and practices based around the primacy of teaching and a view of mathematics as a collection of separate routines and procedures which needed to be taught and practised;
- *discovery* – beliefs and practices based around the primacy of learning and a view of mathematics as being discovered by pupils, especially through the use of practical equipment.

These orientations are described in much greater detail in the full report of the project (Askew *et al.*, 1997). They represent 'ideal types' in that no teacher is likely to fit exactly within the framework of beliefs of any of the three orientations, and many will combine characteristics of two or more. Examples are given below of lessons to illustrate each orientation, taken from field notes of lessons observed.

Example 1: Connectionist orientation

A Y6 class. The teacher has put a chart on the white board which has columns for fractions, decimal fractions, percentages and ratios. One value has been entered in each row and the pupils are working in pairs to convert from one form of representation to another. They are using a variety of methods but working mainly in their heads and most are checking using a different method. As they begin to complete the task the teacher brings the class together. Individuals are invited to provide the answers and explain the method of calculation used. The other pupils are attentive to these explanations. More efficient methods are offered and errors are dealt with in a supportive manner either by the teacher or other pupils. Finally they discuss the sort of contexts where the different representations would be used.

Example 2: Transmission orientation

A class of Y4 pupils are working on equivalent fractions. The teacher draws a diagram on the board to demonstrate a means of converting 1/2 into quarters. She explains that quarters are the fraction to convert to and so the pupils will need to draw a rectangle divided into four equal parts.

$$\frac{1}{2} = \frac{\square}{4}$$

Since a half is required then two of these parts need to be shaded in.

$$\frac{1}{2} = \frac{\boxed{2}}{4}$$

'So, a half is equivalent to two quarters', explains the teacher. 'On the other hand', she continues, ' we could just look at the numbers on the bottom of the fraction. I have to multiply 2 (pointing to the 2 on the bottom of the 1/2) by 2 to make 4 (pointing to 4 on the board of a yet numerator free quarter fraction), so I multiply the 1 (pointing to the 1 on the top of the 1/2) by 2 also. So we get 2/4, which is the same as we got when we drew the diagram.'

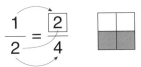

The pupils are given a number of fractions to convert into equivalents and told they can either use the diagram method or the multiplication method. As the teacher moves around the class, once pupils have done a few examples using the diagram, she suggests to them that it will be quicker to use the other method.

Example 3: Discovery orientation

This Y2 class is organised in ability groups. The teacher is working with a low attaining group on doubling. The pupils spend a long time counting out individual cubes, fitting them together and recounting them. The teacher sets them a series of numbers to double, reiterates how to find the answer using the cubes and goes to join another group. The pupils are able to talk about what double four hundred might be and quickly move onto discussing doubling three thousand, six million and so on. After the lesson the teacher explained that she was concerned that the pupils were not ready to be working with large numbers, particularly as no base ten blocks had been got out so that they could see that double three thousand was six thousand.

We found that the five case-study teachers judged to have a *connectionist* orientation were all in the 'highly effective' group, in terms of the gains made by their pupils in the tests. These *connectionist* teachers made up five of the six in the highly effective category; the only other teacher in the group was judged to have no strong orientation herself but to be strongly affected by the practice of other connectionist teachers leading the mathematics policies in her school.

In contrast the two case-study teachers who were judged to be *transmission* and the two who were judged to be *discovery* in orientation were both in the lowest 'moderately effective' group, along with two other teachers judged to have no strong orientation. All the four case study teachers in the intermediate 'effective' group in terms of average gain scores of their pupils were also judged to have no strong orientation.

We were also interested in how the connectionist teachers had come by their orientations, in order to make recommendations. Four of the five had been on 20-day courses run jointly by universities and LEAs, three in mathematics and one in science. The three who had been on recent courses spoke feelingly of the changes that had come about in their thinking and practices as a result of these courses, and in particular of focusing on pupils' strategies and understandings. (The 20-day science course had a similar content, being related to research on pupils' conceptions and how to teach taking these into account.) In the whole sample of 76 teachers, there was a clear relationship between having been on a 10- or 20-day mathematics course and the size of the gains made by pupils. However, there was no clear effect of attending either only mathematics courses of less than ten days, or of attending longer courses unrelated to the teaching of mathematics.

On the other hand, neither initial training nor mathematical qualifications (A-level, or degree-level in mathematics) seemed to be strong factors. Some teachers with recent primary PGCEs felt that there had not been enough time to really come to terms with primary mathematics on such a short course. Surprisingly the possession of A-level mathematics was if anything related with lower average pupil gains; a possible reason for this was that many teachers who had enjoyed the subject to age 16 felt that mathematics teaching at A-level and/or degree level had been so formal that they had developed a negative view of the subject. This finding is supported by some of the work on subject knowledge summarised by Aubrey (1994).

The case-study teachers with high gains who had not attended 20-day courses in mathematics had all had an alternative opportunity of having long conversations over an extended period of time about their beliefs and practices with knowledgeable and experienced people. In one case this was a mathematical brother-in-law, and in the other two cases it was with other teachers in the school.

Implications of the findings in relation to national policy

There seemed to be three important threads running through the findings about effective teachers: *time*, *talk* and *attitudes to mathematics*. The connectionist teachers had developed an integrated orientation of beliefs and practices, and positive *attitudes to mathematics* and its teaching, through *talk* over relatively long *time* spans. This was with people of whom at least some were more expert in and more enthusiastic about mathematics teaching than themselves. This talk took place either in informal circumstances or in more formal arenas such as extended courses.

Perhaps this result is not surprising, since it echoes what we know about effective teaching of mathematics itself. Effective, connectionist teachers themselves have positive attitudes to mathematics and try to teach mathematics in an exciting and challenging way. They use talk and classroom discussion with the pupils they teach, and know that the impact of these methods takes place not in a week but over the course of a year.

Judged against the findings about the development of effective teaching, recent government policy has both strengths and weaknesses. The government funding for 10- and 20-day primary mathematics courses, doubled for 1997–8, was sadly halted in 1998 in order to finance national training, first in literacy and then in numeracy, of a few teachers from each school. At the same time a greater proportion of primary teachers is coming through the 1-year PGCE route which, even when followed by an induction year, appears an inadequate period to establish a good basis of knowledge about mathematics and numeracy teaching. Nor is there much incentive for teachers to engage in sustained professional development courses when they are expected to personally fund them and to attend during the evenings.

On the other hand, the national training for the Numeracy Strategy itself had some of the ingredients of a 20-day course, and was conducted by recently recruited local consultants who, thanks in most cases to their attendance at such courses, were hopefully both enthusiastic and expert. Nevertheless for most schools the training for key staff was short and compacted into three consecutive days. There must be considerable doubt about whether this would have been sufficiently sustained to have a strong effect on one or more teachers in each school, and especially about whether effective cascade from these key teachers to all teachers in primary schools took place in the three further one-day training days. Schools with more identified problems are receiving additional intensive and longer-term support, which should be an appropriate step, with more chance of having a long-term effect.

Although, like the *Framework*, the training materials drew substantially on input from a small number of researchers in higher education, it is a pity that more use was not made in the training process of the very considerable experience and knowledge of mathematics education lecturers in higher education, many of whom ran the very successful 20-day courses.

There must also be some doubt as to whether any focus on the important features of quality, connectionist teaching was overwhelmed by the less important aspects of the National Numeracy Strategy, such as the exact form of class and lesson organisation, and prescription of a curriculum which, as noted earlier, has considerable benefits in elaborating mental arithmetic skills, but does not completely match the needs of the next century. Will practising long division drive out discussion of how and when the operation of division can be applied, and the effect it has, or the enthusiasm of teachers and pupils for solving mathematical problems? Only time will tell.

References

(Books and articles suggested for further reading related to teachers' knowledge and effectiveness are marked with an asterisk.)

*Askew, M., Rhodes, V., Brown, M., Wiliam, D. and Johnson, D. C. (1997) *Effective Teachers of Numeracy: Report of a study carried out for the Teacher Training Agency*, London: King's College London.

*Aubrey, C. (1994) *The Role of Subject Knowledge in the Early Years of Schooling*, London: Falmer Press.

*Brown, M., Askew, M., Baker, D., Denvir, B. and Millett, A. (1998) 'Is the National Numeracy Strategy research-based?', *British Journal of Educational Studies*, 46(4), 362–385.

Department for Education and Employment (DfEE) (1997) *Excellence in Schools*, London: HMSO.

Department for Education and Employment (DfEE) (1998) *The Implementation of the National Numeracy Strategy: The final report of the Numeracy Task Force*, London: DfEE.

Department for Education and Employment (DfEE) (1999) *Framework for Teaching Mathematics from Reception to Year 6*, London: DfEE.

Department of Education and Science (DES), Central Advisory Council for Education (1959) *A Report ('The Crowther Report')*,. London: HMSO.

Department of Education and Science/Welsh Office (DES/WO), Committee of Inquiry into the Teaching of Mathematics in Schools (1982) *Mathematics Counts ('The Cockcroft Report')*, London: HMSO.

Chapter 10

Mental mathematics

Jean Murray

Mental arithmetic (or mental calculation) has long been an established part of the mathematics curriculum. In the 1990s, however, there has been an increasing emphasis on the place of mental methods of calculating at primary school level. The work of the National Numeracy Strategy (NNS), and a series of curriculum documents and research findings (see, for example, Askew and Wiliam, 1995; Askew, 1998; SCAA, 1997) have explored the place of what is now termed mental mathematics in numeracy development. This term includes more than just mental arithmetic, as is explained in the following sections.

This chapter reflects the emphases of these recent developments in primary mathematics in two ways. Firstly, it focuses on mental mathematics as a key element of children's numeracy. Secondly, it uses the term mental mathematics to denote numerical thinking, although in other contexts the term can be used to describe thinking processes across all areas of the mathematics curriculum.

The chapter aims to give an overview of the major issues involved in the teaching and learning of mental mathematics. It looks at the following:

- a definition of mental mathematics and its place in numeracy development;
- a consideration of the nature of numeracy;
- an analysis of the nature of mental calculations;
- an analysis of the components of mental mathematics;
- two accounts of how children 'figure out' (Askew and Wiliam, 1995) answers;
- research findings on the characteristics of children who are confident with mental calculations;
- an indication of the implications of the chapter for teaching.

How is mental mathematics defined?

The broad term mental mathematics needs to be distinguished from the narrower terms of mental arithmetic (or mental calculation). The nature of this distinction can be illustrated by describing the events during a recent teaching session for PGCE students at Brunel University. The session involved the students doing some mental calculations and analysing the ways in which they had calculated. As soon as the focus of the session became clear, some students began to look worried, and a number confessed to feeling tense about the calculating activities. It transpired that this was not because they doubted their own abilities to calculate the answers, but because they had very negative memories of experiences of mental arithmetic in their own schooling. The calculating activities were recalling these memories.

This was a useful starting point both for defusing the anxiety and tension, and for discussing the differences between the nature of the mental arithmetic work the students had experienced as pupils, and the mental mathematics work they would find in contemporary primary schools.

After some discussion we established that the mental arithmetic work which the students had experienced had the following features:

- it claimed to focus on all aspects of mental calculation but correct answers were valued above all else;
- it de-emphasised the processes of thinking by which answers were obtained;
- it involved much testing and practising;
- factual knowledge predominated in the testing and practising routines;
- children tended either to know an answer immediately or to be unable to answer the question at all;
- there was little direct or indirect teaching of useful strategies for calculation;
- there was little discussion of how and why answers were obtained;
- factual knowledge of the correct answers could be achieved by rote learning and was not underpinned by understanding;
- testing and practising routines were often conducted in front of the whole class;
- children could be left feeling tense and anxious about failure or potential failure.

In contrast to this narrow model of teaching and learning, current practice in mental mathematics aims to help children develop more extensive numeracy knowledge and a greater flexibility in using and applying such knowledge in thinking about their mathematics. This means that children have a familiarity and confidence in using the number system which is sometimes referred to as a 'feel for numbers'. Mental mathematics, according to this extended definition, has the following characteristics:

- it emphasises answers alongside the mental processes by which they were obtained;
- it considers children's factual knowledge, their conceptual understanding of the number system, their strategies and their attitudes to mathematics as integrated aspects of numeracy development;
- it involves teaching of relevant strategies, concepts and facts, as well as practising and testing of factual knowledge;
- an emphasis on oral mathematics is used to explore how and why certain answers are obtained and to give the teacher insight into children's thinking;
- teaching aims to develop positive attitudes to numeracy, particularly to develop children's confidence in tackling and solving mental calculations.

Mental mathematics then extends and develops some aspects of previous models of mental arithmetic. It focuses, for example, on mental calculation, but it goes beyond arithmetic to include a focus on the mental images and strategies which underpin such calculation. It attempts to validate the processes of thinking as well as correct answers, and it aims to develop children's confidence and competence in thinking mathematically. Mental mathematics can then be defined as the use of mental images of number and / or of arithmetical thinking undertaken without resource to the manipulation of physical objects or to written representation. It includes, but is not limited to, mental arithmetic. It involves an emphasis on the processes of mathematical thinking and on the use of oral language to explore such processes.

The place of mental arithmetic in numeracy

Numeracy or being numerate can be defined in a number of ways. Nunes and Bryant (1996, p. 19), for example, state that 'being numerate involves thinking mathematically about situations'. This mathematical thinking includes knowing mathematical systems of representation to use as thinking tools, being able to understand these systems and to relate them to the contexts in which they are used, and choosing the most appropriate form of mathematics to use in a given context. The authors make the important point that 'it is not enough to learn procedures; it is necessary to make these procedures into thinking tools'.

The current definition of numeracy offered by the NNS documentation (1999) also stresses the importance of children being able to use and apply numerical knowledge appropriately. In order to do this children need to have a feel for numbers. The NNS 1999, like Nunes and Bryant, sees numeracy as extending beyond knowledge of the structures and operations of the number system. It includes

> an ability and inclination to solve numerical problems, including those involving money or measures. It also demands familiarity with the ways in which numerical information is gathered by counting and measuring, and is presented in graphs, charts and tables. (p. 5).

The NNS sees mental mathematics as an essential part of children's numeracy, both as a means of calculating in its own right and as the underpinning of written arithmetic, work with mathematical resources and appropriate use of calculators. In stating its model of numeracy the NNS draws on well-established ideas about the place of mental mathematics in numeracy. The Cockcroft Report (DES, 1982, para 255), for example, stated that working 'done in the head' occupied a central place in numeracy and underpinned written arithmetic. The National Curriculum (DfE, 1995, p. 3) underlines the importance of mental mathematics by stating that at Key Stage 1 children should be given:

- opportunities to develop flexible methods of working with numbers, orally and mentally;
- opportunities to record number operations in a variety of ways, including ways that relate to mental processes.

At Key Stage 2 children should be taught to:

- develop a variety of mental methods for computation;
- extend their mental methods of calculation to include all four operations of arithmetic;
- develop a range of mental methods for finding unknown facts from known facts;
- chose a method of calculation suited to the context of a particular problem;
- begin to check their answers in different ways (DfE, 1995, p. 7).

The nature of mental ways of working

This section aims to establish some of the characteristics of mental ways of working and of the components of numerical knowledge which come into operation when mental mathematics takes place. In order to collect some examples of mental mathematics in operation, try the practical activity in Figure 10.1 and make notes on the relevant points.

In analysing the notes it should be noticed that most people will have done the calculation in very different ways from the methods which they would use for a written calculation. There should also be evidence that the mental ways of calculating used for any one sum vary from person to person. This is because in mental mathematics there is no single 'proper method' which has to be used (see the Cockcroft Report, DES, 1982, para 256). As Plunkett (1979) has defined in a thought-provoking article on mental mathematics, the methods used are variable, flexible and adaptable. People calculate mentally in ways which feel accessible and appropriate to them. Mental methods require understanding and people often make a choice as to the most appropriate or economical way to calculate an answer. The methods are often holistic in that the calculating method works with at least one complete number rather than separated components of it, as in written arithmetic. Some methods of calculating give an early approximation of the correct answer because of this holistic tendency. (For example, 145 + 37 may be calculated as 145 + 30 (145, 155, 165, 175) + 7 = 182. Doing the same calculation in the standard written format of

$$145$$
$$+ 37$$

would involve calculating the units column first, then the tens, then the hundreds, and would not therefore give the same early sense of the possible size of the answer.

In some mental methods, especially those used by children, it is possible to see iconic mental images underpinning the strategy in use. Children sometimes make use of images of number lines or number squares in their methods of calculation. This usage is often reflected in their oral accounts of how they have calculated. In adults the traces of such mental imagery have often been lost, as numerical ability has increased. Mental methods are not easily accessible to recording on paper, and they are of limited use with large numbers (try calculating a sum like 4567 + 2388 mentally and this point quickly becomes clear for most people). •

In mental ways of working, there is no single set method which must be followed for a particular calculation. But it is possible to identify some recurring types and patterns of mathematical knowledge and strategies which form what I have termed the building blocks of mental mathematics. These are analysed below using the model of looking at mathematics in terms of facts, skills, concepts, strategies and attitudes taken from *Mathematics 5–16* (DES, 1985). (This model of mathematics is discussed in detail in the introduction to this book.)

Returning to the notes taken for practical activity 1, in the different methods of calculation investigated there should be evidence of:

• use of *factual* knowledge, that is knowledge of the results of number calculations (for example, addition bonds, such as 4 + 6 = 10, or multiplication results, such as 3 × 4 = 12). This factual knowledge may be used to give *instant recall* of an answer or to generate a *quick recall*. The distinction between these two methods is examined in more depth below.

The purpose of this activity is to enable you to find out how people use mental mathematics when calculating. In order to do this you need to find out as much as possible about the mental, emotional and physical processes which accompany mental mathematics. The activity is not necessarily about obtaining correct answers. Remember that the focus is mental ways of working, so use of written recording is prohibited!

First try out the calculations below yourself. After calculating each answer, try to think through the methods you used. Make notes on your methods for each calculation. Also record any feelings you had about undertaking the activity.

Next ask two other people to try the calculations. Ideally, these people should be an adult and a child at the top of the primary school age range. It will help if the child you choose is confident in mathematics. If you can't find a child to help you in this activity, ask two adults.

When working with others
1   Tell them that there is no need to hurry. A nervous desire to produce a quick response may hinder later exploration of the methods used.
2   Give each person time to relax.
3   Speak slowly and do not repeat the question unless the person requests it.
4   Do not show the written questions.
5   Do not allow any writing or use of practical resources.

After each answer has been given
1   Ask about the mental methods used. Your aim is to find out as much as you can about the mathematical thinking. Useful questions here may include:
•   How did you get that answer?
•   What was the next stage of your calculation?
•   Tell me what you thought about at the beginning of the calculation.
•   Did any mental images accompany your thinking?
•   How did you feel about doing this calculation?
2   You may need to probe the person's thinking to find out more. Useful questions may include:
•   Where did this number come from?
•   Did you check your answers?
•   What do you mean 'I just added'? How did you add?
•   How exactly did you work that out?
3   Make a note of any body movements which accompany the calculations, especially use of fingers to support calculation, signs of nervousness and changes in body language.
4   Make a note of how easy the person finds it to explain their thinking to you.
5   Take full notes of how the calculation was done. Check with the person that you have noted their ways of thinking correctly.

Calculations

$16 + 7 =$	$76 + 46 =$	$51 \times 19 =$
$16 + 17 =$	$125 - 88 =$	$200 \div 25 =$
$8 \times 7 =$	$26 \times 9 =$	$255 \div 13 =$
$80 \times 7 =$		

Figure 10.1 Practical activity

- re-arranging the sum to make it more manageable
  for example, calculating $7 + 23$ as $23 + 7$ or given the sum $2 \times 50 \times 5$ working it out as $(2 \times 5) \times 50$

- bridging through tens
  for example, $18 + 6$ is worked out by splitting the 6 into 4 and 2, then calculating $(18 + 2) + 4 = 24$

- using doubles and near doubles
  for example, knowing that $12 + 12 = 24$ and deducing the answer to $12 + 13$ from $(12 + 12) + 1 = 25$

- using patterns of similar calculations
  for example, calculating $25 \times 4 = 100$ so 28×4 can be calculated as $100 + (3 \times 4)$

- estimating reasonable answers
  for example, 6.7×3: $7 \times 3 = 21$ and $6 \times 3 = 18$ so these two answers give the upper and lower 'limits' which guide the final calculation

Figure 10.2 Examples of strategies adapted and extended from SCAA (1997) and Circular 4/98 (DfEE, 1998)

- use of *conceptual* knowledge. This may include:
  - knowledge of counting sequences;
  - understanding and use of the commutative law of addition ($3 + 4 = 4 + 3$), under-standing of the relationships between different concepts (for example, that addition can be seen as the inverse of subtraction and therefore that $100 - 67$ can be calculated by counting on from the lower number to the higher as $67 + 3 = 70 + 30 = 100$);
  - knowledge of the place value system (for example, to use when partitioning numbers for calculating – a calculation using 125 may involve partitioning the number into 100, 20 and 5).
- a repertoire of mental *strategies* which can be used to find unknown results, and decisions on the use of a strategy appropriate for the sum. Examples of common strategies are shown in Figure 10.2.
- having *positive attitude to mathematics*, including having the confidence to try out new mental strategies and to implement checking strategies.

Instant recall, quick recall and the creation of new knowledge

Instant Recall

The results of mental calculations may be found by using instant recall of factual knowledge. The importance of instant recall is heavily stressed in the National Curriculum and in the

NNS. It is obviously very important for all children to have an appropriate range of factual knowledge as part of their mathematical knowledge. The research of Gray, Hart and Steffe (cited in Askew and Wiliam, 1995) shows how children who do not develop factual knowledge, but remain reliant on simple arithmetic techniques, such as counting on one by one or calculating multiplication as repeated addition, are disadvantaged in their numeracy work.

Factual knowledge, however, always needs to be supported by understanding of how and why the number system works to produce the relevant results. Askew and Wiliam (1995, p. 8) refer to these two aspects of knowledge as 'knowing by heart' and 'figuring out'. They argue that the two aspects support each other in pupils' progression in number. This is because factual knowledge expands the mathematical knowledge base available to pupils, and deducing number facts helps to develop understanding of the number system. Such understanding in time translates into greater factual knowledge.

If, for example, an answer is not known immediately, then some type of 'figuring out' of the answer may happen. This may be a swift process, resulting in quick recall of the answer, or it may involve a longer process of 'figuring out'. In either case, in moving from known facts to derived facts (Askew, 1998, p. 50) children make use of various aspects of numeracy. Not all children find it easy to make this move, often because they lack either the necessary aspects of numeracy or confidence in using their own strategies for calculation.

Quick recall and the mathematical safety net

Quick recall is a further important element of mental calculation. Figure 10.3. gives an example of a child using quick recall to reconstruct a number fact he had forgotten.

In this case Henry was able to use quick recall to find the answer. In doing this he demonstrated his 'feel for numbers' and used the following building blocks of mathematics:

- known factual knowledge ($10 \times 7 = 70$);
- knowledge of the relationship between 9×7 and 10×7 (10×7 can be seen as $9 \times 7 + 7$ more);
- ability to count back accurately from 70).

Henry used these building blocks to help him construct a quick recall strategy for finding the answer. In other words, his ability to use and apply his numerical knowledge gave him a

Interviewer:	What is 9 x 7?
	(pause of 20 seconds during which Henry is obviously doing some calculations)
Henry:	63
Interviewer:	How did you get that answer?
Henry:	Well, I forgot it, I couldn't remember it …
Interviewer:	So how did you get the answer then?
Henry:	Well, I said 10×7 makes 70 and then I counted back 7 from 70 and that makes 63.

Figure 10.3 Harry's quick recall

mathematical safety net. He forgot the relevant fact, but this did not mean that he was completely stuck. He had an understanding of the number system which enabled him to reconstruct the answer.

The creation of new knowledge in mental calculation: the mathematical springboard

The extract in Figure 10.4 gives a flavour of a more prolonged process of a child 'figuring out' an answer. In this case Gemma is, with the support of her teacher, creating knowledge as she calculates the answer to a sum which seems quite new to her. Incidentally, this extract underlines that some children seem to think that multiplication facts stop at multiplication of a number by 10!

Teacher:	What would 13 × 5 be?
Gemma:	(looking very puzzled and after long pause) You can't do that.
Teacher:	Why not?
Gemma:	(long pause) You can do 10 × 5.
Teacher:	What would that be?
Gemma:	(instantly) 50
Teacher:	Good. So what would 3 × 5 be?
Gemma:	(instantly) 15.
Teacher:	(talking at the same time as writing these sums and their results on a piece of paper) So now we know that, if we wanted to find out 13 × 5 how could we do it?
Gemma:	(long pause, thinking hard) 65?
Teacher:	Well done, that's excellent. How did you do that?
Gemma:	(pause) I said 50 add 15 'cos that's 3 more groups of 5, isn't it?

Figure 10.4 Gemma's creation of new knowledge

In this extract, with the support of careful teacher questioning, Gemma creates a new piece of mathematical knowledge for herself. To do this she uses:

- known factual knowledge (10 × 5; 3 × 5);
- knowledge of multiplication as repeated addition;
- encouraged by the teacher, the strategy of partitioning 13 into 10 + 3 and multiplying these components separately by 5;
- her positive attitudes to mathematics to tackle a new calculation.

This creation of new knowledge in mental mathematics then involves factual knowledge, and selection of a relevant strategy. These aspects are underpinned by relevant conceptual knowledge and by positive attitudes to mathematics. As Figure 10.4 shows, this interweaving of different aspects of knowledge and understanding can be seen as a mathematical springboard for the creation of new knowledge and enhanced confidence in mathematics.

This way of working depends then on children knowing key aspects of the mathematical ideas underpinning the required calculation. The following quotation from a curriculum guidance document underlines this point, 'a sound understanding of the number system is fundamental to developing effective mental strategies' (SCAA, 1997, p. 14).

Research into children's mental mathematics

A research study conducted at Brunel University into children's mental mathematics gives an indication of the characteristics of children who are confident in such work. The findings of the research showed that at the end of Key Stage 2 such children:

- demonstrated a feel for numbers in mental mathematics, although this was not necessarily apparent in all aspects of their numeracy development. Typically, some children who were good at mental mathematics found written calculations difficult, and had sometimes been judged to be low attainers in numeracy work because of this;
- had a good bank of factual knowledge to use in their calculations;
- had a wide range of mental strategies;
- selected from this range a strategy which they felt was most appropriate for that particular calculation;
- could articulate the strategy they had used;
- checked their answers using an alternative strategy;
- often answered the questions rapidly.

All the children who were confident in mental mathematics also shared two further characteristics. Firstly, they showed the ability to 'juggle' with numbers, often opting for solutions which involved a series of number operations and/or a sequence of strategies. This finding is confirmed by the work of Ginsberg (1982) who showed that able children often adopt sophisticated and idiosyncratic methods of calculation in order to celebrate their creativity in calculating. Secondly, the children, again like those in Ginsberg's study, explained their ways of working with obvious confidence and enjoyment in their own creativity. Overall their attitudes to mental mathematics were characterised by the awareness of their own competence and confidence.

At the end of Key Stage 1 children who were confident at mental calculations had:

- a developing range of mental strategies, including strategies which had moved away from counting one by one in addition and subtraction calculations, and sometimes away from using repeated addition in multiplication calculations;
- a bank of instant recall factual knowledge, including typically knowledge of addition and subtraction bonds to 10 and of simple multiplication facts;
- iconic mental images which they used in their mental methods, such as images of numbers as arranged in dice or domino patterns, blocks of tens or hundreds, and number lines or number squares;
- strong knowledge of sequences of numbers. These included conventional sequences such as 10, 20, 30 ... as well as of other sequences such as 4, 14, 24 ... Some children could also count back in such sequences (for example, 60, 55, 50 ...);
- the beginnings of checking strategies and of decision making about how to do the calculation economically.

Like the Key Stage 2 children, the younger children had a sense of confidence in their work, and showed enjoyment of the processes of both calculating and discussing their calculations. The attainment of both groups indicates the power of Askew and Wiliam's (1995) contention that children's self-confidence and beliefs affect their success in mathematics.

The achievements of the confident and competent children in this research stand in contrast to the children in the research reported by Askew and Wiliam whose limited range of calculation strategies have been noted earlier in this chapter.

Implications for the teaching of mental mathematics

As has been noted previously, the NNS structure for the teaching of numeracy includes a heavy emphasis on the teaching of mental mathematics. This approach identifies the importance of:

- giving children opportunities to practise their mental mathematics regularly;
- testing children's knowledge regularly;
- using other assessment tools to monitor and record children's progress;
- integrating mental mathematics work with other aspects of numeracy development;
- direct teaching of relevant strategies.

From the detailed NNS teaching framework I have identified two teaching approaches which had particular significance in developing children's competence and confidence in numeracy in the Brunel University research on confident mental mathematicians. The two approaches are the use of oral mathematics and the importance of connecting children's knowledge of mental mathematics to other aspects of numeracy work.

Oral mathematics

Oral mathematics is defined by Jeffery (1997) as a term referring to all of the contexts of mathematics where talk is involved. It includes processes such as questioning, explaining, discussing, conjecturing and convincing. Oral mathematics is an essential element of the interactive teaching mode which the NNS suggests. Here the teacher's job is to enable children to explore their mathematical ideas orally, particularly in the introduction and the plenary to each lesson.

Encouraging children to talk about their mental mathematics is important for a number of reasons. Firstly, such talk enables the variety of ways of thinking to be demonstrated and celebrated. This opens the way for further discussion of key points such as:

- are there other ways of thinking which could be used here?
- which ways of thinking do the children find particularly useful? why is this?
- why have particular mental methods been used for particular contexts or calculations?
- how could estimates of the likely answers be obtained?
- how could the answers be checked?
- why does a particular mental method work?

The rationale for such discussions is that children will be able to share each other's ways of thinking and learn from one another as well as from the teacher. This will enable them to develop their repertoire of mental methods and their understanding of numeracy. It is also thought that talking about their methods of calculation and the mental images which accompany them helps to develop children's awareness of their thought processes. This 'thinking about thinking' in mathematics is often termed metacognition.

The use of oral mathematics raises further issues about teaching and learning. As the results of the practical activity may have shown, some adults find it difficult to communicate their thought processes. It is therefore not surprising to find that some children also find oral mathematics challenging. There are particular issues about this type of work for children who have English as an additional language and for children for whom speech is difficult. But all children face challenges in learning the appropriate mathematical language in which to communicate their thinking. As Pimm (1987) has identified, part of becoming a mathematician is learning the language of mathematics. Having the confidence to use aspects of this language to develop and communicate ways of working in mental mathematics is something from which children will benefit.

In the Brunel University research on confident mental mathematicians, a high percentage of the children, particularly at Key Stage 1, came from schools where there was a strong emphasis on oral mathematics. The children were therefore accustomed to talking about their ways of working. This had obviously given them increased confidence in using mathematical language to discuss their own strategies. It also seemed to have given them an increased awareness of their own knowledge and that of other children.

Connecting mental mathematics with other areas of number work

As mentioned previously, in the research, some of the children who were confident mental mathematicians at Key Stage 2 found written calculations difficult. Despite their competence in mental mathematics, they had sometimes been judged by their teachers to be low attainers because of these difficulties. It was clear from the research findings that these children could not connect their ability to calculate mentally to their written arithmetic. Their mental mathematics had sometimes been generated in contexts outside school (for example, going shopping or watching parents work with money). The children seemed to see this knowledge as unrelated to their work in school. They did not use their knowledge of mental mathematics when completing written calculations, but instead relied on rules learnt by rote. They rarely checked their work and did not seem to expect the answers to make sense. These findings have been replicated in the research of Carraher *et al.* (1990), Hughes (1986) and Ginsberg (1982). In such research, children are also shown to have difficulties understanding formal written arithmetic and relating its procedures to their informal understanding of numbers.

Mental mathematics work needs to be a central part of numeracy. As stated earlier in this chapter, knowledge of mental mathematics should underpin written arithmetic, work with practical resources and use of calculators. In order to enable children to use their mental mathematics in this way teachers need to encourage children to 'translate' (Hughes, 1986) between different areas of numeracy knowledge. In particular, children need support in translating between mental mathematics and written arithmetic. There are two ways in which this translation can be supported. Firstly, informal written methods can be developed and used. Secondly, mental mathematics can be used alongside formal written methods.

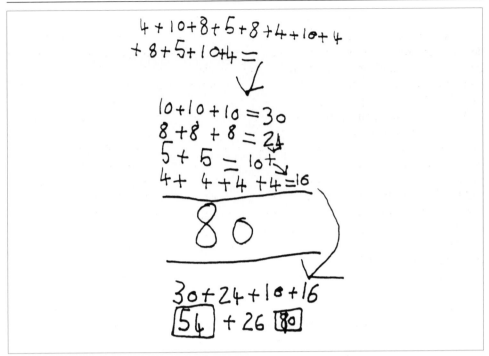

Figure 10.5 A pupil's own recording of addition

In 1989 the Non Statutory Guidance to the National Curriculum emphasised the importance of informal methods of writing down calculations. An example of an informal method is shown in Figure 10.5.

These informal methods can form a bridge between mental mathematics and written arithmetic. There is a growing interest in such methods, including the use of empty number lines (SCAA, 1997; Askew, 1998), horizontally presented sums (NNS, 1999) and encouraging alternative representations of calculations (Askew, 1998). More use of these informal methods in schools will enable children to translate between their mental mathematics knowledge and the written calculations they use.

Formal written methods of calculating can also be learnt in ways which encourage children to make such translations. Children should be encouraged to use mental mathematics to check that answers to formal written methods of calculating make sense. For such calculations a simple rubric for each sum of:

- estimate the likely answer;
- do the written calculation;
- ask yourself 'does this answer look correct?';
- check your answer

will enable most children to begin to connect mental and written methods.

Further development

This chapter has addressed some of the key issues about the teaching and learning of mental mathematics. It has stressed that confidence in mental mathematics is an essential element in numeracy development. Without such confidence children are unlikely to become competent and creative in their use of number knowledge. Mental mathematics can be developed through thinking and talking about methods of calculation and the mental images which accompany them. Mental mathematics needs to be connected to written arithmetic either through use of informal written methods or by ensuring that formal written methods are underpinned by the use of mental mathematics in estimating and checking answers.

In order to develop the ideas in this chapter further, two routes are suggested. Firstly, undertake further reading on the key issues, using the recommendations below as a starting point. Secondly, try out some of the practical activities in the books with children and gain a sense of how and why children at different stages of primary schooling calculate. It may also be possible to try adapted versions of the practical activities with children of different ages. Looking in more depth at children's use and understanding of mental mathematics will provide new starting points for teaching and learning.

Further reading

Askew, M. (1997) *Bridging the Gap in Junior Education*, Leamington Spa: Scholastic.
Askew, M. (1998) *Teaching Primary Mathematics*, London: Hodder and Stoughton.
Gorman, M. (1997) *Rewriting the Rules in Junior Focus*, Leamington Spa: Scholastic.
Mathematical Association (1992) *Mental Methods in Mathematics*, Mathematical Association.
National Numeracy Project (1997) *Mathematical Vocabulary*, BEAM.
SCAA (1997) *The teaching and assessment of number at Key Stages 1–3*.

Activities for children

Bibby, T. (1997) *Developing Mental Mathematics with 9–11 year olds*, Leamington Spa: Scholastic.
Fielker, D. (1993) *Starting From Your Head: Mental Number*, BEAM.
Kurta, J. (1997) *Developing Mental Maths with 7–9 year olds*, Leamington Spa: Scholastic.
Straker, A. (1992) *Talking Points in Mathematics*, Cambridge University Press.
Straker, A. (1994) *Mental Maths for Ages 9–11*, Cambridge University Press.

Acknowledgements

The practical activity included in this chapter was originally devised by Jan Potworowski and Bob Jeffery. It has been refined since then by various tutors and students at Brunel University. I have used an amended version of the original here.

In developing the ideas presented in this chapter, I acknowledge the contribution of many colleagues and students at Brunel. I would particularly like to thank Bob Jeffery and Debbie Robinson for the many discussions I have had with them about the teaching of numeracy.

References

Askew, M. (1998) *Teaching Primary Mathematics*, London: Hodder and Stoughton.
Askew, M. and Wiliam, D. (1995) *Recent Research in Mathematics Education 5–16*, London: Ofsted.

Carraher, T., Carraher, D. and Schliemann, A. (1990) 'Mathematics in the streets and in schools' in V. Lee (ed.) *Children's Learning in School*, London: Hodder and Stoughton.

DES (1982) *Mathematics Counts*, Report of the Inquiry into the teaching of Mathematics in schools under the Chairmanship of Dr. W. H. Cockcroft, London: HMSO.

DES (1985) *Mathematics from 5 to 16*, London: HMSO.

DfE (1995) *Mathematics in the National Curriculum*, London: HMSO.

DfEE (1998) *Teaching: High Status, High Standards. Circular 4/98*, London: HMSO.

Ginsberg, H. (1982) *Children's Arithmetic: the learning process*, New York: Van Nostrand.

Hughes, M. (1986) *Children and Number: Difficulties in Learning Mathematics*, Oxford: Basil Blackwell.

Jeffery, R. (1997) *Mental Arithmetic and Oral Mathematics*, London: Brunel University.

National Curriculum Council (NCC) (1989) *Mathematics Non Statutory Guidance*, London: NCC.

National Numeracy Strategy (NNS) (1999) *Framework for Numeracy,* London: DfEE.

Nunes, T. and Bryant, P. (1996) *Children Doing Mathematics*, Oxford: Blackwell.

Pimm, D. (1987) *Speaking Mathematically*, London: Routledge and Kegan Paul.

Plunkett, S. (1979) *Decomposition and All That Rot*, Mathematics in Schools 8.3, Association of Teachers of Mathematics.

SCAA (1997) *The Teaching and Assessment of Number at Key Stages 1–3*, London: Schools Curriculum and Assessment Authority.

Chapter 11

Children's mistakes and misconceptions

Valsa Koshy

Identifying and correcting children's misconceptions is recommended by the Numeracy Task Force (DfEE, 1998a) as a way of improving standards in mathematics; the new *Framework for Teaching Mathematics* (DfEE, 1999) implemented in primary schools from September 1999 requires teachers to address children's misconceptions and mistakes by a process of probing and questioning. The National Curriculum for Mathematics for initial training which was introduced by the Teacher Training Agency (DfEE, 1998b), requires teacher trainees to be taught how to:

> recognise common pupil errors and misconceptions in mathematics, and to understand how these arise, how they can be prevented and how to remedy them' (p. 370).

I have spent the last few months, with the help of teachers who attend the mathematics in-service courses at Brunel University, exploring issues relating to the identification of children's mistakes and misconceptions. Based on the feedback I received from teachers who took part in the project, I feel that the prominence given to this aspect is timely and justified.

What are mistakes and misconceptions? A clarification of the meanings of these words should in itself be useful. A mistake is described as a wrong idea or wrong action; a misconception is defined as a misunderstanding. A mistake can often be the result of a misconception, but not always so. Many other factors can contribute to children making mistakes.

The main purpose of including this chapter in this book is to assist the reader to consider how children's mistakes and misconceptions can be used to improve mathematics teaching and learning. I intend to do this in four sections devoted to:

- reflecting on the role of mistakes;
- analysing a sample of children's mistakes collected from classrooms;
- providing a commentary on some reasons for children's misconceptions and mistakes and on what action may be appropriate;
- considering the role of the teacher in addressing children's misconceptions.

The role of mistakes

Perhaps one of our first tasks should be to turn the negative connotations attached to mistakes into positive ones and start thinking about them as having a positive role in the teaching and learning of mathematics. This does not mean encouraging children to make mistakes but to encourage teachers to adopt a constructive attitude to their pupils' mistakes. In real life we have often heard people say 'I have learnt so much from that one mistake'. This comment may be made with reference to getting lost whilst travelling or feeling stronger after sorting out one's problems. After facing the consequences of one's wrong actions, whether deliberate or accidental, lessons are often learnt.

As in real life, mistakes made in mathematical lessons can also be very useful. They provide us with very useful insights into children's thinking and mathematical understanding. Mistakes which are persistent can often highlight gaps in the child's knowledge. One teacher who took part in the project explained how she always feels some unease when her children get several pages of sums right, because she feels she is not providing them with enough challenge. Another teacher who participated in the project claimed that as a result of looking for mistakes, she realised that the work she had been setting her children consisted mainly of 'closed' questions which did not encourage much thinking or development of reasoning and logic.

In this context it is useful to consider how children perceive making mistakes. Given the recent advice to teachers about the importance of analysing children's mistakes and remedying deficiencies, children's perceptions about making mistakes may change. But at present the work carried out by our teachers suggests that most children do not perceive mistakes as having any positive effect on their learning. When teachers asked their children to articulate, verbally or in writing, how they feel about making mistakes the following sample of responses was given. These responses display their feelings of anger, frustration and disappointment. Children's comments provide some useful pointers for the teacher.

- 'I think a mistake is something you do what you are not supposed to do. Sometimes you make one accidentally, sometimes it is because you don't understand what you are supposed to do. You shouldn't be told off for it. My teacher gets very cross when I make mistakes. She doesn't mind one mistake, but if you make many, then she does get cross.'
- 'Sometimes I hate you (teacher) when I make a mistake because you don't make sense, then it is your fault, not mine.'
- 'I feel imbarased (embarrassed) and I want to cry or run away. I feel stupid.'
- 'I don't mind when I make mistakes as long as teachers don't cross it out in front of others and show me up.'
- 'The angriest I got was when my teacher crossed my answer out because it was not the same as in the answer book, but when I checked it was really right. I had copied the sum wrong.'
- 'I make mistakes when I try to figure out something I have learnt but can't remember how to do it. I try very hard.'
- 'I make lots of mistakes when I am nervous like when you do a test of mental maths.'

Teachers' awareness of these attitudes possessed by children towards making mistakes is very useful in several respects. They highlight the need for sensitive handling of children who make mistakes. There is a need to create a culture where mistakes are acceptable and useful. It will be useful to remind ourselves that nervousness, fear, pressure of tests and failure and physical exhaustion can all contribute to both adults and children making more mistakes. A teacher needs to make a sensitive selection from a range of possible responses so that a more positive attitude to making mistakes can emerge.

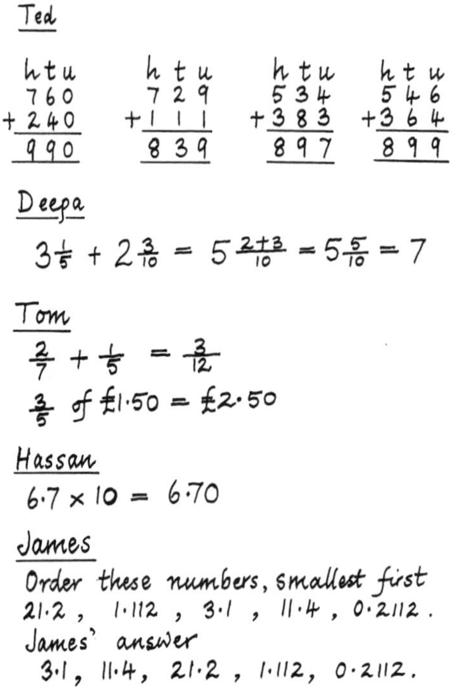

Ted

$$
\begin{array}{r}
h\ t\ u \\
7\ 6\ 0 \\
+\ 2\ 4\ 0 \\
\hline
9\ 9\ 0
\end{array}
\qquad
\begin{array}{r}
h\ t\ u \\
7\ 2\ 9 \\
+\ 1\ 1\ 1 \\
\hline
8\ 3\ 9
\end{array}
\qquad
\begin{array}{r}
h\ t\ u \\
5\ 3\ 4 \\
+\ 3\ 8\ 3 \\
\hline
8\ 9\ 7
\end{array}
\qquad
\begin{array}{r}
h\ t\ u \\
5\ 4\ 6 \\
+\ 3\ 6\ 4 \\
\hline
8\ 9\ 9
\end{array}
$$

Deepa

$$3\tfrac{1}{5} + 2\tfrac{3}{10} = 5\tfrac{2+3}{10} = 5\tfrac{5}{10} = 7$$

Tom

$$\tfrac{2}{7} + \tfrac{1}{5} = \tfrac{3}{12}$$

$$\tfrac{3}{5} \text{ of } £1.50 = £2.50$$

Hassan

$$6.7 \times 10 = 6.70$$

James

Order these numbers, smallest first

21.2 , 1.112 , 3.1 , 11.4 , 0.2112 .

James' answer

3.1 , 11.4 , 21.2 , 1.112 , 0.2112 .

Figure 11.1 Children's mistakes

A teaching environment where children are afraid to make mistakes is less likely to encourage the freedom of enquiry which is required for investigative work. If we want children to develop logic and reasoning, they will need the confidence to follow leads which may prove to be the wrong ones; they will need to feel it is OK to prove a conjecture to be wrong without the fear of failing. A close examination of the comments from children suggests that work needs to be done in this area.

Analysing children's mistakes

Figure 11.1 includes a selection of mistakes made by children from different age groups. It will be useful to analyse them and think about the possible reasons for children making them. This kind of analysis helps us to understand some of the sources of the errors and focus on the possible misconceptions held by children. The information gained through such analysis can then be taken into account in our teaching. You may want to do this task individually, in pairs or small groups. For each set of mistakes, make notes on:

what the child seems to know and do;
what the possible reasons are for making the mistakes;
what action you will take to help her/him.

After undertaking the task, read the next section where I have suggested some reasons for children making these mistakes. My explanations are derived from two sources: from teachers who did some probing of their children's thinking and from our collective attempts to make sense of the child's written responses.

A commentary on possible reasons for children's misconceptions and mistakes

Careless mistakes

Children make accidental mistakes. These are quite common and can be explained in terms of lack of practice, boredom and carelessness. It may be due to feeling pressure or fear. When such a mistake is pointed out to the child, it is useful to probe into the reasons for the mistake having been made. Careless mistakes are made by children of all ability levels. If you take the example of James, aged 7, who writes: $7 + 5 = 11$, it may be that he has recalled the number bond wrongly or started 'counting on' 5 from 7 as 7, 8, 9, 10, 11. Asking children to explain how they have tackled a particular piece of work will help the teacher to take appropriate action. If the reason for making the above mistake is the latter, the teacher will need to do some explicit teaching of the 'counting on' strategy, perhaps using a number line. She will also need to keep a watchful eye to see whether James has now acquired the necessary skills.

Reliance on rules

Learning how to generalise, through a good understanding of the reasoning behind rules, is an effective way of learning mathematics. At the same time, a large number of misconceptions and mistakes also originate from reliance on rules which either have been not understood, forgotten or only partly remembered.

If we refer to Ted's row of sums, in Figure 11.1, it shows that he can add two digits accurately, but is 'mixed up' with the carrying aspect of addition. He has learnt a rule on which the place value system is based. I consider that appreciating this rule – that the largest number you could have in a column is 9 – requires quite a sophisticated level of reasoning. Ted follows the rule correctly, but does not know what to do with the rest of the number, as he has not grasped the underlying principle behind that rule. In Ted's case analysing his written work alone provides valuable information for his teacher. Although he has made mistakes, his level of thinking suggests that this misconception may be remedied quite easily by discussing and perhaps demonstrating the 'grouping' and 'carrying' aspects of the place value concept with him.

Deepa's sum too shows misapplication of a rule; this, however, shows a lack of understanding of the concept of fractions. With 5 as the numerator and 10 as the denominator one would expect her to see that it could not produce an answer of 2 whole ones. The rest of her calculation shows accuracy and competence although it is possible that the correct procedures she has adopted may also be the result of rules that she has remembered. Only a probing interview with her will enlighten the teacher as to the scale of misunderstanding. Adding 'tops and bottoms' of fractions, in the case of Tom, is a common mistake which is based on a forgotten rule. This may be the result of a lack of conceptual understanding of what fractions are about. Asking Tom to describe what a fifth and two fifths means may encourage him to rethink his strategy. 'Learning from one's mistakes' may well be the case here because of the teacher's timely prompt. Tom's answer to what is three fifths of £1.50 suggests that he may have used a partly or wrongly remembered rule to work this sum out.

Although generalisations play an important part in performing mathematics tasks, the generalisations need to be explained carefully. It is easy for a child to over-generalise a rule and apply it in wrong contexts as in the case of Hassan who has learnt and applied the rule 'add a zero when you multiply by 10,' which works for whole numbers. Whether it is a lack of understanding of 'decimal' numbers or whether he chose an easier option of using a generalisation is hard to tell. The importance of highlighting when and how rules are applicable is a useful reminder here.

James too has relied on a generalisation he has made, that 'the larger the number of digits, the larger the size of the number'. He has used this rule to order decimal numbers. James's teacher, Caroline, was surprised to find out that James, who was 'in the top set and did very well usually' had such a misconception which prompted her to investigate how many other children had subcribed to this rule. During the following week, she did some targeted teaching to remedy the misunderstanding using number lines, decimal cakes and so on. Caroline had this to say about her experience:

> It is amazing how the decimal cakes idea helped children to understand the size of decimal *numbers*. It encouraged them to develop an imagery of whole and parts of cakes. It did have a stunning effect on the number of decimal operations they did afterwards.

Many of the mistakes children make with written algorithms are due to their misconceptions relating to 'place value' of numbers. Although the base ten number system provides a sensible and efficient system, many of the mistakes children make are due to a lack of understanding of the grouping aspect on which the system is based. When considering this aspect it is worth pointing out that children tend to make more mistakes with subtraction than with the other operations. Melissa's explanation as to why she has crossed the numbers out was:

$$\require{cancel}{}^3\cancel{6}\,{}^1 0\,{}^1 0\,{}^1 0$$
$$-\qquad\qquad 4$$

Teacher: I see lots of ones and crossings out, Melissa tell me what you are doing here.
Melissa: Well, I said nothing take away 4, you can't do. Normally I would go next door. That is a waste of time here because there are zeros in the next two places. So I thought I'd save time and take 3 from the 6 and put one next to each of the numbers.

Melissa does not seem to be aware of the principles behind the 'crossing out' process used in this method which is usually referred to as 'decomposition'. There are two issues here for her teacher to deal with. First, according to her teacher, if Melissa was asked to take 4 away from 6000, she would have got the correct answer. The text book had presented this sum vertically which led Melissa to believe that she was expected to do a crossing out sum. This poses the question of whether vertical sums are the best way to proceed in this case. The second part of the action is to find out the extent of Melissa's possible misunderstanding in order to ascertain the nature of what needs to be done. Remediation here could involve a step-by-step explanation and modelling using appropriate apparatus. Practical advice , based on research findings, by SCAA (1997) on aspects of teaching place value makes very useful reading. Koshy (1998) provides practical suggestions for discussing place value ideas with children using specially designed place value arrow cards and calculators.

What I have referred to so far is based on the samples of examples in Figure 11.1. Other mistakes children make when operating on whole numbers, such as:

```
  2 4 7
  1 2
  9
+ 8 3
─────────
2 0 9 7
─────────
```

and the insertion of extra zeros when writing numbers, e.g. writing fifty-five as 505, six hundred and thirty-five as 600305, can also be due to a lack of understanding of applying the place value system. To remedy these mistakes, the use of structured apparatus is often recommended. I would add, however, that the use of structured apparatus alone is not enough. Teacher input in the form of discussions is also vital in helping pupils to make the connections between the formal apparatus and related concepts.

Mistakes due to problems with language and mathematical vocabulary

David's mistakes (shown in Figure 11.2) with subtraction puzzled his teacher. Whilst marking his work it took her some time to work out the possible reason for his page full of mistakes. Her speculation that he confused the two words, subtraction and multiplication was confirmed when she asked David to explain what he was doing. He did not know that 'subtraction meant take away'. This highlights the importance of learning the range of words used in mathematics. Section B of this book should offer much help in this respect.

Many children's mistakes arise from their misunderstanding of the vocabulary in use. For example, we cannot assume that a child who has heard the word 'take way' to refer to 'take away' food will readily accept that the same phrase is used to refer to subtraction. The teacher may want to speculate , with the children, on how the phrase 'take away' which means buying food and taking it away from the premises may be related to the process of subtraction.

It is also common for children to be confused about terms such as 'face' 'vertex' and 'parallel' when learning about shapes. They may also have difficulties remembering words such as 'mean', 'median' and 'mode' in handling data. The terminology used in connection with graphical representations, e.g. pie charts, histograms, is another source of confusion and resultant errors. One possible support is the reinforcement of these words through classroom displays of the correct mathematics vocabulary. One teacher asked her children to make up their own 'glossary' of mathematical terms. Children were asked to design and list all the mathematical terms and corresponding illustrations as they learnt new mathematical words. Constructing their own glossary, according to the teacher, was more effective than using mathematical dictionaries and giving photocopied lists of words. The book *Mathematical*

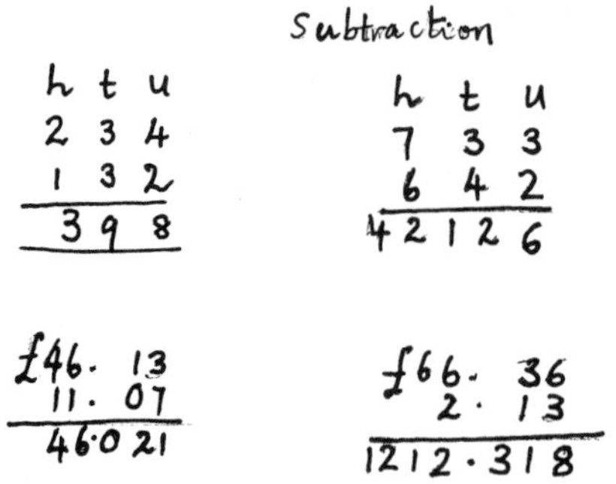

Subtraction

```
  h  t  u              h   t   u
  2  3  4              7   3   3
  1  3  2              6   4   2
 ---------            -----------
  3  9  8            4 2 1 2  6
```

```
 £46.  13            £66.  36
  11.  07             2.  13
 ---------           -----------
 46·0 21            1212·318
```

Figure 11.2 David's subtraction mistakes

Vocabulary, recommended in the National Numeracy framework (BEAM, 1997) is a very useful resource to have in all classrooms.

Most of us are familiar with mistakes children make when they get mixed up between the two words 'area' and 'perimeter'. This type of mistake may not be due to misunderstandings about the concepts involved; some kind of personalised way of remembering these words is often helpful. Memory tricks are useful; for example, the Y coordinate, as opposed to the X coordinate was described by one child as 'the one with the tail coming down'. Index numbers pose another source of confusion for children, as 2^3 is often given as 6 , not as $2 \times 2 \times 2 = 8$. Making up rhymes can act as memory aids. Anticipating these mistakes allows the teacher to address these at the planning and teaching stages.

Mistakes when special cases present themselves

Children make mistakes, as can be seen in Figure 11.3, when they are engaged in calculations which involve the use of different bases. They use an algorithm which they are familiar with (in this case, a base 10 algorithm) without actually thinking about what the task is about. Quite often, asking a child who has made these mistakes to use another method instead of using the vertical format may help to highlight the fact that a wrong base was selected for the calculation. This kind of 'checking' in another way is likely to help the child to remember these ' special cases' in the future.

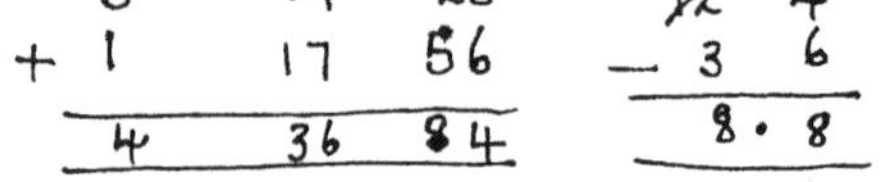

```
  day    hr    min          wk   day
   3    ¹19   ²28          ¹¹ ¹
 +  1     17    56          1Z  ⁴4
 -----------------         -  3    6
   4     36    84          --------
                           8 · 8
```

Figure 11.3 Mistakes in special cases

Mistakes in solving numerical problems

Teachers who took part in our project listed three types of mistakes made by children when they were engaged in solving problems. The first type involved children looking for 'clue' words. This strategy was articulated by 9-year-old Ben who provided a list of such 'helpful' words. His list included: ' "difference" means a subtraction sum, "more" and "altogether" mean addition sums, "times" to do multiplication and "share" to do division.' When faced with a problem: *Natasha has 34 stamps which is 11 more than what her brother Sam has, how many stamps has Sam got?*, a child who uses the 'clue' strategy is likely to use the word clue 'more' to do an addition sum and get the answer 45. Discussion of 'reasonableness' of the solution should encourage the child to question the effectiveness of the 'clue' strategy.

The second type of mistake, relating to the the role of context, is also worth exploring. It is reasonable to assume that a child who has not heard about 'exchange' rates may have difficulties when asked to work out: *Express in pounds the cost of a computer being sold in the Unites States for $3300.* The effect of context does influence the way children interpret problems and make decisions about appropriate calculations; readers are encouraged to read the section on the effects of context in the SCAA (1997) discussion paper for further enlightenment on this aspect.

The third type of mistake, the kind of response to word problems, occurs when children offer unexpected solutions to word problems due to their 'unusual' and sometimes 'creative' interpretations of the contexts. Research being carried out into mathematical performances of higher ability pupils at the able children's education unit at Brunel University suggests that more able pupils tend to question the contexts offered to them, more than their peers, in problem-solving situations. For example, during a test 10-year-old Paul decided not to give an answer to the problem: *What speed was a cyclist travelling if he covered 16 miles in 8 hours?* His answer: 'need more information for this, was the cyclist travelling against gravity? The question suggests so, judging from the distance he covered' *would probably be marked 'wrong' in an examination, although it is based on his reasoning.*

What can teachers do?

In this section, I will briefly discuss how teachers may address children's misconceptions and mistakes. When children's mistakes show consistency, as some of the examples given earlier in this chapter show, it may be relatively easy to work on them by asking the child to explain the method and discussing the strategies in order to clear up the misunderstanding.

Whether planning is done in groups or individually, it will be useful for teachers to reflect on possible misconceptions children hold and be to pro-active in addressing them. In the context of addressing children's misunderstanding of decimals, Discussion paper 10 from SCAA (1997) suggests that two specific approaches can be adopted:

> First, teaching that takes such misconceptions into account, tries to anticipate why pupils might develop them, and structures lessons in such a way as to encourage correct understanding and prevent such misunderstanding developing in the first place. An alternative approach is one that acknowledges pupils' misconceptions and presents pupils with experiences that expose their misconceptions, works explicitly on them and raises pupils' awareness of the inadequacies of their existing ideas, thus making them receptive to the introduction of correct concepts (p. 12).

For example, teachers who are aware of the types of misconception held by children when they 'order' numbers or when working with decimal numbers, may decide to use more appropriate teaching methods and visual aids to facilitate greater understanding of the complex concepts involved. In our 'mistakes' project, teachers claimed that by using carefully selected apparatus, appropriate questioning and discussions to teach place value of both whole numbers and decimal numbers , children showed greater confidence and understanding of the concepts. Another example of the use of practical apparatus and appropriate discussion will be to challenge children's perceptions of the properties of shapes. In Cockburn's (1998) excellent book, she refers to the problems created by the standard representations of triangles with their 'edges parallel to the sides of the page' in textbooks. Children may fail to recognise the same shapes represented in different orientations. A teacher who actively encourages children to discuss properties of triangles or asks children to act as LOGO turtles and follow instructions to draw triangles are likely to help those children avoid such misconceptions.

Indeed, a consideration of teaching styles is important too. A teaching style which encourages children to discuss their methods with the teacher and with other pupils is likely to be more effective in exposing misconceptions. Listening to other children should encourage a reconsideration and refinement of one's own strategies. Probing children through sensitive questioning about their work, both their correct and incorrect responses, should also prove helpful.

Asking children to look at collections of mistakes made by 'imaginary' children and analyse them, in the same way as mentioned previously in this chapter, has also been reported to have a positive impact on those children who did the analysis. Even children who felt anxious about making mistakes enjoyed looking for reasons for other children's mistakes and sensitively suggesting how they could avoid such mistakes in the future. Such opportunities could be incorporated into the daily planning of the Numeracy Hour. This process of analysing mistakes and looking for the rationale behind strategies will almost certainly help children to 'explain' their own methods logically, which is a requirement in the SATs paper.

Final thoughts

If children's misconceptions are anticipated and addressed it is likely that gaps in children's understanding can be remedied, which in turn will help them to develop a more robust framework of conceptual understanding. It is also likely that an enhanced understanding of concepts will enable children to recall rules correctly, or at least reconstruct forgotten or partially remembered rules.

The teachers who took part in the our small project claimed that the awareness created by collecting and analysing children's misconceptions and mistakes and the experience of conducting short interviews with children to ascertain their strategies have helped their planning, choice and use of resources, teaching styles and the way they mark children's work. I too remain convinced that in a classroom where children's responses – both correct and incorrect – are valued, children's self-confidence will be enhanced. That self-confidence will ultimately help them to develop a positive attitude towards mathematics as a subject and raise standards of achievement.

References

BEAM (1997) *Mathematical Vocabulary*, London: BEAM.

Cockburn, A.(1998) *Teaching Mathematics with Insight*, London: Falmer Press.

DfEE (1998a) *Numeracy Matters. The Preliminary Report of the Numeracy Task Force*, London.

DfEE (1998b) *Teaching: High Status, High Standards. Circular Number 4/98*, London.

DfEE (1999) *Framework for Teaching Mathematics*, London.

Koshy, V. (1998) *Mental Maths: Teachers' Guides 1, 2, and 3*, London: Collins Educational.

SCAA (1997) *The Teaching and Assessment of Number at Key Stages 1–3. Discussion Paper 10*, March 1997, London: SCAA.

Useful reading

Dickson, L., Brown, M. and Gibson, O. (eds) (1984) *Children Learning Mathematics: A Teachers' Guide to Recent Research*, Eastbourne: Holt, Rinehart and Winston.

Ginsburg, H. P. (1977) *Children's Arithmetic: The Learning Process*, New York: Van Nostrand.

Hart, K. (1981) *Children's Understanding of Mathematics, 11–16*, London: John Murray.

Hughes, M. (1986) *Children and Number: Difficulties in Learning Mathematics*, Oxford: Basil Blackwell.

Chapter 12

Using writing to scaffold children's explanations in mathematics

Christine Mitchell and William Rawson

Since the 1988 Education Reform Act and the development of a National Curriculum for mathematics, primary teachers have been required to provide children with opportunities to 'explain their thinking' and 'develop their reasoning' (DFE and Welsh Office, 1995). This focus on process skills as well as curriculum content is also given explicit attention in the National Numeracy Strategy (DfEE, 1998a) recommendations. For example, numerate pupils should 'explain their methods and reasoning using correct mathematical terms' as well as 'explain and make predictions from the numbers in graphs, diagrams, charts and tables' (p. 12). Moreover, as part of the daily mathematics lesson, children should receive 'good direct teaching' that 'allows pupils to show what they know, explain their thinking and methods, and suggest alternative ways of tackling problems' (p. 14). Children are also required to provide explanations and reasons as part of the end of Key Stage 2 national assessment tests (see Figure 12.1).

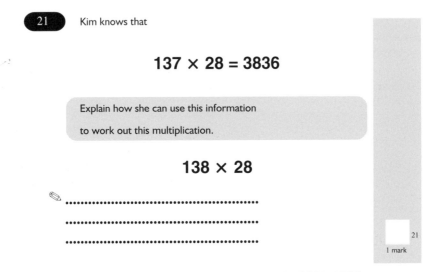

Figure 12.1 Key Stage 2 Standard Assessment Test A Question 21 (SCAA, 1997)

Given the statutory requirement to focus on developing explanations and reasoning skills, we would like to consider the following questions:

- In what ways is explicit attention given to this aspect of children's development in mathematics?
- How can writing in mathematics be used to enhance children's explanations?

Teaching towards developing children's explanations and reasoning

Text-based teaching

The advent of the National Numeracy Strategy may well herald a change in the culture of primary mathematics teaching. However, since the 1960s, many schools have centred their mathematics work on a commercial mathematics scheme with children working in isolation through the text or workbook pages. Under these circumstances, more often than not, children are simply practising skills and rehearsing facts as they respond to imperatives such as: *how many…? find the missing number; find the difference; copy and complete…* Even some texts specifically designed to support the skills of using and applying mathematics have exercise pages which simply lead children through a series of tasks (see Figure 12.2). Children are not required to explain the 'why' or the 'how' of their actions or thinking even for those questions which have the potential for a thoughtful as opposed to largely procedural response. See, for example, the final question in Figure 12.2: *If you could keep either the coins on your foot, or the coins round it, which would you choose?*.

Many commercial mathematics schemes provide teachers' handbooks which encourage teachers to seek explanations from children. For example, *STEPS 1 Mathematics* (Woodman, 1995) has designated sections within the handbook to focus the teacher's attention on children thinking and talking mathematically. At the same time, the suggested activities for children encourage teacher–pupil and pupil–pupil interaction. For example:

> Ask pairs of children to look around the room and choose a set of objects which go together, and to explain their selection. Leave the sets on display so that other children can guess the criteria for sorting (p. 31).

However, there is no firm evidence that teachers make use of such guidance, particularly if they are monitoring a large class of children all working at their own pace on individual tasks. Hence, it is highly likely that many children working on mathematics from published material will not be challenged to explain their thinking either by the text or by the teacher. Neither does the text provide the children with exemplar explanations.

Mental calculations

Since the early 1980s, there has been increasing emphasis on developing children's number competence by promoting mental methods of calculation and giving less attention to standard written procedures or algorithms. Children are encouraged to invent and to share their own informal strategies for working in the head based on an 'at-homeness' (the Cockcroft Report,

Figure 12.2 Extract from *Ginn Mathematics 2 Using and Applying Mathematics* pp 2–3 (original in colour) Merttens (1992), reporduced with the publisher's permission.

DES, 1982) with numbers. In this way, children have access to a range of non-standard methods for calculating. For example, Nasreen (Year 4) explains her methods of adding a pair of two-digit numbers mentally (see Figure 12.3). Similar examples are well documented. One such source is the *Exemplification of Standards* (SCAA, 1995) material circulated to all primary schools.

Rawson (1998) highlights that children need to be challenged to explain both *how* and *why* their method works. In other words, children need to be prompted to move beyond an initial description of their mental method thereby providing a '*means by which children's understanding of the number system is enhanced and … a natural entrance for [our] pupils to work towards higher order mathematical thinking*' (p. 16). Teaching primary children to ask questions, explain their thinking, predict outcomes, recognise patterns and relationships, formulate and investigate generalisations, and check the reasonableness of their results provides them with the essential processes for later work on the higher order thinking represented by mathematical proof. Yet the research evidence shows that providing children with opportunities to develop their explanations and reasoning remains problematic for many teachers.

Research findings

Evidence from the evaluation of the National Curriculum undertaken by Askew *et al.* (1993) suggests that in the early stages of implementing the using and applying programme of study, the mathematical reasoning strand was given very little attention by teachers. Significantly

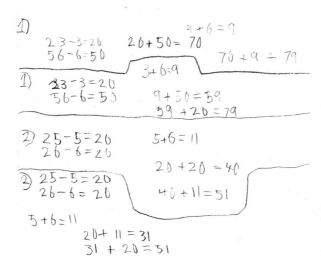

Figure 12.3 Nasreen's explanation of how she calculated 23 + 56 and 25 + 26

more attention was given to the provision of practical activities and using mathematics in 'real-life', everyday situations. Similarly, research by Hughes, Desforges and Mitchell (forthcoming) revealed that making provision for developing mathematical reasoning and providing opportunities for children to explain their thinking were rarely evident in the examples of classroom practice provided by the teachers in their study. Nevertheless, one of their project teachers described how some of her Y6 children had to provide a reasoned, written account for the headteacher to enable him to order building materials to make a science equipment storage area. Another teacher described how her Y2 children had to keep an account of trading at a classroom car boot sale. In both of these examples, some form of explanation was necessary in order to complete the task satisfactorily: the task *prompted* the explanation.

Writing in mathematics to enhance children's explanations and reasoning

Since the early 1980s and the publication of *Mathematics Counts* (the 'Cockcroft Report', DES, 1982), mathematics educators have been giving explicit attention to the use of discussion and the development of mathematical language in mathematics lessons. One of the Cockcroft recommendations states:

> The ability to 'say what you mean and mean what you say' should be one of the outcomes of good mathematics teaching. This ability develops as a result of opportunities to talk about mathematics, to explain and discuss results which have been obtained, and to test hypotheses (para. 246).

Burton (1994) suggests that as many different modes of communication as possible should be available in the mathematics classroom and argues that different forms suit different children. Nevertheless, in this section, we concentrate on writing in mathematics and explore how writing can provide the forum for teachers and children to focus on the development of reasoning.

We have taken writing as the focus of attention, firstly, a response to the challenge from HMI (1985) that *'Writing about mathematics is not generally developed. There is a lot of "written work" connected with "exercises" but there is little communication of mathematical ideas in writing'* (p. 13). This view is reiterated in the research of Marks and Mousley (1990) who identify a paucity of different writing genres in mathematics teaching, children's work and textbooks.

Secondly, we focus on writing in response to the expectation of the National Literacy Strategy (DfEE, 1998b) which directs attention to particular literacy skills relevant across National Curriculum subjects: *'Skills, especially those that focus on reading and writing non-fiction texts should be linked to and applied in every subject'* (p. 3).

And finally, we focus on writing because of the important differences between speech (discussion) and writing. For example, in a spoken explanation the voice can be used to give emphasis to certain points or details (Perera, 1987). Alternatively, body language or gesture can be used, leaving the listener (teacher) to infer, and possibly even voice, the critical features of the explanation. The prompts that are available to children in conversation or discussion with the teacher are not normally available in writing and may have nothing to do with mathematical reasoning anyway. Writing an explanation necessarily involves far more attention to detail and rigour.

Working with writing frames

The Exeter Extending Literacy (EXEL) Project (Lewis and Wray, 1995), funded by the Nuffield Foundation attends to the demands of non-fiction writing placed upon children at primary school. Researchers Lewis and Wray conjecture that children's early attempts at non-fiction writing might successfully be assisted by framing structures. Writing frames consist of skeleton outlines which help children to use the generic structures and language features of recount, report, procedure, explanation, exposition and discussion. Children use these until they become familiar enough with the written structures to have assimilated them into their writing repertoire.

The model of teaching underpinning the EXEL project builds upon the ideas of Vygotsky (1978). Particular attention is given to the teacher as expert and learner as novice relationship. Figure 12.4 summarises the phases of activity as expert and novice collaborate on a new task. Initially, the expert takes the lead modelling or demonstrating. The novice gradually joins in the task, taking more and more responsibility but supported and assisted throughout by the expert. Finally, the novice is experienced and accomplished enough to work independently and the expert becomes supportive audience.

The EXEL project highlighted that in relation to developing children's writing:

> … children are too often expected to move into the independent writing phase before they are really ready and often the pressure to do so is based on the practical problem of teachers being unable to find the time to spend with them in individual support. What is clearly needed is something to span the joint activity and independent activity phase. We have called this the scaffolded phase … (p. 5).

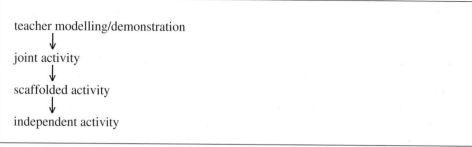

Figure 12.4 The EXEL teaching model

Writing frames provide teachers with a scaffolding strategy to support children in their writing development without an adult necessarily being alongside them. The frames offer prompts for children in their first attempts at independent writing in an unfamiliar genre. An example of a frame which enables children to reflect on their own learning can be seen in Figure 12.5.

Although I already knew that …

I have learnt some new facts …

I also learnt that …

Another fact I learnt …

However the most interesting thing I learnt was …

Figure 12.5 Writing frame example (Wray and Lewis, 1998, p. 7)

Writing frames for mathematics

The early EXEL research work was extended to include 25 teachers from Devon KS1, KS2 and middle schools. The focus for the group was to consider the function of writing in the development of mathematical thinking. Tentative agreement was reached concerning a range of genres that exist in writing mathematics:

- **report** offers a non-chronological description, e.g. *This is what I know about triangles …*
- **recount** retells events in chronological order, e.g. *In order to add 63 + 94, I added 10 to 94 giving 104, then added 50 giving 154, and finally I added 3 to give a total of 157.*
- **enquiry** establishes a way of working through a problem, e.g. *My task is to find out what happens when I draw different shapes all with the same area. I think that they will have different perimeters.*
- **explanation** consists of logical steps that inform how or why something works, e.g. *I turned the pencil until it pointed in the opposite direction. This is called a half turn. When you make a half turn you turn through 180 degrees.*

- **proof** gives evidence of some sort or other and draws logical conclusions from this evidence, e.g. *I know that a triangle is a closed shape made of 3 straight lines. This means that it has 3 interior angles …*
- **planning** provides information on how to tackle a particular investigation, e.g. *I know that I have to fill the jar with something in order to find its capacity. I will then need to measure what I have used to fill the jar.*

Initially, a range of frames were designed to represent each genre. The group of teachers then began to trial, redesign, collect, discuss and analyse examples of children's work using the mathematics writing frames. The following examples demonstrate what can happen as teachers and children use frames to support writing in mathematics with a particular emphasis on extending children's explanations and reasoning skills.

Using recount frames in handling data

Judith wanted her Y1 and Y2 children to concentrate on interpreting graphical representations. She wanted to focus on their ability to read and reason from the data presented. A brainstorming session with the class resulted in the frame in Figure 12.6.

Judith was pleased with the outcomes and highlighted these two comments from different children: 'I noticed only 2 liked oranges.'; 'So I think most people like fruit.' The final prompt of this frame encourages a reasoned conclusion introducing the [and] so form. It is at this point that Judith's children responded at different levels of sophistication:

- 'So I think most people like fruit'
- 'So I think the bananas are most popl (popular)'
- 'So I think I licke (like) bananas'
- 'So I think Mrs Shaw will like my piece of work'

In this way, reviewing several completed frames together with the whole class gave Judith an opportunity to compare and discuss which responses were more appropriate in the mathematical sense. The frames were an excellent reference point in terms of formative assessment, helping to identify individual's successes and pinpointing the focus for the next phase of teacher modelling.

Using recount frames to reveal children's thinking

Many of the recent initiatives in mathematics education have stressed the importance of developing children's mental methods for calculating. Encouraging children to share their idiosyncratic methods with each other helps to extend the range of strategies available to the children. Nevertheless, not only is it important to provide children with opportunities to describe their thinking but also it is essential to challenge them to explain why their approach works. Designing a frame with this in mind is not as easy as it first seems! For example, the frame in Figure 12.7 was trialled by Andy with both Y2 and Y3 children.

Andy commented that the younger children initially needed considerable support in scribing their responses and he found this particular frame needed redesigning with fewer initial starting prompts:

I decided to …

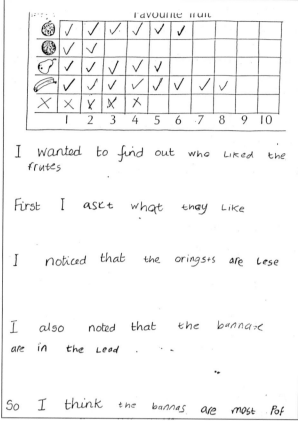

Figure 12.6 Completed mathematics writing frame (Y2 child)

Then I …
I found that …

At the same time, the frame in Figure 12.7 does not move Jessica (Y3) beyond an initial description of how she completed her calculation, whereas the frame in Figure 12.8 *requires* Natasha (Y6) to justify the processes she is using. This frame provides the pupil with a model that helps to keep a chronological order and, at each step, provide and explanation of why this action is taken.

Using a 'proof' frame for investigations

Anne teaches a Year 5/6 class (9–11 year olds). She wanted the children to spend most of the term doing mathematics investigations of one kind or another. She used the writing frame to help them express how and why they had arrived at a particular result in their mathematics work.

My task is to …
I think that …
One reason for thinking that is …
Another reason is …

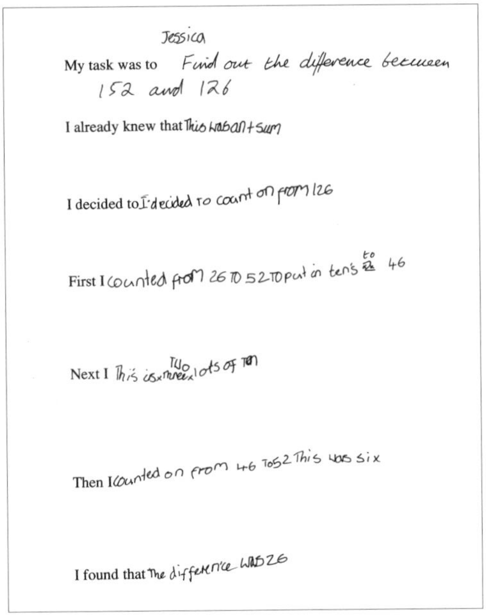

Jessica

My task was to Find out the difference between 152 and 126

I already knew that This was an + sum

I decided to I decided to count on from 126

First I counted from 26 to 52 to put in ten's to 46

Next I This is two lots of ten

Then I counted on from 46 to 52 This was six

I found that The differnce was 26

Figure 12.7 Completed mathematics writing frame: Jessica Y3

In addition to this …

This is why I think that …

Anne commented: ‘The children in my class have been used to exploring and discussing various strategies and sharing with others their reasoning in producing their results in their maths work. They have also written down their reasoning from time to time.’ Anne went on to identify how some of her class could explain their thinking orally but ‘couldn’t get it down the same way on paper’.

Nevertheless, Anne highlighted how her more able children adapted their use of the writing frame. They were confident enough to cross out starting phrases (see Figures 12.9 and 12.10) or complete two tasks using one frame (see Figure 12.10). In relation to the model of teaching described earlier (Figure 12.4), Amy and Michael are operating more at the independent rather than scaffolded phase of the activity continuum. Their written accounts include some of the essential features and vocabulary of reasoning (if, then, therefore, and so...). For example, from Amy’s frame in Figure 12.9:

> Another reason is *If angle D was made into 90°*
> *90 – 55 = 35. Therefore, angle Y is 180 – 35 which equals 145.*

Michael began his use of the writing frame by crossing out two of the prompts (Figure 12.10: ‘One reason for thinking this is …’ and ‘Another reason is …’). However, he changed his mind and, having re-instated them, provided some detailed reasons. His final more free-flowing account includes some of the traditional reasoning vocabulary:

> *The x angle is 125 because the angles of a triangles is 180°*
> *(90 + 35 + 55 = 180 and so 180 – 55 = 125 so the angle x = 125).*

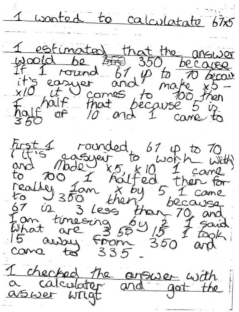

Figure 12.8 Natasha's explanation (Y6)

The initial task for Amy and Michael was to 'calculate the size of angles *x* and y'. The writing frame ensured that they had a *context* for explaining their thinking and the prompts gave some initial focus as to the *form* of the explanation. This can also be seen in the example provided in Figure 12.11. Daniel is described by Anne as in the middle ability range for mathematics work. Once again, the frame has 'forced' Daniel to share his reasons for why he would rather have a present for each day he has lived rather than a present for every second in twelve hours.

The initial prompts led him to connect his reasons with his conclusion and in so doing he began to include the '[and] *so*' form even though there is some error in his calculations!

> Another reason is *that there are 3600 seconds in an hour which is half of the answer for the days* so *it must be the seconds.*

Moreover, the penultimate starting phrase of this frame 'In addition to this ...' prompted Daniel to think beyond the immediate problem and consider other cases:

> In addition to this I think *it might be different for someone older than me because I multiplied 10* [his age] *by 365.*

Turning this additional thought into his next line of enquiry might have resulted in Daniel generating a generalisation for the investigation or at least discovering that you have to be around 119 years old before it is better to have a present for every day that you have lived!

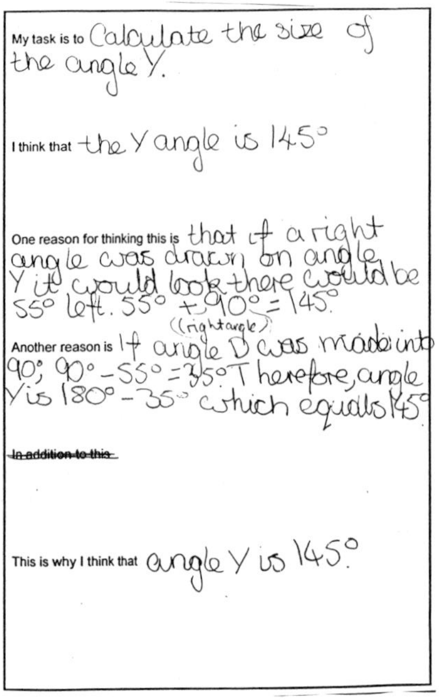

My task is to Calculate the size of the angle Y.

I think that the Y angle is 145°

One reason for thinking this is that if a right angle was drawn on angle Y it would look there could be 55° left. 55° + 90° = 145°. (rightangle)

Another reason is If angle D was made into 90°, 90° - 55° = 35°. Therefore, angle Y is 180° - 35° which equals 145°

~~In addition to this~~

This is why I think that angle Y is 145°

Figure 12.9 Amy's frame (Y6)

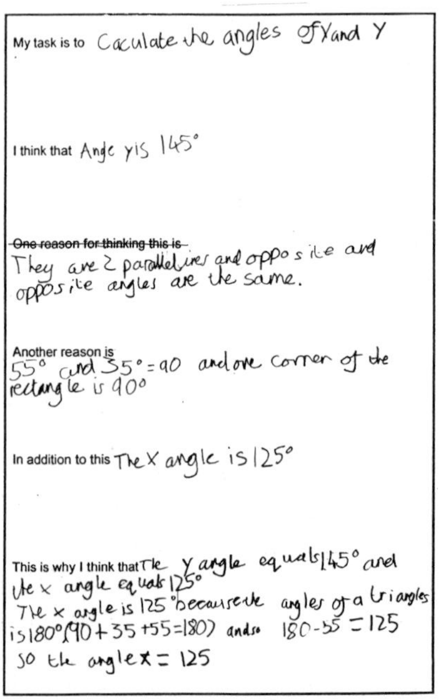

My task is to Caculate the angles of X and Y

I think that Angle y is 145°

~~One reason for thinking this is~~
They are 2 parallel lines and oppo site and opposite angles are the same.

Another reason is
55° and 55° = 90 and one corner of the rectangle is 90°

In addition to this The X angle is 125°

This is why I think that The Y angle equals 145° and the x angle equals 125°
The x angle is 125° because the angles of a triangle is 180° (90 + 35 + 55 = 180) and so 180 - 55 = 125
So the angle x = 125

Figure 12.10 Michael's frame (Y6)

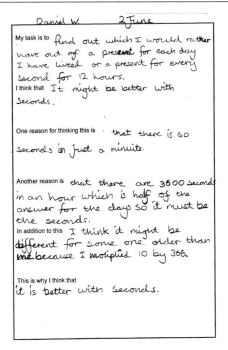

Daniel W.   2 June

My task is to find out which I would rather
have out of a present for each day
I have lived or a present for every
second for 12 hours.
I think that It might be better with
seconds.

One reason for thinking this is : that there is 60
seconds in just a minuite.

Another reason is that there are 3600 seconds
in an hour which is half of the
answer for the days so it must be
the seconds.
In addition to this I think it might be
different for some one older than
me because I motiplied 10 by 365.

This is why I think that
it is better with seconds.

Figure 12.11 Daniel's frame (Y6)

Conclusion

Many of the project teachers commented that introducing the frames to the children takes time initially. Anne highlighted how it was necessary for the content side of her mathematics work to be given less attention for a while:

> the focus of the lesson became explain your reasoning and that was what I was wanting the children to get better at in that particular lesson. In other words, using the frames throws up the importance of the section in the National Curriculum that concentrates on explaining reasoning and while children are learning that skill the forward movement of the rest of the maths curriculum is slowed down. Once the skill is on board the two move forward together.

Nevertheless, writing frames provide both teachers and children with a common focus to *force awareness* (Gattegno, 1987) of the nature of mathematical explanation. This awareness is rarely explicitly addressed in commercial primary mathematics schemes. The writing frame 'prompts' enable children to concentrate on communicating their thinking. Moreover, the frames provide children with experience of the particular vocabulary and form of the early stages of mathematical reasoning. We believe that writing frames are tools that help to make transparent some of the thinking associated with the process of the solving of mathematical problems.

An important feature of the frames is the link with an explicit, structured teaching model. Work of this kind is teacher intensive if the children are to be challenged to stretch their thinking. This is only a temporary state. It must be remembered that the child moves from a state of dependence as a spectator through taking over some of the work before accepting full responsibility when eventually the frame is no longer needed. A warning is appropriate at this juncture. Already we have shown how one teacher needed to spend some time introducing the idea of writing frames. She also noted that the forward movement of the rest of the maths curriculum was *slowed down* while she gave more emphasis to explanation and reasoning. It can only be assumed, however, that this period of specific attention to reasoning will have beneficial effects towards later aspects of mathematical understanding.

Written fluency for some young learners comes through a slow, difficult and often painful process. It might be argued that the use of writing frames to help pupils with their non-fiction writing is too prescriptive and may obstruct their creativity. Many teachers in primary schools will be familiar with those occasions when pupils, faced with non-fiction writing tasks, have found no other way than copying large chunks of text from information books. The use of writing frames could also be interpreted as a violation of choice and imposition of style. Nevertheless, given that our aim is to support and encourage young learners to express their mathematical understanding in the written form, the frames provide a way forward in the scaffolded learning process.

Acknowledgements

Anne Jones, Christow Primary School, Devon.
Judith Shaw, Charlton Horethorne C of E Grant Maintained School, Dorset.
Ruth Trundley, Advisory Teacher for Mathematics, Devon.
Andy Whelan, Montgomery Combined School, Exeter.

We would also like to thank Maureen Lewis and David Wray, for inviting us to participate in the original EXEL Project in relation to writing frames in mathematics.

References

Askew, M. (1993) *Evaluation of the Implementation of National Curriculum Mathematics*, London: SCAA.

Burton, L. (1994) *Children Learning Mathematics Patterns and Relationships*, Herts: Simon and Schuster.

DES (1982) *Mathematics Counts: Report of the Committee of Inquiry into the Teaching of Mathematics in Schools* (The Cockcroft Report), London: HMSO.

DFE and Welsh Office (1995) *Mathematics in the National Curriculum*, London: HMSO.

DfEE (1998a) *The Implementation of the National Numeracy Strategy: The Final Report of the Numeracy Task Force*, London: HMSO.

DfEE (1998b) *The National Literacy Strategy Framework for Teaching*, London: HMSO.

Gattegno, C. (1987) *The Science of Education Part 1 Theoretical Considerations*, New York: Educational Solutions.

HMI (1985) *Mathematics from 5 to 16, Curriculum Matters 3*, London: HMSO.

Hughes, M., Desforges, C. and Mitchell, C. (1999) *Numeracy and Beyond: Applying Mathematics in the Primary School*, Buckingham: Open University Press.

Lewis, M. and Wray, D. (1995) *Developing Children's Non-Fiction Writing*, Leamington Spa: Scholastic.

Marks, G. and Mousley, J. (1990) 'Mathematics education and genre: Dare we make the process writing mistake?', *Language and Education*, (2), 117–135.

Merttens, R. (1992) *Ginn Mathematics 2 Using and Applying Mathematics*, Bucks: Ginn.

Perera, K. (1987) *Understanding Language*, Sheffield: National Association of Advisers in English.

Rawson, W. (1998) *Teaching Mathematics at Key Stage 2*, Cambridge: Chris Kington Publishing

SCAA (1995) *Exemplification of Standards Key Stages 1 and 2*, London: SCAA.

SCAA (1997) *Mathematics Key Stage 2 Test A*, London: SCAA.

Vygotsky, L. (1978) *Mind in Society: The Development of Higher Psychological Processes*, Cambridge, MA: Harvard University Press.

Woodman, A. (ed.) (1995) *STEPS 1 Mathematics Teacher's Handbook*, London: Collins Educational.

Wray, D. and Lewis, M. (1998) *From Learning to Teaching: Towards a Model of Teaching Literacy*, http:/www.ex.ac.uk.

Chapter 13

Differentiation

Lesley Jones and Barbara Allebone

There are many different ways in which the term differentiation is used and interpreted in the educational context. In this chapter we will attempt to clarify what we do and do not mean in our use of the term and consider some of the approaches frequently employed. In the not-so-distant past the UK school system was very much more differentiated than it is now. There was a widespread division between grammar and 'secondary modern' schools, there was a large section of special schools and there were technical schools. The curriculum within each of these different schools was very clearly differentiated. The grammar schools followed a traditional 'classical' curriculum. The secondary schools used a modified version of this with the inclusion of many more practical aspects. The technical school curriculum was intended as a more vocational curriculum, leading directly into certain sections of the workplace. The special schools had a curriculum which was largely focused on 'basic skills'; both academic and day-to-day living skills.

This method for schools to shape a divided society was not new. Indeed it has roots within the classical literature. Plato wrote of his vision of society,

> You are, all of you in this land, brothers. But when God fashioned you, he added gold in the composition of those of you who are qualified to be Rulers (which is why their prestige is greatest); He put silver in the Auxiliaries, and iron and bronze in the farmers and the rest (Lee, 1955, p. 160).

The three groups were to lead different life styles and, most importantly, follow different educational experiences, for

> on education everything else depends, and it is an illusion to imagine that mere legislation without it can effect anything of consequence (p. 166).

In 1965 comprehensive education became official government policy. The 1990 Education Act introduced the National Curriculum and led to many of the children identified as having special educational needs being catered for in mainstream schools. Each of these changes has led to a more inclusive view of education in which the child is seen as having the right to equal access to a common curriculum. This means that structurally the school system is far less differentiated than it was a few years ago.

Within schools, however, there are often structures which lead to differentiated provision for children. Some schools stream or set the children according to ability. Primary schools have not had a tradition of setting or streaming, though this is becoming more frequent in recent years. Ofsted (1993) in a survey of primary schools noted that: 'grouping, particularly by ability in mathematics and English, was a frequent feature of the primary classes in the survey'.

Mathematics education in the UK has been the subject of much criticism. International surveys have indicated that children in the UK perform badly in comparison with their counterparts world-wide. An influential report published in 1996 (Reynolds and Farrell, 1996) reviewed a number of international comparative reports and suggested that a major problem in the UK was the very extensive range of achievement, and in particular the long 'tail' of children underachieving. The authors postulated that a systemic factor associated with the high achievement scores of children in Pacific Rim countries was,

> the prevalent belief that all children are able to acquire certain core skills in core subjects, and that there is no need for a 'trailing edge' of low performing pupils. This contrasts with the belief in Western societies of the normal distribution, with an elongated tail and 'built in' failure of fifty percent of the distribution to acquire more than the average level of skill (Reynolds and Farrell, 1996, p. 54).

The report suggested that key classroom factors which contributed to this finding included:

- mechanisms to ensure that things are taught properly the first time around, and that there is no 'trailing edge' of children who have to be returned to later (an example from Taiwan is that children have to repeat in their homework books any exercises they got wrong in their previous homework);
- high quantities of whole-class interactive instruction, in which the teacher attempts to ensure the entire class have grasped the information being given;
- mechanisms to ensure that the range of achievement is kept small (in Taiwan children who have fallen behind finish their work in lesson breaks, at break times and sometimes after school).

Other reports reviewed by Reynolds and Farrell (1996) concentrated on comparisons with other European countries which showed significantly higher achievements than in the UK (e.g. Bierhoff and Prais, 1995; Smithers and Robinson, 1991; Bierhoff, 1996; Burghes and Blum, 1995). Suggested reasons for these differences included the following:

- Teaching groups are more homogeneous, partly because the school system is selective (for most German states) thus reducing the range and making teaching less difficult.
- Students can be 'kept down a grade' until they have acquired the levels of achievement in all subjects necessary for the next grade up.
- The use of textbooks as a resource prevents teachers from re-inventing the wheel and diverting their energies into the preparation of worksheets.
- High proportion of lesson time (50–70%) being used for whole class teaching. This is not simply of the 'lecture to the class' variety, but high quality interactive teaching in which the teacher starts with a problem and develops solutions and concepts through a series of graded questions addressed to the whole class. Pupils working on their own and in groups are correspondingly much rarer than in England.

The education press (Neumark, 1996) put their own blunt 'spin' on the findings:

> Put simply individual children and individual schools are being deprived of the chance to learn much mathematics. The likely culprit is differentiation where pupils in the same class learn a different syllabus, depending on their ability.

They go on to contrast this with Taiwan, Switzerland and Germany, and then to present the remedies suggested by Dr John Marks, in a pamphlet for the right-wing Centre for Policy Studies. These include interactive whole-class teaching, narrowing the scope of the mathematics curriculum in the primary years, banning calculators and introducing better and more standardised textbooks.

This report had considerable impact in the UK and gained extensive media attention. Professor David Reynolds, one of the authors, moved on to chair the Numeracy Task force, thus acquiring a very influential position in relation to primary mathematics. This body added its weight to an already evolving trend to encourage whole class teaching and move away from the notion of individualised learning. Recent policy documents emphasise the importance of teaching, rather than learning and there is a clear trend towards the idea of keeping the teaching group together, rather than catering for differences between children's attainment and ability. Ofsted (1993) followed up the discussion paper known as the 'Three Wise Men' report (Alexander *et al.,* 1992) with a report in which they state that,

> Being taught together as a class provided (children) with richer opportunities to internalise, communicate and explore ideas than was often achieved by individual work or group work where the teacher's input was often fleeting and constrained by the need to attend several groups or many individuals within a short period of time (p. 9).

and

> Although teachers frequently exploited the potential of whole class teaching for younger pupils in the case of literature, there was much less evidence of their doing so in subjects where it might have brought similar benefits … (p. 9).

These views are in contrast with advice offered in the 1980s by HMI and the then Department of Education and Science. In 1980 HMI noted the seemingly contrary requirements of the curriculum:

> On the one hand it has to reflect the broad aims of education which hold good for all children, whatever their abilities and whatever the schools they attend. On the other hand it has to allow for difference in the abilities and other characteristics of children, even of the same age (HMI, 1980).

And the DES, in 1986, identified differentiation as one of the four marks of the acceptable curriculum (broad, balanced, relevant and differentiated).

As so often happens with educational trends the pressure to bring about change has resulted in a swing from one extreme (individualised working) to the other (whole class teaching) at least in terms of what is advocated, if not in what is generally practised. The Numeracy Task Force Final Report (DfEE, 1998) states that the aim of their proposed strategy is to allow all children in a class to progress steadily, so that all of them reach a satisfactory standard and *the range of attainment is much narrower.* They express concern that 'children should not continue to work at many different levels, with the teacher placing them in a wide range of differentiated groups'. They recommend that the whole class should be taught together for a high proportion of the time so that the teacher spends more time interacting directly with the pupils and less time troubleshooting with individuals. They do, however, acknowledge the need for 'a certain amount of differentiation in the group work' and targeted questions for individuals during whole-class work.

Clearly there is a tension between the conflicting desire for all children to reach a satisfactory level of attainment and for each child to achieve their full potential. The resolution of this tension lies in the ability of teachers to plan and organise their lessons in a way which allows challenge for children at different levels of attainment. Within the rest of this chapter we detail some practical strategies for differentiation within the classroom which can bring about this aim.

Approaches to differentiation in the mathematics classroom

Within any classroom there are a wide range of abilities, interests and learning styles. Children learn in different ways, at different speeds and need different kinds of support. Differentiation is not primarily about helping the slower learners or extending the more able. It is about all children and how we as teachers can cater for the needs of individuals through the methods we employ in the classroom. In theory the ways of differentiating are limitless – every learner (and teacher) is unique. In practice however, teachers are constrained by the realities of classroom organisation and achieving a balance between what is manageable, the needs of the individual and needs of the whole class.

Some approaches to differentiation are unplanned and arise as a response to the on-going situation. Teachers enable differentiation to occur by intervening in the learning at an individual or small-group level in a number of ways. A comment or word of encouragement may help in maintaining the progress in learning; there may be an opportunity to discuss in greater depth, to explain and ask and answer questions. Skilled questioning can encourage children to higher levels of thinking (what do you think would happen if …?). Individual goals may be set, alternative resources provided or the teacher may decide that progress in learning can best be achieved by not intervening.

A range of planned approaches to differentiating the curriculum has been identified (DES, 1992; Lewis, 1992; Dickinson and Wright, 1993). It can be useful to consider these individually, although in practice these are not discrete – rarely is one method exclusively employed. Teachers may focus on one main planned approach, for example by providing different tasks for the perceived abilities of the children. In this case children may be encouraged to select their own resources or they will be provided with specific resources for the task. Teachers will support individual children or intervene in response to the learning styles employed.

Frequently used planned approaches to differentiation include the following.

Differentiation by outcome

Pupils are given a common task to elicit different levels of response.
Issues arising:

- Open-ended tasks with accessible starting points are provided for all the children.
- Activities can be introduced and discussed with the whole class.

- Children can work at their own pace.
- Whole class, mixed ability or ability grouping can be in operation.
- Clear questioning is essential to provide individual challenges for all children.
- Pupils have the opportunity to demonstrate their potential.
- Pupils can make choices about how to proceed with a problem from a given starting point.

An example of differentiating by outcome is illustrated in 'Polite Numbers' below.

Polite Numbers – differentiation by outcome (support through use of materials)

The children were asked to find out which numbers are 'polite'. They were told that polite numbers are those that you can make from the sum of any sequence of consecutive numbers, e.g. $6 = 1 + 2 + 3$ and $15 = 7 + 8$ so both 6 and 15 are 'polite'. Children investigated which numbers less than 50 could be made in this way. The least able children were able to use trial and error, adding short sequences of numbers and, in some cases, using equipment. Some children were encouraged to work systematically and look for a pattern in the numbers that could be made out of a sequence of 3. The most able were asked to find out which numbers could not be made and to generalise their findings. The teacher was supporting and extending the children through the level of questioning and interventions.

Differentiation by task

Pupils are set different tasks within a common theme or topic, some that require greater sophistication than others. These will be built into the scheme of work and the subsequent planning of lessons.

This approach encompasses the idea of *enrichment* to cater for the needs of the more able children. In this case, pupils are given supplementary tasks intended to 'broaden or deepen skills or understanding' (DES, 1992). Such tasks will be outside the core of learning which most pupils undertake.

Issues arising from differentiating by task:

- Tasks can be selected and 'tailored' to address specific learning objectives for the perceived needs of groups of children.
- Grouping by ability within that topic.
- Poor planning and assessment can deny pupils access to mathematics by giving them tasks which are inappropriate for their level of ability. If the tasks are too difficult they may lead to frustration and/or lowering of self-esteem, too easy and there is a danger of boredom and feeling devalued.
- Selecting appropriate tasks assumes the teacher has knowledge and understanding of the topic to a suitable level, has some notion of the likely progression of understanding in the

topic and is aware of the previous knowledge, skills and understanding required to underpin the topic and form a basis on which to build.

Place Value – differentiating by task (support through equipment)

Developing an understanding of place value using Dienes equipment.
Children choose a target number and find it on a 1–100 number line. They scoop up some ten rods and some unit cubes and work out the number, marking it on the number line. The child who is nearest to the target number takes a cube.

Developing an understanding of numerals to 100
Children have a 100 square cut up into pieces. They try and fit the pieces back together to make a complete 100 square. Children can be encouraged to make their own hundred square jigsaw and challenge a friend to complete it.

Extending an understanding of the number system
Children each have a 100 square written in a different script but with some numerals missing. Children work out the missing numerals and complete the 100 square. Children cut up their 100 square to make a jigsaw and challenge a friend to put it together. Number squares in different 'bases' could also be a challenge.

Differentiation by rate of progress

Pupils are encouraged to proceed through a course or topic at their own speed. For the able child this is likely to take the form of extension in which the child is allowed to move through the curriculum at a faster rate either by covering it more quickly or by skipping sections which the child clearly understands and will not provide a challenge.

This approach encompasses the idea of *acceleration* to meet the needs of the more able. Exceptionally able children may work with older children or be moved into a higher age group.

This move can be full-time or could be for certain periods of the week for particular curriculum areas. However, this response requires very careful consideration on an individual basis in terms of the child's maturity and the ability to interact with older children and reintegrate.

Issues arising from differentiating by rate of progress:

- Pupils can work at their own pace.
- Grouping by ability within that topic or individual.
- Children may become de-motivated and measure their ability according to the work they are doing rather than their own achievements.
- More able children have sometimes been set simply more work of the same kind when they have completed allotted tasks, e.g. when they have finished multiplying 3-digit numbers the children are asked to multiply 4-digit numbers.

- Acceleration into a 'higher' class can cause social problems. This approach to catering for able children needs to be part of a broader policy and needs to be considered carefully for each individual.

Differentiation by support

Additional support is offered to learners of all abilities in terms of time, materials and tasks. This may involve the presence of a support or general assistant who works alongside specific groups of pupils during the lesson. Alternatively, whilst children are working in groups or individually, the teacher is freed to work with a small group or with an individual learner. Support does not necessarily have to be in the form of extra teachers or helpers in a room – it may involve alternative materials or tasks.

Issues arising:

- Pupils can work on similar tasks using different equipment or with added support.
- Grouping by perceived ability within that topic.
- More able children can be isolated and left to their own devices. Croll and Moses (1985) found that children with learning difficulties in mainstream primary classes tend to receive more individual teacher time and more non-task orientated interactions (e.g. comments about behaviour) than other children.

Differentiation by interest

Pupils are allowed to pursue something which interests them personally, and are given a degree of choice or 'guided' choice in selecting activities.

Issues arising:

- Children who are given the opportunity to study something they are really interested in will be more highly motivated.
- Grouping by interest – mixed ability groups.
- Limiting the choice makes this approach manageable.

Exploring 500 – differentiation by interest (task)

A Year 5 class had been studying the Tudors and the teacher used the fact that they lived about 500 years ago as a starting point to explore 500. The class was asked to brainstorm ways in which they could investigate 500 and their ideas were recorded on the board. The children drew on their previous experiences and their suggestions included finding $\sqrt{500}$, 'exploding' 500 and expressing it in different ways, finding ways of multiplying two numbers to make 500, making 500 using a limited number of keys on the calculator. Children selected their activity and worked in friendship groups. The teacher worked with a focus group of more able children investigating the number of generations in 500 years. This involved defining the average length of one generation and evaluating the validity of their findings.

Differentiation by context

Pupils work on the same aspect of mathematics in a range of different contexts. Presenting the topic in a variety of meaningful contexts will help pupils to gain access to mathematical concepts by:

- helping them to see the relevance;
- helping them to generalise the concepts and skills into other situations.

The context in which learning takes place is very important in achieving successful learning. Children have a variety of experiences of successful learning which are not solely school-based, but come from their daily experiences of living. Often these experiences involve skills and abilities which are needed in school but, because the context of the learning is not familiar to the child, the child fails to use them. Children may fail to make the conceptual links between the task as presented by the teacher and the task they solve in the real world. Knowledge relevant to the task in school sometimes fails to be used by the pupil because of the approach taken.

Exploring decimals – differentiating by context

Children in a Year 5 class were designing a game using decimals. Some children were encouraged to use the context of money. They were using decimal notation and collected amounts to make £1. Others were designing a game using the context of length with variable lengths. The most able children were making a game which focused on the relationship between decimal fractions, vulgar fractions and percentages.

Whatever approach is taken, we need to ensure that we are encouraging children to learn in the most effective way for them; we need to recognise that there will be different responses to the same stimuli and while we plan different approaches, we are also differentiating through the level of questioning and our expectations.

Differentiating through the level of questioning

The structure of the Numeracy Hour encourages a 'good deal of whole class teaching' with the emphasis on 'minimising the range of levels of attainment between the most and least able children in the class'. (DfEE, 1998). Within this structure, teachers are encouraged to differentiate through the level of questioning in whole-class work, using planned approaches to differentiation in the main activity/ies within a common theme.

During whole class sessions in the daily mathematics lesson, the teacher directs some questions towards the pupils in the class who are most able, in the same way that some questions are directed towards those who find mathematics most difficult. These [most able] pupils can be stretched through differentiated work in the sessions of group work, extra challenges they can do towards the end of a topic when other pupils are working through exercises to consolidate their understanding and harder problems given to them for homework (DfEE, 1998, p. 57).

It is important to consider what kind of thinking a question generates and how the question can help children engage with a task. Analysis of the types of questions asked by teachers in the classroom has shown that many teachers ask questions to test recall and procedures; questions that promote higher order thinking skills, those of analysis, synthesis and reasoning occur with decreasing frequency (Kerry, 1983; Allebone, 1996). Some inquiries have shown that pupils learn more in classrooms where 'the teachers use a mix of both "higher" and "lower" level questions than in those in which teachers ask pupils mainly to recall or recognise' (Askew and Wiliam, 1995).

Bloom and Krathwohl's taxonomy (1965) of the cognitive and affective domains provides a framework through which to consider the processes of logical thinking. This divides learning into six categories: knowledge, comprehension, application, analysis, synthesis and evaluation. The taxonomy suggests that you cannot value or judge until you:

> know the facts, understand the facts, can apply the facts, can take the facts apart and analyse them, can put the facts together in such a way that new perspectives are revealed (Bloom and Krathwohl, 1965).

'Lower level' thinking skills are considered to be those of:

- **developing knowledge (recall).** Acquiring knowledge requires memory, repetition and description and includes knowledge of appropriate materials, methods, processes, patterns, structures (e.g. mathematical symbols). Questions may be characterised by key words such as: Who? What? When? Where? (Morgan and Saxton, 1991). E.g. What is this shape? What is 3 times 2?
- **developing understanding at its most basic level.** Developing understanding of the knowledge acquired requires translating (e.g. paraphrasing, explaining the meaning of words), interpreting (e.g. grouping or classifying according to specific criteria) and extrapolating (e.g. using given data to determine consequences and effects). Teachers generally concentrate on the acquisition of knowledge and the first level of comprehension, i.e. translation (Wallace, 1992). Questions may be characterised by phrases such as: What is meant by …? What is the difference …? Can you describe …? What is the main idea …? E.g. What is the difference between a square and a triangle? What is an even number?
- **developing application.** Knowledge is static unless it is applied to solving problems. Application involves using acquired knowledge in different areas of study, applying acquired practices and theories to solving problems, transferring methods or techniques to new situations. Questions may be characterised by phrases such as: What would happen if …? How would you find out if …? How would you …? If … how can …? E.g. How can we find out if all triangles tessellate? What are the multiples of two? How can we find out?

'Higher level' thinking skills are considered to be those of:

- **developing analysis.** This involves the process of breaking down the whole to clarify the relationship between constituent parts. Analysis involves finding patterns and relationships, differentiating between facts and hypothesis, understanding the system or organisation. Questions may be characterised by words or phrases such as: Why? What if …? What was the purpose …? Is it a fact that …? E.g. Why do triangles tessellate? How many ways can you subtract 43 from 82?
- **developing synthesis or creative thinking (creating).** This is the process of creating or recombining elements to form a new whole, rearranging or reclassifying to make a new pattern or structure. Questions may be characterised by phrases such as: How could we …? How can …? What if …? I wonder how …? Do you suppose that …? What would happen if …? E.g. What would happen if we tessellated with hexagons? What if we multiplied odd numbers together?. What would happen?
- **developing evaluation (judging).** This requires perhaps the greatest cognitive demand. It is the process of appraising and assessing on the basis of specific criteria. The process of evaluation involves verifying, proving, comparing and discriminating between theories and generalisations. Questions may be characterised by phrases such as: How do you know that it is true? Would you agree that …? Would it be better if …? Were we right to …? E.g. Can you explain why all triangles tessellate?

The characteristic which identifies able children is their ability to use the higher order thinking skills with ease and in depth at an earlier age than other children. In order to identify and to provide for able children, we have to ensure that there are opportunities to use and develop higher order thinking skills in the tasks provided for all children and the level of questions asked.

Planning for differentiation

We could plan an individual programme for each child based on careful observation and assessment to meet their particular learning needs. In practice, however, this is not realistic. Teachers tend to group children, taking into consideration the needs of each child in terms of ability, social skills, the learning styles encouraged and the teaching styles employed. Teachers may plan differentiated activities for different groups of children or plan how they aim to differentiate for the different needs of the children, perhaps through targeted questions or interventions.

One approach to planning for the different abilities is to include the categories of extension and support in every lesson plan and scheme of work to encourage planning for at least three different levels.

Another approach is to differentiate the learning objectives in planning – to consider what all the children *must* know/understand/be able to do, what most children *should* know/understand/be able to do and what some children *could* know/understand/develop/ be able to do by the end of the lesson/unit of work.

- Children must … (**all** children will be able to achieve this aspect of the work).
- Children should … (**many** children will be able to achieve this aspect of the work).
- Children could … (**some** children will be able to achieve this aspect of the work).

This ensures that you differentiate your expectations and can apply the levels progressively throughout a scheme of work or individual lesson.

Teachers generally put a high value on children assimilating the curriculum content. Whilst not under-emphasising its value, this is only one aspect of curriculum development. Rather than absorbing large numbers of facts, the most important skills which pupils need to acquire are those concerned with learning how to learn. By over-emphasising content, teachers may omit to pay attention to the ways in which individuals will respond to what they are going to teach.

All approaches to differentiation need very careful planning to be successful. It is important for the teacher to identify beforehand precise learning objectives which may form the basis of an Individual Educational Programme and/or curriculum related assessment.

Grouping

Grouping is a powerful tool in organising differentiated learning. Groupings can be created for different activities and aspects of mathematics. When pupils are grouped by ability for a particular lesson or series of lessons, material can be matched closely to the needs of the particular group, either to reinforce existing understanding in new contexts or to provide a fresh challenge with aims just beyond their existing 'platform of experience'. At other times mixed ability groups may be created to allow children to extend their competence and understanding by working collaboratively supporting their peers, while providing slower learners with peer support. Teaching others can be an effective way to consolidate and develop understanding. Many primary teachers have commented on how an aspect of mathematics finally 'made sense' when teaching it. One of our initial training students had learned the rule that to divide one fraction by another you 'turn the second one upside down and multiply'. When discussing and with a Year 5 class, she asked the children how many quarters there were in a half and suddenly the learnt rule began to make sense to her.

Research from Maine, USA (reproduced in George, 1995) considered the average retention rates for different approaches to learning as shown in Fig.13.1.

It is important to recognise that children learn and develop at different rates. Rigid ability groupings can result in children 'living up to' the teacher's expectations and may result in negative attitudes to mathematics and low-esteem. A child who demonstrates good computational skills may have difficulty in applying these skills to other aspects of mathematics, to analysing and solving problems. Conversely, a child put in a group of 'perceived low achievers' may not be given the opportunity to demonstrate their ability to use higher level thinking skills.

Assessment

Assessment of the children, their attainment and potential, is an essential aspect of providing a differentiated curriculum. It is in fact a central and vital aspect of any curriculum planning. Teachers can only plan an appropriate curriculum for their pupils if they have some understanding of each child's present level of understanding and their ability to tackle the work set. However, teachers can sometimes be subject to misconceptions or pre-conceived ideas about the children's level of ability. An instance of this is detailed in relation to some teachers working on an observation task in connection with a 20-day mathematics course they were following.

	Average retention rate
Lecture	5%
Reading	10%
Audio visual	20%
Demonstration	30%
Discussion group	50%
Practice by doing	75%
Teach others immediate use of learning	90%

Figure 13.1 The learning pyramid

In this the authors (Thumpston and Jones, 1992) describe how teachers dismissed the evidence of their own observations of children's performance in favour of their previously formed opinion of the children's work. One teacher stated that 'The youngest and brightest didn't show her ability' and another that, 'Stephen, who is meant to be a bit brighter, said the pattern goes up in 8's, so he was wrong, but I'm sure he knew really'. A third teacher noted that, 'the most sensible answers came from the boy who is statemented'.

In this study teachers also made assumptions about children in the affective domain. One teacher claimed that, 'The girls were more timid, which you could see by the softer way they used their crayons'. And another that, 'The girls looked up to me for reassurance'. There is a substantial body of research which indicates that teachers' assumptions about children's levels of confidence can have far-reaching effects on their school careers (see, for instance, Walden and Walkerdine, 1985).

It is for this reason that we maintain that assessment of children's attainment should be firmly grounded in evidence, and that teachers should be constantly using the feedback cycle of observation and assessment in providing a suitable differentiated curriculum.

Within this chapter we have aimed to put the idea of differentiation in the broader context and to provide some practical approaches for the classroom. Education must always be centrally concerned with making appropriate curriculum provision for individual children. To do this we need to provide opportunities for children to demonstrate their potential and to ensure that our expectations of children do not act as a 'ceiling', limiting their achievements. Teachers therefore need to consider carefully the kind of activities they introduce, ensuring that they have sufficient potential for extension to challenge all children at their own level.

The ways in which this can be implemented necessitate systematic planning, assessment and careful use of questioning.

References and further reading

Alexander, R., Rose, J. and Woodhead, C. (1992) *Curriculum Organisation and Classroom Practice in Primary Schools*, A Discussion Paper, London: DES.

Allebone, B. (1996) *An Investigation into the Provision Made for Able Children Focusing on Mathematically Able Children at Key Stage 2*, Unpublished MEd Thesis, Brunel University.

Askew, M. and Wiliam, D. (1995) *Recent Research in Mathematics Education 5–16*, London: HMSO.

Barnes, D. (1985) *Practical Curriculum Study*, London: Routledge & Kegan Paul.

Barthorpe, T. and Visser, J. (1991) *Differentiation: Your Responsibility*, NARE Publications.

Bierhoff, H. (1996) *Laying the Foundation for Numeracy: A Comparison of Primary School Textbooks in Britain, Germany and Switzerland*, London: National Institute for Economic and Social Research.

Bierhoff, H. and Prais, S. (1995) Schooling as a Preparation for Life and Work in Switzerland and Britain, London: National Institute for Economic and Social Research.

Bloom, B. and Krathwohl, D. (1965) *The Taxonomy of Educational Objectives, the Classification of Educational Goals. Handbook 1: Cognitive Domain*, New York: D. McKay.

Burghes, D. and Blum, W. (1995) *The Exeter Kassel Comparative project: A Review of Year 1 and 2 Results in Gatsby Foundation: Proceedings of a Seminar in Mathematics Education*, London: Gatsby.

Casey, R. and Koshy, V. (1995) *Bright Challenge*, Gloucester: Stanley Thornes.

Croll, P. and Moses, D. (1985) *One in Five*, London: Routledge.

DES (1986) *Better Schools*, London: HMSO.

DES (1987) *Better Mathematics*, London: HMSO.

DES (1992) *The Education of Very Able Children in Maintained Schools*, London: HMSO.

Desforges, C. and Cockburn, A. (1987) *Understanding the Mathematics Teacher*, London: Falmer Press.

DfE (1993) *Exceptionally Able Children – Report of Conferences*, London: HMSO.

DfEE (1998) *The Implementation of the National Numeracy Strategy*, London: DfEE.

Dickinson, C. and Wright J. (1993) *Differentiation: A Practical Handbook of Classroom Strategies*, National Council for Educational Technology.

George, D. (1995) *Gifted Education – Identification and Provision*, London: David Fulton.

HMI (1980) *A View of the Curriculum*, London: HMSO.

HMI (1992) *The Education of Very Able Children in Maintained Schools*, London: HMSO.

Kerry, T. (1983) *Finding and Helping the Able Child*, Croom Helm.

Koshy, V. and Casey, R. (1997) *Effective Provision for Able and Exceptionally Able Children*, London: Hodder and Stoughton.

Lee, H. D. L. (1955) *Plato: the Republic*, Penguin.

Lewis, A. (1992) 'From planning to practice', in Peters, M. *Differentiation: Ways Forward*, NASEN.

McNamara, S. and Moreton, G. (1997) *Understanding Differentiation*, London: David Fulton.

Morgan, N. and Saxton, J. (1991) *Teaching Questioning and Learning*, London: Routledge.

NCC (1989) *Curriculum Guidance 2 – A Curriculum for All*, London: HMSO.

Neumark, V. (1996) 'Dispatches from the front', *Times Educational Supplement, Mathematics Extra*, 4 October 1996, page II.

Ofsted (1993) *Curriculum Organisation and Classroom Practice in Primary Schools*, DfEE.

Peter, M. (1992) *Differentiation: Ways Forward*, NASEN.

Reynolds, D. and Farrell, S. (1996) *Worlds Apart? A Review of International Surveys of Educational Achievement Involving England*, London: Ofsted.

Smithers, A. and Robinson, D. (1991) *Beyond Compulsory Schooling: A Numerical Picture*, London: Council for Industry and Higher Education.

Thumpston, G. and Jones, L. (1992) 'Developing observational skills in teacher assessment', *British Journal of Curriculum and Assessment*, 2(3).

Walden, R. and Walkerdine, V. (1985) *Girls and Mathematics: From Primary to Secondary Schooling*, Bedford Way Papers 26, University of London, Institute of Education.

Wallace, B. (1992) *Teaching the Very Able Child*, Professional Library.

Appendices

Answers to self-study questions

Chapter 2

1. The result of 156 may be obtained in various ways. One method is to think of the difference between 100 and 243 and the 13 difference between 87 and 100; 143 + 13 equals 156.

2. (a) $1237 + 637 \approx 1200 + 700 = 1900$. Exact result is 1874.
   (b) $350 + 351 \approx 700 = 701$ exactly.
   (c) $432 - 179 \approx 450 - 200 = 250$. The result is 253 exactly.
   (d) $23 \times 9 \approx 20 \times 10 = 200$. The result is 207 exactly.
   (e) $76 \times 34 \approx 80 \times 30 = 2400$. The result is 2584 exactly.
   (f) $416 \div 6 \approx 400 \div 5 = 80$. The result is 69.3, with the 3 recurring.
   (g) $376 \div 22 \approx 360 \div 20 = 18$. The exact result is 17.09, with the digits 09 recurring.

4. Addition and multiplication are commutative.
   $8 + 6 = 14$; $6 + 8 = 14$.
   $8 \times 6 = 48$; $6 \times 8 = 48$.

5. (b) $631 + 542 = 1173$ is the biggest possible.
   (c) $213 - 165 = 48$ is the smallest possible.
   (d) $642 \times 531 = 340\ 902$ is the largest possible.
   (e) $2516 \div 34 = 74$, after a bit of trial and error.

6. (a) –5, –4, –3, –2, –1, 0, 1, 2 and 3.
   (b) It shows –1 degree. After a rise of another 3 degrees it will read 2 degrees.
   (c) The required order is –8, –3, –2, 0, 2.

7. The required multiples of 7 are: 56, 63, 70, 77, 84, 91, 98.

9. (a) 2 is a prime number and is even, so the statement is false.
   (b) There are more than 12 primes between 10 and 80.
   (c) Just 23 and 59 are prime, so the statement is true.

Chapter 3

1   (a) 20/12 or 5/3; an estimate would be 'a bit less than 2'.
    (b) 14/16; the numerator must be estimated as 'less than 16'.
    (c) 43.61
    (d) 5.03

2   (a) 3/5 > 4/7;   (b) 2/3 < 4/5;   (c)1.901 >1.222

3   15% of £180 = £27

4   1/2 = 0.5 = 50%
    3/5 = 0.6 = 60%
    2/5 = 0.4 = 40%
    1/4 = 0.25 = 25%
    3/4 = 0.75 = 75%
    1/20 = 0.05 = 5%
    1/5 = 0.2 = 20%

5   (a) $5 = 5^1$
    (b) $25 = 5^2$
    (c) $125 = 5^3$
    (d) $625 = 5^4$
    (e) $3125 = 5^5$
    (f) $1 = 5^0$
    (g) $1/5 = 5^{-1}$
    (h) $1/25 = 5^{-2}$
    (i) $1/125 = 5^{-3}$

6   (a) $0.025 = 2.5 \times 10^{-2}$
    (b) $0.25 = 2.5 \times 10^{-1}$
    (c) $0.79 = 7.9 \times 10^{-1}$
    (d) $0.0079 = 7.9 \times 10^{-3}$
    (e) $0.926 = 9.26 \times 10^{-1}$
    (f) $0.0805 = 8.05 \times 10^{-2}$
    (g) $0.000018 = 1.8 \times 10^{-5}$
    (h) $0.0000000062 = 6.2 \times 10^{-9}$
    (i) $36 = 3.6 \times 10^1$
    (j) $84 = 8.4 \times 10^1$

Chapter 4

1   You will get £162 in the fifth week.

2   The number is 16.

3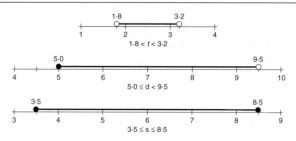

4 (a) The total of the first 10 odd numbers is 100.
(b) The total of the first 30 odd numbers is 900.
(c) The total of the first n odd numbers is n squared.

6 (a) For a 6-sided shape there are 9 diagonals (1/2 of 6 times 3)
(b) For a 20-sided shape there are 170 diagonals (1/2 of 20 times 17)
(c) For an n-sided shape there are $\frac{n}{2}(n-3)$ diagonals.

Chapter 5

1 The number of tiles required is 200 times 30 which is 6000.

2 The required areas are:
(a) $144 + 24 = 168$ square metres.
(b) $256 + 48 = 304$ square metres.

3 The volume of the box is 192 cubic centimetres, so the number of cubes which will fit into it is 192.

4 (a) The real lengths are 400 metres and 275 metres.
(b) The perimeter is 1350 metres.

5 (a) $a = 90°$ (b) $a = 120°$ (c) $a = 120°$.

Chapter 7

1 No, it is not true.
(a) There are 36 possible outcomes.
(b) The probability of throwing a double is 6/36 or 1/6.
(c) The probability of throwing a total of 7 is 6/36 or 1/6.
(d) No, since the probability of getting a total of 6 is 5/36, it is more difficult to get than either a double or a total of 7.

3 The mean daily wage is £79.

4 The numbers may be rearranged as: 1, 5, 6, 18, 22, 22, 22, 23, 25, 25.
The median is, therefore, 22.

5 There are three modes. They are 19, 22 and 27; each of them occurs twice.

Answers to self-assessment questions

1 (a) 7, 186
 (b) $\frac{3}{4}$, $72\frac{1}{3}$
 (c) $\sqrt{2}$, π
 (d) -2, $-14\frac{1}{5}$
 (e) 8.76, 407.0
 (f) $\frac{7}{8}$, $\frac{82}{5}$

2 0.422, 3.79, 4.10, 4.2, 4.22

3 2.300 km

4 £33 360

5 $8+5 = 13; 5+8 = 13$
   $8\times5 = 40; 5\times8 = 40$

6 (a) 324   (b) 3822   (c) 262   (d) 93.84

7 25: 1, 5, 25   3 factors
   88: 1, 2, 4, 8, 11, 22, 44, 88   8 factors
   93: 1, 3, 31, 93   4 factors
   64: 1, 2, 4, 8, 16, 32, 64   7 factors

8 (a) 32, 64. The tenth term is 1024.
 (b) 64 is the eighth term; the nt. term is n^2.

9. The right-most digit in a decimal number refers to a power of 10, equal to the number of decimal places – ignoring the negative sign. So the 5 in 23.65 and in 1.45 stands for 5×10^{-2}. When these 5s are multiplied together the result is 25×10^{-4}. It is the 4 in the negative 4 which indicates that the product has 4 digits to the right of the decimal point.

10 Changing the fractions into equivalent ones with common denominator 120:
   $\frac{4}{10} = \frac{48}{120}$; $\frac{3}{5} = \frac{72}{120}$; $\frac{7}{8} = \frac{105}{120}$; $\frac{3}{4} = \frac{90}{120}$; $\frac{2}{3} = \frac{80}{120}$.
   105 is the largest numerator, so $\frac{7}{8}$ would most suit a glutton.

11 It is a rise in temperature of 15 degrees.

12 (a) 25% of £160 $= \frac{1}{4} \times$ £160 $=$ £40..
    (b) (i) 0.23 $= \frac{23}{100} = 23\%$
         (ii) A quarter $= \frac{25}{100} = 25\%$
         (iii) 0.20 $= \frac{20}{100} = 20\%$
    (iv) $\frac{1}{8} = \frac{125}{1000} = \frac{12.5}{100} = 12.5\%$

13 (a) $5^1 = 5$ (f) $5^0 = 1$
    (b) $5^2 = 25$ (g) $5^{-1} = 1/5$
    (c) $5^3 = 125$ (h) $5^{-2} = 1/25$
    (d) $5^4 = 625$ (i) $5^{-3} = 1/125$
    (e) $5^5 = 3125$ (j) $5^{-4} = 1/625$

14 (a) $\frac{6}{12}$ or $\frac{1}{2}$ (b) $\frac{2}{5} \times \frac{10}{5} = \frac{4}{5}$ (c) $\frac{2}{5} + \frac{1}{10} = \frac{5}{10}$ or $\frac{1}{2}$ (d) $\frac{3}{8} - \frac{1}{4} = \frac{1}{8}$

15 (a) $4000 = 4.0 \times 10^3$
    (b) $0.673 = 6.73 \times 10^{-1}$
    (c) $0.00000076 = 7.6 \times 10^{-7}$

16 $x = 5$

17 $a = 120$ degrees

18 £120

19 The total number of results is $6 \times 6 = 36$
    A total of 8 is obtained with (2,6), (3,5), (4,4), (5,3) and (6,2); it can be obtained in 5
    ways. So the probability of getting 8 is 5/36.

20 (a) 20 sq m + 12 sq m = 32 sq m.
    (b) The perimeter $= 5 + 4 + 11 + \sqrt{(4^2 + 6^2}$
                      $= 20 + \sqrt{52}$
                      $= 20 + 7.2$
                      $= 27.2$ m

21.

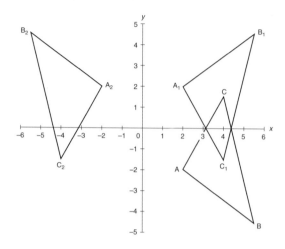

ABC is the object with $A = (2,-2)$, $B = (5\frac{1}{2},-4\frac{1}{2})$, $C = (4,1\frac{1}{2})$.
$A_1B_1C_1$ is the reflection image.
$A_1 = (2,2)$, $B_1 = (5\frac{1}{2},4\frac{1}{2})$, $C_1 = (4,-1\frac{1}{2})$
$A_2B_2C_2$ is the rotation image.
$A_2 = (-2,2)$, $B_2 = (-5\frac{1}{2},4\frac{1}{2})$, $C_2 = (-4,-1\frac{1}{2})$.

22

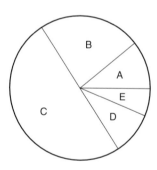

$\frac{1}{30}$ of 360 is 12. The angle for A is 36°; for B it is 84°; for C it is 180°; for D it is 36° and for E it is 24°.

23   The concert lasted for 2 hours and 40 minutes.

24   $\frac{18}{8} = 2\frac{1}{4}$; $2\frac{1}{4} \times £28.60 = £64.35$
    The eighteen books cost £64.35

25        $(476 \times 81)/39 \approx (480 \times 80)/40$

            $= 480 \times 2$

            $= 960$ approximately

Answers to multiple-choice mathematics

1   (b)
2   (c)
3   (c)
4   (b)
5   (d)
6   (d)
7   (b)
8   (a)
9   (d)
10 (a)
11 (a)
12 (a)
13 (d)
14 (b)
15 (a)
16 (c)

Record of achievement

This grid is for recording your progress. After trying the questions at the end of chapters 2 to 7 or the self-assessment questions at the end of Chapter 8, you can make a record of *what you can do, what you can do but not really understand* and *what you just cannot do.*

This process will help you evaluate the nature of the support you may need and to set targets for personal learning. For example, you may try some questions at the end of the chapter on whole numbers before you read the chapter. You may have chosen this because you are planning to teach it to children or because the lecture at the training institution may be focusing on that topic. After trying a set of questions, make an assessment of what you know and what you need to work on. A blank grid is provided in the appendix for you to photocopy and use.

When you have identified a topic or an aspect of a topic which needs further study, the first thing you can do is to read about it in Section B of this book. Read it carefully and systematically. Always have pencil and paper available to make notes. You may need to read it a second time. If you need further help, you may refer to other books or enlist the help of your friends or tutor.

After seeking help, evaluate your progress and make notes about your achievement. At this stage you may want to give yourself further exercises to do as well as make notes about areas which still cause you concern.

Record of achievement

Date

Topic

What I can do	
What I can do, but need to understand the principles	
What I need to work on	

Mathematical glossary

Add to your glossary as you neet new mathematical vocabulary and new ideas. You may want to use this format or use a notebook

Addition

Additon is 'counting on'. The sign is +; the words ususally related to additon are: total, sum of . . .

    Addition is commutative which means . . . give example.

Angle

Angles are made when two straight lines meet each other. Here are the illustrations of right angles, obtuse angles . . .

Index

Animal Hats to Knit

**20 WILD PROJECTS
FOR YOU TO CREATE**

LUISE ROBERTS

First published 2014 by
Guild of Master Craftsman Publications Ltd
Castle Place, 166 High Street, Lewes,
East Sussex BN7 1XU

ISBN 978 1 86108 989 2

The publishers and author can accept no legal responsibility
for any consequences arising from the application of
information, advice or instructions given in this publication.

A catalogue record for this book is available from the
British Library.

Publisher Jonathan Bailey
Production Manager Jim Bulley
Managing Editor Gerrie Purcell
Senior Project Editor Virginia Brehaut
Editor Nicola Hodgson
Managing Art Editor Gilda Pacitti
Designer Simon Goggin
Photographers Chris Gloag, Andrew Perris
and Anthony Bailey

Set in ClanPro and Cooper Black
Colour origination by GMC Reprographics
Printed and bound in China

Animal Hats
to Knit

**20 WILD PROJECTS
FOR YOU TO CREATE**

Contents

TECHNIQUES

Introduction

Can the world have too many animal hats? We all have an animal that we warm to, some of us have favourite animals and most of us like to dress up – even if dressing up means carefully styling everyday clothes to make them not quite so everyday. *Animal Hats to Knit* has 20 animal patterns but contains an animal-world of possibilities. There are at least five different shapes of ear, several different ways of making an eye and an abundance of noses. Like Mary Shelley's character, Victor Frankenstein, you can take the parts you need and make the animal of your choice. The snout of the pig could, with a few more rounds, become an elephant trunk; the tiger could, with cat ears, become a domestic ginger cat; the chicken beak could become owl ears when placed on a recoloured penguin beanie. Add a bit of loop stitch to the mix and you could make yourself a lion hat, a hairy monkey or a Highland cow. Add i-cords or lengths of French knitting for eyebrows and make your animal happy or sad, cheeky or fearsome. Finally, I could not help but decorate the hats as they sat in my office at home: bandanas, knitted flowers, bows, masks and eye patches as well as metal rings and jewellery all found their way onto the hats. After all, we get ready to go out; why shouldn't our animal hats?

THE PROJECTS

Cat

Is this hat too pretty? If so, work the rib in a contrast colour
to resemble a collar; flatten off the top of the nose; embroider
some scars and sew some tucks into the ears – so it looks like
the cat that comes in after a long night out on the town.
You could even add a bell and name barrel to the back.

SIZE

To fit: child[adult] (see page 94)
A close fit that covers the top of the ears.

TENSION

24 sts and 36 rows to 4in (10cm) measured over
stocking stitch using 3.75mm needles. Use larger
or smaller needles if necessary to obtain the
correct tension.

MATERIALS

• Light-weight yarn: Patons Diploma Gold DK, 55% wool,
  25% acrylic, 20% nylon (131yds/120m per 50g ball)
• 1 x 50g ball in 6187 (white) (A)
• 1 x 50g ball in 6305 (pink) (B)
• 1 x 50g ball in 6184 (grey) (C)
• Short lengths of tapestry wool or scraps of yarn
  in blue (D) and dark blue (E)
• Pair of 3.75mm (UK9:US5) straight needles
• Pair of 3.25mm (UK10:US3) straight needles
• Tapestry needle

HAT

Using yarn A, 3.25mm needles and the thumb method (see page 96), cast on 110[122] sts.

Row 1 (RS): K1, (k1, p1) to last st, k1.

Row 2: (P1, k1) to last 2 sts, p2.

Rows 3–6: Rep Rows 1–2 twice.

Row 7: K10, k2tog, k to end (109[121]) sts.

Change to 3.75mm needles.

Begin to work from chart, using the intarsia technique (see page 106) around each shape but Fair Isle stranding (see page 106) within the shape.

Rows 8–31: Working in stocking stitch, 21[27]A; work chart from right to left on RS rows and left to right on WS rows; work 21[27]A. Cont in yarn A only.

CHILD SIZE ONLY

Rows 32–35: Work in stocking stitch as set.

Row 36: P16, (p2tog, p23) 3 times, p2tog, p16 (105 sts).

ADULT SIZE ONLY

Rows 32–36: Work in stocking stitch as set.

Row 37: (K13, k2tog) 4 times, k1, (ssk, k13) 4 times (113 sts).

Rows 38–40: Work in stocking stitch as set.

Row 41: (K12, k2tog) 4 times, k1, (ssk, k12) 4 times (105 sts).

Row 42: Purl.

BOTH SIZES
CROWN

Row 1: (K11, k2tog) 4 times, k1, (ssk, k11) 4 times (97 sts).

Row 2 and 6 following alternate rows: Purl.

Row 3: (K10, k2tog) 4 times, k1, (ssk, k10) 4 times (89 sts).

Row 5: (K9, k2tog) 4 times, k1, (ssk, k9) 4 times (81 sts).

Row 7: (K8, k2tog) 4 times, k1, (ssk, k8) 4 times (73 sts).

Row 9: (K7, k2tog) 4 times, k1, (ssk, k7) 4 times (65 sts).

Row 11: (K6, k2tog) 4 times, k1, (ssk, k6) 4 times (57 sts).

Row 13: (K5, k2tog) 4 times, k1, (ssk, k5) 4 times (49 sts).

Row 15: (K4, k2tog) 4 times, k1, (ssk, k4) 4 times (41 sts).

Row 16: (P3, p2togtbl) 4 times, p1, (p2tog, p3) 4 times (33 sts).

Row 17: (K2, k2tog) 4 times, k1, (ssk, k2) 4 times (25 sts).

Row 18: (P1, p2togtbl) 4 times, p1, (p2tog, p1) 4 times (17 sts).

Row 19: (K2tog) 4 times, k1, (ssk) 4 times (9 sts).

Cut yarn, thread through rem sts and draw tight.

EARS (MAKE 4)

Using yarn A, 3.75mm needles and the thumb method, cast on 27 sts.

Row 1 (WS): Purl.

Rows 2–7: Work in stocking stitch.

Row 8: K1, ssk, k to the last 3 sts, k2tog, k1. (25 sts)

Row 9 and each alternate row: Purl.

Rows 10–27: Rep Rows 8–9, 9 times. (7 sts)

Cast off knitwise in decrease patt set.

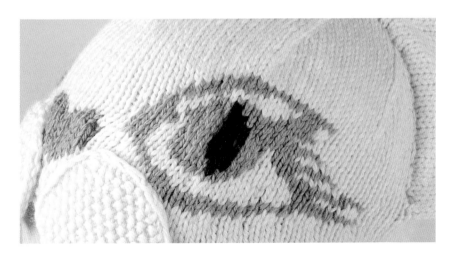

UPPER LIP (MAKE 2)

Using yarn A, 3.75mm needles and the cable method (see page 97), cast on 8 sts.
Slip stitches purlwise.

Row 1 (WS): K1tbl, inc, (p1, k1) twice, inc, sl1 (10 sts).

Row 2: K1tbl, inc, (p1, k1) 3 times, inc, sl1 (12 sts).

Row 3: K1tbl, inc, (p1, k1) 4 times, inc, sl1 (14 sts).

Row 4: K1tbl, (k1, p1) 6 times, sl1.

Row 5: K1tbl, inc, (k1, p1) 5 times, inc, sl1 (16 sts).

Row 6: K1tbl, (p1, k1) 7 times, sl1.

Row 7: K1tbl, (k1, p1) 7 times, sl1.

Rows 8–17: Rep Rows 6–7, 5 times.

Row 18: Rep Row 6.

Row 19: K1tbl, p2tog, (k1, p1) 5 times, k2tog, sl1 (14 sts).

Row 20: K1tbl, (k1, p1) 6 times, sl1.

Row 21: K1tbl, k2tog, (p1, k1) 4 times, p2tog, sl1 (12 sts).

Row 22: K1tbl, k2tog, (p1, k1) 3 times, p2tog, sl1 (10 sts).

Row 23: K1tbl, k2tog, (p1, k1) twice, p2tog, sl1 (8 sts).
Cast off, at the same time: K1tbl, k2tog, p1, k1, p2tog, sl1.

FINISHING

Sew in ends. Block and press the knitted pieces. Using yarn E, Swiss darn (see page 107) the detail to the eyes. Using mattress stitch (see page 108), sew the back seam allowing one stitch on each edge for the seam allowance, and join the outer edges of ear pieces to form a pair. Using the photograph as a guide, use whip stitch (see page 108) to attach both ears and upper lips to the hat.

KNITTING AND SWISS DARNING CHART FOR CAT

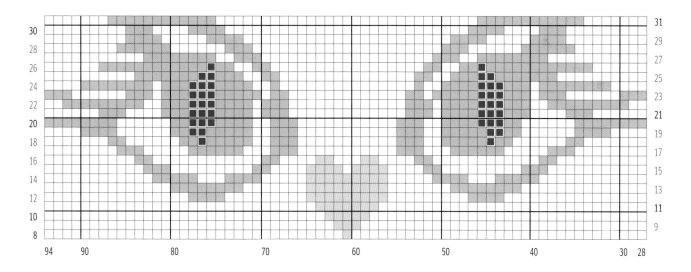

KEY

STITCH NUMBERS ALONG THE BOTTOM OF THE CHART REFER TO THE ADULT SIZE.

☐ K on RS, P on WS
☐ Yarn A (white)
▨ Yarn B (pink)
▨ Yarn C (grey)
▨ Yarn D (blue)
■ Swiss darn, yarn E (dark blue)

Eagle

Why not wear this hat with the eyes to the side or to the back and give the person next to you a surprise? Change the colour scheme to blues, greens and oranges and you will have a parrot; change the colours to blacks and blues and you will have a crow.

SIZE

To fit: child[adult] (see page 94)
A close fit that covers the top of the ears.

TENSION

26 sts and 38 rows to 4in (10cm) measured over stocking stitch using 3.25mm needles. Use larger or smaller needles if necessary to obtain the correct tension.

MATERIALS

- Light-weight yarn: Rowan Felted Tweed DK, 50% merino wool, 25% alpaca, 25% viscose (191yds/175m per 50g ball)
- 1 x 50g ball in 178 Seafarer (dark blue) (A)
- 1 x 50g ball in 177 Clay (white) (B)
- 1 x 50g ball in 181 Mineral (yellow) (C)
- Short lengths of tapestry wool or scraps of yarn in blue (D)
- Two 3.25mm (UK10:US3) circular needles
- Tapestry needle

LOWER BEAK

Using yarn C, one 3.25mm circular needle and the thumb method (see page 96), cast on 10 sts.

Row 1 and each alternate row: Purl.

Row 2: (K1, M1R) twice, ssk, k2, k2tog, (M1L, k1) twice (12 sts).

Row 4: (K1, M1R) twice, k1, ssk, k2, k2tog, k1, (M1L, k1) twice (14 sts).

Row 6: (K1, M1R) 3 times, k1, ssk, k2, k2tog, k1, (M1L, k1) 3 times (18 sts).

Row 8: (K1, M1R) twice, k4, ssk, k2, k2tog, k4, (M1L, k1) twice (20 sts). Leave the sts on the needle.

HAT

Using yarn A, one 3.25mm circular needle and the thumb method, cast on 114[122] sts.

Row 1 (RS): K1, (k1, p1) to last st, k1.

Row 2: (P1, k1) to last 2 sts, p2.

Rows 3-12: Rep Rows 1-2, 5 times. Using the Fair Isle technique (see page 106), cont as follows.

Row 13: K1B, (k1B, k3A) to last st, k1A.

Row 14: P2B, (p1A, p3B) to end.

Row 15: K2A, (k3B, k1A) to last 4 sts, k4B.

Row 16: P1A, (p1A, p1B) to last st, p1B.

Fasten off yarn A, cont in yarn B.

Rows 17-19: Work in stocking stitch. Two circular needles are used on the following rows.

Using the intarsia technique (see page 106), work the yarns as presented by the sts below.

Row 20: Needle 1: P57[61], p10 from the Lower Beak; Needle 2: P10 from the Lower Beak, p57[61] from the hat (134[142] sts).

To work as presented, work keeping the stitch pattern and colours as presented on the left-hand needle. Cont working with the needles as set.

Row 21: Yarn B, k57[61]; yarn C, M1R, k7, ssk, k2, k2tog, k7, M1L; yarn B, k57[61] (134[142]) sts.

Row 22: Purl, working the yarns as presented.

Row 23-24: Rep Rows 21-22, once.

Row 25: Yarn B, k57[61]; yarn C, k7, ssk, k2, k2tog, k7; yarn B, k57[61] (132[140] sts).

Row 26: Purl, working the yarns as presented.

On the following row, two blocks of yarn C are started for the Eyes so two more lengths of yarn C and two more lengths of yarn B are joined in.

Row 27: Needle 1: K44[48]B; join in C, k5C; join in B, k8B; yarn C, work sts as presented to 3 sts before the end of needle, ssk, k1. Needle 2: Yarn C, K1, k2tog, knit sts as presented; k8B; join in yarn C, k5C; join in B, k44[48]B (130[138] sts). The yarn C blocks for the Eyes become 2 sts wider.

Row 28: Needle 1: P43[47]B, p7C, p7B; yarn C, purl to end of needle. Needle 2: Yarn C, purl sts as presented; p7B, p7C, p43[47]B.

Row 29: Work the yarns as presented. Needle 1: Knit to 3 sts before end of needle, ssk, k1. Needle 2: K1, k2tog, knit to end of needle (128[136] sts).

Row 30: Work the yarns as presented. Needle 1: Purl to 3 sts before end of needle, p2tog, p1. Needle 2: P1, p2togtbl, purl to end of needle (126[134] sts).

Rows 31-34: Rep Rows 29-30 twice more (118[126] sts).

The two blocks of yarn C for the Eyes have now been completed.

Row 35: Needle 1: K57[61]B, sskC. Needle 2: K2togC, k57[61]B (116[124] sts).

Cont working on one circular needle only.

Row 36: Purl the yarns as presented. Fasten off yarn C; cont in yarn B only.

Row 37: K55[59], ssk, k2, k2tog, k55[59] (114[122] sts).

CHILD SIZE ONLY

Row 38: P14, (p2tog, p10) 7 times, p2tog, p14 (106 sts).

ADULT SIZE ONLY

Row 38: Purl.

Row 39: (K13, ssk) 4 times, k2, (k2tog, k13) 4 times (114 sts).

Rows 40-42: Work in stocking stitch.

Row 43: (K12, ssk) 4 times, k2, (k2tog, k12) 4 times (106 sts).

Row 44: Purl.

BOTH SIZES

CROWN

Row 1: (K11, ssk) 4 times, k2, (k2tog, k11) 4 times (98 sts).

Row 2 and 6 following alternate rows: Purl.

Row 3: (K10, ssk) 4 times, k2, (k2tog, k10) 4 times (90 sts).

Row 5: (K9, ssk) 4 times, k2, (k2tog, k9) 4 times (82 sts).

Row 7: (K8, ssk) 4 times, k2, (k2tog, k8) 4 times (74 sts).

Row 9: (K7, ssk) 4 times, k2, (k2tog, k7) 4 times (66 sts).

Row 11: (K6, ssk) 4 times, k2, (k2tog, k6) 4 times (58 sts).

Row 13: (K5, ssk) 4 times, k2, (k2tog, k5) 4 times (50 sts).

Row 15: (K4, ssk) 4 times, k2, (k2tog, k4) 4 times (42 sts).

Row 16: (P3, p2tog) 4 times, p2, (p2togtbl, p3) 4 times (34 sts).

Row 17: (K2, ssk) 4 times, k2, (k2tog, k2) 4 times (26 sts).

Row 18: (P1, p2tog) 4 times, p2, (p2togtbl, p1) 4 times (18 sts).

Row 19: (K2tog) 4 times, k2, (k2tog) 4 times (10 sts).

Cut yarn, thread through rem sts and draw tight.

FINISHING

Sew in ends. Block and press the hat. Swiss darn (see page 107) the detail to the eyes. Note that the dark blue (D) stitch in the centre front top corner is embroidered over a yellow (C) stitch. Using mattress stitch (see page 108), sew the back seam allowing one stitch on each edge for the seam allowance.

SWISS DARNING CHART FOR EAGLE'S EYES

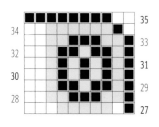 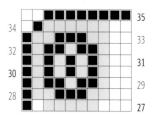

KEY

- ■ Swiss darn, yarn A (dark blue)
- ▨ Swiss darn, yarn D (blue)
- ▦ Yarn C (yellow)
- □ Yarn B (white)

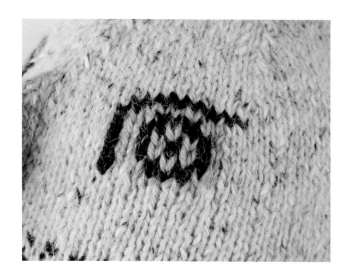

Penguin

It is all in the eyes. This hat has a small amount of
Swiss-darned detail around the eyes but there is no reason
why there shouldn't be more. A pair of eyebrows, perhaps
some spectacles or laughter lines would mean this fellow
could say a lot more to the world. Change the colours
and it could be the bird of your choice.

SIZE

To fit: child[adult] (see page 94)
A close fit that covers the top of the ears.

TENSION

24 sts and 36 rows to 4in (10cm) measured over
stocking stitch using 3.75mm needles. Use larger
or smaller needles if necessary to obtain the
correct tension.

MATERIALS

- Light-weight yarn: Rowan Felted Tweed DK,
  50% merino wool, 25% alpaca, 25% viscose
  (191yds/175m per 50g ball)
- 1 x 50g ball 159 Carbon (blue) (A)
- 1 x 50g ball 177 Clay (white) (B)
- 1 x 50g ball 181 Mineral (yellow) (C)
- Short lengths of tapestry wool or scraps of yarn
  in orange (D) and black (E)
- Short length of waste cotton yarn
- Pair of 3.75mm (UK9:US5) straight needles
- Pair of 3.25mm (UK10:US3) straight needles
- Set of five 3.25mm (UK10:US3) double-pointed needles
- Tapestry needle
- 2 x ¾in (20mm) black buttons for eyes

HAT

Using yarn A, 3.25mm needles and the thumb method (see page 96), cast on 110[122] sts.

Row 1 (RS): K1, (k1, p1) to last st, k1.

Row 2: (P1, k1) to last 2 sts, p2.

Rows 3-6: Rep Rows 1-2 twice.

Row 7: K10, k2tog, k to end (109[121] sts).

Change to 3.75mm needles.

Row 8: Purl.

Begin to work from chart using the intarsia technique (see page 106). When working the 17 sts in waste cotton yarn (Row 9), leave long ends at either end so that the yarn may be removed easily.

Rows 9-35: Working in stocking stitch, work 31[37] sts in A, work chart from right to left on RS rows and left to right on WS rows, work 31[37] sts in A.

Cont in yarn A only.

CHILD SIZE ONLY

Rows 36-37: Work in stocking stitch.

Rows 38: P16, (p2tog, p23) 3 times, p2tog, p16 (105 sts).

ADULT SIZE ONLY

Rows 36-38: Work in stocking stitch.

Row 39: (K13, k2tog) 4 times, k1, (ssk, k13) 4 times (113 sts).

Rows 40-42: Work in stocking stitch.

Row 43: (K12, k2tog) 4 times, k1, (ssk, k12) 4 times (105 sts).

Row 44: Purl.

BOTH SIZES
CROWN

Row 1: (K11, k2tog) 4 times, k1, (ssk, k11) 4 times (97 sts).

Row 2 and 6 following alternate rows: Purl.

Row 3: (K10, k2tog) 4 times, k1, (ssk, k10) 4 times (89 sts).

Row 5: (K9, k2tog) 4 times, k1, (ssk, k9) 4 times (81 sts).

Row 7: (K8, k2tog) 4 times, k1, (ssk, k8) 4 times (73 sts).

Row 9: (K7, k2tog) 4 times, k1, (ssk, k7) 4 times (65 sts).

Row 11: (K6, k2tog) 4 times, k1, (ssk, k6) 4 times (57 sts).

Row 13: (K5, k2tog) 4 times, k1, (ssk, k5) 4 times (49 sts).

Row 15: (K4, k2tog) 4 times, k1, (ssk, k4) 4 times (41 sts).

Row 16: (P3, p2togtbl) 4 times, p1, (p2tog, p3) 4 times (33 sts).

Row 17: (K2, k2tog) 4 times, k1, (ssk, k2) 4 times (25 sts).

Row 18: (P1, p2togtbl) 4 times, p1, (p2tog, p1) 4 times (17 sts).

Row 19: (K2tog) 4 times, k1, (ssk) 4 times (9 sts).

Cut yarn, draw through rem sts.

BEAK

Gently remove the waste yarn and, using two 3.25mm double-pointed needles (one for the top or face edge and one for the bottom or ribbed edge), pick up the loose stitch loops: 19 sts along the lower edge (1B, 17A, 1B); 17 sts along the upper edge (2B, 13A, 2B) (36 sts). Divide the lower and upper stitches over two double-pointed needles each.

Join in yarn D to the right side of the lower edge.

Round 1: *Pick up and knit 1 st to the right of the first st on the needle, knit to end of next needle, pick up and knit 1 st to the left of the last st on the needle; rep from * once more (40 sts).

Round 2 and each alternate round: Knit.

Round 3: Lower needles: (K1, ssk, k5, k2tog) twice, k1. Upper needles: (K1, ssk, k4, k2tog) twice, k1 (32 sts).

Round 5: Lower needles: (K1, ssk, k3, k2tog) twice, k1. Upper needles: (K1, ssk, k2, k2tog) twice, k1 (24 sts).

Round 7: Lower needles: K1, ssk, k7, k2tog, k1. Upper needles: K1, ssk, k5, k2tog, k1 (20 sts).

Round 9: Lower needles: K1, ssk, k5, k2tog, k1. Upper needles: K1, ssk, k3, k2tog, k1 (16 sts).

Round 11: Lower needles: K1, ssk, k3, k2tog, k1. Upper needles: K1, ssk, k1, k2tog, k1 (12 sts).

Round 12: Knit.
Cast off.

FINISHING

Sew in ends. Block and press the hat. Using yarn D, Swiss darn (see page 107) the detail to the eyes. Using mattress stitch (see page 108), sew up the back seam allowing one stitch on each edge for the seam allowance. Using the photograph as reference, attach the buttons using yarn E; add the highlights using yarn B.

KNITTING AND SWISS DARNING CHART FOR PENGUIN

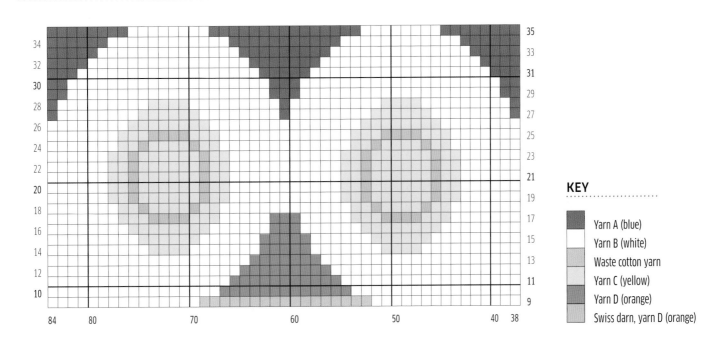

KEY

- Yarn A (blue)
- Yarn B (white)
- Waste cotton yarn
- Yarn C (yellow)
- Yarn D (orange)
- Swiss darn, yarn D (orange)

STITCH NUMBERS ALONG THE BOTTOM OF THE CHART REFER TO THE ADULT SIZE.

Fox

This hat is flighty and feisty with the attitude that can take you from home to work without the need to compromise or look back. To soften the look, reposition the ears and make the eyes slightly bigger – you could even choose to work the eyes from another project in the book.

SIZE

To fit: child[adult] (see page 94)
A close fit that covers the ears.

TENSION

18 sts and 24 rows to 4in (10cm) measured over stocking stitch using two strands of yarn held together and 5mm needles. Use larger or smaller needles if necessary to obtain the correct tension.

MATERIALS

- Aran-weight and light-weight yarn: Rowan Felted Tweed DK, 50% merino wool, 25% alpaca, 25% viscose (191yds/175m per 50g ball); double-stranded for the hat and single for the ears
- 2 x 50g balls in 154 Ginger (rust) (A)
- 1 x 50g ball in 177 Clay (white) (B)
- 1 x 50g ball in 185 Frozen (pink) (D)
- Short lengths of tapestry wool or scraps of yarn in black (C) and brown (E)
- Pair of 5mm (UK6:US8) straight needles
- Set of five 3.25mm (UK10:US3) double-pointed needles
- Pair of 3.25mm (UK10:US3) straight needles, or two needles from the set of double-pointed needles
- Tapestry needle

HAT

Using two strands of yarn worked together, 5mm needles and the thumb method (see page 96), cast on: 16[20]A, 8B, 11A, 9C, 11A, 8B, 15[19]A (78[86] sts).

Work the following using the intarsia technique (see page 106).

Row 1 (WS): P1A, (k1A, p1A) 7[9] times, p8B, p11A, p9C, p11A, p8B, (p1A, k1A) 7[9] times, p2A.

Row 2: K1A, (k1A, p1A) 7[9] times, k1A, k8B, M1RB, k11A, k2C, sskC, k1C, k2togC, k2C, k11A; M1LB, k8B, (k1A, p1A) 7[9] times, k1A.

Row 3: Work keeping stitch pattern and colours as presented on the left-hand needle.

Row 4: K1A, (k1A, p1A) 7[9] times, k1A, k9B, M1RB, k11A, k1C, sskC, k1C, k2togC, k1C, k11A, M1LB, k9B, (k1A, p1A) 7[9] times, k1A.

Row 5: Rep Row 3.

Row 6: K1A, (k1A, p1A) 7[9] times, k1A, k10B, M1RB; k11A, sskC, k1C, k2togC, k11A, M1LB, k10B, (k1A, p1A) 7[9] times, k1A.

Fasten off yarn C.

Row 7: P1A, (k1A, p1A) 7[9] times, p11B, p25A, p11B, (p1A, k1A) 7[9] times, p2A.

Row 8: K1A, (k1A, p1A) 7[9] times, k1A, k11B, M1RB, k10A, sskA, k1A, k2togA, k10A, M1LB, k11B, (k1A, p1A) 7[9] times, k1.

Row 9: Rep Row 3.

Row 10: K1A, (k1A, p1A) 7[9] times, k1A, k12B, M1RB, k9A, sskA, k1A, k2togA, k9A, M1LB, k12B, (k1A, p1A) 7[9] times, k1A.

Row 11: Rep Row 3.

Row 12: K17[21]A, k12B, M1RB, k8A, sskA, k1A, k2togA, k8A, M1LB, k12B, k16[20]A.

Row 13: Rep Row 3.

Row 14: K18[22]A, k12B, M1RB, k7A, sskA, k1A, k2togA, k7A, M1LB, k12B, k17[21]A.

CHILD SIZE ONLY

Fasten off yarn B. Working in yarn A only:

Row 15: Purl.

Row 16: K31, M1R, k6, ssk, k1, k2tog, k6, M1L, k27, M1L, k to end (79 sts).

Row 17: Purl.

Row 18: K32, M1R, k5, ssk, k1, k2tog, k5, M1L, k to end.

Row 19: Purl.

Row 20 (buttonhole row): K28, cast off 6 sts, M1R, k2, ssk, k1, k2tog, k2, M1L, k1, cast off 6 sts, k to end.

Row 21: P28, cast on 6 sts, p11, cast on 6 sts, p to end.

Row 22: K36, M1R, k1, ssk, k1, k2tog, k1, M1L, k to end.

Row 23: Purl.

ADULT SIZE ONLY

Row 15: P22A, p12B, p17A, p12B, p23A.

Row 16: K25A, k10B, M1RB, k6A, sskA, k1A, k2togA, k6A, M1LB, k10B, k21A, M1LA, using yarn A, k to end (87 sts).

Fasten off yarn B. Working in yarn A only:

Row 17: Purl.

Row 18: K36, M1R, k5, ssk, k1, k2tog, k5, M1L, k to end.

Row 19: Purl.

Row 20: K37, M1R, k4, ssk, k1, k2tog, k4, M1L, k to end.

Row 21: Purl.

Row 22: K38, M1R, k3, ssk, k1, k2tog, k3, M1L, k to end.

Row 23: Purl.

Row 24 (buttonhole row): K32, cast off 6 sts, M1R, k2, ssk, k1, k2tog, k2, M1L, k1, cast off 6 sts, k to end.

Row 25: P32, cast on 6 sts, p11, cast on 6 sts, p to end.

Row 26: K40, M1R, k1, ssk, k1, k2tog, k1, M1L, k to end.

Rows 27–31: Work in stocking stitch.

CROWN

CHILD SIZE ONLY

Row 1 (RS): K7, (ssk, k14) twice, k1, (k2tog, k14) twice, k7 (75 sts).

Rows 2–4: Work in stocking stitch.

ADULT SIZE ONLY

Row 1 (RS): K1, (k5, ssk) 6 times, k1, (k2tog, k5) 6 times, k1 (75 sts).

Rows 2–4: Work in stocking stitch.

BOTH SIZES

Row 5: K1, (k4, ssk) 6 times, k1, (k2tog, k4) 6 times, k1 (63 sts).

Rows 6–8: Work in stocking stitch.

Row 9: K1, (k3, ssk) 6 times, k1, (k2tog, k3) 6 times, k1 (51 sts).

Row 10: Purl.

Row 11: K1, (k2, ssk) 6 times, k1, (k2tog, k2) 6 times, k1 (39 sts).

Row 12: Purl.

Row 13: K1, (k1, ssk) 6 times, k1, (k2tog, k1) 6 times, k1 (27 sts).

Row 14: Purl.

Row 15: K1, (ssk) 6 times, p1, (k2tog) 6 times, k1 (15 sts).

Row 16: P1, (p2tog) 3 times, k1, (p2tog) 3 times, p1 (9 sts).

Cut yarn, thread through rem sts and draw tight.

OUTER EAR (MAKE 2)

Using a single strand of yarn A, 3.25mm needles and the thumb method, cast on 27 sts.

Row 1 (WS): Purl.
Rows 2–7: Work in stocking stitch.
Row 8: K1, ssk, k to the last 3 sts, k2tog, k1 (25 sts).
Row 9: Purl.
Rows 10–29: Rep Rows 8–9, 10 times (5 sts).
Cast off knitwise, working 2 sts together at the beg and end of the row before casting them off.

INNER EAR (MAKE 2)

Using a single strand of yarn D, 3.25mm needles and the thumb method, cast on 27 sts.
Work as for Outer Ear.

EYE CENTRE (MAKE 2)

Using a single strand of yarn B, 3.25mm double-pointed needles and the thumb method, cast on 36 sts. Arrange the stitches to work in the round.

Rounds 1–2: Knit.
Round 3: (K1, k2tog) 12 times (24 sts).
Fasten off yarn B. Join in yarn E.
Round 4: Knit.
Round 5: (K2tog) 12 times (12 sts).
Round 6: (K2tog) 6 times (6 sts).
Cut yarn, thread through rem sts and draw tight.

FINISHING

Sew in ends. Block and press the knitted pieces. Using mattress stitch (see page 108), sew the back seam and the inner ear to the outer ear, in both cases allowing one stitch on each edge for the seam allowance. Using the photograph as a guide, position the eyes inside the hat behind the buttonholes. Use whip stitch (see page 108) to attach both the ears and the eyes to the hat. Add the highlights to the eyes using French knots (see page 107) and yarn B.

Mouse

The gentle shaping around the face flatters the wearer and covers the forehead. This mouse has been worked in grey, but there is no reason why you couldn't make it a golden field mouse. For a quirky touch, add a tuft of grey yarn between the ears and a satin bow or place an eye patch across one eye.

SIZE
To fit: child[adult] (see page 94)
A loose fit that covers the ears.

TENSION
18 sts and 24 rows to 4in (10cm) measured over stocking stitch using two strands of yarn held together and 5mm needles. Use larger or smaller needles if necessary to obtain the correct tension.

MATERIALS
• Aran-weight and light-weight yarn: Rowan Felted Tweed DK, 50% merino wool, 25% alpaca, 25% viscose (191yds/175m per 50g ball); double-stranded for the hat and single for the ears

• 2 x 50g balls in 172 Ancient (grey) (A)
• 1 x 50g ball in 185 Frozen (pink) (B)
• Short lengths of tapestry wool or scraps of yarn in white (C) and brown (D)
• 5mm (UK6:US8) 16in (40cm) circular knitting needle
• Set of five 3.25mm (UK10:US3) double-pointed needles
• Set of five 5mm (UK6:US8) double-pointed needles
• Pair of 3.25mm (UK10:US3) straight needles, or two needles from the set of double-pointed needles
• Tapestry needle

SPECIAL ABBREVIATION
Pspo = p1, slip stitch back to left-hand needle, pass the second st on left needle over first.

HAT

Using two strands of yarn A held together, 5mm circular needle and the thumb method (see page 96), cast on 81[97] sts.

Arrange the stitches to work in the round.

Round 1: (K1, p1) to the last st, k1.
Round 2: K26[34], M1R, k12, ssk, k1, k2tog, k12, M1L, k26[34].
Rounds 3-4: Knit.
Round 5: K27[35], M1R, k11, ssk, k1, k2tog, k11, M1L, k27[35].
Rounds 6-7: Knit.
Round 8: K28[36], M1R, k10, ssk, k1, k2tog, k10, M1L, k28[36].
Rounds 9-10: Knit.
Round 11: K29[37], M1R, k9, ssk, k1, k2tog, k9, M1L, k29[37].
Rounds 12-13: Knit.
Round 14: K30[38], M1R, k8, ssk, k1, k2tog, k8, M1L, k30[38].
Rounds 15-16: Knit.
Round 17: K31[39], M1R, k7, ssk, k1, k2tog, k7, M1L, k31[39].
Rounds 18-19: Knit.
Round 20: K32[40], M1R, k6, ssk, k1, k2tog, k6, M1L, k32[40].
Rounds 21-22: Knit.

ADULT SIZE ONLY

Round 23: K41, M1R, k5, ssk, k1, k2tog, k5, M1L, k41.
Rounds 24-25: Knit.
Round 26: K42, M1R, k4, ssk, k1, k2tog, k4, M1L, k42.
Rounds 27-28: Knit.

BOTH SIZES
CROWN

Change to 5mm double-pointed needles when required.
Round 1: (K8[10], ssk) 4 times, k1, (k2tog, k8[10]) 4 times (73[89] sts).
Rounds 2-3: Knit.

Round 4: (K7[9], ssk) 4 times, k1, (k2tog, k7[9]) 4 times (65[81] sts).
Rounds 5-6: Knit.
Round 7: (K6[8], ssk) 4 times, k1, (k2tog, k6[8]) 4 times (57[73] sts).
Round 8: Knit.
Round 9: (K5[7], ssk) 4 times, k1, (k2tog, k5[7]) 4 times (49[65] sts).
Round 10: Knit.
Round 11: (K4[6], ssk) 4 times, k1, (k2tog, k4[6]) 4 times (41[57] sts).
Round 12: Knit.
Round 13: (K3[5], ssk) 4 times, k1, (k2tog, k3[5]) 4 times (33[49] sts).
Round 14: Knit.
Round 15: (K2[4], ssk) 4 times, k1, (k2tog, k2[4]) 4 times (25[41] sts).
Round 16: Knit.
Round 17: (K1[3], ssk) 4 times, k1, (k2tog, k1[3]) 4 times (17[33] sts).

ADULT SIZE ONLY

Round 18: Knit.
Round 19: (K2, ssk) 4 times, k1, (k2tog, k2) 4 times (25 sts).
Round 20: Knit.
Round 21: (K1, ssk) 4 times, k1, (k2tog, k1) 4 times (17 sts).

BOTH SIZES

Next round: (K2tog) 4 times, k1, (k2tog) 4 times (9 sts).
Cut yarn, thread through rem sts and draw tight.

OUTER EAR (MAKE 2)

Using a single strand of yarn A, 3.25mm double-pointed needles and the thumb method, cast on 26 sts. Arrange the stitches to work in the round.
Ear Front: Needle 1, 5 sts; Needle 2, 6 sts.
Ear Back: Needle 3, 8 sts; Needle 4, 7 sts.
Round 1: Knit.
Round 2: K16, ssk, k1, k2tog, k5 (24 sts).
Round 3: Knit.
Round 4: K15, ssk, k1, k2tog, k4 (22 sts).
Round 5: Knit.
Cont as follows: first repeat is worked on Ear Front; second on Ear Back.
Round 6: (K1, M1R, k9, M1L, k1) twice (26 sts).
Round 7: (K1, M1R, k11, M1L, k1) twice (30 sts).
Round 8: Knit.
Round 9: (K1, M1R, k13, M1L, k1) twice (34 sts).
Rounds 10-11: Knit.
Round 12: (K1, M1R, k15, M1L, k1) twice (38 sts).

Rounds 13–21: Knit.
Round 22: (K1, ssk, k13, k2tog, k1) twice (34 sts).
Round 23: Knit.
Round 24: (K1, ssk, k11, k2tog, k1) twice (30 sts).
Round 25: Knit.
Round 26: (K1, ssk, k9, k2tog, k1) twice (26 sts).
Round 27: [(K1, ssk) twice, k1, (k2tog, k1) twice] twice (18 sts).
Round 28: [(Ssk) twice, k1, (k2tog) twice] twice (10 sts).
Cast off in patt. Join Front Ear to Back Ear using mattress stitch (see page 108) or Kitchener stitch (see page 107).

INNER EAR (MAKE 2)

Using a single strand of yarn B, 3.25mm needles and the thumb method, cast on 4 sts.
Row 1: Purl.
Row 2: (K1, M1R) 3 times, k1 (7 sts).
Row 3: P1, M1R, p5, M1L, p1 (9 sts).
Row 4: K1, M1R, k7, M1L, k1 (11 sts).
Row 5: P1, M1R, p9, M1L, p1 (13 sts).
Rows 6–7: Work in stocking stitch.
Row 8: K1, M1R, k11, M1L, k1 (15 sts).
Rows 9–11: Work in stocking stitch.
Row 12: Ssk, k11, k2tog (13 sts).
Rows 13–14: Work in stocking stitch.
Row 15: P2tog, p9, pspo (11 sts).
Row 16: Ssk, k7, k2tog (9 sts).
Row 17: P2tog, p5, pspo (7 sts).
Row 18: Ssk, k3 k2tog (5 sts).
Cast off in decrease patt as set.

NOSE

Work as for Inner Ear.
Cut yarn, leaving a 4in (10cm) tail.
Sew a line of running stitch along the outer edge of the Nose.
Draw tight, gathering the outer edges towards the centre.
Secure with a few small backstitches.

LEFT EYE WHITE

Using yarn C, 3.25mm needles and the thumb method, cast on 11 sts.
Row 1: Purl.
Row 2: K10, M1L, turn.
Row 3: Sl1, p until 1 st rem, M1R, turn.
Row 4: Sl1, k until 3 sts rem, M1L, turn.
Row 5: Sl1, p until 3 sts rem, M1R, turn.
Row 6: Sl1, k until 5 sts rem, M1L, turn.
Row 7: Sl1, p until 5 sts rem, M1R, turn.
Row 8: Sl1, k until 7 sts rem, M1L, turn.
Row 9: Sl1, p to end.
Cast off knitwise.

RIGHT EYE WHITE

Using yarn C, 3.25mm needles and the thumb method, cast on 11 sts. Work as for Left Eye White but work a knit stitch in place of a purl stitch and a purl stitch in place of a knit stitch.

EYE CENTRE (MAKE 2)

Using yarn D, 3.25mm needles and the thumb method, cast on 3 sts.
Row 1: Purl.
Row 2: K1, M1R, k1, M1L, k1 (5 sts).
Row 3: P1, M1L, p3, M1R, p1 (7 sts).
Row 4: Knit.
Row 5: Purl.
Row 6: Ssk, k3, k2tog (5 sts).
Cast off in decrease patt as set.

FINISHING

Sew in ends. Block and press the knitted pieces. Using the photograph as a guide, use whip stitch (see page 108) to attach the inner ear to the outer ear and the eye centre to the eye white. Then attach both ears, eyes and the nose to the hat. Add highlights to the eyes using French knots (see page 107) and yarn C.

Ladybird

This cloche hat is flattering, warm and cute. If you don't like colour knitting, then fear not, the hat is worked from brim to crown around the head – so if you can already knit stripes, you can knit this. For a hat shape that you can lightly steam and mould, choose a 100% wool yarn to make this project.

SIZE

To fit: child[adult] (see page 94)
A loose fit that covers the ears.

TENSION (CHILD'S HAT)

24 sts and 32 rows to 4in (10cm) measured over stocking stitch using 3.75mm needles and light-weight yarn. Use larger or smaller needles if necessary to obtain the correct tension.

TENSION (ADULT'S HAT)

18 sts and 24 rows to 4in (10cm) measured over stocking stitch using 5mm needles and Aran-weight yarn. Use larger or smaller needles if necessary to obtain the correct tension.

MATERIALS (CHILD'S HAT)

• Light-weight yarn: Rowan Pure Wool DK, 100% super-wash wool (142yds/130m per 100g ball)
• 1 x 100g ball in 004 Black (A)
• 1 x 100g ball in 036 Kiss (red) (B)
• Short length of waste yarn
• Pair of 3.75mm (UK9:US5) straight needles
• Pair of 3.25mm (UK10:US3) straight needles
• Set of five 3.25mm (UK10:US3) double-pointed needles
• Tapestry needle
• 3.5mm (UK9:US4) crochet hook
• 2 x 12in (30cm) lengths of pipe cleaner
(Materials list for adult's hat on page 34.)

MATERIALS (ADULT'S HAT)

- Aran-weight yarn: James Brett Chunky with merino, 70% acrylic, 20% siliconized soft polyamide, 10% merino wool (164yds/150m per 100g ball)
- 1 x 100g ball in CM2 (black) (A)
- 1 x 100g ball in CM5 (red) (B)
- Short length of waste yarn
- Pair of 5mm (UK6:US8) straight needles
- Pair of 4mm (UK8:US6) straight needles
- Set of five 4mm (UK8:US6) double-pointed needles
- 4mm (UK8:US6) crochet hook
- 2 x 12in (30cm) lengths of pipe cleaner
- Tapestry needle

CHILD'S HAT

Work as for Adult's hat using light-weight yarn and smaller needles.

ADULT'S HAT

Using the crochet hook and a provisional cast-on (see page 97), cast on 34 sts.
Join in yarn A.
Using 5mm needles, work in stocking stitch throughout.

RIGHT BACK SECTION

Row 1 and 5 following alternate rows: Purl.
Row 2: K20, yf, sl1r, yb, sl1l, turn.
Row 4: K14, yf, sl1r, yb, sl1l, turn.
Row 6: K8, yf, sl1r, yb, sl1l, turn.
Row 8: K11, yf, sl1r, yb, sl1l, turn.
Row 10: K17, yf, sl1r, yb, sl1l, turn.
Fasten off yarn A, join in yarn B.

RIGHT WING

Row 12: Knit.
Row 13: Purl.
Row 14: K1, M1R, k32, yf, sl1r, yb, sl1l, turn.
Row 15: Purl.
Rows 16–33: Rep Rows 14–15, 9 times.
Row 34: K1, M1R, k31, yf, sl1r, yb, sl1l, turn.
Row 35 and 4 following alternate rows: Purl.
Row 36: K1, M1R, k30, yf, sl1r, yb, sl1l, turn.
Row 38: Knit.
Row 40: K1, K2tog, k29, yf, sl1r, yb, sl1l, turn.

Row 42: K1, k2tog, k30, yf, sl1r, yb, sl1l, turn.
Row 44: K1, k2tog, k31, yf, sl1r, yb, sl1l, turn.
Row 45: Purl.
Rows 46–63: Rep Rows 44–45, 9 times.
Row 64: Knit.
Row 65: Purl.
Fasten off yarn B, join in yarn A.

FRONT SECTION

Row 66: K20, yf, sl1r, yb, sl1l, turn.
Row 67 and 12 following alternate rows: Purl.
Row 68: K19, yf, sl1r, yb, sl1l, turn.
Row 70: K18, yf, sl1r, yb, sl1l, turn.
Row 72: K17, yf, sl1r, yb, sl1l, turn.
Row 74: K16, yf, sl1r, yb, sl1l, turn.
Row 76: K15, yf, sl1r, yb, sl1l, turn.
Row 78: Knit.
Row 80: K15, yf, sl1r, yb, sl1l, turn.
Row 82: K16, yf, sl1r, yb, sl1l, turn.
Row 84: K17, yf, sl1r, yb, sl1l, turn.
Row 86: K18, yf, sl1r, yb, sl1l, turn.
Row 88: K19, yf, sl1r, yb, sl1l, turn.
Row 90: K20, yf, sl1r, yb, sl1l, turn.
Fasten off yarn A, join in yarn B.

LEFT WING

Rows 92–145: Rep Rows 12–65. (34 sts)
Fasten off yarn B, join in yarn A.

LEFT BACK SECTION

Rows 146–155: Rep Rows 2–11.
Row 156: Knit.
Place the sts onto a straight needle so that the last st worked is nearest to the point.

BLACK DOTS (MAKE 6)

Using yarn A, 4mm double-pointed needles and the thumb method (see page 96), cast on 6 sts.

Round 1: (Inc) 6 times (12 sts).
Round 2: (K1, inc) 6 times (18 sts).
Round 3: Knit.
Round 4: (K2, inc) 6 times (24 sts).
Round 5: Knit.
Round 6: (K2, inc) 8 times (32 sts).
Cast off.

ANTENNAE (MAKE 2)

Using yarn B, 4mm needles and the thumb method, cast on 30 sts.

Row 1: Knit.
Row 2: Purl.
Fasten off yarn B, join in yarn A.
Row 3: Purl.
Row 4: Knit.
Rows 5–10: Rep Rows 3–4, 3 times.
Cast off knitwise.
Fold the pipe cleaners so the two points are folded to meet in the middle.

Use mattress stitch (see page 108) to stitch the cast-off edge to Row 3, encasing the rows of red knitted fabric and the pipe cleaner, stopping 2in (5cm) from the end.
Do not sew in the end. Don't be tempted to miss the cast-off and work Kitchener stitch too close the seam. The skeletal strength of the cast-off makes a difference.
Using 4mm double-pointed needles, pick up and knit 9 sts along the remaining short edge.
Arrange the stitches over 3 double-pointed needles.

Round 1: (Inc) 9 times (18 sts).
Round 2: Knit.
Round 3: (K1, inc) 9 times (27 sts).
Cast off.
Finish working mattress stitch along the long edge.

FINISHING

Sew in ends. Block and press the hat. Gently unpick the provisional cast-on and place the live stitches onto a spare needle so that the stitch at the bottom edge of the hat is nearest the point. Use Kitchener stitch (see page 107) to close the back seam. Flatten the hat with the front facing and the double decrease along the fold. Using mattress stitch, sew the flattened top seam. Using the photograph as a guide and whip stitch (see page 108), attach the black dots to the wings. Attach the antennae in the same way but adding a line of running stitch around the base.

Tiger

Perfect for the urban jungle, this hat is bound to attract attention when viewed from the front or when viewed from the back. For a subtler colour scheme make the stripes dark brown rather than black. To make a lioness hat, work this pattern without the black stripes.

SIZE

To fit: child[adult] (see page 94)
A close fit that covers the top of the ears.

TENSION

24 sts and 36 rows to 4in (10cm) measured over stocking stitch using 3.75mm needles. Use larger or smaller needles if necessary to obtain the correct tension.

MATERIALS

- Light-weight yarn: Rowan Tweed, 100% wool (129yds/118m per 50g ball)
- 1 x 50g ball in 600 Tissington (orange) (A)
- 1 x 50g ball in 585 Askrigg (black) (B)
- 1 x 50g ball in 584 Buckden (white) (C)
- Short lengths of tapestry wool or scraps of yarn in green (D) and pink (E)
- Pair of 3.75mm (UK9:US5) straight needles
- Set of five 3.25mm (UK10:US3) double-pointed needles
- Tapestry needle

HAT

Using 3.75mm needles and the thumb method (see page 96), cast on 43[49]A, 23B, 43[49]A, (109[121] sts).
Fasten off yarn B.
Work the following using the intarsia technique (see page 106).
Row 1 (RS): (K1A, p1A) 21[24] times, k1A, k23C, (k1A, p1A) 21[24] times, k1A.
Row 2: (P1A, k1A) 20[23] times, p1A, (k1C, p1C) 13 times, k1C, (p1A, k1A) 20[23] times, p1A.
Row 3: (K1A, p1A) 20[23] times, (k1C, p1C) 14 times, k1C, (p1A, k1A) 20[23] times.
Row 4: Work keeping stitch pattern and colours as presented on the left-hand needle.
Rows 5–6: Rep Rows 3–4.
Begin to work from chart in stocking stitch.

CHILD SIZE ONLY
Rows 7–29: Yarn A, work 5 sts; work chart from right to left on RS rows and left to right on WS rows, between the vertical red rules; yarn A, work 5 sts.
Row 30: P1A, p2togA, p2A; work from chart; p2A, p2togA, p1A (107 sts).
Rows 31–35: Yarn A, work 4 sts; work from chart; yarn A, work 4 sts.
Row 36: P2A, p2togA; work from chart; p2togA, p2A (105 sts).
Fasten off all strands of yarn B except the strand attached to the centre 5 sts.

ADULT SIZE ONLY
Rows 7–36: Yarn A, work 6 sts; work the entire chart from right to left on RS rows and left to right on WS rows; yarn A, work 6 sts (121 sts).
Row 37: (K13A, k2togA) 3 times, k13A, k2togB, k1B, sskB, k13A, (sskA, k13A) 3 times (113 sts).
Rows 38–40: Work in stocking stitch as set, keeping the centre 3 sts in B.
Row 41: (K12A, k2togA) 3 times, k12A, k2togB, k1B, sskB, k12A, (sskA, k12A) 3 times (105 sts).
Row 42: Purl.

BOTH SIZES
CROWN
Work keeping stitch pattern and colours as presented on the left-hand needle: the fourth k2tog, the centre black st and the first ssk are worked in yarn B.
Row 1: (K11, k2tog) 4 times, k1, (ssk, k11) 4 times (97 sts).
Row 2 and 6 following alternate rows: Purl.
Row 3: (K10, k2tog) 4 times, k1, (ssk, k10) 4 times (89 sts).
Row 5: (K9, k2tog) 4 times, k1, (ssk, k9) 4 times (81 sts).
Row 7: (K8, k2tog) 4 times, k1, (ssk, k8) 4 times (73 sts).
Row 9: (K7, k2tog) 4 times, k1, (ssk, k7) 4 times (65 sts).
Row 11: (K6, k2tog) 4 times, k1, (ssk, k6) 4 times (57 sts).
Row 13: (K5, k2tog) 4 times, k1, (ssk, k5) 4 times (49 sts).
Row 15: (K4, k2tog) 4 times, k1, (ssk, k4) 4 times (41 sts).
Row 16: (P3, p2togtbl) 4 times, p1, (p2tog, p3) 4 times (33 sts).

Row 17: (K2, k2tog) 4 times, k1, (ssk, k2) 4 times (25 sts).
Row 18: (P1, p2togtbl) 4 times, p1, (p2tog, p1) 4 times (17 sts).
Row 19: (K2tog) 4 times, k1, (ssk) 4 times (9 sts).
Cut yarn, thread through rem sts and draw tight.

EARS (MAKE 2)
Using yarn A, 3.25mm double-pointed needles and the thumb method, cast on 34 sts. Arrange the stitches to work in the round.
Ear Front: Needle 1, 7 sts; Needle 2, 7 sts.
Ear Back: Needle 3, 10 sts; Needle 4, 10 sts.
Round 1: Knit.
Round 2: K21, ssk, k2, k2tog, k7 (32 sts).
Round 3: K20, ssk, k2, k2tog, k6 (30 sts).
Round 4: K19, ssk, k2, k2tog, k5 (28 sts).
Cont as follows: first repeat is worked on Ear Front; second repeat on Ear Back.
Round 5: (K1, M1R, k12, M1L, k1) twice (32 sts).
Round 6: Knit.
Round 7: (K1, M1R, k14, M1L, k1) twice (36 sts).
Round 8: Knit.
Round 9: (K1, M1R, k16, M1L, k1) twice (40 sts).
Rounds 10–14: Knit.

Round 15: (K1, ssk, k14, k2tog, k1) twice (36 sts).

Round 16: (K1, ssk, k12, k2tog, k1) twice (32 sts).

Round 17: (K1, ssk, k10, k2tog, k1) twice (28 sts).

Round 18: (K1, ssk, k8, k2tog, k1) twice (24 sts).

Round 19: (K1, ssk, k6, k2tog, k1) twice (20 sts).

Round 20: (K1, ssk, k4, k2tog, k1) twice (16 sts).

Round 21: (K1, ssk, k2, k2tog, k1) twice (12 sts).

Cast off in pattern as set. Join Ear Front to Ear Back using mattress stitch (see page 108) or Kitchener stitch (see page 107).

FINISHING

Sew in ends. Block and press the knitted pieces. Using the chart as a guide, Swiss darn (see page 107) the detail to the eyes, nose and mouth. Using mattress stitch (see page 108), sew the back seam allowing half a stitch on each edge for the seam allowance. Using the photograph as a guide, use whip stitch (see page 108) to attach both ears to the hat.

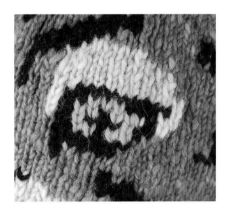

KNITTING AND SWISS DARNING CHART FOR TIGER

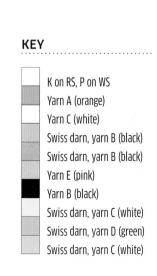

STITCH NUMBERS ALONG THE BOTTOM OF THE CHART REFER TO THE ADULT SIZE.

KEY

☐	K on RS, P on WS
	Yarn A (orange)
☐	Yarn C (white)
	Swiss darn, yarn B (black)
	Swiss darn, yarn B (black)
	Yarn E (pink)
■	Yarn B (black)
	Swiss darn, yarn C (white)
	Swiss darn, yarn D (green)
	Swiss darn, yarn C (white)

Brown Bear

The squish on the nose of this hat is irresistible. You may
decide to fill it with toy stuffing, but for me the soft nose
suggests cuddles and comfort – that is, until it gets very wet.
To make this hat bigger, add half the stitches to the front panel
and half the extra stitches required to the back panel.

SIZE

To fit: child[adult] (see page 94)
A standard fit that covers the ears.

TENSION

9½ sts and 15 rows to 4in (10cm) measured over
stocking stitch using 10mm needles. Use larger
or smaller needles if necessary to obtain the
correct tension.

MATERIALS

- Chunky-weight yarn: Rowan Big Wool, 100% wool
  (87yds/80m per 100g ball)
- 1 x 100g ball in 071 Stag (brown) (A)
- A short length or scrap of chunky-weight yarn to
  be worked as a double strand in black (B)
- Short lengths of tapestry wool or scraps of yarn
  in dark brown (C), white (D) and black (E)
- Short length of waste yarn
- 9mm (UK00:US13) circular needle
- 10mm (UK000:US15) circular needle
- Set of five 9mm (UK00:US13) double-pointed needles
- Set of five 10mm (UK000:US15) double-pointed needles
- Set of five 3.25mm (UK10:US3) double-pointed needles
- 2 x 1in (24mm) black buttons
- Tapestry needle

HAT

Using 9mm circular needle, yarn A and the cable method (see page 97), cast on 56[64] sts.
Arrange the stitches to work in the round.

Rounds 1–3: (K1, p1) to end.
Change to 10mm circular needle.

Round 4: Knit.

Round 5: K2[3], ssk, k20[22], k2tog, k4[6] (this is the Front Panel), ssk, k20[22], k2tog, k2[3] (52[60] sts).

Rounds 6–7: Knit.

Round 8: K2[3], ssk, k18[20], k2tog, k4[6], ssk, k18[20], k2tog, k2[3] (48[56] sts).

Rounds 9–10: Knit.

Round 11: K2[3], ssk, k16[18], k2tog, k4[6], ssk, k16[18], k2tog, k2[3] (44[52] sts).

Rounds 12–13: Knit.

Round 14: K2[3], ssk, k14[16], k2tog, k4[6], ssk, k14[16], k2tog, k2[3] (40[48] sts).

Rounds 15–16: Knit.

Round 17: K2[3], ssk, k12[14], k2tog, k4[6], ssk, k12[14], k2tog, k2[3] (36[44] sts).

Round 18: Knit.

Round 19: K2[3], ssk, k10[12], k2tog, k4[6], ssk, k10[12], k2tog, k2[3] (32[40] sts).

Round 20: Knit.

Round 21: K2[3], ssk, k8[10], k2tog, k4[6], ssk, k8[10], k2tog, k2[3] (28[36] sts).

Round 22: Knit.
Change to 10mm double-pointed needles.

CHILD SIZE ONLY

Round 23: K2, ssk, k6, k2tog, k4, ssk, k6, k2tog, k2 (24 sts).

Round 24: K2, ssk, k4, k2tog, k4, ssk, k4, k2tog, k2 (20 sts).

Round 25: K2, ssk, k2, k2tog, k4, ssk, k2, k2tog, k2 (16 sts).

Round 26: K2, ssk, k2tog, k4, ssk, k2tog, k2 (12 sts).

Round 27: K3.
Rearrange the sts onto two needles so that the next 6 sts are on one needle and the remainder are on the other.
Use Kitchener stitch (see page 107) or three-needle cast off (see page 98) to join the two sets of stitches.

ADULT SIZE ONLY

Round 23: K3, ssk, k8, k2tog, k6, ssk, k8, k2tog, k3 (32 sts).

Round 24: Knit.

Round 25: K3, ssk, k6, k2tog, k6, ssk, k6, k2tog, k3 (28 sts).

Round 26: K3, ssk, k4, k2tog, k6, ssk, k4, k2tog, k3 (24 sts).

Round 27: K3, ssk, k2, k2tog, k6, ssk, k2, k2tog, k3 (20 sts).

Round 28: K3, ssk, k2tog, k6, ssk, k2tog, k3 (16 sts).

Round 29: K4.
Rearrange the sts onto two needles so that the next 8 sts are on one needle and the remainder are on the other.
Use Kitchener stitch or three-needle cast off to join the two sets of stitches.

EAR (MAKE 2)

Using 9mm double-pointed needles, yarn A and the thumb method (see page 96), cast on 12 sts.
Arrange the stitches to work in the round.
Ear Front: needle 2 and 3. Ear Back: needle 1 and 4.

Round 1: Knit.

Round 2: (K1, M1R, k4, M1L, k1) twice (16 sts).

Round 3: (K1, M1R, k6, M1L, k1) twice (20 sts).

Rounds 4–5: Knit.

Round 6: (K1, ssk, k4, k2tog, k1) twice (16 sts).

Round 7: (K1, ssk, k2, k2tog, k1) twice (12 sts).
Cast off in pattern set and join the Front Ear to the Back Ear using mattress stitch (see page 108) or Kitchener stitch.

Note: The decreases align with the centre front and centre back of the Ear.

NOSE

Using waste yarn, mark the edge of the Front panel and Row 1[1] and Row 12[14].

Using 9mm double-pointed needles, yarn A, and starting from the centre front 1 row above the rib, pick up and knit: 3[4] sts across half the bottom edge of the Front Panel; 10[12] sts up the left-hand side of the Front Panel ending at Row 11[13]; 6[8] sts across the top edge of the Front Panel; 10[12] sts down the right-hand side of the Front Panel ending at Row 1[1]; 3[4] sts across half the bottom edge of the Front Panel (32[40] sts).

Arrange the stitches over three needles to work in the round. Starting at the centre front: needle 1, 12[14] sts; needle 2, 8[12] sts; needle 3, 12[14] sts (32[40] sts).

Rounds 1-3: Knit.

Round 4: K2, k2tog, k7[10], ssk, k6[8], k2tog, k7[10], ssk, k2 (28[36] sts).

Round 5: K1, k2tog, k to the last 3 sts, ssk, k1 (26[34] sts).

Round 6: K2tog, k to the last 2 sts, ssk (24[32] sts).

Round 7: K2tog, k6[9], k2tog, k4[6], ssk, k6[9], ssk (20[28] sts).

Rounds 8-9: Rep Row 6 twice (16[24] sts).

Round 10: K2tog, k3[6], k2tog, k2[4], ssk, k3[6], ssk (12[20] sts).

ADULT SIZE ONLY

Rounds 11-12: Rep Row 6 twice (16 sts).

Round 13: K2tog, k3, k2tog, k2, ssk, k3, ssk (12 sts).

BOTH SIZES

Fasten off yarn A, join in yarn B.

Next round: Knit.

Rep the last round twice more.

Next round: (K2tog, k1) 4 times.

Cut yarn, thread through rem sts and draw tight.

EYE (MAKE 2)

Leaving a 4in (10cm) tail, using yarn C, 3.25mm double-pointed needles and the thumb method, cast on 14 sts. Arrange the stitches to work in the round.

Rounds 1-4: Knit.

Round 5: (K2tog) 7 times (7 sts).

Cut yarn, thread through rem sts, place a button into the tube of knitted fabric and draw tight.

Using the cast-on tail, sew a line of running stitch along the outer edge of the Eye.

Draw together but not too tightly, gathering the outer edges towards the centre.

Secure with a few small backstitches.

FINISHING

Sew in ends. Block and press the knitted pieces. Add highlights to the eyes using French knots (see page 107) and yarn D. Using yarn E, attach the eyes to the hat. Using the photograph as a guide and whip stitch (see page 108), attach the ears to the hat.

Chicken

Now this is a hat to strut your stuff in. The fact that
the eyes are looking skyward stops people from talking to the
hat rather than to the wearer. To make this hat into a chick,
change the main colour to yellow and do not add a wattle
or comb to the design.

SIZE

To fit: child[adult] (see page 94)
A close fit that covers the top of the ears.

TENSION

20½ sts and 27 rows to 4in (10cm) measured
over stocking stitch using 4.5mm needles. Use
larger or smaller needles if necessary to obtain
the correct tension.

MATERIALS

- Aran-weight yarn: Sublime Luxurious Aran Tweed,
  40% wool, 40% cotton, 20% llama (109yds/100m
  per 50g ball)
- 1 x 50g ball in 371 Oxblood (rust) (A)
- Short lengths of tapestry wool or scraps of tweed
  yarn in red (B), pink (C), yellow (D), brown (E)
  and white (F)
- 5mm (UK6:US8) circular needle
- 4.5mm (UK7:US7) circular needle
- Set of four or five 4.5mm (UK7:US7) double-pointed
  needles (if required to work the last few rounds)
- Set of five 5 x 3.25mm (UK10:US3) double-pointed
  needles
- Tapestry needle

HAT

Using 5mm circular needle, yarn A and the cable method (see page 97), cast on 98[112] sts.
Arrange the stitches to work in the round.
Round 1: Purl.
Round 2 and 4 following alternate rounds: Knit.
Round 3: (K2, ssk, k7, k2tog, k1) 7[8] times (84[96] sts).
Round 5: (K1, yo, k1, ssk, k5, k2tog, k1, yo) 7[8] times.
Round 7: (K2, yo, k1, ssk, k3, k2tog, k1, yo, k1) 7[8] times.
Round 9: (K3, yo, k1, ssk, k1, k2tog, k1, yo, k2) 7[8] times.
Round 11: (K4, yo, k1, sl2tog, k1, psso, k1, yo, k3) 7[8] times.
Change to 4.5mm circular needle.
Round 12 and 3 following alternate rounds: Knit to the last st; the last st becomes part of the first-stitch decrease on the next round.
Round 13: (Sl2tog, k1, psso, k4, yo, k1, yo, k4) 7[8] times.
Round 15: (Sl2tog, k1, psso, k3, yo, k3, yo, k3) 7[8] times.
Round 17: (Sl2tog, k1, psso, k2, yo, k5, yo, k2) 7[8] times.
Round 19: (Sl2tog, k1, psso, k1, yo, k7, yo, k1) 7[8] times.
Round 20 and 4[6] following alternate rounds: Knit.
Round 21: (K1, yo, k4, sl2tog, k1, psso, k4, yo) 7[8] times.
Round 23: (K2, yo, k3, sl2tog, k1, psso, k3, yo, k1) 7[8] times.
Round 25: (K3, yo, k2, sl2tog, k1, psso, k2, yo, k2) 7[8] times.
Round 27: (K4, yo, k1, sl2tog, k1, psso, k1, yo, k3) 7[8] times.

ADULT SIZE ONLY

Round 29: (K3, k2tog, k1, M1R, k1, M1L, k1, ssk, k2) 8 times.
Round 31: (K2, k2tog, k1, M1R, k3, M1L, k1, ssk, k1) 8 times.
Round 33: (K1, k2tog, k1, M1R, k5, M1L, k1, ssk) 8 times.
Round 34: Knit to the last st; the last st becomes part of the first double-decrease on the next round.
Round 35: (Sl2tog, k1, psso, k1, M1R, k7, M1L, k1) 8 times.
Round 36: Knit.

BOTH SIZES
CROWN

Round 1: (K2, ssk, k5, k2tog, k1) 7[8] times (70[80] sts).
Round 2: Knit.
Round 3: (K1, M1R, k1, ssk, k3, k2tog, k1, M1L) 7[8] times.
Round 4: Knit.
Round 5: (K3, ssk, k1, k2tog, k2) 7[8] times (56[64] sts).
Round 6: Knit.
Round 7: (K2, M1R, k1, sl2tog, k1, psso, k1, M1L, k1) 7[8] times.
Rounds 8–9: Knit.
Round 10: (K3, sl2tog, k1, psso, k2) 7[8] times (42[48] sts).
Rounds 11–12: Knit.
Round 13: (K2, sl2tog, k1, psso, k1) 7[8] times (28[32] sts).
Rounds 14–15: Knit.
Round 16: (K1, sl2tog, k1, psso) 7[8] times (14[16] sts).
Round 17: Knit.
Round 18: (K2tog) 7[8] times (7[8] sts).
Cut yarn, thread through rem sts and draw tight.

COMB

Using yarn B, 3.25mm two double-pointed needles and the thumb method (see page 96), cast on 8 sts.
Rows 1–2: Knit.
Row 3: Cast off 4 sts, k to end (4 sts).
Row 4: K to end, cast on 8 sts.
Rows 5–8: Knit.
Row 9: Cast off 4 sts, k to end (8 sts).
Row 10: K to end, cast on 4 sts (12 sts).
Rows 11–14: Knit.
Rows 15–20: Rep Rows 9–14 once.
Row 21: Cast off 8 sts, k to end (4 sts).
Row 22: K to end, cast on 4 sts (8 sts).
Rows 23–26: Knit.
Cast off.

OUTER EYE (MAKE 2)

Using yarn C, 3.25mm double-pointed needles and the thumb method, cast on 36 sts.
Arrange the stitches to work in the round.
Rounds 1–2 (WS): Knit.
Round 3: (K1, k2tog) 12 times (24 sts).
Round 4: Knit.
Round 5: (K2tog) 12 times (12 sts).
Round 6: (K2tog) 6 times (6 sts).
Cut yarn, thread through rem sts and draw tight.

EYE CENTRE (MAKE 2)

Using yarn D, two 3.25mm double-pointed needles and the thumb method, cast on 3 sts.

Row 1 (RS): Purl.
Row 2: K1, M1R, k1, M1L, k1 (5 sts).
Row 3: P1, M1L, p3, M1R, p1 (7 sts).
Row 4: Knit.
Row 5: Purl.
Row 6: Ssk, k3, k2tog (5 sts).
Cast off in the decrease pattern set.

BEAK

Using yarn D, 3.25mm double-pointed needles and the thumb method, cast on 18 sts.
Arrange the stitches to work in the round.

Rounds 1–4: Knit.
Round 5: K2tog, k4, ssk, k2, k2tog, k4, ssk (14 sts).
Round 6: K2tog, k to the last 2 sts, ssk (12 sts).
Round 7: K2tog, k2, ssk, k2tog, k2, ssk (8 sts).
Round 8: K2tog, k to the last 2 sts, ssk (6 sts).
Rounds 9–10: Knit.
Cut yarn, thread through rem sts and draw tight.

WATTLE

Using yarn B, 3.25mm double-pointed needles and the thumb method, cast on 6 sts.
Arrange the stitches to work in the round.

Round 1: (Inc) 6 times (12 sts).
Round 2: (K1, inc) 6 times (18 sts).
Round 3: (K2, inc) 6 times (24 sts).
Rounds 4–6: Knit.
Round 7: (K2, k2tog) 6 times (18 sts).
Rounds 8–10: Knit.
Round 11: (K1, k2tog) 6 times (12 sts).
Rounds 12–14: Knit.
Round 15: (K2tog) 6 times (6 sts).
Rounds 16–23: Knit.
Cut yarn, thread through rem sts and draw tight.

FINISHING

Sew in ends. Block and press the knitted pieces. Using yarn E and Swiss darning (see page 107), embroider the pupil on the eye centre. Using yarn E and a French knot (see page 107), add a highlight to the outer eye. Attach the eye centres to the reverse stocking stitch side of the outer eye. With the comb edge aligned along a line of double decreases, and its centre slightly back from the last stitches of the hat, starting at the front, whip stitch (see page 108) the comb to the line of double decreases. Using the photograph as a guide and whip stitch, attach the eyes, beak and the narrower end of the wattle to the hat.

SWISS DARNING CHART FOR CHICKEN'S EYES

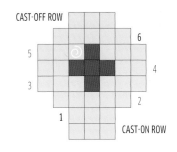

CAST-OFF ROW

5

3

1

CAST-ON ROW

6

4

2

KEY

- Yarn D (yellow)
- Swiss darn, yarn E (brown)
- French knot, yarn F (white)

Zebra

....

This hat is very versatile. Without its ears, it makes a gentle
nod (get it?) towards the animal hat trend. Change the colours
and this hat becomes more Punk rock than African rock.
Most of the adult hats in this book would look good on older
children, but the child's version of this hat looks cute
on a medium-sized adult head.

SIZE
To fit: child[adult] (see page 94)
A loose fit that covers the ears, but the
child's hat also makes a cute adult hat.

TENSION
17 sts and 22 rows to 4in (10cm) measured over
stocking stitch using 5.5mm needles. Use larger
or smaller needles if necessary to obtain the
correct tension.

MATERIALS
• Chunky-weight yarn: Rowan Cocoon, 80% wool,
  20% mohair (126yds/115m per 100g ball)
• 3 x 100g balls in 805 Mountain (black) (A)
• 1 x 100g ball in 801 Polar (white) (B)
• Pair of 5.5mm (UK5:US9) straight needles
• Set of five 5mm (UK6:US8) double-pointed needles
• Tapestry needle

NOTE
Pattern instructions have been given for wrapping
stitches on short rows. Remember to pick up and knit
the wraps when the wrapped stitch is next worked.

CHILD SIDE PANEL (MAKE 2)

Using 5.5mm needles and yarn A, cast on 25 sts.

Row 1 (WS): P to the last 3 sts, k1, p1, k1.

Row 2: K1, M1R, k18, yf, sl1r, yb, sl1l, turn.

Row 3: Rep Row 1.

Join in yarn B.

Using the intarsia technique (see page 106), work the first 3 sts of each RS row and the last 3 sts of each WS row in yarn A. Carry the yarn not in use on WS rows before the last 3 sts in yarn A are worked.

Row 4: Yarn A, k1, M1R, k1; yarn B, k19, yf, sl1r, yb, sl1l, turn.

Row 5: Yarn B, p to the last 3 sts; yarn A, k1, p1, k1.

Row 6: Yarn A, k1, M1R, k12, yf, sl1r, yb, sl1l, turn.

Row 7: Yarn A, p to the last 3 sts, k1, p1, k1.

Row 8: Yarn A, k1, M1R, k1; yarn B, k22, yf, sl1r, yb, sl1l, turn.

Row 9: Rep Row 5.

Row 10: Yarn A, k1, M1R, k25, yf, sl1r, yb, sl1l, turn.

Row 11: Rep Row 7.

Row 12: Yarn A, k1, M1R, k27, yf, sl1r, yb, sl1l, turn.

Row 13: Rep Row 7.

Row 14: Yarn A, k1, M1R, k1; yarn B, k28, yf, sl1r, yb, sl1l, turn.

Row 15: Rep Row 5.

Row 16: Yarn A, k1, M1R, k to end.

Row 17: Rep Row 7.

Row 18: Yarn A, k1, M1R, k1; yarn B, k24, yf, sl1r, yb, sl1l, turn.

Row 19: Rep Row 5.

Row 20: Yarn A, k1, k2tog, k to end.

Row 21: Rep Row 7.

Row 22: Yarn A, k1, k2tog, k1; yarn B, k28, yf, sl1r, yb, sl1l, turn.

Row 23: Rep Row 5.

Row 24: Yarn A, k1, k2tog, k27, yf, sl1r, yb, sl1l, turn.

Row 25: Rep Row 7.

Row 26: Yarn A, k1, k2tog, k25, yf, sl1r, yb, sl1l, turn.

Row 27: Rep Row 7.

Row 28: Yarn A, k1, k2tog, k1; yarn B, k22, yf, sl1r, yb, sl1l, turn.

Row 29: Rep Row 5.

Row 30: Yarn A, k1, k2tog, k12, yf, sl1r, yb, sl1l, turn.

Row 31: Rep Row 7.

Row 32: Yarn A, k1, k2tog, k1; yarn B, k19, yf, sl1r, yb, sl1l, turn.

Row 33: Rep Row 5.

Fasten off yarn B.

Row 34: Yarn A, k1, k2tog, k18, yf, sl1r, yb, sl1l, turn.

Row 35: Rep Row 1.

Row 36: Yarn A, k1, k2tog, k to end. Cast off purlwise.

ADULT SIDE PANEL (MAKE 2)

Using 5.5mm needles and yarn A, cast on 33 sts.

Row 1 (WS): P to the last 3 sts, k1, p1, k1.

Row 2: K1, M1R, k26, yf, sl1r, yb, sl1l, turn.

Row 3: Rep Row 1.

Join in yarn B.

Using the intarsia technique, work the first 3 sts of each RS row and the last 3 sts of each WS row in yarn A. Carry the yarn not in use on WS rows before the last 3 sts in yarn A are worked.

Row 4: Yarn A, k1, M1R, k1; yarn B, k27, yf, sl1r, yb, sl1l, turn.

Row 5: Yarn B, p to the last 3 sts; yarn A, k1, p1, k1.

Row 6: Yarn A, k1, M1R, k20, yf, sl1r, yb, sl1l, turn.

Row 7: Yarn A, p to the last 3 sts, k1, p1, k1.

Row 8: Yarn A, k1, M1R, k1; yarn B, k30, yf, sl1r, yb, sl1l, turn.

Row 9: Rep Row 5.

Row 10: Yarn A, k1, M1R, k33, yf, sl1r, yb, sl1l, turn.

Row 11: Rep Row 7.

Row 12: Yarn A, k1, M1R, k35, yf, sl1r, yb, sl1l, turn.

Row 13: Rep Row 7.

Row 14: Yarn A, k1, M1R, k1; yarn B, k36, yf, sl1r, yb, sl1l, turn.

Row 15: Rep Row 5.

Row 16: Yarn A, k1, M1R, k1; yarn B, k to end.

Row 17: Rep Row 5.

Row 18: Yarn A, k1, M1R, k to end.

Row 19: Rep Row 7.

Row 20: Yarn A, k1, M1R, k1; yarn B, k32, yf, sl1r, yb, sl1l, turn.

Row 21: Rep Row 5.

Row 22: Yarn A, k1, k2tog, k to end.

Row 23: Rep Row 7.

Row 24: Yarn A, k1, k2tog, k1; yarn B, k to end.

Row 25: Rep Row 5.

Row 26: Yarn A, k1, k2tog, k1; yarn B, k36, yf, sl1r, yb, sl1l, turn.

Row 27: Rep Row 5.

Row 28: Yarn A, k1, k2tog, k35, yf, sl1r, yb, sl1l, turn.

Row 29: Rep Row 7.

Row 30: Yarn A, k1, k2tog, k33, yf, sl1r, yb, sl1l, turn.

Row 31: Rep Row 7.

Row 32: Yarn A, k1, k2tog, k1; yarn B, k30, yf, sl1r, yb, sl1l, turn.

Row 33: Rep Row 5.

Row 34: Yarn A, k1, k2tog, k20, yf, sl1r, yb, sl1l, turn.

Row 35: Rep Row 7.
Row 36: Yarn A, k1, k2tog, k1; yarn B, k27, yf, sl1r, yb, sl1l, turn.
Row 37: Rep Row 5.
Fasten off yarn B.
Row 38: Yarn A, k1, k2tog, k26, yf, sl1r, yb, sl1l, turn.
Row 39: Rep Row 1.
Row 40: Yarn A, k1, k2tog, k to end.
Cast off purlwise.

MANE (BOTH SIZES)

Using 5.5mm needles and two strands of yarn A worked together, cast on 12[14] sts.
Row 1: Knit.
Row 2: Purl.
Row 3: K1, ML 10[12] times, k1.
Row 4: Purl.
Rep Rows 3–4, 26[32] times.
Next row: K1, ML 10[12] times, k1.
Cast off purlwise.

EAR (MAKE 2)

Using 5mm double-pointed needles, yarn A and the thumb method (see page 96), cast on 14 sts.
Arrange the stitches to work in the round.
Ear Front: needle 2 and 3. Ear Back: needle 1 and 4.
Rounds 1–6: Knit.
Round 7: (K1, M1R, k5, M1L, k1) twice (18 sts).
Round 8: Knit.
Round 9: (K1, M1R, k7, M1L, k1) twice (22 sts).
Round 10: Knit.
Round 11: (K1, M1R, k9, M1L, k1) twice (26 sts).
Rounds 12–18: Knit.
Round 19: (K1, ssk, k7, k2tog, k1) twice (22 sts).
Round 20: Knit.
Round 21: (K1, ssk, k5, k2tog, k1) twice (18 sts).
Round 22: Knit.
Round 23: (K1, ssk, k3, k2tog, k1) twice (14 sts).
Round 24: Knit.
Round 25: (K1, ssk, k1, k2tog, k1) twice (10 sts).
Round 26: Knit.
Round 27: (Ssk, k1, k2tog) twice (6 sts).
Round 28: Knit.
Cut yarn, thread through rem sts and draw tight.
Note: The decreases align with the centre front and centre back of the Ear.

CORD (MAKE 2)

Make an i-cord as follows.
Using a pair of 5mm double-pointed needles, yarn A and the thumb method, cast on 4 sts.
Row 1: Knit.
*Without turning work, slide sts along the needle to the right-hand point and draw the working yarn across the back of the sts.
Row 2: Knit.
Rep from *until the cord measures 16in (38cm) or the required length.
Cut yarn, thread through sts and draw tight.

FINISHING

Sew in ends. Block and press the side panels. Using mattress stitch (see page 108), join the mane to the side panels from the back corner of the side panel to a point level with the top of the first, partial, black stripe. Fold the first 6 rounds of the ear to the inside of the ear. Using the photograph as a guide and using whip stitch (see page 108), attach the ears and the cords to the hat. Using yarn A, make two pompoms (see page 109) – the pompoms on this hat are 2in (5cm) in diameter. Attach a pompom to each cord.

Panda

Can you have too many pompoms? The pompoms in this project are quite modest; don't be tempted to make them too big as they might overbalance the hat. If you don't want to have pompom ears, you can work the ears from the Brown Bear pattern on page 40.

SIZE
To fit: child[adult] (see page 94)
A close fit that covers the top of the ears.

TENSION
22 sts and 32 rows to 4in (10cm) measured over stocking stitch using 4mm needles. Use larger or smaller needles if necessary to obtain the correct tension.

MATERIALS
- Aran-weight yarn: Rowan Creative Focus Worsted, 75% wool, 25% alpaca (220yds/200m per 100g ball)
- 1 x 100g ball in 500 Ebony (black) (A)
- 1 x 100g ball in 100 Natural (white) (B)
- Small amount of worsted-weight yarn in cream (C)
- Short lengths of tapestry wool or scraps of yarn in smooth black yarn (D) and white (E)
- Pair of 3.75mm (UK9:US5) straight needles
- Pair of 4mm (UK8:US6) straight needles
- Set of five 3.25mm (UK10:US3) double-pointed needles
- 2 x ¾in (20mm) black buttons
- Tapestry needle

HAT

Using 3.75mm needles and the thumb method (see page 96), cast on 28[30]A, 15[19]B, 23D, 15[19]B, 28[30]A (109[121] sts).

Fasten off yarn D, join in yarn C. Using the intarsia technique (see page 106), work chart from right to left on RS rows and left to right on WS rows, unless otherwise indicated by the chart, keeping the colours and stitches as presented - work yarn A into yarn A stitches and yarn B into yarn B stitches; purl stitches into purl stitches and knit stitches into knit stitches.

Row 1 (RS): (K1, p1) 17[20] times, k1; work chart; (k1, p1) 17[20] times, k1.

Row 2: (P1, k1) 17[20] times, p1; work chart; (p1, k1) 17[20] times, p1.

Rows 3-6: Rep Rows 1-2 twice. Change to 4mm needles. Working in stocking stitch, keeping the colours and stitches as presented.

Row 7: Yarn A, k28[30] sts; yarn B, k7[11] sts; work chart; yarn B, k7[11] sts; yarn A, k28[30] sts.

Row 8: Yarn A, p28[30] sts; yarn B, p7[11] sts; work chart; yarn B, p7[11]sts; yarn A, p28[30] sts.

CHILD SIZE ONLY

Rows 9-28: Rep Rows 7-8, 10 times.

Row 29: Rep Row 7.

Row 30: Yarn A, p1, p2tog, p25; yarn B, p7; work from chart, yarn B, p7; yarn A, p25, p2tog, p1 (107 sts).

Row 31: Yarn A, k27; yarn B, k7; work chart; yarn B, k7; yarn A, k27.

Row 32: Yarn A, p27; yarn B, p53; yarn A, p27.

Rows 33-35: Work keeping the colours and stitches as presented.

Row 36: Yarn A, p1, p2tog, p24; yarn B, p53; yarn A, p24, p2tog, p1 (105 sts).

ADULT SIZE ONLY

Rows 9-30: Rep Rows 7-8, 11 times.

Row 31: Rep Row 7.

Rows 32-36: Work keeping the colours and stitches as presented, cont in yarn B across chart sts.

Row 37: Yarn A, (k13, k2tog) twice; yarn B, (k13, k2tog) twice, k1, (ssk, k13) twice; yarn A, (ssk, k13) twice (113 sts).

Rows 38-40: Work keeping the colours and stitches as presented.

Row 41: Yarn A, (k12, k2tog) twice; yarn B, (k12, k2tog) twice, k1, (ssk, k12) twice; yarn A, (ssk, k12) twice (105 sts).

Row 42: Work keeping the colours and stitches as presented.

BOTH SIZES
CROWN

Work keeping the colours as presented.

Row 1: (K11, k2tog) 4 times, k1, (ssk, k11) 4 times (97 sts).

Row 2 and 6 following alternate rows: Purl.

Row 3: (K10, k2tog) 4 times, k1, (ssk, k10) 4 times (89 sts).

Row 5: (K9, k2tog) 4 times, k1, (ssk, k9) 4 times (81 sts).

Row 7: (K8, k2tog) 4 times, k1, (ssk, k8) 4 times (73 sts).

Row 9: (K7, k2tog) 4 times, k1, (ssk, k7) 4 times (65 sts).

Row 11: (K6, k2tog) 4 times, k1, (ssk, k6) 4 times (57 sts).

Row 13: (K5, k2tog) 4 times, k1, (ssk, k5) 4 times (49 sts).

Row 15: (K4, k2tog) 4 times, k1, (ssk, k4) 4 times (41 sts).

Row 16: (P3, p2togtbl) 4 times, p1, (p2tog, p3) 4 times (33 sts).

Row 17: (K2, k2tog) 4 times, k1, (ssk, k2) 4 times (25 sts).

Row 18: (P1, p2togtbl) 4 times, p1, (p2tog, p1) 4 times (17 sts).

Row 19: (K2tog) 4 times, k1, (ssk) 4 times (9 sts).

Cut yarn, thread through rem sts and draw tight.

EYE (MAKE 2)

Leaving a 4in (10cm) tail, using yarn A, 3.25mm double-pointed needles and the thumb method, cast on 12 sts.

Arrange the stitches to work in the round.

Rounds 1–4: Knit.

Round 5: (K2tog) 6 times (6 sts).

Cut yarn, thread through rem sts, place a button into the tube of knitted fabric and draw tight.

Using the cast-on tail, sew a line of running stitch along the outer edge of the Eye.

Draw together but not tightly, gathering the outer edges towards the centre.

Secure with a few small backstitches.

FINISHING

Sew in ends. Block and press the knitted pieces. Using the photograph as a guide and yarn D, Swiss darn (see page 107) the detail to the nose. Using mattress stitch (see page 108), sew the back seam, allowing half a stitch on each edge for the seam allowance. Add highlights to the eyes using French knots (see page 107) and yarn E. Using yarn A, attach the eyes to the hat. Using yarn A, make two pompoms (see page 109) – the pompoms on this hat are 2in (5cm) in diameter. Attach the pompoms to the hat as shown.

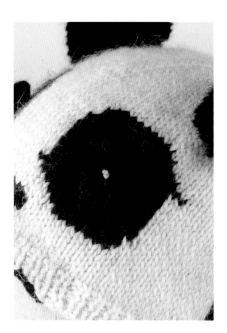

CHART FOR PANDA

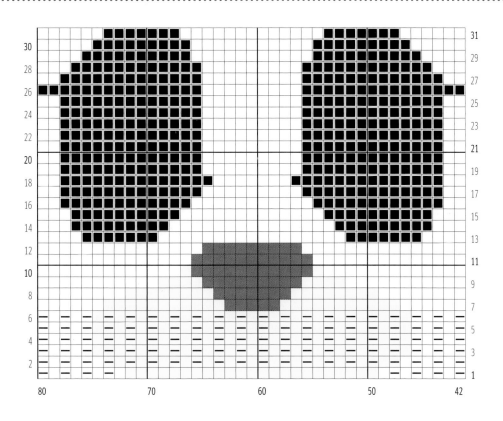

STITCH NUMBERS ALONG THE BOTTOM OF THE CHART REFER TO THE ADULT SIZE.

KEY

	K on RS, P on WS
—	P on RS, K on WS
■	Yarn A (black)
	Yarn B (white)
	Yarn C (cream)
	Yarn D (smooth black yarn)

Fly

Do you want to create a buzz when you enter a room? Well, this might be the hat for you. A lame joke, but the buzz may be about the flattering shaping and the unusual design. It is an animal hat but it is also an elegant hat. Change the colour scheme to create an insect of your choice.

SIZE

To fit: child[adult] (see page 94)
A loose fit which covers the ears.

TENSION (CHILD'S HAT)

24 sts and 32 rows to 4in (10cm) measured over stocking stitch using 4mm needles and light-weight yarn. Use larger or smaller needles if necessary to obtain the correct tension.

TENSION (ADULT'S HAT)

18 sts and 24 rows to 4in (10cm) measured over stocking stitch using 5mm needles and chunky-weight yarn. Use larger or smaller needles if necessary to obtain the correct tension.

MATERIALS (CHILD'S HAT)

- Light-weight yarn: Rowan Pure Wool DK, 100% wool (142yds/130m per 50g ball)
- 1 x 50g ball in 011 Navy (dark blue) (A)
- Aran-weight yarn: Rowan Creative Focus Worsted, 75% wool, 25% alpaca (220yds/200m per 100g ball)
- 1 x 100g ball in 500 Ebony (black) (B)
- Short length of waste yarn
- 4mm (UK8:US6) circular needle
- Pair of 3.25mm (UK10:US3) straight needles
- Set of four 3.75mm (UK9:US5) double-pointed needles
- 3.5mm (UK9:US4) crochet hook
- 2 x 12in (30cm) lengths of pipe cleaner
- Tapestry needle

(Materials list for adult's hat on page 58.)

MATERIALS (ADULT'S HAT)

- Chunky-weight yarn: Rowan Pure Wool Aran, 100% wool (186yds/170m per 100g ball)
- 1 x 100g ball in 683 Marine (dark blue) (A)
- Aran-weight yarn: Rowan Creative Focus Worsted, 75% wool, 25% alpaca (220yds/200m per 100g ball)
- 1 x 100g ball in 500 Ebony (black) (B)
- Short length of waste yarn
- 5mm (UK6:US8) circular needle
- Pair of 3.25mm (UK10:US3) straight needles
- Set of four 3.75mm (UK9:US5) double-pointed needles
- 4mm (UK8:US6) crochet hook
- 2 x 12in (30cm) lengths of pipe cleaner
- Tapestry needle

CHILD'S HAT

Work as for Adult hat using light-weight yarn and smaller needles.

ADULT'S HAT

Using the crochet hook and a provisional cast on (see page 97), cast on 34 sts.
Join in yarn B.
Change to 5mm needles.

RIGHT BACK SECTION

Row 1: Knit.
Row 2: Purl.

RIGHT EYE

Fasten off yarn B, join in yarn A.
Row 3: K1, M1R, k32, yf, sl1r, yb, sl1l, turn (35 sts).
Row 4: (P1, k1), rep to end (35 sts).
Rows 5–26: Rep Rows 3–4, 11 more times (46 sts).
Row 27: K31, yf, sl1r, yb, sl1l, turn.
Row 28: (P1, k1), rep to last st, k1.
Row 29: K28, yf, sl1r, yb, sl1l, turn.
Row 30: (P1, k1), rep to end.
Row 31: K25, yf, sl1r, yb, sl1l, turn.
Row 32: (P1, k1), rep to last st, k1.
Row 33: K22, yf, sl1r, yb, sl1l, turn.
Row 34: (P1, k1), rep to end.
Row 35: K22, yf, sl1r, yb, sl1l, turn.
Row 36: (K1, p1), rep to last 2 sts, k2.
Row 37: K25, yf, sl1r, yb, sl1l, turn.
Row 38: (K1, p1), rep to last st, k1.
Row 39: K28, yf, sl1r, yb, sl1l, turn.
Row 40: (K1, p1), rep to last 2 sts, k2.
Row 41: K31, yf, sl1r, yb, sl1l, turn.
Row 42: (K1, p1), rep to last st, k1.
Row 43: K1, k2tog, k31, yf, sl1r, yb, sl1l, turn (45 sts).
Row 44: (K1, p1), rep to last st, k1.
Rows 45–66: Rep Rows 43–44, 11 more times (34 sts).

FRONT SECTION

Fasten off yarn A, join in yarn B.
Row 67: K20, sl1r, yf, sl1l, turn.
Row 68 and 4 following alternate rows: Knit.
Row 69: K14, sl1r, yf, sl1l, turn.
Row 71: K8, sl1r, yf, sl1l, turn.
Row 73: K11, sl1r, yf, sl1l, turn.
Row 75: K17, sl1r, yf, sl1l, turn.
Rows 77–80: Knit.
Rows 81–94: Rep Rows 67–80.
Rows 95–104: Rep Rows 67–76.

LEFT EYE

Fasten off yarn B, join in yarn A.
Rows 105–168: Rep Rows 3–66.

LEFT BACK SECTION

Fasten off yarn A, join in yarn B.
Row 169: Knit.
Row 170: Purl.
Place the sts onto a straight needle so that the last st worked is nearest to the point.

ANTENNAE (MAKE 2)

Using yarn A, 3.75mm double-pointed needles and the thumb method (see page 96), cast on 60 sts.

Row 1: Knit.

Row 2: Purl.

Fasten off yarn A, join in yarn B.

Row 3: Purl.

Row 4: Knit.

Rows 5–10: Rep Rows 3–4, 3 times.

Row 11: Purl.

Cast off knitwise.

Fold the pipe cleaners so the two points are folded to meet in the middle, then hook two pipe cleaners together to form one antenna.

Use mattress stitch (see page 108) to stitch cast-off edge to Row 3, encasing the pipe cleaner and stopping 2in (5cm) from the end. Using 3.75mm double-pointed needles, pick up and knit 9 sts along remaining short edge. Arrange the sts over 3 double-pointed needles.

Round 1: (Inc) 9 times (18 sts).

Round 2: Knit.

Round 3: (K1, inc) 9 times (27 sts). Cast off.

Finish working mattress stitch along the long edge.

FINISHING

Sew in ends. Block and press the hat. Gently unpick the provisional cast-on and place the live stitches onto a spare needle so that the stitch at the bottom edge of the hat is nearest the point. Use Kitchener stitch (see page 107) to close the back seam. Flatten the hat with the front facing and the double-decrease along the fold. Then, using mattress stitch, sew the flattened top seam. Using the photograph as a guide and whip stitch (see page 108), attach the antennae to the hat, then stitch a line of running stitch around the base of the knitted tube that encloses the pipe cleaners.

Grasshopper

This hat shape has huge potential because it is so flattering.
The decreases are arranged at four points around the hat,
up its entire length, providing large uninterrupted areas for
complex designs. This hat has been described as a grasshopper
but you could make any bug in the colours of your choice.

SIZE

To fit: child[adult] (see page 94)
A close fit that covers the top of the ears and extends
slightly beyond the top of the head.

TENSION

22 sts and 30 rows to 4in (10cm) measured over
stocking stitch using 4mm needles. Use larger or smaller
needles if necessary to obtain the correct tension.

MATERIALS

- Light-weight yarn: Sublime Luxurious DK, 60% wool,
  40% cotton (148yds/135m per 50g ball)
- 1 x 50g ball in 389 Wild at Heart (lime) (A)
- 1 x 50g ball in 395 Down to Earth (grey) (B)
- Pair of 3.75mm (UK9:US5) straight needles
- Pair of 4mm (UK8:US6) straight needles
- Set of four 3.75mm (UK9:US5) double-pointed needles
- 4 x 12in (30cm) lengths of pipe cleaners
- Tapestry needle

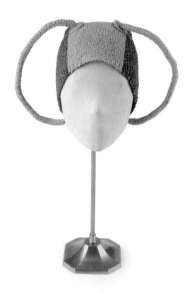

HAT

Using 3.75mm needles and the thumb method (see page 96), cast on, 1[13]A, 33[37]B, 20[24]A, 33[37]B, 11[13]A (108[124] sts). Work the appropriate chart (child or adult) using the intarsia technique (see page 106).

Row 1: K1, [work chart from right to left] twice, k1.

Row 2: P1, [work chart from left to right] twice, p1.

Rep the last two rows twice more. Change to 4mm needles. Rep Rows 1-2 until the chart has been worked.

Cast off, using yarn A, knitwise.

ANTENNA (MAKE 2)

Using yarn B, 3.75mm needles and the thumb method, cast on 60 sts.

Row 1: Knit.

Row 2: Purl.

Fasten off yarn B, join in yarn A.

Row 3: Purl.

Row 4: Knit.

Rows 5-10: Rep Rows 3-4, 3 times.

Row 11: Purl.

Cast off knitwise.

Fold the pipe cleaners so the two points are folded to meet in the middle, then hook two pipe cleaners together to form one antenna.

Use mattress stitch (see page 108) to stitch cast-off edge to Row 3, encasing the pipe cleaner and stopping 2in (5cm) from the end. Using 3.75mm double-pointed needles, pick up and knit 9 sts along remaining short edge.

Arrange the stitches over 3 double-pointed needles.

Round 1: [Inc] 9 times (18 sts).

Round 2: Knit.

Round 3: [K1, inc] 9 times (27 sts).

Cast off.

Finish working mattress stitch along the long edge.

FINISHING

Sew in ends. Block and press the hat. Using mattress stitch, sew the back seam, allowing a stitch on each edge for the seam allowance. Flatten the hat with the fold halfway through the grey panels. Then, using mattress stitch, sew a flat, straight seam joining the front and back yarn A stitches. Using the photograph as a guide and whip stitch (see page 108), attach the antennae to the hat, then stitch a line of running stitch around the base of the tube enclosing the pipe cleaners.

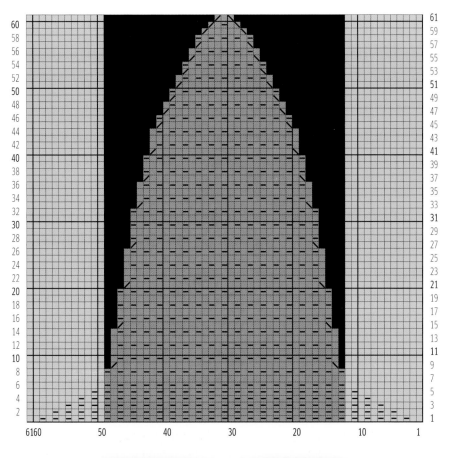

CHART FOR
GRASSHOPPER (ADULT)
·······························

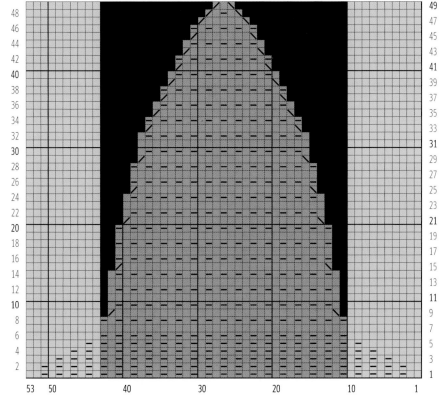

CHART FOR
GRASSHOPPER (CHILD)
·······························

KEY
·······························

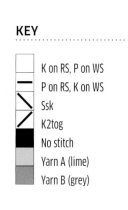

K on RS, P on WS

P on RS, K on WS

Ssk

K2tog

No stitch

Yarn A (lime)

Yarn B (grey)

Rabbit

As you prepare to go out, you could also dress your
animal hat to suit the occasion. Styling this hat is great fun.
You can tie the ears into a faux knot, add a tattoo-like
brooch, a large satin ribbon or even a small top hat.
A white pompom tail at the back would be cute too.

SIZE

To fit: child[adult] (see page 94)
A loose fit that covers the ears.

TENSION

17 sts and 22 rows to 4in (10cm) measured over
stocking stitch using 5.5mm needles. Use larger
or smaller needles if necessary to obtain the
correct tension.

MATERIALS

- Chunky-weight yarn: Rowan Cocoon, 80% wool,
  20% mohair (126yds/115m per 100g ball)
- 2 x 100g ball in 801 Polar (white) (A)
- Short length of waste cotton yarn
- Short lengths of tapestry wool or scraps of yarn in pale
  pink (B), bright white (C), light pink (D) and dark pink (E)
- 5.5mm (UK5:US9) circular needle
- Set of five 5mm (UK6:US8) double-pointed needles
- Set of five 3.25mm (UK10:US3) double-pointed needles
- Pair of 3.25mm (UK10:US3) straight needles
- Tapestry needle

NOTE

- A 5.5mm (UK5:US9) circular knitting needle is specified
  because it is more flexible than straight needles.
- All stitches are slipped (sl) purlwise, with yarn at wrong
  side of work.
- Mark the stitches indicated with a length of waste
  cotton yarn looped loosely through the stitch.

BONNET

Using 5.5mm needles, yarn A and the thumb method (see page 96), cast on 57[73] sts.

Row 1 (RS): K1tbl, k to the end.
Row 2: Sl1, k to last st, sl1.
Rows 3–12: Rep Rows 1–2, 5 times.
Row 13: K1tbl, k to the end.
Fasten off yarn.
Row 14: Sl21[27] sts, mark the last st worked, (k1, sl1) 8[10] times, mark the last sl st, turn.
Row 15: Knit 17[21] sts.
Row 16: (Sl1, k1) 8[10] times, sl1.
Cont to work on the centre 17[21] sts.

CHILD SIZE ONLY

Rows 17–46: Rep Rows 15–16, 15 times.
Fasten off.
With RS facing, rejoin yarn to the marked st on Row 14.
Row 47: Starting with the marked st on Row 14, pick up and knit 16 sts through the 16 edge sts, k17, pick up and knit 16 sts through the edge sts finishing with the marked st, turn (49 sts).
Cont working on the centre 49 sts.
Row 48: (Sl1, k1) 24 times, p2tog the next st with the next st on the needle (last worked on Row 13).
Row 49: Sl1, k47, ssk the next st with the next st on the needle (last worked on Row 13).
Rows 50–87: Rep Rows 48–49 until all the sts from Row 13 have been worked.
Cast off at the same time: p2, (p2tog,p3) to the last 2 sts, p2.

ADULT SIZE ONLY

Rows 17–54: Rep Rows 15–16, 19 times.
Fasten off.

With RS facing, rejoin yarn to the marked st on Row 14.
Row 55: Starting with the marked st on Row 14, pick up and knit 20 sts through the 20 edge sts, k21, pick up and knit 20 sts through the edge sts finishing with the marked st, turn (61 sts).
Cont working on the centre 61 sts.
Row 56: (Sl1, k1) 30 times, p2tog the next st with the next st on the needle (last worked on Row 13).
Row 57: Sl1, k59, ssk the next st with the next st on the needle (last worked on Row 13).
Rows 58–107: Rep Rows 56–57 until all the sts from Row 13 have been worked.
Cast off at the same time: p3, (p2tog, p4) to last 4 sts, p2tog, p2.

EAR (MAKE 2)

Using 5mm double-pointed needles, yarn A and the thumb method, cast on 22 sts.
Arrange the stitches to work in the round.
Ear Front: needle 1, 4 sts; needle 2, 5 sts. Ear Back: needle 3, 6 sts; needle 4, 7 sts.
Round 1: Knit.
Round 2: K13, ssk, k1, k2tog, k4 (20 sts).
Round 3: Knit.
Round 4: K12, ssk, k1, k2tog, k3 (18 sts).
Round 5: Knit.
Cont as follows: first repeat is worked on Ear Front; second repeat is worked on Ear Back.
Round 6: (K1, M1R, k7, M1L, k1) twice (22 sts).
Round 7: (K1, M1R, k9, M1L, k1) twice (26 sts).

Round 8: Knit.
Round 9: (K1, M1R, k11, M1L, k1) twice (30 sts).
Rounds 10–35: Knit.
Round 36: (K1, ssk, k9, k2tog, k1) twice (26 sts).
Rounds 37–38: Knit.
Round 39: (K1, ssk, k7, k2tog, k1) twice (22 sts).
Rounds 40–41: Knit.
Round 42: (K1, ssk, k5, k2tog, k1) twice (18 sts).
Round 43: Knit.
Round 44: (K1, ssk, k3, k2tog, k1) twice (14 sts).
Round 45: Knit.
Round 46: (K1, ssk, k1, k2tog, k1) twice (10 sts).
Round 47: (Ssk, k1, k2tog) twice (6 sts).
Cut yarn, thread through rem sts and draw tight.

NOSE

Using yarn B, 3.25mm double-pointed needles and the thumb method, cast on 10 sts. Arrange the stitches to work in the round.
Nose Front: needle 1, 3 sts; needle 2, 2 sts. Nose Back: needle 3, 3 sts; needle 4, 2 sts.
Cont as folls: first repeat is worked on Nose Front; second repeat is worked on Nose Back.
Round 1: Knit.
Round 2: (K1, M1R, k3, M1L, k1) twice (14 sts).
Round 3: Knit.
Round 4: (K1, M1R, k5, M1L, k1) twice (18 sts).
Round 5: Knit.
Round 6: (K1, M1R, k7, M1L, k1) twice (22 sts).
Rounds 7–8: Knit.

Round 9: (K1, M1R, k9, M1L, k1) twice (26 sts).

Rounds 10–11: Knit.

Round 12: (K1, ssk, k7, k2tog, k1) twice (22 sts).

Round 13: (K1, ssk, k5, k2tog, k1) twice (18 sts).

Cast off and join the Front Ear to the Back Ear using mattress stitch (see page 108) or Kitchener stitch (see page 107). Use mattress stitch to join the cast-on stitches.

CORD (MAKE 2)

Make an i-cord as follows.

Using 5mm double-pointed needles, yarn A and the thumb method, cast on 4 sts.

Row 1: Knit.

*Without turning work, slide sts along the needle to the right-hand point and draw the working yarn across the back of the sts.

Row 2: Knit.

Rep from *until the cord measures 12in (30cm) or the required length. Cut yarn, thread through sts and draw tight.

LEFT EYE WHITE

Using yarn C, a pair of 3.25mm needles and the thumb method, cast on 11 sts.

Row 1: Purl.

Row 2: K10, M1L, turn.

Row 3: Sl1, p until 1 st rem, M1R, turn.

Row 4: Sl1, k until 3 sts rem, M1L, turn.

Row 5: Sl1, p until 3 sts rem, M1R, turn.

Row 6: Sl1, k until 5 sts rem, M1L, turn.

Row 7: Sl1, p until 5 sts rem, M1R, turn.

Row 8: Sl1, k until 7 sts rem, M1L, turn.

Row 9: Sl1, p to end.

Cast off knitwise (top edge of the Eye White).

RIGHT EYE WHITE

Using yarn C, a pair of 3.25mm needles and the thumb method, cast on 11 sts. Work as for Left Eye White but work a knit stitch in place of a purl stitch and a purl stitch in place of a knit stitch.

EYE CENTRE (MAKE 2)

Using yarn D, a pair of 3.25mm needles and the thumb method, cast on 3 sts.

Row 1: Purl.

Row 2: K1, M1R, k1, M1L, k1 (5 sts).

Row 3: P1, M1L, p3, M1R, p1 (7 sts).

Row 4: Knit.

Row 5: Purl.

Row 6: Ssk, k3, k2tog (5 sts).

Cast off in the decrease pattern set.

SWISS DARNING CHART FOR RABBIT'S EYES

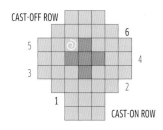

CAST-OFF ROW

5

3

6

4

1

2

CAST-ON ROW

KEY

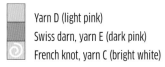

Yarn D (light pink)

Swiss darn, yarn E (dark pink)

French knot, yarn C (bright white)

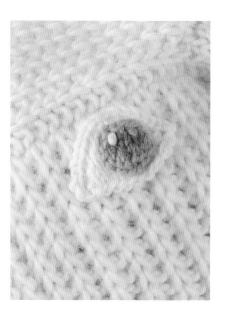

FINISHING

Sew in ends. Block and press the knitted pieces. Using yarn E, Swiss darn (see page 107) the pupil on the eye centre. Using yarn C and a French knot (see page 107) add a highlight to the outer eye. The chart shows the highlight position for the right eye. Move the French knot two stitches to the left for the left eye. Attach the eye centres to the whites. Fold the ear in half and oversew the edges of the front at the narrowest point. Open out the edges below the narrowest point and fold up the cast-on edge to meet the edges. Secure the cast-on edge in place – the seam should look like an upside down 'T'. Attach the ears to the bonnet so that the front follows the line of the slip stitches that form the corner of the bonnet. The centre of the ear is aligned with the centre of the corner. Using whip stitch (see page 108), attach the eyes, nose and the cords to the bonnet. Using yarn A, make two 2in (5cm)-diameter pompoms (see page 109). Attach to each cord.

Snake

What is there not to love about this headband? The concept
is so simple and is perfect for all the multi-coloured yarns
available now. Choose a yarn you like, match the needle size
to the yarn and make this project. You could even forget the
intarsia and the embroidery – keep it simple and go bold.

SIZE
One size
A headband that covers the top of the ears.

TENSION
24 sts and 30 rows to 4in (10cm) measured over
stocking stitch using 3.75mm needles. Use larger
or smaller needles if necessary to obtain the
correct tension.

MATERIALS
- Light-weight yarn: Sublime Luxurious DK, 60% wool,
  40% cotton (148yds/135m per 50g ball)
- 1 x 50g ball in 390 Greengrass (jade) (A)
- 1 x 50g ball in 389 Wild at heart (lime) (B)
- 1 x 50g ball in 393 Pomegranate (rust) (C)
- Short lengths of tapestry wool or yarn in black (D)
- Pair of 3.75mm (UK9:US5) straight needles
- Set of 3.75mm (UK9:US5) double-pointed needles
- Tapestry needle

NOTE
This project is knitted using the intarsia method
(see page 106) to knit vertical yarn A and yarn B
stripes. The single yarn A stitch in the centre of
the row and the yarn C stitches are Swiss darned
(see page 107) onto the knitted fabric at the end.

HAT

Using yarn A and straight needles, cast on 3 sts.

SPIRAL ROUND ONE

A narrow strip of stitches is worked.
Row 1 (RS): Knit.
Row 2: K1, p to the last st, M1R, k1 (4 sts).
Row 3: K1, M1R, k to end (5 sts). Join in yarn B.
Row 4: Yarn A, k1, p1; yarn B, p1; yarn A, p1, M1R, k1 (6 sts).
Row 5: Yarn A, k1, M1R, k1; yarn B, k1; yarn A, k3 (7 sts).
Row 6: Yarn A, k1, p3; yarn B, p1; yarn A, p1, k1.
Row 7: Yarn A, k1, M1R, k1; yarn B, k1; yarn A, k4 (8 sts).
Row 8: Yarn A, k1, p3; yarn B, p2; yarn A, p1, k1.
Row 9: Yarn A, k1, M1R, k1; yarn B, k2; yarn A, k4 (9 sts).
Row 10: Yarn A, k1, p3; yarn B, p3; yarn A, p1, k1.
Row 11: Yarn A, k1, M1R, k1; yarn B, k3; yarn A, k4 (10 sts).
Row 12: Yarn A, k1, p2; yarn B, p5; yarn A, p1, k1.
Row 13: Yarn A, k1, M1R, k1; yarn B, k5; yarn A, k3 (11 sts).
Row 14: Yarn A, k1, p2; yarn B, p5; yarn A, p2, k1.
Row 15: Yarn A, k3; yarn B, k5; yarn A, k3.
Row 16: Yarn A, k1, p2; yarn B, p5; yarn A, p2, k1.
Rep Rows 15–16 until the strip fits snugly around the head.

SPIRAL ROUND TWO

The strip is curled to form a loop and Spiral round two is joined to the right-hand edge of the strip of stitches worked for Spiral round one.
Next row: Yarn A, k3; yarn B, k5; yarn A, k2, p1, pick up and knit a stitch through the knot of stitches at the start (right-hand edge) of the first full row of sts (Row 13) (12 sts).
Next row: Yarn A, k2tog, p2; yarn B, p5; yarn A, p2, k1 (11 sts).
Next row: Yarn A, k3; yarn B, k5; yarn A, k2, p1, pick up and knit a stitch through the next knot of stitches along the edge (12 sts).
Next row: Yarn A, k2tog, p2; yarn B, p5; yarn A, p2, k1 (11 sts).
Rep the last two rows until a full round of rows has been worked.

SPIRAL ROUND THREE

Cont working as for Spiral round two.

SPIRAL ROUND FOUR

The next rows are not joined to previous rows.
Rep Rows 15–16 until the strip measures half the distance around the top edge.
Next row: Yarn A, k2; yarn B, k7; yarn A, k2.
Next row: Yarn A, k1, p1; yarn B, p7; yarn A, p1, k1.
Rep the last two rows 8 more times.
Next row: Yarn A, k1; yarn B, k9; yarn A, k1.
Next row: Yarn A, k1; yarn B, p9; yarn A, k1.
Rep the last two rows 8 more times.
Fasten off yarn A.
Cont with yarn B only.
Next row: Knit, cast on 11 sts (22 sts).
Change to set of double-pointed needles. Arrange the stitches to work in the round.

HEAD

Rounds 1–10: Knit.

Cont as follows: first repeat is worked on Head Front; second on Head Back.

Round 11: [K1, M1R, k9, M1L, k1] twice (26 sts).

Round 12: Knit.

Round 13: [K1, M1R, k11, M1L, k1] twice (30 sts).

Round 14: Knit.

Round 15: [K1, M1R, k13, M1L, k1] twice (34 sts).

Rounds 16–24: Knit.

Round 25: [K1, ssk, k11, k2tog, k1] twice (30 sts).

Rounds 26–27: Knit.

Round 28: [K1, ssk, k9, k2tog, k1] twice (26 sts).

Rounds 29–30: Knit.

Round 31: [K1, ssk, k7, k2tog, k1] twice (22 sts).

Rounds 32–33: Knit.

Round 34: [K1, ssk, k5, k2tog, k1] twice (18 sts).

Rounds 35–36: Knit.

Round 37: [K1, ssk, k3, k2tog, k1] twice (14 sts).

Rounds 38–39: Knit.

Round 40: [K1, ssk, k1, k2tog, k1] twice (10 sts).

Round 41: Knit.

Cast off.

FINISHING

Sew in ends. Block and press the hat. Using the chart as reference, Swiss darn (see page 107) the detail onto the knitted fabric. For the eyes, using yarn C, sew two extended Swiss-darned stitches over four rows. Using yarn D, stitch a French knot (see page 107) into the apex of each extended Swiss darning stitch.

SWISS DARNING CHART FOR SNAKE

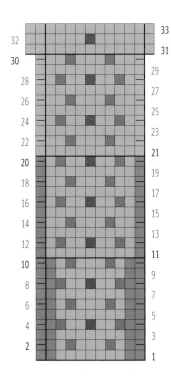

KEY

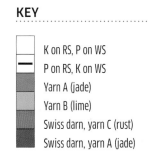

	K on RS, P on WS
—	P on RS, K on WS
	Yarn A (jade)
	Yarn B (lime)
	Swiss darn, yarn C (rust)
	Swiss darn, yarn A (jade)

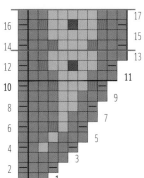

Pig

It is hard to look at this hat and not have perky, happy thoughts. All that is missing from this pig hat is a curly tail; you could easily make one by casting on 12in (30cm) of stitches onto the larger needle and casting off the stitches firmly with a smaller needle.

SIZE

To fit: child[adult] (see page 94)
A close fit that covers the ears.

TENSION

18 sts and 24 rows to 4in (10cm) measured over stocking stitch using two strands of yarn worked together and 5mm needles. Use larger or smaller needles if necessary to obtain the correct tension.

MATERIALS

• Light-weight yarn: Rowan Felted Tweed DK, 50% merino wool, 25% alpaca, 25% viscose (191yds/175m per 50g ball); double-stranded throughout
• 1 x 50g ball in 157 Camel (light brown) (A)
• 1 x 50g ball in 185 Frozen (light pink) (B)
• 1 x 50g ball in 171 Paisley (dark pink) (C)

• Short lengths of tapestry wool or scraps of yarn in white (D) and brown (E)
• Pair of 5mm (UK6:US8) straight needles
• Set of four 5mm (UK6:US8) double-pointed needles
• Set of four 3.25mm (UK10:US3) double-pointed needles
• Tapestry needle

NOTE

• The hat is worked with two strands of yarn held together throughout.
• Yarn AB denotes that the stitches are worked with one strand of yarn A and one strand of yarn B held together.
• Yarn AC denotes that the stitches are worked with one strand of yarn A and one strand of yarn C held together.

HAT

Using 5mm needles and the thumb method (see page 96), cast on, 14[18]AB, 19AC, 11AB, 19AC, 15[19] AB, (78[86] sts).

Using the intarsia technique (see page 106):

Row 1 (RS): Yarn AB, k1, (k1, p1) 6[8] times, k2; yarn AC, k19; yarn AB, (k1, p1) 5[5] times, k1; yarn AC, k19; yarn AB, k1, (k1, p1) 6[8] times, k1.

Row 2: Yarn AB, p1, (k1, p1) 6[8] times, p1; yarn AC, p19; yarn AB, (p1, k1) 5[5] times, p1; yarn AC, p19; yarn AB, p1, (p1, k1) 6[8] times, p2.

Rows 3-6: Rep Rows 1-2 twice.

Row 7: Yarn AB, k15[19]; yarn AC, k19; yarn AB, k11; yarn AC, k19; yarn AB, k14[18].

Row 8: Yarn AB, p14[18]; yarn AC, p19; yarn AB, p11; yarn AC, p19; yarn AB, p15[19].

Row 9: Rep Row 7.

Row 10: Yarn AB, p15[19]; yarn AC, p17; yarn AB, p13; yarn AC, p17; yarn AB, p16[20].

Row 11: Yarn AB, k16[20]; yarn AC, k17; yarn AB, k13; yarn AC, k17; yarn AB, k15[19].

Row 12: Yarn AB, p16[20]; yarn AC, p15; yarn AB, p15; yarn AC, p15; yarn AB, p17[21].

Row 13: Yarn AB, k18[22]; yarn AC, k13; yarn AB, k17; yarn AC, k13; yarn AB, k17[21].

Row 14: Yarn AB, p19[23]; yarn AC, p9; yarn AB, p21; yarn AC, p9; yarn AB, p20[24].

Cont in yarn AB only.

Row 15: K to the last 3 sts, M1R, k3 (79[87] sts).

Rows 16-20: Work in stocking stitch.

CHILD SIZE ONLY

Row 21 (buttonhole row): K21, cast off 7 sts, k22, cast off 7 sts, k to end.

Row 22: P21, cast on 7 sts, p23, cast on 7 sts, p to end.

Rows 23-24: Work in st st.

Row 25: K12, ssk, k23, ssk, k1, k2tog, k23, k2tog k to end (75 sts).

ADULT SIZE ONLY

Rows 21-22: Work in stocking stitch.

Row 23 (buttonhole row): K25, cast off 7 sts, k22, cast off 7 sts, k to end.

Row 24: P25, cast on 7 sts, p23, cast on 7 sts, p to end.

Rows 25-30: Work in stocking stitch.

Row 31: K1, (k5, ssk) 6 times, k1, (k2tog, k5) 6 times, k1 (75 sts).

Rows 32-34: Work in stocking stitch.

CROWN

Row 1: K1, (k4, ssk) 6 times, k1, (k2tog, k4) 6 times, k1 (63 sts).

Rows 2-4: Work in stocking stitch patt as set.

Row 5: K1, (k3, ssk) 6 times, k1, (k2tog, k3) 6 times, k1 (51 sts).

Row 6: Purl.

Row 7: K1, (k2, ssk) 6 times, k1, (k2tog, k2) 6 times, k1 (39 sts).

Row 8: Purl.

Row 9: K1, (k1, ssk) 6 times, k1, (k2tog, k1) 6 times, k1 (27 sts).

Row 10: Purl.

Row 11: K1, (ssk) 6 times, k1, (k2tog) 6 times, k1 (15 sts).

Row 12: P1, (p2tog) 3 times, p1, (pspo) 3 times, p1 (9 sts).

Cut yarn, thread through rem sts and draw tight.

EAR (MAKE 2)

Using a pair of 5mm needles and yarn AB, cast on 3 sts.

Row 1 and 7 following alternate rounds: Purl.

Row 2: K1, M1R, k1, M1L, k1 (5 sts).

Row 4: K1, M1R, k3, M1L, k1 (7 sts).

Row 6: K1, M1R, k5, M1L, k1 (9 sts).

Row 8: K1, M1R, k7, M1L, k1 (11 sts).

Row 10: K1, M1R, k9, M1L, k1 (13 sts).

Row 12: K1, M1R, k11, M1L, k1 (15 sts).

Row 14: K1, M1R, k13, M1L, k1 (17 sts).

Row 16: K1, M1R, k15, M1L, k1 (19 sts).

Rows 17-25: Work in stocking stitch.

Row 26: Ssk, k15, k2tog (17 sts).

Row 27: Purl.

Row 28: Ssk, k13, k2tog (15 sts).

Row 29: Purl.

Row 30: Ssk, k11, k2tog (13 sts).

Row 31: P2tog, p9, pspo (11 sts).

Row 32: Ssk, k7, k2tog (9 sts).

Rows 33-35: Work in stocking stitch. Cast off.

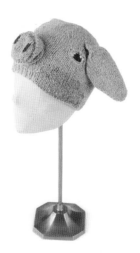

SNOUT FRONT

Using a pair of 5mm needles and yarns AC, cast on 7 sts.

Row 1: Purl.
Row 2: K1, M1R, k5, M1L, k1 (9 sts).
Row 3: P1, M1L, p7, M1R, p1 (11 sts).
Row 4: K1, M1R, k9, M1L, k1 (13 sts).
Rows 5–11: Work in stocking stitch.
Row 12: Ssk, k9, k2tog (11 sts).
Row 13: P2tog, p7, pspo (9 sts).
Row 14: Ssk, k5, k2tog (7 sts).
Cast off in the pattern set.

SNOUT SIDES

Using 5mm double-pointed needles and yarns AC, pick up and knit 39 sts around the circumference of the Snout Front.

Round 1: Knit.
Round 2: Purl.
Fasten off yarn C, join in yarn B and work double-stranded with yarn A.
Rounds 3–7: Knit.
Cast off.

EYE CENTRE (MAKE 2)

Using a single strand of yarn D, 3.25mm double-pointed needles and the thumb method, cast on 36 sts. Arrange the stitches to work in the round.

Rounds 1–2: Knit.
Round 3: (K1, k2tog) 12 times (24 sts).
Fasten off yarn D. Join in yarn E.
Round 4: Knit.
Round 5: (K2tog) 12 times (12 sts).
Round 6: (K2tog) 6 times (6 sts).
Cut yarn, thread through rem sts and draw tight.

FINISHING

Sew in ends. Block and press the knitted pieces. Using mattress stitch (see page 108), sew the back seam. Using the photograph as a guide, position the eyes inside the hat behind the buttonholes, using whip stitch (see page 108) to attach both ears and snout to the hat. Add highlights to the eyes using French knots (see page 107) and yarn D. Using the photograph as reference, Swiss darn (see page 108) nostrils in yarn E onto the snout.

Sheep

Wear this hat with big hair and a big personality or make it slightly smaller for a more subdued look. The shaggy nature of this hat won't be to everyone's taste, so if you prefer you could add the head, ears and eyes to another basic hat shape in the book – try the monkey on page 88.

SIZE

To fit: child[adult] (see page 94)
A generous fit that covers the ears.

CHILD TENSION

14 sts and 18 rows to 4in (10cm) measured over stocking stitch using yarn A and 4.5mm needles. Use larger or smaller needles if necessary to obtain the correct tension.

ADULT TENSION

14 sts and 18 rows to 4in (10cm) measured over stocking stitch using yarn A and 5.5mm needles. Use larger or smaller needles if necessary to obtain the correct tension.

MATERIALS

- Chunky-weight yarn: Drops Alpaca Bouclé, 80% alpaca, 15% wool, 5% polyamide (153yds/140m per 50g ball)
- 2 x 50g balls in 100 Off White (A)
- Light-weight yarn: Rowan Tweed DK, 100% wool (129yds/118m per 50g ball)
- 1 x 50g ball in 595 Pendle (black) (B)
- Short lengths of tapestry wool or scraps of yarn in white (C) and brown (D)
- Toy filling
- 5.5mm (UK5:US9) circular needle
- Set of four 5.5mm (UK5:US9) double-pointed needles (if required to work the last few rounds)
- Set of five 3.25mm (UK10:US3) double-pointed needles
- Pair of 3.75mm (UK9:US5) straight needles
- Set of five 3.75mm (UK9:US5) double-pointed needles
- Tapestry needle

SPECIAL ABBREVIATION

MB (make bobble): (knit into the front and back of the next st) twice, (turn, purl, turn knit) twice, pass the second, third and then fourth st on the right-hand needle over the first.

CHILD'S HAT

Work as for Adult hat using the same yarn but work the Earflaps and Hat using a 4.5mm (UK7:US7) circular needle and double-pointed needles (as required).

EARFLAP (MAKE 2)

Using 5.5mm circular needle, yarn A and the thumb method (see page 96), cast on 19 sts. Work back and forth.

Row 1: Purl.
Row 2 (RS): (ML, k5) 3 times, ML.
Row 3: Purl.
Row 4: K1, M1R, k2, (ML, k5) twice, ML, k2, M1L, k1 (21 sts).
Row 5: Purl.
Row 6: K1, M1R, (ML, k5) 3 times, ML, M1L, k1 (23 sts).
Row 7: Purl.
Row 8: K5, (ML, k5) 3 times.
Place the sts onto a double-pointed needle or stitch holder.

ADULT'S HAT

Using 5.5mm circular needle, yarn A and the cable method (see page 97), cast on 13 sts; with RS facing, knit across one Earflap, cast on 25 sts, knit across second Earflap, cast on 12 sts (96 sts).
Arrange the sts to work in the round.
Round 1: K15, (ML, k5) 3 times, ML, k29, (ML, k5) 3 times, ML, k14.
Round 2 and each alternate round: Knit.
Round 3: K18, (ML, k5) twice, ML, k35, (ML, k5) twice, ML, k17.
Round 5: K3, (ML, k5) 15 times, ML, k2.
Round 7: (ML, k5) 16 times.
Rounds 9–12: Rep Rounds 5–8.

Round 13: K3, (MB, k5, ML, k5) 7 times, MB, k5, ML, k2.
Round 15: (ML, k5, MB, k5) 8 times.
Rounds 17–20: Rep Rounds 13–16.
Round 21: (ML, k2, MB, k2) to end.
Rounds 23–26: Rep Rounds 21–22 twice.
Rounds 27–37: Knit.

CROWN

Round 1: (K2, ssk, k5, k2tog, k1) 8 times (80 sts).
Rounds 2–4: Knit.
Round 5: (K2, ssk, k3, k2tog, k1) 8 times (64 sts).
Rounds 6–8: Knit.
Round 9: (K2, ssk, k1, k2tog, k1) 8 times (48 sts).
Rounds 10–11: Knit.
Change to 5.5mm double-pointed needles as required.
Round 12: (K2, sl2tog, k1, psso, k1) 8 times (32 sts).
Rounds 13–14: Knit.
Round 15: (K1, sl2tog, k1, psso) 8 times (16 sts).
Round 16: Knit.
Cut yarn, thread through rem sts and draw tight.

EAR (MAKE 2)

Using 3.75mm needles and yarn B, cast on 7 sts.

Row 1: Purl

Rows 2-5: Work in stocking stitch.

Row 6: K1, M1R, k5, M1L, k1 (9 sts).

Row 7: Purl.

Row 8: K1, M1R, k7, M1L, k1 (11 sts).

Rows 9-21: Work in stocking stitch.

Row 22: Ssk, k7, k2tog (9 sts).

Row 23: Purl.

Row 24: Ssk, k5, k2tog (7 sts).

Row 25: Purl.

Row 26: Ssk, k3, k2tog (5 sts).

Row 27: Purl.

Row 28: Ssk, k1, k2tog (3 sts). Cast off.

HEAD

Using 3.75mm double-pointed needles, yarn B and the thumb method, cast on 44 sts.

Arrange the sts to work in the round. Head Front: needle 1, 11 sts; needle 2, 11 sts. Head Back: needle 3, 11 sts; needle 4, 11 sts.

Rounds 1-20: Knit.

EYE SOCKETS

Round 21: (K1, M1R, k20, M1L, k1) twice (48 sts).

Round 22: (K1, M1R, k22, M1L, k1) twice (52 sts).

Round 23: (K1, M1R, k24, M1L, k1) twice (56 sts).

Round 24: (K1, M1R, k26, M1L, k1) twice (60 sts).

Rounds 25-28: Knit.

Round 29: (K1, ssk, k24, k2tog, k1) twice (56 sts).

Round 30: (K1, ssk, k22, k2tog, k1) twice (52 sts).

Round 31: (K1, ssk, k20, k2tog, k1) twice (48 sts).

Round 32: (K1, ssk, k18, k2tog, k1) twice (44 sts).

FOREHEAD

Rounds 33-34: Knit.

Round 35: (K1, ssk, k16, k2tog, k1) twice (40 sts).

Rounds 36-38: Knit.

Round 39: (K1, ssk, k14, k2tog, k1) twice (36 sts).

Round 40: Knit.

Round 41: (K1, ssk, k12, k2tog, k1) twice (32 sts).

Round 42: Knit.

Round 43: (K1, ssk, k10, k2tog, k1) twice (28 sts).

Round 44: (K1, ssk, k8, k2tog, k1) twice (24 sts).

Round 45: (K1, ssk, k6, k2tog, k1) twice (20 sts).

Round 46: (K1, ssk, k4, k2tog, k1) twice (16 sts).

Cast off in pattern as set and join the Head Front to the Head Back using mattress stitch (see page 108) or join the stitches using Kitchener stitch (see page 107).

EYEBALL (MAKE 2)

Using 3.25mm double-pointed needles, yarn C and the thumb method, cast on 6 sts.

Arrange the sts to work in the round.

Round 1: (Inc) 6 times (12 sts).

Round 2: (K1, inc) 6 times (18 sts).

Rounds 3-4: Knit.

Fasten off yarn C. Join in yarn D.

Rounds 5-6: Knit.

Gently start to stuff the eyeball with toy filling. Add more filling after the following rounds as required.

Fasten off yarn D. Join in yarn B.

Round 7: (K2tog, k1) 6 times (12 sts).

Round 8: (K2tog) 6 times (6 sts).

Cut yarn, thread through rem sts and draw tight.

FINISHING

Sew in ends. Block and press the knitted pieces. Using the photograph as a guide, tuck in the corners of the lower head to form nostrils. Tuck the eye sockets into the head and, using whip stitch (see page 108), sew the eyes in the sockets. Using whip stitch, attach the ears to the head and then the head to the hat.

Dog

There is endless fun to be had in making the ears longer and adjusting how they sit on the head, so you might want to buy an extra ball of the main yarn colour. For several days this hat wore a red bandana with one ear pinned up – the old sea dog.

SIZE

To fit: child[adult] (see page 94)
A close fit that covers the top of the ears.

TENSION

22 sts and 32 rows to 4in (10cm) measured over stocking stitch and 4mm needles. Use larger or smaller needles if necessary to obtain the correct tension.

MATERIALS

- Light-weight yarn: Rowan Felted Tweed DK, 50% merino wool, 25% alpaca, 25% viscose (191yds/175m per 50g ball)
- 1 x 50g ball in 160 Gilt (brown) (A)
- 1 x 50g ball in 177 Clay (white) (B)
- 1 x 50g ball in 185 Frozen (pink) (C)
- Short lengths of tapestry wool or scraps of yarn in black (D) and chestnut (E)
- Pair of 3.75mm (UK9:US5) straight needles
- Pair of 4mm (UK8:US6) straight needles
- Tapestry needle

HAT

Using 3.75mm needles and the thumb method (see page 96), cast on, 43[49]A; black yarn 23 sts; 43[49]A (109[121] sts).

Fasten off black yarn, join in yarn B. Using the intarsia technique (see page 106), work the knitting chart from right to left on RS rows and left to right on WS rows.

Row 1 (RS): (K1, p1) 20[23] times; work chart; (p1, k1) 20[23] times.

Row 2: (P1, k1) 20[23] times; work chart; (k1, p1) 20[23] times.

Rows 3-6: Rep Rows 1-2 twice. Change to 4mm needles. Work in stocking stitch, keeping the colours and stitches as presented.

Row 7: Yarn A, k40[46] sts; work chart; yarn A, k40[46] sts.

Row 8: Yarn A, p40[46] sts; work chart; yarn A p40[46] sts.

Rows 9-22: Rep Rows 7-8, 7 times.

Row 23: Rep Row 7.

CHILD SIZE ONLY

Rows 24-29: Work keeping the colours and stitches as presented.

Row 30: Yarn A, p1, p2tog, p to the last 3 sts keeping the colours as presented, p2tog, p1 (107 sts).

Rows 31-35: Work keeping the colours and stitches as presented.

Row 36: Yarn A, p1, p2tog, p to the last 3 sts keeping the colours as presented, p2tog, p1 (105 sts).

ADULT SIZE ONLY

Rows 24-36: Work keeping the colours and stitches as presented.

Row 37: Yarn A, (k13, k2tog) 3 times, k11; yarn B, k2, k2tog, k1, ssk, k2; yarn A, k11, (ssk, k13) 3 times (113 sts).

Rows 38-40: Work keeping the colours and stitches as presented.

Row 41: Yarn A, (k12, k2tog) 3 times, k9; yarn B, k3, k2tog, k1, ssk, k3; yarn A, k9, (ssk, k12) 3 times (105 sts).

Row 42: Work keeping the colours and stitches as presented.

CROWN
BOTH SIZES

Work keeping the colours as presented.

Row 1: (K11, k2tog) 4 times, k1, (ssk, k11) 4 times (97 sts).

Row 2 and 6 following alternate rows: Purl.

Row 3: (K10, k2tog) 4 times, k1, (ssk, k10) 4 times (89 sts).

Row 5: (K9, k2tog) 4 times, k1, (ssk, k9) 4 times (81 sts).

Row 7: (K8, k2tog) 4 times, k1, (ssk, k8) 4 times (73 sts).

Row 9: (K7, k2tog) 4 times, k1, (ssk, k7) 4 times (65 sts).

Row 11: (K6, k2tog) 4 times, k1, (ssk, k6) 4 times (57 sts).

Row 13: (K5, k2tog) 4 times, k1, (ssk, k5) 4 times (49 sts).

Row 15: (K4, k2tog) 4 times, k1, (ssk, k4) 4 times (41 sts).

Row 16: (P3, p2togtbl) 4 times, p1, (p2tog, p3) 4 times (33 sts).

Row 17: (K2, k2tog) 4 times, k1, (ssk, k2) 4 times (25 sts).

Row 18: (P1, p2togtbl) 4 times, p1, (p2tog, p1) 4 times (17 sts).

Row 19: (K2tog) 4 times, k1, (ssk) 4 times (9 sts).

Cut yarn, thread through rem sts and draw tight.

OUTER EAR (MAKE 2)

Using yarn A, 4mm needles and the thumb method, cast on 14 sts.

Row 1: Knit.

Row 2: P1, M1L, p12, M1R, p1 (16 sts).

Row 3: K1, M1R, k14, M1L, k1 (18 sts).

Row 4: Purl.

Row 5: K1, M1R, k16, M1L, k1 (20 sts).

Row 6: Purl.

Row 7: K1, M1R, k18, M1L, k1 (22 sts).

Rows 8-9: Work in stocking stitch.

Row 10: P1, M1R, p20, M1L, p1 (24 sts).

Rows 11-12: Work in stocking stitch.

Row 13: K1, M1R, k22, M1L, k1 (26 sts).

Rows 14-16: Work in stocking stitch.

Row 17: K1, M1R, k24, M1L, k1 (28 sts).

Rows 18-20: Work in stocking stitch.

Row 21: K1, M1R, k26, M1L, k1 (30 sts).

Rows 22-60: Work in stocking stitch. Cast off knitwise.

INNER EAR (MAKE 2)

Using yarn C, 4mm needles and the thumb method, cast on 14 sts. Work as for Outer ear. Cast off knitwise.

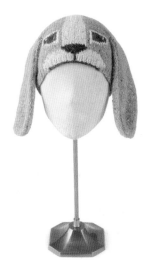

CHART FOR DOG

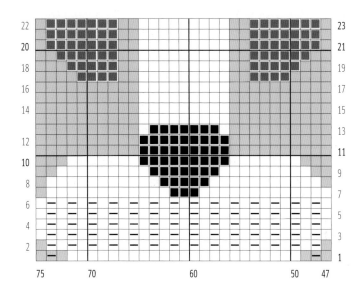

FINISHING

Sew in ends. Block and press the knitted pieces. Using mattress stitch (see page 108), sew the back seam, allowing half a stitch on each edge for the seam allowance. Sew the outer ears to the inner ears. Using the Swiss darning chart as a guide, Swiss darn (see page 107) the detail to the nose and eyes. Add highlights to the eyes using French knots (see page 107) and yarn B. Attach the ears to the hat.

SWISS DARNING CHART FOR DOG'S EYES AND NOSE

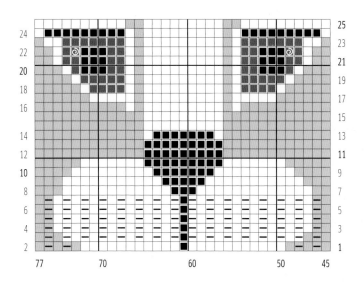

STITCH NUMBERS ALONG THE BOTTOM OF
THE CHART REFER TO THE ADULT SIZE.

KEY

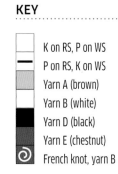

	K on RS, P on WS
—	P on RS, K on WS
	Yarn A (brown)
	Yarn B (white)
	Yarn D (black)
	Yarn E (chestnut)
	French knot, yarn B

Bull

A statement hat if ever there were one. Known to make cats
flee, children scream and adults smile, you are sure to make
an entrance wherever you go. There are two sizes of horns
– the adult hat shown has the larger size. Knit both sizes to
find the one that will suit you best – scary or terrifying!

SIZE

To fit: child[adult] (see page 94)
A loose fit that covers the ears.

TENSION

17 sts and 22 rows to 4in (10cm) measured over
stocking stitch using 5.5mm needles. Use larger
or smaller needles if necessary to obtain the
correct tension.

MATERIALS

• Chunky-weight yarn: Berroco Comfort Chunky, 50%
  nylon, 50% acrylic (150yds/138m per 100g ball)
• 2 x 100g balls in 5720 Humus (tan) (A)
• Light-weight yarn: Debbie Bliss Eco Baby 100% cotton
  (136yds/124m per 50g ball)
• 1 x 50g ball in 01 White (B)

• Waste cotton yarn
• Toy filling
• 5.5mm (UK5:US9) circular needle
• Set of four 5.5mm (UK5:US9) double-pointed needles
  (if required to work the last few rounds)
• 2 x 5mm (UK6:US8) double-pointed needles
• Set of four 3.25mm (UK10:US3) double-pointed needles
• Tapestry needle

NOTE

• A 5.5mm (UK5:US9) circular needle is specified
  because they are more flexible than straight needles.
• All stitches are slipped (sl) purlwise, with yarn at
  wrong side of work.
• Mark the stitches indicated with a length of waste
  cotton yarn looped loosely through the stitch.

BONNET

Using 5.5mm circular needle, yarn A and the thumb method (see page 96), cast on 57[73] sts. Work back and forth.

Row 1 (RS): K1tbl, k to the end.
Row 2: Sl1, k to last st, sl1.
Rows 3–12: Rep Rows 1–2, 5 times.
Row 13: K1tbl, k to the end.
Fasten off yarn.
Row 14: Sl21[27] sts, mark the last st worked, (k1, sl1) 8[10] times, mark the last sl st, turn.
Row 15: Knit 17[21] sts.
Row 16: (Sl1, k1) 8[10] times, sl1.
Cont working on the centre 17[21] sts.

CHILD SIZE ONLY

Rows 17–36: Rep Rows 15–16, 10 times.
Row 37: K1tbl, k to the end.
Row 38: Sl1, k to last st, sl1.
Rows 39–66: Rep Rows 37–38, 14 times.

Base of the horns

Row 67: K1tbl, k to the end.
Using a 5.5mm double-pointed needle and with the wrong side facing, slide the tip of the needle under the top bump of each stitch on the first row of garter stitch, Row 37, storing each top-bump loop on the needle. Hold the double-pointed needle in front and parallel with the working needle with the live stitches.
Row 68: Knit through the next st on the double-pointed needle and the next stitch on the working needle to the end of the row.
Rows 69–78: Rep Rows 15–16, 5 times.
Fasten off. With RS facing, rejoin yarn to the marked st on Row 14.

Row 79: Starting with the marked st on Row 14, pick up and knit 16 sts through the 16 edge sts, k17, pick up and knit 16 sts through the edge sts finishing with the marked st, turn (49 sts).
Cont working on the centre 49 sts.
Row 80: (Sl1, k1) 24 times, p2tog the next st with the next st on the needle (last worked on Row 13).
Row 81: Sl1, k47, ssk the next st with the next st on the needle (last worked on Row 13).
Rows 82–119: Rep Rows 48–49 until all the sts from Row 13 have been worked.
Cast off at the same time: p2, (p2tog, p3) to the last 2 sts, p2.

ADULT SIZE ONLY

Rows 17–44: Rep Rows 15–16, 14 times.
Row 45: K1tbl, k to the end.
Row 46: Sl1, k to last st, sl1.
Rows 47–74: Rep Rows 45–46, 14 times.

Base of the horns

Row 75: K1tbl, k to the end.
Using a 5.5mm double-pointed needle and with the wrong side facing, slide the tip of the needle under the top bump of each stitch on the first row of garter stitch, Row 45, storing each top-bump loop on the needle. Hold the double-pointed needle in front and parallel with the working needle with the live stitches.
Row 76: Knit through the next st on the double-pointed needle and the next stitch on the working needle to the end of the row.
Rows 77–86: Rep Rows 15–16, 5 times.

Fasten off. With RS facing, rejoin yarn to the marked st on Row 14.
Row 87: Starting with the marked st on Row 14, pick up and knit 20 sts through the 20 edge sts, k21, pick up and knit 20 sts through the edge sts finishing with the marked st, turn (61 sts).
Cont working on the centre 61 sts.
Row 88: (Sl1, k1) 30 times, p2tog the next st with the next st on the needle (last worked on Row 13).
Row 89: Sl1, k59, ssk the next st with the next st on the needle (last worked on Row 13).
Rows 90–139: Rep Rows 88–89 until all the sts from Row 13 have been worked.
Cast off at the same time: (p3, p2tog) to the last st, p1.

EAR (MAKE 2)

Using 5.5mm circular needle, yarn A and the thumb method, cast on 15 sts. Work back and forth.
Row 1: Purl.
Rows 2–9: Work in stocking stitch.
Row 10: K1, M1R, k13, M1L, k1 (17 sts).
Row 11: P1, M1R, p15, M1L, p1 (19 sts).
Row 12: Knit.
Row 13: P1, M1R, p17, M1L, p1 (21 sts).
Rows 14–23: Work in stocking stitch.
Row 24: K1, ssk, k15, k2tog, k1 (19 sts).
Row 25 and each alternate row: Purl.
Row 26: K1, ssk, k13, k2tog, k1 (17 sts).
Row 28: K1, ssk, k11, k2tog, k1 (15 sts).
Row 30: K1, ssk, k9, k2tog, k1 (13 sts).

Row 32: K1, ssk, k7, k2tog, k1 (11 sts).
Row 34: K1, ssk, k5, k2tog, k1 (9 sts).
Row 36: K1, ssk, k3, k2tog, k1 (7 sts). Cast off at the same time: K1, ssk, k1, k2tog, k1.

CHILD HORNS (MAKE 2)

Using 3.25mm double-pointed needles, yarn B and the thumb method, cast on 6 sts.
Arrange the sts to work in the round.
Round 1: (Inc) 6 times (12 sts).
Round 2: Knit.
Round 3: (Inc, k1) 6 times (18 sts).
Rounds 4–15: Knit.
Round 16: K8, yf, sl1r, yb, sl1l, turn; p7, yb, sl1r, yf, sl1l, turn; k6, yf, sl1r, yb, sl1l, turn; p5, yb, sl1r, yf, sl1l, turn; k4, yf, sl1r, yb, sl1l, turn; p3, yb, sl1r, yf, sl1l, turn; k to the end of the round, picking up and knitting any st wraps.
Round 17: Knit to the end of the round, picking up and knitting any st wraps.
Rounds 18–27: Knit.
Round 28: (K4, k2tog) 3 times (15 sts).
Rounds 29–30: Knit.
Round 31: (K3, k2tog) 3 times (12 sts).
Rounds 32–33: Knit.
Gently start to stuff the horn with toy filling. Add more filling after the following rounds as required.
Round 34: (K2, k2tog) 3 times (9 sts).
Rounds 35–36: Knit.
Round 37: (K1, k2tog) 3 times (6 sts).
Rounds 38–39: Knit.
Cut yarn, thread through rem sts and draw tight.

ADULT HORNS (MAKE 2)

Using 3.25mm double-pointed needles, yarn B and the thumb method, cast on 6 sts.
Arrange the sts to work in the round.
Round 1: (Inc) 6 times (12 sts).
Round 2: Knit.
Round 3: (Inc, k1) 6 times (18 sts).
Round 4: Knit.
Round 5: (Inc, k2) 6 times (24 sts).
Rounds 6–20: Knit.
Round 21: K11, yf, sl1r, yb, sl1l, turn; p10, yb, sl1r, yf, sl1l, turn; k9, yf, sl1r, yb, sl1l, turn; p8, yb, sl1r, yf, sl1l, turn; k7, yf, sl1r, yb, sl1l, turn; p6, yb, sl1r, yf, sl1l, turn; k to the end of the round, picking up and knitting any st wraps.
Round 22: Knit to the end of the round, picking up and knitting any st wraps.
Rounds 23–30: Knit.
Round 31: (K6, k2tog) 3 times (21 sts).
Rounds 32–33: Knit.
Round 34: (K5, k2tog) 3 times (18 sts).
Rounds 35–36: Knit.
Round 37: (K4, k2tog) 3 times (15 sts).
Rounds 38–39: Knit.
Round 40: (K3, k2tog) 3 times (12 sts).
Rounds 41–42: Knit.
Gently start to stuff the horn with toy filling. Add more filling after the following rounds as required.
Round 43: (K2, k2tog) 3 times (9 sts).
Rounds 44–45: Knit.
Round 46: (K1, k2tog) 3 times (6 sts).
Rounds 47–48: Knit.
Cut yarn, thread through rem sts and draw tight.

CORD (MAKE 2)

Make an i-cord as follows.
Using 5mm double-pointed needles, yarn A and the thumb method, cast on 4 sts.
Row 1: Knit.
*Without turning work, slide sts along the needle to the right-hand point and draw the working yarn across the back of the stitches.
Row 2: Knit.
Rep from *until the cord measures 18in (45cm) or the required length.
Cut yarn, thread through sts and draw tight.

FINISHING

Sew in ends. Block and press the knitted pieces. Fold the ears wrong sides together, using mattress stitch (see page 108), stitch the first 10 rows together. Using yarn A, make four 2in (5cm)-diameter pompoms (see page 109). Attach a pompom to each end of each cord. Using the photograph as reference, attach the cords, ears and horns to the bonnet.

Monkey

This is a hat for when you just want to swing on by, but be careful – with the generous fit and a mouth that flops and droops, you may suggest surprise at the most inopportune moment. For an expression that is less surprised, do not stretch the face as you stitch it to the hat base.

SIZE
To fit: child[adult] (see page 94)
A close fit that covers the top of the ears.

TENSION
9½ sts and 15 rows to 4in (10cm) measured over stocking stitch, using yarn A and 10mm needles. Use larger or smaller needles if necessary to obtain the correct tension.

MATERIALS
• Bulky-weight yarn: Rowan Big Wool, 100% wool (87yds/80m per 100g ball)
• 1 x 100g ball in 008 Black (A)
• Light-weight yarn: Knitpicks Cotlin, 70% Tanguis cotton, 30% linen (123yds/112m per 50g ball)

• 1 x 50g ball in 694 Linen (flesh) (B)
• Short lengths of tapestry wool or scraps of yarn in white (C) and brown (D)
• 9mm (UK00:US13) circular needle
• 10mm (UK000:US15) circular needle
• Set of four 10mm (UK000:US15) double-pointed needles (if required to work the last few rounds)
• Pair of 3.75mm (UK9:US5) straight needles
• Set of five 3.75mm (UK9:US5) double-pointed needles
• Set of five 3.25mm (UK10:US3) double-pointed needles
• Stitch holder
• Tapestry needle
• Sewing pins
• Sewing needle and matching thread

HAT

Using 9mm circular needle, yarn A and the cable method (see page 97), cast on 48[60] sts.
Arrange the sts to work in the round.
Rounds 1–3: (K1, p1) to end.
Change to 10mm needle.

CHILD SIZE ONLY
Rounds 4–12: Knit.

ADULT SIZE ONLY
Rounds 4–16: Knit.

CROWN
BOTH SIZES
Round 1: (K2, ssk, k4, k2tog, k2) 4[5] times (40[50] sts).
Rounds 2–4: Knit.
Round 5: (K2, ssk, k2, k2tog, k2) 4[5] times (32[40] sts).
Round 6: Knit.
Round 7: (K2, ssk, k2tog, k2) 4[5] times (24[30] sts).
Round 8: Knit.
Round 9: (K1, ssk, k2tog, k1) 4[5] times (16[20] sts).
Round 10: Knit.
Round 11: (Ssk, k2tog) 4[5] times (8[10] sts).
Round 12: Knit.
Cut yarn, thread through rem sts and draw tight.

FACE

Using 3.75mm needles and yarn B, cast on 10 sts.
Row 1: Purl.
Row 2: K1, M1R, k8, M1L, k1 (12 sts).
Row 3: P1, M1R, p10, M1L, p1 (14 sts).
Row 4: K1, M1R, k12, M1L, k1 (16 sts).
Row 5: Purl.
Row 6: K1, M1R, k14, M1L, k1 (18 sts).
Row 7: Purl.
Row 8: K1, M1R, k16, M1L, k1 (20 sts).
Row 9: Purl.
Row 10: K1, M1R, k18, M1L, k1 (22 sts).
Row 11: Purl.
Row 12: K1, M1R, k20, M1L, k1 (24 sts).
Row 13: Purl.
Row 14: K4, cast off 16 sts, k to end.
Row 15: P4, cast on 16 sts, p4.
Rows 16–17: Work in stocking stitch.
Row 18: Ssk, k to the last 2 sts, k2tog (22 sts).
Row 19: Purl.
Rows 20–21: Rep Rows 18–19 (20 sts).
Row 22: Ssk, k to the last 2 sts, k2tog (18 sts).
Row 23: P2tog, p to the last 2 sts, pspo (16 sts).
Rows 24–27: Work in stocking stitch.
Row 28: K1, M1R, k14, M1L, k1 (18 sts).
Row 29: Purl.
Row 30: K1, M1R, k16, M1L, k1 (20 sts).
Row 31: Purl.
Row 32: K1, M1R, k18, M1L, k1 (22 sts).
Row 33: Purl.

Row 34: K1, M1R, k20, M1L, k1 (24 sts).
Row 35: Purl.
Row 36: K1, M1R, k22, M1L, k1 (26 sts).
Row 37: Purl.
Row 38: K1, M1R, k24, M1L, k1 (28 sts).
Row 39: Purl.
Row 40: K3, cast off 9 sts, k to last 12 sts, cast off 9 sts, k to end.
Row 41: P3, cast on 9 sts, p4, cast on 9 sts, p3.
Rows 42–43: Work in stocking stitch.
Row 44: Ssk, k to the last 2 sts, k2tog (26 sts).
Row 45: P12, cast off 2 sts, p to end (24 sts).

LEFT EYEBROW
Row 46: Ssk, k10, place rem sts onto a stitch holder, turn (11 sts).
Row 47: P2tog, p9 (10 sts).
Row 48: Ssk, k to the last 2 sts, k2tog (8 sts).
Cast off at the same time: p2tog, p4, pspo.

RIGHT EYEBROW
Transfer the sts from the stitch holder.
With the RS facing join yarn to the rem sts.
Row 46: K to last 2 sts, k2tog, (11 sts).
Row 47: P9, p2tog, (10 sts).
Row 48: Ssk, k to the last 2 sts, k2tog (8 sts).
Cast off at the same time: p2tog, p4, pspo.

EAR (MAKE 2)

Using 3.75mm double-pointed needles, yarn B and the thumb method (see page 96), cast on 28 sts.

Arrange the sts to work in the round.
Ear Front: needle 2 and 3.
Ear Back: needle 1 and 4.

Rounds 1–4: Knit.

Round 5: (K1, M1R, k12, M1L, k1) twice (32 sts).

Round 6: (K1, M1R, k14, M1L, k1) twice (36 sts).

Round 7: (K1, M1R, k16, M1L, k1) twice (40 sts).

Round 8: Knit.

Round 9: (K1, M1R, k18, M1L, k1) twice (44 sts).

Rounds 10–13: Knit.

Round 14: (K1, ssk, k16, k2tog, k1) twice (40 sts).

Round 15 and 2 following alternate rounds: Knit.

Round 16: (K1, ssk, k14, k2tog, k1) twice (36 sts).

Round 18: (K1, ssk, k12, k2tog, k1) twice (32 sts).

Round 20: (K1, ssk, k10, k2tog, k1) twice (28 sts).

Round 21: (K1, ssk, k8, k2tog, k1) twice (24 sts).

Round 22: (K1, ssk, k6, k2tog, k1) twice (20 sts).

Cast off in pattern set and join the Front ear to the Back ear using mattress stitch (see page 108) or join the stitches using Kitchener stitch (see page 107).

Note: The decreases align with the centre front and centre back of the Ear.

EYE CENTRE (MAKE 2)

Using a single strand of yarn C, 3.25mm double-pointed needles and the thumb method, cast on 36 sts. Arrange the sts to work in the round.

Rounds 1–2: Knit.

Round 3: (K1, k2tog) 12 times (24 sts).

Fasten off yarn C. Join in yarn D.

Round 4: Knit.

Round 5: (K2tog) 12 times (12 sts).

Round 6: (K2tog) 6 times (6 sts).

Cut yarn, thread through rem sts and draw tight.

FINISHING

Sew in ends. Block and press the knitted pieces. Add a highlight to each eye using yarn C and a French knot (see page 107). Pin the face to the hat, stretching the eyes towards the top of the hat. Using a sewing needle and matching thread, sew the face to the front of the hat. Place the eyes through the eye slits. Using a sewing needle and matching thread, sew the eyes to the reverse of the face, stitching around the edge of the eye slits. Using the photograph as reference, attach the ears to either side of the hat.

TECHNIQUES

Getting started

SIZING

Most of the hats in this book are sized to fit a child of four to five years old or an adult with a medium-sized head. The adult size is a more generous, but pleasing, fit on an older child. Some of the hats have a closer fit than others, but the fit of the hat is described at the start of each pattern.

To enlarge a hat to fit a larger head or provide a more generous fit, either work the hat in a yarn in which you can achieve a tension with slightly less than 10% fewer stitches over 4in (10cm) than that stated in the pattern. Alternatively, if the pattern is worked on two needles, add 5% more stitches at either end of the row at the cast-on stage.

Separate the extra stitches from those described in the pattern with stitch markers and decrease one extra stitch at the beginning of each decrease row on the crown shaping until no extra stitches remain. The hat will have a more pronounced curve at the back of the head, but that could be said to be in keeping with the head of the animal being depicted. Some of the yarns in this book have been worked with slightly more stitches over 4in (10cm) than recommended by the manufacturer and could easily be worked at a slightly looser tension to create a larger hat.

There are usually a few rows of plain stocking stitch before the crown shaping. It is always useful to measure the hat at this stage and gauge whether or not you will need all these rows or whether you need a few more. Look at the pattern, note the number of rows or rounds in the crown shaping, measure this number of rows or rounds from the cast-on edge, add this measurement to the work you have already completed and make your decision. You are in charge.

> **CAUTION**
> Remember to allow more yarn if you are working a larger hat.

TENSION

Having just encouraged you to look at the tension recommendations with a critical eye, if you want a hat identical to the one in the project photograph you will need to match the tension stated at the beginning of each pattern. As already discussed, a variation of 10% – or two to three stitches over 4in (10cm) – can make a difference of 2in (5cm) to the width of the brim; the subsequent difference in the row count could make the difference between a youthful version of the animal and a wrinkly, double-chinned version!

To work a tension swatch, cast on slightly more stitches than those stated in the tension recommendation and work slightly more rows. Lightly block the swatch, place pins 4in (10cm) apart across the width and depth of the swatch, and count the number of stitches and rows between. If there are too few stitches, rework the swatch with a smaller needle size; if there are too many stitches, rework the swatch with a slightly larger needle size. Continue to work swatches until you have matched the tension recommendation as closely as possible. The wise knitter will check the tension again as they work the project.

MATERIALS AND EQUIPMENT

KNITTING NEEDLES

This is up to personal preference. Bamboo and wooden needles provide more friction and may make colour knitting slightly easier. Smoother needles make textured yarns move more easily along the needles and often require less physical effort to knit with. In general, however, it is the length of the needle or its tip that makes the most difference; try to use shorter needles for smaller pieces of work and longer needles for wider sections of the projects. Using circular needles for the main hat pieces has the added advantage of allowing you to wrap the work around a head to check the size and fit.

> **TIP**
> Always use the same knitting equipment to knit the project as you used to knit the tension swatch.

OTHER EQUIPMENT

Although it is easy to be seduced by the various knitting bags and cases, tapestry needles and knitter's needles, tape measures and stitch markers available, knitting is a hobby that has quite light equipment requirements. Check that your knitting bag is clean, your tape measure is accurate, that your stitch markers and needles won't snag, and enjoy your knitting.

SUBSTITUTING YARN

When choosing yarn for a pattern in this book, one of the most important things to consider is the shade of the yarn, and this includes its texture. This consideration is closely followed by the weight of the yarn, and finally the fibre content. Many of the projects in this book use yarns with a high percentage of alpaca because this helps the edges and the narrow bands of rib lie flat.

One way to gauge whether or not a yarn would make a suitable substitute is to examine the wraps per inch produced by a yarn. Some websites provide this information, but otherwise you can measure this yourself. Wrap a strand of yarn in a single layer, with the wraps side by side, around a ruler for several inches, then divide the total number of wraps by the number of inches covered to produce an average number of wraps per inch. The received wisdom is that you should use a yarn that has twice as many wraps per inch as you require stitches per inch. However, this will only ever be a rough guide; there is no substitute for knitting a swatch and assessing the fabric's suitability for your project with your eyes and hands.

Finding the correct shade of knitting yarn may prove difficult. One solution is to use tapestry yarn or threads used for crewel embroidery. These threads are produced in a huge range of shades and are perfect for small pieces or sections of knitting. To knit thread that is slightly too fine, hold two strands together or work one strand together with a fine silk mohair yarn.

> **TIP**
> You can treat yarns like pigments and mix two shades together to create a third shade. Have another look at the Pig hat on page 72: it uses two strands of yarn held together to produce the main colours in the project. This method is also a good way of introducing a subtle echo of a shade in your favourite scarf or gloves to a hat.

Knitting techniques

SLIP KNOT

The first stitch is not a stitch but a slip knot, which is counted as a stitch. To make a slip knot, wrap the yarn around the fingers of your left hand with the second wrap behind the first wrap and further from your fingertips than the first. Holding a knitting needle in your right hand, insert the needle under the first wrap and, using the tip of the needle, draw the yarn from the second wrap under the yarn of the first wrap to form a loop on the needle. Gently release the yarn wraps from around the fingers and pull the yarn ends to tighten the loop around the knitting needle.

THUMB CAST ON

This cast on is particularly elastic and is perfect for the brim of a hat. It is worked using the tail of yarn beyond the slip knot as well as the working yarn – the yarn that emerges from the ball of yarn.

1 Leaving a long yarn tail, make a slip knot and place it onto a knitting needle. To ensure the yarn tail is long enough for the cast on, allow at least three times the length of the cast-on and a bit extra to weave in the end.

2 Holding the needle in the right hand, wind the yarn tail around the left thumb from front to back and insert the needle tip through the thumb loop from front to back. Wrap the working yarn around the tip of the needle so that it goes under the needle and crosses the top of the needle from left to right.

3 Draw the yarn wrapped around the needle through the thumb loop and remove the thumb from the loop. Gently pull the yarn tail to tighten the new loop on the needle. Repeat steps 2–3 until the required number of cast-on stitches are on the needle.

1

2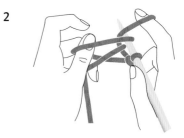

3

CABLE CAST ON

This type of cast on creates a firm decorative edge.

1 Leaving a 4in (10cm) yarn tail, make a slip knot in the yarn and place it onto a knitting needle. Holding the needle with the slip knot in the left hand, pick up a second knitting needle in the right hand and insert the needle tip, from front to back, through the slip knot. Wrap the working yarn around the tip of the needle so that it goes under the needle and crosses the top of the needle from left to right.

2 Draw the yarn wrapped around the right-hand needle through the slip knot to create a new loop on the right-hand needle.

3 Place the new loop onto the left-hand needle and gently pull the working yarn to tighten the new loop.

4 Insert the right-hand needle tip, from front to back, between the last two stitch loops on the left-hand needle.

5 Wrap the working yarn around the tip of the right-hand needle as if to knit and draw the yarn wrapped around the right-hand needle through the gap.

6 Place the new loop onto the left-hand needle and gently pull the working yarn to tighten the new loop. Repeat this step until the required number of cast-on stitches are on the left-hand needle.

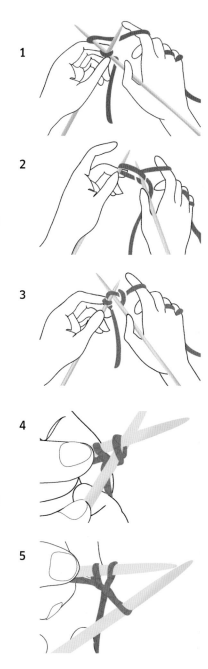

1

2

3

4

5

6

PROVISIONAL CAST ON

This is a type of cast on that can be unravelled to reveal loops that can then be picked up and worked. One method is to work a crochet chain around a knitting needle.

1 Make a slip knot and place it onto a crochet hook. Holding the slip knot steady, wrap the working yarn around the crochet hook and draw the yarn through the loop on the hook to complete a chain stitch. Repeat this last step until you have 2–3 chain stitches hanging from the hook.

2 Holding a knitting needle in the left hand, with the working yarn under and behind the needle, wrap the yarn across the top of the needle and around the hook to complete another stitch. Take the working yarn under and behind the needle and repeat this step until the required number of cast-on stitches are on the needle.

3 To fasten off, work a few chain stitches without wrapping around the needle, cut the working yarn, draw the cut yarn end through the last loop, and pull the yarn end to secure. Work from the pattern, knitting through the loops on the knitting needle as directed.

4 To unravel the cast-on, unpick the last chain by drawing the yarn end back through the last loop, and pulling it to unravel the stitches. With a needle, pick up the loops that are revealed along the knitted edge. Work from the pattern, knitting through the loops on the needle as directed.

CAST OFF KNITWISE

Casting off is a method of securing stitches so that they won't unravel when the knitting needle is removed. This method produces a firm edge that is easy to seam.

1 Knit two stitches. Insert the left-hand knitting needle through the stitch furthest from the tip of the right-hand knitting needle; lift this stitch over the stitch closest to the tip of the right-hand needle and over the tip of the right-hand needle. Drop the lifted stitch off the left-hand needle. This is one cast-off stitch.

2 Knit one stitch. Insert the left-hand knitting needle through the stitch furthest from the tip of the right-hand needle and repeat as before. Repeat this step until one stitch remains on the right-hand needle. To fasten off, cut the working yarn, leaving a 4in (10cm) tail, and draw the yarn tail through the remaining stitch on the needle.

CAST OFF PURLWISE

Work as for casting off knitwise but work purl stitches instead of knit stitches.

THREE-NEEDLE CAST-OFF

This cast-off secures the stitches from two knitting needles, holding parallel lines of stitches, using a knitted cast-off. With the wrong side facing outwards, the two needles are held parallel in the left hand and an empty third knitting needle is held in the right hand. Insert the tip of the right-hand needle through the next stitch on the nearest needle and then through the next stitch on the needle behind. Wrap the yarn around the needle as if to knit and complete the stitch, drawing the yarn through both stitch loops. Knitting through one stitch on each needle, repeat the process. Insert the tip of one of the left-hand needles through the stitch furthest from the tip of the right-hand needle; lift this stitch over the stitch closest to the tip of the right-hand needle and over the tip of the right-hand needle. Drop the lifted stitch off the left-hand needle. Continue to work as for casting off knitwise (see opposite, left), but work each new stitch with the right-hand needle through one stitch from each of the left-hand needles.

CAST OFF GATHER

To gather the remaining stitches, cut the yarn 4in (10cm) from the last stitches, thread the yarn end through a tapestry needle and, starting with the stitch furthest from the tip of the needle, pass the needle through the remaining stitches. Gently pull the yarn end to draw the stitches together. Secure the stitches by weaving in the yarn end on the reverse of the project.

1

2

KNIT STITCH

This is one of the two basic stitches used in knitting.

1 Start with the knitting needle with the cast-on stitches or live stitches in the left hand, an empty needle in the right hand and the points of each needle pointing into the middle. Insert the right-hand needle tip through the stitch loop nearest the tip of the left-hand needle from left to right. Then wrap the working yarn around the tip of the right-hand knitting needle so that it goes under the knitting needle and crosses the top of the knitting needle from left to right.

2 Draw the yarn wrapped around the right-hand knitting needle through the stitch loop to create a new loop on the right-hand needle.

3 Slide the stitch loop just worked off the left-hand needle. Repeat steps 1–3 for each stitch on the left-hand needle. This is one knit row.

To work in rows, transfer the knitting needle in the right hand to the left hand and repeat the sequence described above.

KNIT THROUGH THE BACK OF THE LOOP (KTBL)

Work as the knit stitch described above but insert the right-hand needle through the next stitch loop on the left-hand needle from right to left.

Knit stitch

1

2

3

Purl stitch

1
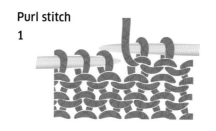

2

3

PURL STITCH

This is the other of the two basic stitches used in knitting.

1 Start with the knitting needle with the cast-on or live stitches in the left hand, an empty needle in the right hand, and the points of each needle pointing into the middle. Insert the right-hand needle tip through the stitch loop nearest the tip of the left-hand needle from right to left. Wrap the working yarn around the tip of the right-hand knitting needle so that it goes over the knitting needle and crosses the top of the knitting needle from right to left.

2 Draw the yarn wrapped around the right-hand knitting needle through the stitch loop to create a new loop on the right-hand needle.

3 Slide the stitch loop just worked off the left-hand needle. Repeat steps 1–3 for each stitch on the left-hand needle. This is one purl row.

To work in rows, transfer the knitting needle in the right hand to the left hand and repeat the sequence described above.

PURL THROUGH THE BACK OF THE LOOP (PTBL)

Work as for the purl stitch described above but insert the right-hand needle through the next stitch loop on the left-hand needle from back-left to front.

STITCH VARIATIONS

Once the knit and purl stitches have been mastered a variety of stitch patterns can be worked. The method of working these patterns may vary depending on whether you are working in rows or in the round on circular or double-pointed needles. The right side is the side of the project that is intended for display. The wrong side is the side that would not normally be seen. When a side is described as facing, it means the side that is at the front, facing towards you, as you hold your work in your left hand, ready to knit.

GARTER STITCH
This stitch appears the same on both right and wrong sides and looks like a series of horizontal ridges. Each ridge denotes two rows or rounds.

Working in rows: Knit every row.
Working in the round: Knit one round, purl the next; repeat to the end.

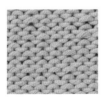

REVERSE STOCKING STITCH (REV ST ST)
This stitch is also known as reverse stockinette stitch (mainly in the US). On the right side it looks like a series of interlocking offset bumps. Each pair of bumps denotes one row or round.

Working in rows: Purl when the right side is facing and knit when the wrong side is facing.
Working in the round: Purl all rounds.

STOCKING STITCH (ST ST)
This stitch is also known as stockinette stitch (mainly in the US). On the right side it looks like a series of interlocking V-shapes. Each V-shape denotes one row or round.

Working in rows: Knit when the right side is facing and purl when the wrong side is facing.
Working in the round: Knit all rounds.

MOSS STITCH
This stitch is also known as seed stitch (mainly in the US). It appears the same on both right and wrong sides and is a chequer pattern of knit and purl stitches. Each raised bump denotes one row or round.

Working in rows and rounds: If the next stitch on the left-hand needle has the appearance of a purl stitch when viewed from the side facing, then knit the next stitch; if the next stitch on the left-hand needle has the appearance of a knit stitch when viewed from the side facing, then purl the next stitch.

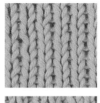

SINGLE AND DOUBLE RIB
These stitch patterns are vertical stripe patterns of stocking stitch and reverse stocking stitch and appear the same on both the right and wrong sides. Single rib is made up of stitch columns one stitch wide. Double rib is made up of stitch columns two stitches wide. Each V-shape denotes one row or round.

Working in rows and rounds: If the next stitch on the left-hand needle has the appearance of a purl stitch when viewed from the side facing, then purl the next stitch; if the next stitch on the left-hand needle has the appearance of a knit stitch when viewed from the side facing, then knit the next stitch.

LOOP STITCH (ML)

Loop stitch is a variation of a knit stitch.

1 With the knitting needle with the live stitches in the left hand and a working knitting needle in the right hand, work to the position of the next 'make loop' and insert the right-hand needle through the next stitch loop on the left-hand needle. Work as if to knit but do not slide the stitch on the left-hand needle off the needle. Move the working yarn between the two needles to the front of the work, loop it around your left thumb.

2 Move the yarn back between the needles to the back of the work. Insert the right-hand needle into the next stitch on the left-hand needle for the second time, wrap the working yarn around the tip of the right-hand needle as if to knit, and draw the yarn through the stitch loop as before. This time, slide the worked stitch off the left-hand needle.

3 Insert the left-hand needle through the second stitch loop from the tip of the right-hand needle and lift this stitch over the stitch closest to the tip of the right-hand needle and over the tip of the right-hand needle. Drop the lifted stitch off the left-hand needle. Gently pull the yarn loop to tighten the stitch.

INCREASING

Increasing is usually associated with increasing the number of stitches in a row or round; however, the total number of stitches may remain the same because stitches may be added in one part of the fabric and removed in another. This may be done for decorative reasons or to manipulate the direction in which the knitted stitches lie. All these methods of adding stitches create one extra loop on the right-hand needle each time they are worked. These extra loops should be counted as stitches and worked as directed on subsequent rows or rounds.

INCREASE (INC)

This increase adds one extra stitch by working twice into the same stitch. Work to an 'increase' instruction, then insert the right-hand knitting needle through the next stitch loop on the left-hand knitting needle from left to right. Wrap the working yarn around the tip of the right-hand needle as if to knit and draw the yarn through the loop. Do not slide the stitch on the left-hand needle off the needle. Insert the right-hand needle into the next stitch on the left-hand needle for the second time, from right to left (through the back of the loop), wrap the working yarn around the tip of the right-hand needle as if to knit and draw the yarn through the stitch loop as before. This time, slide the worked stitch off the left-hand needle.

YARNOVER (YO)

This method of adding stitches adds one extra stitch by looping the yarn around the right-hand knitting needle before working the next stitch. Work to a 'yarnover' instruction, move the working yarn between the two knitting needles to the front of the work, and wrap the yarn across the top of the right-hand needle from front to back. Work the next stitch as directed by the pattern.

> **NOTE**
>
> The base of the bobble in this book is worked by knitting into the front and back of a stitch four times. This creates three extra stitches on the right-hand knitting needle.

MAKE ONE LEFT OR RIGHT (M1L OR M1R)

This method of adding stitches adds an extra stitch by lifting and working a strand between two stitches. It creates left-slanting or right-slanting stitches – a description of the appearance of the new stitch when viewed from the right side of the work. The increases follow the pattern set by the stitch pattern.

Make one left (M1L): Insert the tip of the left-hand knitting needle from front to back under the strand between the last stitch worked and the next. Insert the right-hand knitting needle into the loop as if to knit or purl into the back of the loop, wrap the working yarn around the tip of the right-hand needle, and draw the yarn through the loop. Slide the lifted loop off the left-hand needle.

Make one right (M1R): Insert the tip of the left-hand knitting needle from back to front under the strand between the last stitch worked and the next. Insert the right-hand knitting needle into the loop as if to knit or purl into the loop in the usual way, wrap the working yarn around the tip of the right-hand needle and draw the yarn through the loop. Slide the lifted loop off the left-hand needle.

DECREASING

Decreasing is usually associated with decreasing the number of stitches in a row or round; however, the total number of stitches may remain the same for the same reasons that increases may not increase the number of stitches in a row or round. Many of these decreases are described as left- or right-slanting, which describes the appearance of the stitches when viewed from the right side of the work. All these methods of removing stitches lose one stitch loop on the right-hand needle each time they are worked.

KNIT TWO STITCHES TOGETHER (K2TOG)

This is a right-slanting knit decrease.
1 Work to a 'knit two stitches together' instruction. Insert the right-hand knitting needle into two stitches on the left-hand knitting needle, starting with the second stitch from the tip of the left-hand needle and then through the next stitch on the left-hand needle, nearest the tip. Wrap the working yarn around the tip of the right-hand needle as if to knit.

2 Draw the yarn through both stitch loops to complete the knit stitch. Slide both stitches off the left-hand needle.

KNIT TWO STITCHES TOGETHER THROUGH THE BACK OF THE LOOP (K2TOGTBL)

This is a left-slanting knit decrease. Work to a 'knit two stitches together through the back of the loop' instruction. Insert the right-hand knitting needle through the next two stitches on the left-hand knitting needle, from right to left, starting with the stitch nearest the tip of the needle. Wrap the working yarn around the tip of the right-hand knitting needle as if to knit and draw the yarn through both stitch loops to complete the knit stitch. Slide both stitches off the left-hand needle.

PURL TWO STITCHES TOGETHER (P2TOG)

This is a right-slanting purl decrease. Work to a 'purl two stitches together' instruction. Insert the right-hand knitting needle through the next two stitches on the left-hand knitting needle, from right to left and starting with the stitch nearest the tip of the needle. Wrap the working yarn around the tip of the right-hand needle as if to purl, then draw the yarn through both stitch loops to complete the purl stitch. Slide both stitches off the left-hand needle.

SLIP, SLIP, KNIT (SSK)

This is a left-slanting knit decrease. Work to a 'slip, slip, knit' instruction. Insert the right-hand knitting needle into the next stitch on the left-hand knitting needle as if to knit and slip it onto the right-hand needle, twice. Then insert the left-hand needle from left to right through the front loops of the slipped stitches. The knitting needle positions should look similar to knitting two stitches together through the back of the loop. Wrap the working yarn around the tip of the right-hand needle as if to knit, and draw the yarn through both stitch loops to complete the knit stitch. Slide both stitches off the left-hand needle.

PURL, SLIP STITCH BACK, PASS SECOND STITCH OVER (PSPO)

This is a left-slanting purl decrease. Work to a 'purl, slip stitch back, pass second stitch over' instruction. Purl the next stitch on the left-hand knitting needle, insert the tip of the left-hand needle into the stitch on the right-hand knitting needle from left to right, and slip it back onto the left-hand needle. Insert the right-hand knitting needle through the stitch furthest from the tip of the left-hand needle and lift this stitch over the stitch closest to the tip of the right-hand needle and over the tip of the left-hand needle. Drop the lifted stitch off the right-hand needle.

TIP

The secret of a neat decrease is not to stretch the stitches as you work them; in particular the stitch that will lie on top. Keep the right-hand needle tip pointing down and towards the work for the best results.

WORKING IN THE ROUND

A knitted fabric may be produced using two knitting needles worked back and forth in rows or in the round using double-pointed needles or circular needles worked in one direction in a spiral. Double-pointed needles have a point at each end and are used in groups of four or five with one needle in the right hand and the remaining needles in the left hand holding the stitch loops. To work in the round, cast on as described in the pattern, onto one double-pointed or circular needle.

USING DOUBLE-POINTED NEEDLES

1 To start working using double-pointed needles, keep one needle as the working right-hand needle and divide the cast-on stitches over the remaining double-pointed needles. Place a stitch marker onto the double-pointed needle after the last cast-on stitch. Lay the double-pointed needles in a rough round, onto a flat surface, and arrange the stitches on the needles so that the cast-on edge runs along the inner edge of each double-pointed needle. This is a check to ensure the line of stitches have not twisted around the double-pointed needles like a candy stripe.

2 Holding the double-pointed needles carefully in the left hand and an empty needle in the right hand, insert the right-hand needle into the first stitch loop (originally the slip knot) and work as described in the pattern copy. Continue until the stitches on one double-pointed needle have been worked. This needle then becomes the working needle used to work the next double-pointed needle of stitches. When the stitch marker is reached, this marks the end of the round and is simply slipped from the left-hand needle to the right-hand needle.

USING CIRCULAR NEEDLES

To start working using a circular needle, place a stitch marker onto the circular needle after the last cast-on stitch. Lay the circular needle in a rough round onto a flat surface and arrange the stitches on the needle so that the cast-on edge runs along the inner edge of the circular needle. Holding the circular needle tip nearest the slip knot in the left hand and the circular needle tip nearest the last cast-on stitch in the right hand, insert the right-hand tip into the first stitch loop (originally the slip knot) and work as described in the project pattern.

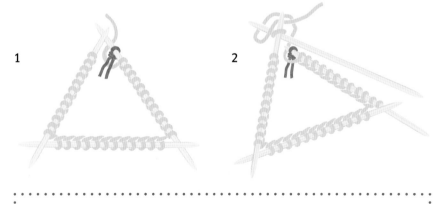

TIP

Work the first few stitches on each double-pointed needle firmly to prevent looser stitches or ladders appearing in the knitted fabric.

Animal Hats to Knit

PICKING UP AND KNITTING STITCHES

To pick up and knit stitches, with the right side facing, hold the knitted edge along which the stitches are to be picked up in the left hand and an empty knitting needle in the right hand.

If working along a cast-on or cast-off edge, with the working yarn at the back, insert the right-hand needle under the edge strands above or below the edge.

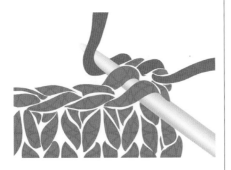

If working along a selvedge, insert the needle into the space between the edge stitch and the next stitch.

Wrap the working yarn around the tip of the needle as if to knit and draw the yarn wrapped around the needle through the fabric.

To avoid loose stitches, work picked-up stitches through the back of the loop on the following row or round.

SHORT-ROW SHAPING

Sometimes a project pattern may ask you to work a partial row, turn the work and work back along the stitches just worked. These rows are called short rows. Unfortunately, if that were all that the knitter was required to do, a hole would appear at the end of the short row the next time a full row was worked. To avoid a hole, the last stitch of a short row may be linked to the next stitch by a wrap of yarn around the base of the next stitch. In this book, the process of wrapping the stitch is described in the pattern copy by a series of yarn movements between the needles and slipped stitches. The wraps can remain in place: on textured stitch patterns they become almost invisible to the casual glance; on stocking stitch they appear as short horizontal strands of yarn across the base of some stitches.

If their appearance does not bother you, then you need not do any more. There are a variety of methods for hiding a stitch wrap, but this is the method that will work best for the wraps you will find in this book. Work until the next stitch on the left-hand needle has a wrap around its base, then insert the tip of the right-hand knitting needle from the front, under the yarn strand wrapping the stitch, and lift it onto the left-hand needle. Insert the right-hand needle through the wrap loop and the stitch that it wrapped and knit the two together through the back of the loops. The wrap should fall to the wrong side of the work, but you may wish to give it a gentle tug with the tip of a needle to neaten the appearance of the stitches on the right side of the work.

NOTE

Some eye patterns in this book use yarnovers to create an extra stitch to fill the gap at the end of short rows. These extra stitches remain and help to create a curved shape to the eye.

FAIR ISLE

This colour knitting technique is ideal when a knitting design is made of small groups of repeated colours across a section of knitting. The colours are picked up and worked as required – the yarn is carried or stranded from one stitch or group of stitches of a colour to the next and a layer of yarn strands is created on the reverse of the fabric. As a result, a project worked using the Fair Isle technique has a thicker fabric and sections of a project worked in Fair Isle may appear slightly raised.

Knit the stitches in the colours indicated in the chart or pattern copy. At each colour change, simply pick up the colour required and continue knitting. There is no need to link the old and new yarns because in a few stitches the same length of old yarn will be used again. For a smooth finish, try not to loop the yarns around each other. For example, in the image below, one yarn is held in each hand and the yarns naturally lie in parallel strands across the back of the work. If you can't knit with two hands, think of the two yarns as being an upper and lower yarn and keep them in these relative positions as you work.

1

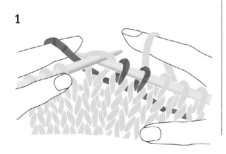

INTARSIA

This colour knitting technique is ideal when a knitting design is made of blocks of colour larger than a few stitches in any direction. Each block of colour is worked using a separate short length of yarn, and the blocks are joined at each colour change by overlapping and linking the yarns. This technique creates a single-layer fabric, which means it has a similar drape to that of a single-colour design and no one colour is raised above another.

Start by winding the yarn required, in short lengths, onto bobbins or into twists of yarn. For a rough guide of how much yarn to wind in each bobbin or twist, wrap the yarn around the knitting needle you are about to use 30 times, unwind the yarn and measure its length. This should be enough for ten stitches. This measure can be multiplied according to the number of stitches in the block. Remember to allow extra yarn for weaving in the ends.

To start a new intarsia block, work to one stitch before the start of a new colour block, lay the yarn end of the new yarn over the working yarn, and work the final stitch in the old colour.

To work an intarsia block, work the first stitch of a new colour, pass the old yarn over the new yarn so that the new yarn loops around or links the old yarn when the first stitch of the new colour is worked. Once a block has been completed, weave in the ends through the linked yarn strands in a clockwise direction.

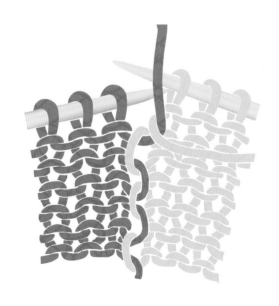

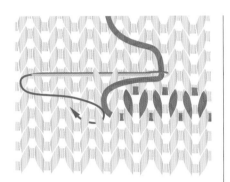

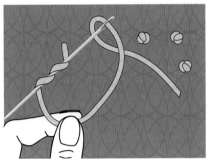

KITCHENER STITCH

This technique secures the stitches from two knitting needles, holding parallel lines of stitches, using a sewn cast-off to create an almost invisible join between the two groups of stitches.

Cut the working yarn to a length about three times the length of the stitches to be joined plus a little extra, and thread this through a tapestry needle. With the right side facing outwards, hold the two knitting needles parallel in the left hand pointing right, with the working yarn coming from the back needle and the tapestry needle in the right hand.

Start the sequence by threading the yarn tail through the first stitch on the front knitting needle as if to purl and through the first stitch on the back needle as if to knit. Then pass the tapestry needle and yarn through the stitches in the following sequence, repeating the sequence until no stitches remain on the knitting needles:

Front needle: First stitch as if to knit; slip the stitch off the needle.
Front needle: Second stitch as if to purl; leave the stitch on the needle.
Back needle: First stitch as if to purl; slip the stitch off the needle.
Back needle: Second stitch as if to knit; leave the stitch on the needle.

It is important to keep your tension even and match the stitch size of the knitted stitches, although you can go back and adjust your sewn stitches at the end.

SWISS DARNING

Also known as duplicate stitch, Swiss darning is an embroidery stitch that mimics or duplicates the appearance of stocking stitch. It is often used for narrow or small blocks of colour, where the intarsia technique is more difficult to use. It is a relatively simple stitch to work because it is worked on the knitted fabric it is trying to match.

Start by threading a tapestry needle with yarn. Select a stitch near the top and right of the section to be embroidered. Working from the back of the work to the front, bring the needle up through the gap at the base V-shape of the selected stitch, then, following the yarn strand that connects the two sections of the V-shape of the selected stitch, pass the needle under both legs of the V-shape of the stitch above. Then take the needle back, from front to back, down through the gap at the base V-shape of the selected stitch. This completes one stitch. Continue to work down and left, across the area to be embroidered.

FRENCH KNOTS

This lovely stitch provides a highlight in the eyes of many of the hats in this book. It is smaller than a knitted stitch and can be positioned anywhere on the knitted fabric.

Start by threading a tapestry needle with yarn. Working from the back of the work to the front, bring the needle up through the knitted fabric. With the finger and thumb of your less dominant hand, hold the yarn taut about 2in (5cm) from where it emerges from the fabric, wind the yarn below where it is held around the tip of the needle, insert the needle back through the fabric close to the point from which it emerged, then, as the needle passes through the fabric, release your hold on the yarn and allow the twist of yarn to form on the surface of the fabric.

WHIP STITCH

This is a flat seam stitch used to join knitted edges to knitted edges or flat knitted fabric without tucking the selvedge to the wrong side, using evenly spaced stitches worked, wherever possible, through the centre of the knitted stitches so that the whip stitches recede. In this book, whip stitch is often used to apply knitted pieces to the knitted fabric of the hat. Prepare the knitted edges that will be visible by lightly blocking or pressing them. Start by threading a tapestry needle with yarn matching the knitted piece to be applied or the sections to be joined. Secure the yarn end to the reverse of the piece to be applied, finishing with the yarn end close to the knitted edge. Then, with the right sides of the knitted fabrics facing outwards, and the knitted piece in place, insert the needle down through the centre of a stitch on the background fabric close to or slightly under the edge of the piece to be applied and then up through the next stitch around the edge of the piece to be applied. Continue working around the piece to be applied and secure the end.

MATTRESS STITCH

This seam stitch is used to create an almost invisible seam with part of or all of the edge stitches hidden within the seam on the wrong side of the work. It is worked with the right side of both edges facing outwards and can be worked through the centre of the edge stitch so that half a stitch along either edge becomes part of the seam and the seam allowance on the wrong side, or it can be worked to the outside of either seam stitch (between it and the next stitch) so a whole stitch on either side becomes the seam allowance.

If mattress stitch is used to join two selvedges, then begin by threading a tapestry needle with matching yarn and placing the two edges side by side. Starting at the bottom edge and working alternate edges, insert the needle from back to front through the cast-on edge loop of one edge either one stitch in or half a stitch in from the edge (as specified in the pattern copy) and repeat on the other edge. Then, insert the needle from front to back through the cast-on loop on

the first edge and from back to front either through the centre of a stitch or to one side of the edge stitch as specified, and repeat on the other side. Now, insert the needle from front to back through the place it last emerged on the first edge and from back to front either through the centre of a stitch or to one side of the edge stitch as specified, two stitches up, and repeat on the other side. Continue working through the fabric of one edge and then the next. Carefully, making the stitches along either edge two rows deep each time will ensure that the rows will align and the top edges will meet.

TIP

It is easier to keep the left-hand edge of a stocking-stitch fabric neat because the passage of the yarn through the stitches causes the stitches to twist slightly in a clockwise direction and into the edge. To create neater edges on the right-hand edge of stocking-stitch fabric, knit the first stitch of every knit row through the back of the loop and purl the last stitch of each purl row as a twisted stitch: insert the tip of the right-hand needle into the stitch as usual, but wrap the working yarn around the tip of the right-hand knitting needle so that it goes under the knitting needle and crosses the top of the knitting needle from right to left. The result is that the stitches on the right-hand edge twist slightly in an anti-clockwise direction.

If mattress stitch is used to join two cast-on or cast-off edges, then begin by threading a tapestry needle with matching yarn and placing the two edges top and bottom, horizontally. Starting at the right edge and working alternate edges, insert the needle from back to front through the centre of the stitch on the lower edge, then pass the needle behind the two V-shaped strands of the corresponding stitch on the upper edge. Insert the needle from front to back through the stitch the yarn last emerged from on the lower edge and from back to front through the centre of the next stitch to the left. Continue working along the edge until the seam is complete.

If mattress stitch is used to join a cast-on or cast-off edge and a selvedge, then begin by threading a tapestry needle with matching yarn and placing the two edges side by side. Starting at the right edge and working alternate edges, work from stitch centre to stitch centre along the cast-on or cast-off edge and between each selvedge stitch and its neighbouring stitch.

POMPOMS

In this book all the pompoms are a single colour and quite small but you can let your creativity run wild. Use several yarns of a single shade but different yarn weights to add texture or, for an ear, wind a small section in pink yarn for instance to create a pink inner ear. The method described below allows you the most creativity but there are several pompom making tools available that speed up the process.

1 Cut out two circles of cardboard a bit smaller than the size of pompom you would like to make. They should have circles cut out of the middle that are about a third of the overall diameter. Wrap lengths of yarn evenly around both circles and through the centre holes until the cardboard is completely covered and the centre hole is very small.

2 Cut through the yarn on the outer edge and through the middle of the two cardboard circles.

3 Place a length of yarn in between the two cardboard circles and tie in a knot to secure the strands of yarn. Pull away the circles of cardboard and trim any untidy strands.

1

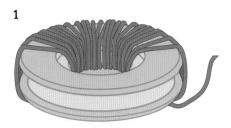

2

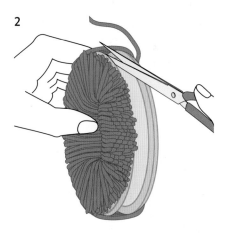

3

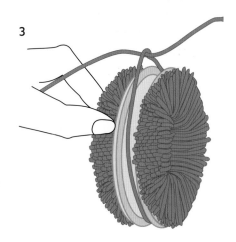

ABBREVIATIONS

cm	centimetre(s)
dpn(s)	double-pointed needle(s)
g	gram(s)
in	inch(es)
inc	knit into the front and back (see page 102)
k	knit (see page 99)
k2tog	knit two stitches together (see page 103)
k2togtbl	knit two stitches together through the back loops (see page 103)
m	metre(s)
M1L	make one left (see page 102)
M1R	make one right (see page 102)
MB	make bobble (see special abbreviations with pattern)
ML	make loop
mm	millimetre(s)
purl	purl (see page 99)
p2tog	purl two stitches together (see page 103)
pspo	purl one stitch, slip stitch back to left-hand needle, pass the second st on left needle over first (see page 103)
psso	pass slipped stitch(es) over
rev st st	reverse stocking stitch
RS	right side
sl	slip
sl1r	slip 1 st right
sl1l	slip 1 st left
sl2, k1, psso	slip two stitches together, knit one stitch, pass the slipped stitches over the knit st
ssk	slip two stitches one at a time, knitwise, knit these two stitches through the back of the loops; see page 103)
st st	stocking stitch (stockinette stitch)
st(s)	stitch(es)
tbl	through the back of the loop(s)
tog	together
WS	wrong side
yb	yarn back between the needles
yf	yarn forward between the needles
yo	yarnover (see page 102)
*	work instructions following *, then repeat as directed
( )	additional information including instructions that vary according to size worked; repeat instructions inside the brackets as directed

CONVERSIONS
KNITTING NEEDLE SIZES

UK	Metric	US
11	3mm	–
10	3.25mm	3
9	3.5mm	4
9	3.75mm	5
8	4mm	6
7	4.5mm	7
6	5mm	8
5	5.5mm	9
4	6mm	10
3	6.5mm	10.5
2	7mm	10.5
1	7.5mm	11
0	8mm	11
00	9mm	13
000	10mm	15

ABOUT THE AUTHOR

Born in Edinburgh, Luise Roberts was taught to knit, sew and crochet at an early age by her German mother. These skills gave her an advantage when she went on to take an Art Foundation Course, where she won an award for the most promising art student of her year. Specialising professionally in graphic design and then book design, Luise continued to work with textiles in her spare time, exhibiting as an embroiderer, before turning her attention back to knitting and crochet. Luise has written several books and contributed to books and magazines with the aim of making techniques more accessible and showing that the time spent on a project can be as rewarding was the final product.

GMC Publications would like to thank the following people: Main photography: Chris Gloag and Andrew Perris; still life photography: Anthony Bailey; Models: Amy from Zone Models and Grace; Hair and make-up: Jen Dodson; Pattern checking: Marilyn Wilson

Index